Z 24
£ 95
RAV
(Hob)

archaeology, politics, religion, psychology,
philosophy and science are all represented
in Canto's specially selected list of titles,
which now offers some of the best and
most accessible of Cambridge publishing to
a wider readership.

ed on or before
below.

0521437733

The Invention of Tradition

Edited by
ERIC HOBSBAWM
and
TERENCE RANGER

CAMBRIDGE
UNIVERSITY PRESS

Published by the Press Syndicate of the University of Cambridge
The Pitt Building, Trumpington Street, Cambridge CB2 1RP
40 West 20th Street, New York, NY 10011-4211, USA
10 Stamford Road, Oakleigh, Victoria 3166, Australia

First published 1983
First paperback edition 1984
Reprinted 1985, 1986, 1987, 1988, 1989
Canto edition 1992

Printed in Great Britain by the
University Press, Cambridge

Library of Congress Catalogue card number: 82–14711

British Library cataloguing in publication data

The invention of tradition – (Past and present publications)
1. Sociology   2. Folklore – History
I. Hobsbawm, E. J.   II. Ranger, Terence
III. Series
303.3′72   HM201

ISBN 0 521 43773 3 paperback

Contents

v

Contributors

DAVID CANNADINE is Professor of History at Columbia University. His books include *Lords and Landlords: The Aristocracy and the Towns, 1774–1967* (1980) and *The Decline and Fall of the British Aristocracy* (1990).

BERNARD S. COHN is Professor of Anthropology at the University of Chicago. He is the author of many articles on the interactions of history and anthropology and on the study of Indian society.

ERIC HOBSBAWM is Emeritus Professor of Economic and Social History at Birkbeck College, University of London, and a founder-member of the journal *Past & Present*. Among his many publications is *Nations and Nationalism since 1780: Programme, Myth, Reality* (1990).

PRYS MORGAN is Reader in History at University College, Swansea. He has published extensively in Welsh and has contributed chapters to many books on Welsh history.

TERENCE RANGER is Rhodes Professor of Race Relations at the University of Oxford, and a Fellow of St Antony's College. He is the author of *The Historical Study of African Religion* (1972) and *Dance and Society in Eastern Africa* (1975).

HUGH TREVOR-ROPER (Lord Dacre of Glanton) was Master of Peterhouse, Cambridge, from 1980 to 1987. He was previously Regius Professor of History at the University of Oxford, from 1957.

1. *Introduction: Inventing Traditions*

ERIC HOBSBAWM

Nothing appears more ancient, and linked to an immemorial past, than the pageantry which surrounds British monarchy in its public ceremonial manifestations. Yet, as a chapter in this book establishes, in its modern form it is the product of the late nineteenth and twentieth centuries. 'Traditions' which appear or claim to be old are often quite recent in origin and sometimes invented. Anyone familiar with the colleges of ancient British universities will be able to think of the institution of such 'traditions' on a local scale, though some – like the annual Festival of Nine Lessons and Carols in the chapel of King's College, Cambridge on Christmas Eve – may become generalized through the modern mass medium of radio. This observation formed the starting-point of a conference organized by the historical journal *Past & Present*, which in turn forms the basis of the present book.

The term 'invented tradition' is used in a broad, but not imprecise sense. It includes both 'traditions' actually invented, constructed and formally instituted and those emerging in a less easily traceable manner within a brief and dateable period – a matter of a few years perhaps – and establishing themselves with great rapidity. The royal Christmas broadcast in Britain (instituted in 1932) is an example of the first; the appearance and development of the practices associated with the Cup Final in British Association Football, of the second. It is evident that not all of them are equally permanent, but it is their appearance and establishment rather than their chances of survival which are our primary concern.

'Invented tradition' is taken to mean a set of practices, normally governed by overtly or tacitly accepted rules and of a ritual or symbolic nature, which seek to inculcate certain values and norms of behaviour by repetition, which automatically implies continuity with the past. In fact, where possible, they normally attempt to establish continuity with a suitable historic past. A striking example is the deliberate choice of a Gothic style for the nineteenth-century

1

rebuilding of the British parliament, and the equally deliberate decision after World War II to rebuild the parliamentary chamber on exactly the same basic plan as before. The historic past into which the new tradition is inserted need not be lengthy, stretching back into the assumed mists of time. Revolutions and 'progressive movements' which break with the past, by definition, have their own relevant past, though it may be cut off at a certain date, such as 1789. However, insofar as there is such reference to a historic past, the peculiarity of 'invented' traditions is that the continuity with it is largely factitious. In short, they are responses to novel situations which take the form of reference to old situations, or which establish their own past by quasi-obligatory repetition. It is the contrast between the constant change and innovation of the modern world and the attempt to structure at least some parts of social life within it as unchanging and invariant, that makes the 'invention of tradition' so interesting for historians of the past two centuries.

'Tradition' in this sense must be distinguished clearly from 'custom' which dominates so-called 'traditional' societies. The object and characteristic of 'traditions', including invented ones, is invariance. The past, real or invented, to which they refer imposes fixed (normally formalized) practices, such as repetition. 'Custom' in traditional societies has the double function of motor and fly-wheel. It does not preclude innovation and change up to a point, though evidently the requirement that it must appear compatible or even identical with precedent imposes substantial limitations on it. What it does is to give any desired change (or resistance to innovation) the sanction of precedent, social continuity and natural law as expressed in history. Students of peasant movements know that a village's claim to some common land or right 'by custom from time immemorial' often expresses not a historical fact, but the balance of forces in the constant struggle of village against lords or against other villages. Students of the British labour movement know that 'the custom of the trade' or of the shop may represent not ancient tradition, but whatever right the workers have established in practice, however recently, and which they now attempt to extend or defend by giving it the sanction of perpetuity. 'Custom' cannot afford to be invariant, because even in 'traditional' societies life is not so. Customary or common law still shows this combination of flexibility in substance and formal adherence to precedent. The difference between 'tradition' and 'custom' in our sense is indeed well illustrated here. 'Custom' is what judges do; 'tradition' (in this instance invented tradition) is the wig, robe and other formal paraphernalia and ritualized practices surrounding their substantial action. The decline of 'custom' inevitably changes the 'tradition' with which it is habitually intertwined.

A second, less important, distinction that must be made is between 'tradition' in our sense and convention or routine, which has no significant ritual or symbolic function as such, though it may acquire it incidentally. It is evident that any social practice that needs to be carried out repeatedly will tend, for convenience and efficiency, to develop a set of such conventions and routines, which may be de facto or de jure formalized for the purposes of imparting the practice to new practitioners. This applies to unprecedented practices (such as the work of an aircraft pilot) as much as to long-familiar ones. Societies since the industrial revolution have naturally been obliged to invent, institute or develop new networks of such convention or routine more frequently than previous ones. Insofar as they function best when turned into habit, automatic procedure or even reflex action, they require invariance, which may get in the way of the other necessary requirement of practice, the capacity to deal with unforeseen or inhabitual contingencies. This is a well-known weakness of routinization or bureaucratization, particularly at the subaltern levels where invariant performance is generally considered the most efficient.

Such networks of convention and routine are not 'invented traditions' since their functions, and therefore their justifications, are technical rather than ideological (in Marxian terms they belong to 'base' rather than 'superstructure'). They are designed to facilitate readily definable practical operations, and are readily modified or abandoned to meet changing practical needs, always allowing for the inertia which any practice acquires with time and the emotional resistance to any innovation by people who have become attached to it. The same applies to the recognized 'rules' of games or other patterns of social interaction, where these exist, or to any other pragmatically based norms. Where these exist in combination with 'tradition', the difference is readily observable. Wearing hard hats when riding makes practical sense, like wearing crash helmets for motor-cyclists or steel helmets for soldiers; wearing a particular type of hard hat in combination with hunting pink makes an entirely different kind of sense. If this were not so, it would be as easy to change the 'traditional' costume of fox-hunters as it is to substitute a differently shaped helmet in armies – rather conservative institutions – if it can be shown to provide more effective protection. Indeed, it may be suggested that 'traditions' and pragmatic conventions or routines are inversely related. 'Tradition' shows weakness when, as among liberal Jews, dietary prohibitions are justified pragmatically, as by arguing that the ancient Hebrews banned pork on grounds of hygiene. Conversely, objects or practices are liberated for full symbolic and ritual use when no longer fettered by practical use. The spurs of Cavalry officers' dress uniforms are more important for 'tradition' when there are no horses, the umbrellas of Guards officers in civilian dress lose their significance when not carried tightly furled (that is, useless), the wigs of lawyers could hardly acquire their modern significance until other people stopped wearing wigs.

Inventing traditions, it is assumed here, is essentially a process of formalization and ritualization, characterized by reference to the past, if only by imposing repetition. The actual process of creating such ritual and symbolic complexes has not been adequately studied by historians. Much of it is still rather obscure. It is presumably most clearly exemplified where a 'tradition' is deliberately invented and constructed by a single initiator, as for the Boy Scouts by Baden-Powell. Perhaps it is almost as easily traced in the case of officially instituted and planned ceremonials, since they are likely to be well documented, as in the case of the construction of Nazi symbolism and the Nuremberg party rallies. It is probably most difficult to trace where such traditions are partly invented, partly evolved in private groups (where the process is less likely to be bureaucratically recorded), or informally over a period of time as, say, in parliament and the legal profession. The difficulty is not only one of sources but also of techniques, though there are available both esoteric disciplines specializing in symbolism and ritual, such as heraldry and the study of liturgy, as well as Warburgian historic disciplines for the study of such subjects. Unfortunately neither are usually familiar to historians of the industrial era.

There is probably no time and place with which historians are concerned which has not seen the 'invention' of tradition in this sense. However, we should expect it to occur more frequently when a rapid transformation of society weakens or destroys the social patterns for which 'old' traditions had been designed, producing new ones to which they were not applicable, or when such old traditions and their institutional carriers and promulgators no longer prove sufficiently adaptable and flexible, or are otherwise eliminated: in short, when there are sufficiently large and rapid changes on the demand or the supply side. Such changes have been particularly significant in the past 200 years, and it is therefore reasonable to expect these instant formalizations of new traditions to cluster during this period. This implies, incidentally, against both nineteenth-century liberalism and more recent 'modernization' theory that such formalizations are not confined to so-called 'traditional' societies, but also have their place, in one form or another, in 'modern' ones. Broadly speaking this is so, but one must beware of making the further assumptions, firstly that older forms of community and authority structure, and consequently the traditions associated with them, were unadaptable and became rapidly unviable, and secondly that 'new' traditions simply resulted from the inability to use or adapt old ones.

Adaptation took place for old uses in new conditions and by using old models for new purposes. Old institutions with established functions, references to the past and ritual idioms and practices might need to adapt in this way: the Catholic Church faced with new political and ideological challenges and major changes in the composition of the faithful (such as the notable feminization both of lay piety and of clerical personnel);[1] professional armies faced with conscription; ancient institutions such as law-courts now operating in a changed context and sometimes with changed functions in new contexts. So were institutions enjoying nominal continuity, but in fact turning into something very very different, such as universities. Thus Bahnson[2] has analysed the sudden decline, after 1848, of the traditional practice of mass student exodus from German universities (for reasons of conflict or demonstration) in terms of the changed academic character of universities, the rising age of the student population, its embourgeoisement which diminished town/gown tensions and student riotousness, the new institution of free mobility between universities, the consequent change in student associations and other factors.[3] In all such cases novelty is no less novel for being able to dress up easily as antiquity.

---

[1] See for instance G. Tihon, 'Les religieuses en Belgique du XVIIIe au XXe siècle: Approche Statistique', *Belgisch Tijdschrift v. Nieuwste Geschiedenis/Revue Belge d'Histoire Contemporaine*, vii (1976), pp. 1–54.
[2] Karsten Bahnson, *Akademische Auszüge aus deutschen Universitäts und Hochschulorten* (Saarbrücken, 1973).
[3] Seventeen such exoduses are recorded in the eighteenth century, fifty in 1800–48, but only six from 1848 to 1973.

More interesting, from our point of view, is the use of ancient materials to construct invented traditions of a novel type for quite novel purposes. A large store of such materials is accumulated in the past of any society, and an elaborate language of symbolic practice and communication is always available. Sometimes new traditions could be readily grafted on old ones, sometimes they could be devised by borrowing from the well-supplied warehouses of official ritual, symbolism and moral exhortation – religion and princely pomp, folklore and freemasonry (itself an earlier invented tradition of great symbolic force). Thus the development of Swiss nationalism, concomitant with the formation of the modern federal state in the nineteenth century, has been brilliantly studied by Rudolf Braun,[4] who has the advantage of training in a discipline ('Volkskunde') which lends itself to such studies, and in a country where its modernization has not been set back by association with Nazi abuses. Existing customary traditional practices – folksong, physical contests, marksmanship – were modified, ritualized and institutionalized for the new national purposes. Traditional folksongs were supplemented by new songs in the same idiom, often composed by schoolmasters, transferred to a choral repertoire whose content was patriotic–progressive ('Nation, Nation, wie voll klingt der Ton'), though it also embodied ritually powerful elements from religious hymnology. (The formation of such new song-repertoires, especially for schools, is well worth study.) The statutes of the Federal Song Festival – are we not reminded of the eisteddfodau? – declare its object to be 'the development and improvement of the people's singing, the awakening of more elevated sentiments for God, Freedom and Country, union and fraternization of the friends of Art and the Fatherland'. (The word 'improvement' introduces the characteristic note of nineteenth-century progress.)

A powerful ritual complex formed round these occasions: festival pavilions, structures for the display of flags, temples for offerings, processions, bell-ringing, tableaux, gun-salutes, government delegations in honour of the festival, dinners, toasts and oratory. Old materials were again adapted for this:

The echoes of baroque forms of celebration, display and pomp are unmistakable in this new festival architecture. And as, in the baroque celebration, state and church merge on a higher plane, so

[4] Rudolf Braun, *Sozialer und kultureller Wandel in einem ländlichen Industriegebiet im 19. und 20. Jahrhundert*, ch. 6 (Erlenbach-Zürich, 1965).

an alloy of religious and patriotic elements emerges from these new forms of choral, shooting and gymnastic activity.[5]

How far new traditions can thus use old materials, how far they may be forced to invent new languages or devices, or extend the old symbolic vocabulary beyond its established limits, cannot be discussed here. It is clear that plenty of political institutions, ideological movements and groups – not least in nationalism – were so unprecedented that even historic continuity had to be invented, for example by creating an ancient past beyond effective historical continuity, either by semi-fiction (Boadicea, Vercingetorix, Arminius the Cheruscan) or by forgery (Ossian, the Czech medieval manuscripts). It is also clear that entirely new symbols and devices came into existence as part of national movements and states, such as the national anthem (of which the British in 1740 seems to be the earliest), the national flag (still largely a variation on the French revolutionary tricolour, evolved 1790–4), or the personification of 'the nation' in symbol or image, either official, as with Marianne and Germania, or unofficial, as in the cartoon stereotypes of John Bull, the lean Yankee Uncle Sam and the 'German Michel'.

Nor should we overlook the break in continuity which is sometimes clear even in traditional *topoi* of genuine antiquity. If we follow Lloyd,[6] English Christmas folk carols ceased to be created in the seventeenth century, to be replaced by hymn-book carols of the Watts–Wesley kind, though a demotic modification of these in largely rural religions like Primitive Methodism may be observed. Yet carols were the first kind of folksong to be revived by middle-class collectors to take their place 'in novel surroundings of church, guild and women's institute' and thence to spread in a new urban popular setting 'by street-corner singers or by hoarse boys chanting on doorsteps in the ancient hope of reward'. In this sense 'God rest ye merry, Gentlemen' is not old but new. Such a break is visible even in movements deliberately describing themselves as 'traditionalist', and appealing to groups which were, by common consent, regarded as the repositories of historic continuity and tradition, such as peasants.[7] Indeed, the very appearance of movements for the defence

[5] Rudolf Braun, *op. cit.*, pp. 336–7.
[6] A. L. Lloyd, *Folk Song in England* (London, 1969 ed.), pp. 134–8.
[7] This is to be distinguished from the revival of tradition for purposes which actually demonstrated its decline. 'The farmers' revival (around 1900) of their old regional dress, folk dances and similar rituals for festive occasions was *neither* a bourgeois *nor* a traditionalistic feature. On the surface it could be viewed as

or revival of traditions, 'traditionalist' or otherwise, indicates such a break. Such movements, common among intellectuals since the Romantics, can never develop or even preserve a living past (except conceivably by setting up human natural sanctuaries for isolated corners of archaic life), but must become 'invented tradition'. On the other hand the strength and adaptability of genuine traditions is not to be confused with the 'invention of tradition'. Where the old ways are alive, traditions need be neither revived nor invented.

Yet it may be suggested that where they are invented, it is often not because old ways are no longer available or viable, but because they are deliberately not used or adapted. Thus, in consciously setting itself against tradition and for radical innovation, the nineteenth-century liberal ideology of social change systematically failed to provide for the social and authority ties taken for granted in earlier societies, and created voids which might have to be filled by invented practices. The success of nineteenth-century Tory factory masters in Lancashire (as distinct from Liberal ones) in using such old ties to advantage shows that they were still there to be used – even in the unprecedented environment of the industrial town.[8] The long-term inadaptability of pre-industrial ways to a society revolutionized beyond a certain point is not to be denied, but is not to be confused with the problems arising out of the rejection of old ways in the short term by those who regarded them as obstacles to progress or, even worse, as its militant adversaries.

This did not prevent innovators from generating their own invented traditions – the practices of freemasonry are a case in point. Nevertheless, a general hostility to irrationalism, superstition and customary practices reminiscent of the dark past, if not actually descended from it, made impassioned believers in the verities of the Enlightenment, such as liberals, socialists, and communists, unreceptive to traditions old or novel. Socialists, as we shall see below, found themselves acquiring an annual May Day without quite knowing

a nostalgic longing for the old-time culture which was so rapidly disappearing, but in reality it was a demonstration of class identity by which prosperous farmers could distance themselves horizontally relative to the townspeople and vertically from the cottars, craftsmen and labourers.' Palle Ove Christiansen, 'Peasant Adaptation to Bourgeois Culture? Class Formation and Cultural Redefinition in the Danish Countryside', *Ethnologia Scandinavica* (1978), p. 128. See also G. Lewis, 'The Peasantry, Rural Change and Conservative Agrarianism: Lower Austria at the Turn of the Century', *Past & Present*, no. 81 (1978), pp. 119–43.

[8] Patrick Joyce, 'The Factory Politics of Lancashire in the Later Nineteenth Century', *Historical Journal*, xviii (1965), pp. 525–53.

how; National Socialists exploited such occasions with liturgical sophistication and zeal and a conscious manipulation of symbols.[9] The liberal era in Britain at best tolerated such practices, insofar as neither ideology nor economic efficiency were at issue, sometimes as a reluctant concession to the irrationalism of the lower orders. Its attitude to the sociable and ritual activities of Friendly Societies was a combination of hostility ('unnecessary expenses' such as 'payments for anniversaries, processions, bands, regalia' were legally forbidden) and toleration of events such as annual feasts on the grounds that 'the importance of this attraction, especially as respects the country population, cannot be denied'.[10] But a rigorous individualist rationalism dominated not only as an economic calculus but as a social ideal. Chapter 7 will investigate what happened in the period when its limitations became increasingly recognized.

These introductory notes may be concluded with some general observations about the invented traditions of the period since the industrial revolution.

They seem to belong to three overlapping types: a) those establishing or symbolizing social cohesion or the membership of groups, real or artificial communities, b) those establishing or legitimizing institutions, status or relations of authority, and c) those whose main purpose was socialization, the inculcation of beliefs, value systems and conventions of behaviour. While traditions of types b) and c) were certainly devised (as in those symbolizing submission to authority in British India), it may be tentatively suggested that type a) was prevalent, the other functions being regarded as implicit in or flowing from a sense of identification with a 'community' and/or the institutions representing, expressing or symbolizing it such as a 'nation'.

One difficulty was that such larger social entities were plainly not *Gemeinschaften* or even systems of accepted ranks. Social mobility, the facts of class conflict and the prevalent ideology made traditions combining community and marked inequality in formal hierarchies (as in armies) difficult to apply universally. This did not much affect traditions of type c) since general socialization inculcated the same values in every citizen, member of the nation and subject of the crown,

---

[9] Helmut Hartwig, 'Plaketten zum 1. Mai 1934–39', *Aesthetik und Kommunikation*, vii, no. 26 (1976), pp. 56–9.

[10] P. H. J. H. Gosden, *The Friendly Societies in England, 1815–1875* (Manchester, 1961), pp. 123, 119.

and the functionally specific socializations of different social groups (such as public school pupils as distinct from others) did not usually get in each others' way. On the other hand, insofar as invented traditions reintroduced, as it were, status into a world of contract, superior and inferior into a world of legal equals, they could not do so directly. They could be smuggled in by formal symbolic assent to a social organization which was de facto unequal, as by the restyling of the British coronation ceremony.[11] (See below pp. 282–3.) More commonly they might foster the corporate sense of *superiority* of élites – particularly when these had to be recruited from those who did not already possess it by birth or ascription – rather than by inculcating a sense of obedience in inferiors. Some were encouraged to feel more equal than others. This might be done by assimilating élites to pre-bourgeois ruling groups or authorities, whether in the militarist/bureaucratic form characteristic of Germany (as with the duelling student corps), or the non-militarized 'moralized gentry' model of the British public schools. Alternatively, perhaps, the *esprit de corps*, self-confidence and leadership of élites could be developed by more esoteric 'traditions' marking the cohesiveness of a senior official mandarinate (as in France or among whites in the colonies).

Granted that 'communitarian' invented traditions were the basic type, their nature remains to be studied. Anthropology may help to elucidate the differences, if any, between invented and old traditional practices. Here we may merely note that while rites of passage are normally marked in the traditions of particular groups (initiation, promotion, retirement, death), this was not usually the case in those designed for all-embracing pseudo-communities (nations, countries), presumably because these underlined their eternal and unchanging character – at least since the community's foundation. However, both new political régimes and innovatory movements might seek to find their own equivalents for the traditional rites of passage associated with religion (civil marriage, funerals).

One marked difference between old and invented practices may be observed. The former were specific and strongly binding social practices, the latter tended to be quite unspecific and vague as to the nature of the values, rights and obligations of the group membership they inculcate: 'patriotism', 'loyalty', 'duty', 'playing the game', 'the school spirit' and the like. But if the content of British patriotism

---

[11] J. E. C. Bodley, *The Coronation of Edward the VIIth: A Chapter of European and Imperial History* (London, 1903), pp. 201, 204.

or 'Americanism' was notably ill-defined, though usually specified in commentaries associated with ritual occasions, the *practices* symbolizing it were virtually compulsory – as in standing up for the singing of the national anthem in Britain, the flag ritual in American schools. The crucial element seems to have been the invention of emotionally and symbolically charged signs of club membership rather than the statutes and objects of the club. Their significance lay precisely in their undefined universality:

> The National Flag, the National Anthem and the National Emblem are the three symbols through which an independent country proclaims its identity and sovereignty, and as such they command instantaneous respect and loyalty. In themselves they reflect the entire background, thought and culture of a nation.[12]

In this sense, as an observer noted in 1880, 'soldiers and policemen wear badges for us now', though he failed to predict their revival as adjuncts to individual citizens in the era of mass movements which was about to begin.[13]

The second observation is that it seems clear that, in spite of much invention, new traditions have not filled more than a small part of the space left by the secular decline of both old tradition and custom; as might indeed be expected in societies in which the past becomes increasingly less relevant as a model or precedent for most forms of human behaviour. In the private lives of most people, and in the self-contained lives of small sub-cultural groups, even the invented traditions of the nineteenth and twentieth centuries occupied or occupy a much smaller place than old traditions do in, say, old agrarian societies.[14] 'What is done' structures the days, seasons and life-cycles of twentieth-century western men and women very much less than it did their ancestors', and very much less than the external compulsions of the economy, technology, bureaucratic state organization, political decision and other forces which neither rely on nor develop 'tradition' in our sense.

However, this generalization does not apply in the field of what might be called the public life of the citizen (including to some extent

---

[12] Official Indian government commentary, quoted in R. Firth, *Symbols, Public and Private* (London, 1973), p. 341.

[13] Frederick Marshall, *Curiosities of Ceremonials, Titles, Decorations and Forms of International Vanities* (London, 1880), p. 20.

[14] Not to mention the transformation of long-lasting rituals and signs of uniformity and cohesion into rapidly changing fashions – in costume, language, social practice etc., as in the youth cultures of industrialized countries.

public forms of socialization, such as schools, as distinct from private ones such as the mass media). There is no real sign of weakening in the neo-traditional practices associated either with bodies of men in the public service (armed forces, the law, perhaps even public servants) or in practices associated with the citizens' membership of states. Indeed most of the occasions when people become conscious of citizenship as such remain associated with symbols and semi-ritual practices (for instance, elections), most of which are historically novel and largely invented: flags, images, ceremonies and music. Insofar as the invented traditions of the era since the industrial and French revolutions have filled a permanent gap – at all events up to the present – it would seem to be in this field.

Why, it may be asked finally, should historians devote their attention to such phenomena? The question is in one sense unnecessary, since a growing number of them plainly do, as the contents of this volume and the references cited in it bear witness. So it is better rephrased. What benefit can historians derive from the study of the invention of tradition?

First and foremost, it may be suggested that they are important symptoms and therefore indicators of problems which might not otherwise be recognized, and developments which are otherwise difficult to identify and to date. They are evidence. The transformation of German nationalism from its old liberal to its new imperialist–expansionist pattern is more exactly illuminated by the rapid replacement of the old black–red–gold colours by the new black–white–red ones (especially by the 1890s) among the German gymnastic movement, than by official statements of authorities or spokesmen for organizations. The history of the British football cup finals tells us something about the development of an urban working-class culture which more conventional data and sources do not. By the same token, the study of invented traditions cannot be separated from the wider study of the history of society, nor can it expect to advance much beyond the mere discovery of such practices unless it is integrated into a wider study.

Second, it throws a considerable light on the human relation to the past, and therefore on the historian's own subject and craft. For all invented traditions, so far as possible, use history as a legitimator of action and cement of group cohesion. Frequently it becomes the actual symbol of struggle, as in the battles over the monuments to Walther von der Vogelweide and Dante in South Tyrol in 1889 and

1896.[15] Even revolutionary movements backed their innovations by reference to a 'people's past' (Saxons versus Normans, 'nos ancêtres les Gaulois' against the Franks, Spartacus), to traditions of revolution ('Auch das deutsche Volk hat seine revolutionäre Tradition' as Engels claimed in the first words of his *Peasant War in Germany*)[16] and to its own heroes and martyrs. James Connolly's *Labour in Irish History* exemplifies this union of themes excellently. The element of invention is particularly clear here, since the history which became part of the fund of knowledge or the ideology of nation, state or movement is not what has actually been preserved in popular memory, but what has been selected, written, pictured, popularized and institutionalized by those whose function it is to do so. Oral historians have frequently observed how in the actual memories of the old the General Strike of 1926 plays a more modest and less dramatic part than interviewers anticipated.[17] The formation of such an image of the French Revolution in and by the Third Republic has been analysed.[18] Yet all historians, whatever else their objectives, are engaged in this process inasmuch as they contribute, consciously or not, to the creation, dismantling and restructuring of images of the past which belong not only to the world of specialist investigation but to the public sphere of man as a political being. They might as well be aware of this dimension of their activities.

In this connection, one specific interest of 'invented traditions' for, at all events, modern and contemporary historians ought to be singled out. They are highly relevant to that comparatively recent historical innovation, the 'nation', with its associated phenomena: nationalism, the nation–state, national symbols, histories and the rest. All these rest on exercises in social engineering which are often deliberate and always innovative, if only because historical novelty implies innovation. Israeli and Palestinian nationalism or nations

---

[15] John W. Cole and Eric Wolf, *The Hidden Frontier: Ecology and Ethnicity in an Alpine Valley* (N.Y. and London, 1974), p. 55.

[16] For the popularity of books on this and other militant historical subjects in German workers' libraries, see H.-J. Steinberg, *Sozialismus und deutsche Sozialdemokratie. Zur Ideologie der Partei vor dem ersten Weltkrieg* (Hanover, 1967), pp. 131–3.

[17] There are perfectly sound reasons why participants at the bottom do not usually see historic events they live through as top people or historians do. One might call this (after the hero of Stendhal's *Chartreuse de Parme*) the 'Fabrice syndrome'.

[18] E.g. Alice Gérard, *La Révolution Française: Mythes et Interprétations, 1789–1970* (Paris, 1970).

must be novel, whatever the historic continuities of Jews or Middle Eastern Muslims, since the very concept of territorial states of the currently standard type in their region was barely thought of a century ago, and hardly became a serious prospect before the end of World War I. Standard national languages, to be learned in schools and written, let alone spoken, by more than a smallish élite, are largely constructs of varying, but often brief, age. As a French historian of Flemish language observed, quite correctly, the Flemish taught in Belgium today is not the language which the mothers and grand-mothers of Flanders spoke to their children: in short, it is only metaphorically but not literally a 'mother-tongue'. We should not be misled by a curious, but understandable, paradox: modern nations and all their impedimenta generally claim to be the opposite of novel, namely rooted in the remotest antiquity, and the opposite of constructed, namely human communities so 'natural' as to require no definition other than self-assertion. Whatever the historic or other continuities embedded in the modern concept of 'France' and 'the French' – and which nobody would seek to deny – these very concepts themselves must include a constructed or 'invented' com-ponent. And just because so much of what subjectively makes up the modern 'nation' consists of such constructs and is associated with appropriate and, in general, fairly recent symbols or suitably tailored discourse (such as 'national history'), the national phenomenon cannot be adequately investigated without careful attention to the 'invention of tradition'.

Finally, the study of the invention of tradition is interdisciplinary. It is a field of study which brings together historians, social anthro-pologists and a variety of other workers in the human sciences, and cannot adequately be pursued without such collaboration. The present book brings together, in the main, contributions by historians. It is to be hoped that others will also find it useful.

2. *The Invention of Tradition: The Highland Tradition of Scotland*

HUGH TREVOR-ROPER

Today, whenever Scotchmen gather together to celebrate their national identity, they assert it openly by certain distinctive national apparatus. They wear the kilt, woven in a tartan whose colour and pattern indicates their 'clan'; and if they indulge in music, their instrument is the bagpipe. This apparatus, to which they ascribe great antiquity, is in fact largely modern. It was developed after, sometimes long after, the Union with England against which it is, in a sense, a protest. Before the Union, it did indeed exist in vestigial form; but that form was regarded by the large majority of Scotchmen as a sign of barbarism: the badge of roguish, idle, predatory, blackmailing Highlanders who were more of a nuisance than a threat to civilized, historic Scotland. And even in the Highlands, even in that vestigial form, it was relatively new: it was not the original, or the distinguishing badge of Highland society.

Indeed, the whole concept of a distinct Highland culture and tradition is a retrospective invention. Before the later years of the seventeenth century, the Highlanders of Scotland did not form a distinct people. They were simply the overflow of Ireland. On that broken and inhospitable coast, in that archipelago of islands large and small, the sea unites rather than divides and from the late fifth century, when the Scots of Ulster landed in Argyll, until the mid-eighteenth century, when it was 'opened up' after the Jacobite revolts, the West of Scotland, cut off by mountains from the East, was always linked rather to Ireland than to the Saxon Lowlands. Racially and culturally, it was a colony of Ireland.

Even politically these two Celtic societies, of Ireland and the Western Highlands, merged into each other. The Scots of Dalriada retained, for a century, their foothold in Ulster. The Danes ruled equally over the Western Islands, the coasts of Ireland and the Isle of Man. And in the later Middle Ages the Macdonald Lords of the Isles were nearer and more effective rulers both in Western Scotland and in Northern Ireland than their nominal sovereigns, the kings of

15

Scotland and England. Under their rule, the Hebridean culture was purely Irish. Their hereditary bards, physicians, harpers (for their musical instrument was the harp, not the pipes) came from Ireland.[1] Even after the destruction of that lordship, the Macdonalds continued to be a force in both countries. It was not till the mid-seventeenth century that the Plantation of Ulster under English authority, and the rise of the Campbells to hegemony in the Western Highlands, broke that potential political unity. But the cultural unity, though weakened, continued. In the eighteenth century, the Western Islands were still essentially an Irish overflow, and the Gaelic language spoken there was regularly described, in the eighteenth century, as Irish.

Being a cultural dependency of Ireland under the 'foreign', and somewhat ineffective, rule of the Scottish crown, the Highlands and Islands of Scotland were culturally depressed. Their literature, such as it was, was a crude echo of Irish literature. The bards of the Scottish chieftains came from Ireland or went thither to learn their trade. Indeed, we are told by an early eighteenth-century writer – an Irishman – that the Scottish bards were the rubbish of Ireland periodically cleared out of Ireland and deposited in that convenient dump.[2] Even under the oppressive rule of England in the seventeenth and eighteenth centuries, Celtic Ireland remained, culturally, an historic nation while Celtic Scotland was, at best, its poor sister. It had – could have – no independent tradition.

The creation of an independent Highland tradition, and the imposition of that new tradition, with its outward badges, on the whole Scottish nation, was the work of the later eighteenth and early nineteenth centuries. It occurred in three stages. First, there was the cultural revolt against Ireland: the usurpation of Irish culture and the re-writing of early Scottish history, culminating in the insolent claim that Scotland – Celtic Scotland – was the 'mother-nation' and Ireland the cultural dependency. Secondly, there was the artificial creation of new Highland traditions, presented as ancient, original and distinctive. Thirdly, there was the process by which these new traditions were offered to, and adopted by, historic Lowland Scotland: the Eastern Scotland of the Picts, the Saxons and the Normans.

The first of these stages was achieved in the eighteenth century. The claim that the Celtic, Irish-speaking Highlanders of Scotland

---

[1] See J. Bannerman, 'The Lordship of the Isles', in Jennifer Brown (ed.), *Scottish Society in the 15th Century* (1977).

[2] *A Collection of Several Pieces by Mr John Toland* (1726), i, pp. 25–9.

were not merely invaders from Ireland in the fifth century A.D., but had an ancient history in Scotland and were in fact the Caledonians who had resisted the Roman armies, was of course an old legend which had done good service in the past. It was effectively refuted in 1729 by the first and greatest of Scottish antiquaries, the Jacobite *émigré* priest, Thomas Innes. But it was reasserted in 1738 by David Malcolm[3] and, more effectively, in the 1760s, by two writers of the same surname: James Macpherson, the 'translator' of Ossian, and the Rev. John Macpherson, minister of Sleat in the island of Skye. These two Macphersons, though unrelated, were known to each other – James Macpherson had stayed with the minister on his visit to Skye in search of 'Ossian' in 1760, and the minister's son, afterwards Sir John Macpherson, governor general of India, would be his close friend and accomplice later – and they worked in concert. Between them, by two distinct acts of bold forgery, they created an indigenous literature for Celtic Scotland and, as a necessary support to it, a new history. Both this literature and this history, in so far as they had any connection with reality, had been stolen from the Irish.

The sheer effrontery of the Macphersons must excite admiration. James Macpherson picked up Irish ballads in Scotland, wrote an 'epic' in which he transferred the whole scenario from Ireland to Scotland, and then dismissed the genuine ballads thus maltreated as debased modern compositions and the real Irish literature which they reflected as a mere reflection of them. The minister of Sleat then wrote a *Critical Dissertation* in which he provided the necessary context for 'the Celtic Homer' whom his namesake had 'discovered': he placed Irish-speaking Celts in Scotland four centuries before their historical arrival and explained away the genuine, native Irish literature as having been stolen, in the Dark Ages, by the unscrupulous Irish, from the innocent Scots. To complete the picture, James Macpherson himself, using the minister's papers, wrote an 'independent' *Introduction to the History of Great Britain and Ireland* (1771) repeating the minister's assertions. Of the success of the Macphersons no more need be said than that they seduced even the normally careful and critical Edward Gibbon, who acknowledged as his guides in early Scottish history those 'two learned Highlanders', James Macpherson and the Rev. John Macpherson, and thus perpetuated what has rightly been called 'a chain of error in Scottish history'.[4]

---

[3] David Malcolm, *Dissertations on the Celtic Languages* (1738).
[4] E. Gibbon, *Decline and Fall of the Roman Empire*, Everyman edn, ii, p. 496; M. V. Hay, *A Chain of Error in Scottish History* (1927).

It took a full century to clear Scottish history – if it has ever been cleared – of the distorting and interdependent fabrications of the two Macphersons.[5] Meanwhile, these two insolent pretenders had achieved a lasting triumph: they had put the Scottish Highlanders on the map. Previously despised alike by the Lowland Scots, as disorderly savages, and by the Irish as their unlettered poor kinsmen, they were now celebrated throughout Europe as a *Kulturvolk* which, when England and Ireland had been sunk in primitive barbarism, had produced an epic poet of exquisite refinement and sensibility, equal (said Madame de Staël), superior (said F. A. Wolf), to Homer. Nor was it only in literature that they had thus drawn the attention of Europe. For once the links with Ireland had been cut, and the Scottish Highlands had acquired – however fraudulently – an independent ancient culture, the way was open to signalize that independence by peculiar traditions. The tradition which was now established was a peculiarity of dress.

In 1805 Sir Walter Scott wrote, for publication in the *Edinburgh Review*, an essay on Macpherson's Ossian. In it he showed, characteristically, sound scholarship and good sense. He decisively rejected the authenticity of the epic which the Scottish literary establishment in general, and the Highlanders in particular, continued to defend. But, in the same essay he remarked, parenthetically, that it was undeniable that the ancient Caledonian of the third century A.D. had worn 'a tartan philibeg'. In so rational and critical an essay, this confident assertion is surprising. Never before – as far as I know – had such a claim been made. Even Macpherson had never suggested it: his Ossian had always been represented in a flowing robe, and his instrument, incidentally, had been not the bagpipe but the harp. But then Macpherson was himself a Highlander and he was a generation older than Scott. This, in such a matter, made a great difference.

When did the 'tartan philibeg', the modern kilt, come to be the costume of the Highlander? The facts are not really in doubt, especially since the publication of Mr J. Telfer Dunbar's excellent work.[6] Whereas tartan – that is, cloth woven in a geometrical pattern

---

[5] Thus – as was pointed out by the most learned scholar in the subject, Ludwig Stern, in his important essay 'Die Ossianischen Heldenlieder', translated in *Transactions of the Gaelic Society of Inverness*, xxii (1897–8) – the article on Macpherson in the *D.N.B.* 'homologates the views of imperfectly informed apologists' and the Albanogaelic lexicographers have damaged their work by taking part of their material from Macpherson's 'faulty and un-gaelic Ossian': i.e. the spurious Gaelic version of Ossian's poems published in 1807.

[6] J. Telfer Dunbar, *History of the Highland Dress* (1962).

of colours – was known in Scotland in the sixteenth century (it seems to have come from Flanders and reached the Highlands through the Lowlands), the philibeg – name and thing – is unknown before the eighteenth century. So far from being a traditional Highland dress, it was invented by an Englishman after the Union of 1707; and the differentiated 'clan tartans' are an even later invention. They were designed as part of a pageant devised by Sir Walter Scott in honour of a Hanoverian king; and owe their present form to two other Englishmen.

Since the Scottish Highlanders were, in origin, merely Irishmen who had crossed from one island to another, it is natural to suppose that originally their dress was the same as that of the Irish. And indeed this is what we find. It is not till the sixteenth century that any writer records any peculiarities of the Highland dress, but all the accounts of that time are in substantial agreement. They show that the ordinary dress of the Highlanders was a long 'Irish' shirt (in Gaelic, *leine*) which the higher classes – as in Ireland – dyed with saffron (*leine-croich*); a tunic or *failuin*; and a cloak or plaid which the higher classes had woven in many colours or stripes but which in general was of a russet or brown effect, as protective colouring in the heather. In addition, the Highlanders wore shoes with a single sole (the higher classes might wear buskins) and flat soft caps, generally blue. In battle, the leaders wore chain mail while the lower classes wore a padded linen shirt painted or daubed with pitch and covered with deer skins. Besides this normal dress, chieftains and great men who had contact with the more sophisticated inhabitants of the Lowlands might wear trews: a combination of breeches and stockings. Trews could only be worn out of doors in the Highlands by men who had attendants to protect or carry them: they were therefore a mark of social distinction. Both plaid and trews were probably of tartan.[7]

In the course of the seventeenth century – the century in which the link between the Highlands and Ireland was broken – the Highland costume was changed. The changes occurred irregularly over the century. First, the long shirt fell into disuse. In the islands it was replaced by the Lowland coat, waistcoat and breeches early in the century.[8] On the other hand, a Scottish minister long afterwards

---

[7] These accounts came from John Major, *Historia Maioris Britanniae* (1521); James Leslie, *De Moribus et Gestis Scotorum* (1570); Lindsay of Pitscottie, *Chronicle* (1573); G. Buchanan, *Rerum Scoticarum Historia* (1583); Nicolay d'Arfeville, *La Navigation du Roy d'Escosse* (1583). The evidence is set out in D. W. Stewart, *Old and Rare Scottish Tartans* (Edinburgh, 1893), Introduction.

[8] M. Martin, *A Description of the Western Islands of Scotland* (1703).

recalled that the wild Highlanders in the Jacobite army which passed through his parish in 1715 wore 'neither plaid nor philibeg' but merely a home-made close-fitting coat of one colour, stretching below mid-leg, with a belt.[9] This is the latest evidence, as far as I know, of the survival of the *leine* in Scotland.

Throughout the seventeenth century, Highland armies fought in the civil wars of Britain, and, whenever they are described, we find that the officers wore trews while the common soldiers had their legs and thighs bare. Both officers and men wore the plaid, the former as an upper garment, the latter covering the whole body, belted round the waist so that the lower part, below the belt, formed a kind of skirt. In this form, it was known as the *breacan* or 'belted plaid'. The essential fact is that, as yet, there was no mention of the kilt, as we know it. The alternative was the gentlemanly trews or the 'servile' belted plaid.[10]

The name 'kilt' first appears twenty years after the Union. Edward Burt, an English officer posted to Scotland as chief surveyor under General Wade, then wrote a series of letters, mainly from Inverness, describing the character and customs of the country. In these he gives a careful description of the 'quelt', which, he explains, is not a distinct garment but simply a particular method of wearing the plaid,

> set in folds and girt round the waist to make of it a short petticoat that reaches half-way down the thigh, and the rest is brought over the shoulders and then fastened before... so that they make pretty near the appearance of the poor women in London when they bring their gowns over their heads to shelter them from the rain.

This petticoat, Burt adds, was normally worn 'so very short that in a windy day, going up a hill, or stooping, the indecency of it is plainly discovered'. His description makes it clear that he is describing not the modern kilt but the belted plaid.

Burt was explicit about the Highland dress because already, in his time, it was the object of political controversy. After the Jacobite rebellion of 1715 the British parliament had considered banning it by law, as the Irish dress had been banned under Henry VIII: such

---

[9] John Pinkerton, *Literary Correspondence* (1830), i, p. 230. The minister was the father of the philosopher Adam Ferguson.

[10] This is shown by the evidence presented by Stewart, *op. cit.*, p. 21. It is illustrated most graphically in the supporters of the arms of Skene of that Ilk – two Highlanders, one (a sword-bearing gentleman) wearing trews, the other in 'a servill habit', i.e. a belted plaid (*not* as Stewart supposes a kilt: on this see Dunbar, *op. cit.*, pp. 34–5).

a ban, it was thought, would help to break up the distinct Highland way of life and integrate the Highlanders into modern society. However, in the end the proposed law was not passed. The Highland dress, it was conceded, was convenient and necessary in a country where a traveller must 'skip over the rocks and bogs and lie all night in the hills'. It was also a necessity for the poor, for it was very cheap: 'a few shillings will buy this dress for an ordinary Highlander' who could never afford even the coarsest 'Lowland suit'.

It is ironical that if the Highland dress had been banned after 'the Fifteen' instead of after 'the Forty Five', the kilt, which is now regarded as one of the ancient traditions of Scotland, would probably never have come into existence. It came into existence a few years after Burt wrote, and very close to the area in which he wrote. Unknown in 1726, it suddenly appeared a few years later; and by 1746 it was sufficiently well established to be explicitly named in the act of parliament which then forbade the Highland dress. Its inventor was an English Quaker from Lancashire, Thomas Rawlinson.

The Rawlinsons were a long-established family of Quaker iron-masters in Furness. By the early eighteenth century, in association with other prominent Quaker families – Fords, Crosfields, Back-houses – they controlled 'a wide meshwork of furnaces and forges' in Lancashire. But their supplies of charcoal had run low and they needed wood for fuel. Fortunately, after the suppression of the rebellion, the Highlands were being opened up, and the forests in the north could be exploited by the industry of the south. So in 1727 Thomas Rawlinson made an agreement with Ian MacDonell, chief of the MacDonells of Glengarry near Inverness, for a thirty-one year lease of a wooded area at Invergarry. There he built a furnace and smelted the iron-ore which he shipped specially from Lancashire. The enterprise was not an economic success: it was wound up after seven years; but during those seven years, Rawlinson came to know the area, established regular relations with the MacDonells of Glengarry, and of course employed 'a throng of Highlanders' to fell the timber and work the furnace.[11]

During his stay at Glengarry, Rawlinson became interested in the Highland costume but he also became aware of its inconvenience. The belted plaid might be appropriate to the idle life of the

[11] On Rawlinson's Scottish venture see Alfred Fell, *The Early Iron Industry of Furness and District* (Ulverston, 1908), pp. 346ff.; Arthur Raistrick, *Quakers in Science and Industry* (1950), pp. 95–102.

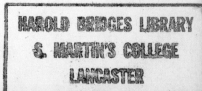

Highlanders – for sleeping in the hills or lying hidden in the heather. It was also conveniently cheap, since all agreed on the fact that the lower class could not afford the expense of trousers or breeches. But for men who had to fell trees or tend furnaces it was 'a cumbrous, unwieldy habit'. Therefore, being 'a man of genius and quick parts', Rawlinson sent for the tailor of the regiment stationed at Inverness and, with him, set out 'to abridge the dress and make it handy and convenient for his workmen'. The result was the *felie beg*, philibeg, or 'small kilt', which was achieved by separating the skirt from the plaid and converting it into a distinct garment, with pleats already sewn. Rawlinson himself wore this new garment, and his example was followed by his associate, Ian MacDonell of Glengarry. After that, the clansmen, as always, obediently followed their chief, and the innovation, we are told, 'was found so handy and convenient that in the shortest space the use of it became frequent in all the Highland countries and in many of the Northern Lowland countries also'.

This account of the origin of the kilt was first given in 1768 by a Highland gentleman who had known Rawlinson personally. It was published in 1785 and excited no dissent.[12] It was confirmed by the two greatest authorities on Scottish customs then living,[13] and by independent testimony, from the Glengarry family.[14] It was not challenged for another forty years. It has never been refuted. All the evidence that has since been accumulated is consistent with it. Pictorial evidence also comes to its aid, for the first person to be painted wearing a recognizable modern kilt, not a belted plaid, appears in a portrait of Alexander MacDonell of Glengarry, the son of the chief who was Rawlinson's friend. It is interesting to note that, in that portrait, the kilt is worn not by the chief but by his servant – thus emphasizing, once again, its 'servile' status.[15] On all this evidence, the best modern authorities accept the story as true.[16] We may thus conclude that the kilt is a purely modern costume, first designed, and first worn, by an English Quaker industrialist, and that it was bestowed by him on the Highlanders in order not to preserve their traditional way of life but to ease its transformation: to bring them out of the heather and into the factory.

[12] The account is by Ivan Baillie of Abereachen, and it was published in the *Edinburgh Magazine*, March 1785 (vol. I, p. 235).

[13] I refer to Sir John Sinclair and John Pinkerton. See below p. 27.

[14] I refer to the evidence of the Sobieski Stuarts. See below p. 36.

[15] For the portrait see Dunbar, *op. cit.*, pp. 69–70. It appears to have been painted about 1747.   [16] Dunbar, *loc. cit.*

But if this was the origin of the kilt, another question immediately forces itself on our mind. What tartan did the kilted Quaker wear? Was a distinctive 'sett' or pattern of colours devised for a Lancashire Rawlinson, or did he become an honorary member of the clan of MacDonell? Were there, indeed, any such 'setts' in the eighteenth century? When did the differentiation of patterns by clans begin?

The sixteenth-century writers who first noticed the Highland dress clearly did not know any such differentiation. They describe the plaids of the chiefs as coloured, those of their followers as brown, so that any differentiation of colour, in their time, was by social status, not by clan. The earliest evidence which has been adduced in support of differentiation by clan is a remark by Martin Martin, who visited the Western Islands at the end of the seventeenth century. But Martin merely assigns different patterns to different localities: he does not differentiate them by clans; and in fact the evidence against differentiation by clans is strong. Thus, a carefully painted series of portraits of the different members of the Grant family by Richard Waitt in the eighteenth century shows all of them in different tartans; the portraits of the Macdonalds of Armadale show 'at least six distinct setts of tartan'; and contemporary evidence concerning the rebellion of 1745 – whether pictorial, sartorial or literary – shows no differentiation of clans, no continuity of setts. The only way in which a Highlander's loyalty could be discerned was not by his tartan but by the cockade in his bonnet. Tartans were a matter of private taste, or necessity, only.[17] Indeed, in October 1745, when the Young Chevalier was in Edinburgh with his army, the *Caledonian Mercury* advertised a 'great choice of tartans, the newest patterns'. As D. W. Stewart reluctantly admits,

> this is a great stumbling-block in the way of those who argue for the antiquity of the patterns; for it seems peculiar that, when the city was filled with Highlanders of all ranks and many clans, they should be offered not their ancient setts but 'a great choice of the newest patterns'.

Thus when the great rebellion of 1745 broke out, the kilt, as we know it, was a recent English invention and 'clan' tartans did not exist. However, that rebellion marked a change in the sartorial as well as in the social and economic history of Scotland. After the rebellion had been crushed, the British government decided at last to do what

[17] The evidence on this point is set out conclusively by H. F. McClintock, *Old Highland Dress and Tartans*, 2nd edn (Dundalk, 1940) and Dunbar, *op. cit.*

had been considered in 1715 (and indeed before) and to destroy finally the independent Highland way of life. By the various acts of parliament which followed the victory at Culloden not only were the Highlanders disarmed and their chiefs deprived of their hereditary jurisdictions, but the wearing of Highland costume – 'plaid, philibeg, trews, shoulder-belts... tartans or parti-coloured plaid or stuff' – was forbidden throughout Scotland under pain of imprisonment without bail for six months and, for a second offence, transportation for seven years.[18] This draconian law remained in force for thirty-five years, during which the whole Highland way of life quickly crumbled. In 1773, when Johnson and Boswell made their famous tour, they found that they were already too late to see what they had expected, 'a people of peculiar appearance and a system of antiquated life'. In the whole of their tour, Johnson recorded, they had never seen the tartan worn. The law (of which he disapproved) had everywhere been enforced. Even the bagpipe, he noted, 'begins to be forgotten'. By 1780 the Highland dress seemed extinct, and no rational man would have speculated on its revival.

However, history is not rational: or at least it is rational only in parts. The Highland costume did indeed die out among those who had been accustomed to wear it. After a generation in trousers, the simple peasantry of the Highlands saw no reason to resume the belted plaid or the tartan which they had once found so cheap and serviceable. They did not even turn to the 'handy and convenient' new kilt. On the other hand, the upper and middle classes, who had previously despised the 'servile' costume, now picked up with enthusiasm the garb which its traditional wearers had finally discarded.[19] In the years when it had been banned, some Highland noblemen had taken pleasure in wearing it, and being portrayed in it, in the safety of their homes. Now that the ban was lifted, the fashion spread. Anglicized Scottish peers, improving gentry, well-educated Edinburgh lawyers and prudent merchants of Aberdeen – men who were not constrained by poverty and who would never have to skip over rocks and bogs or lie all night in the hills – would exhibit themselves publicly not in the historic trews, the traditional costume

---

[18] 19 Geo. II c. 39; 20 Geo. II c. 51; 21 Geo. II c. 34.

[19] Thus John Hay Allan (see below p. 32), in his *Bridal of Caölchairn*, pp. 308–9, remarks that, at Highland weddings, of the unfashionable tartan 'little or nothing is to be seen'. This was published in 1822, the year when King George IV's visit caused tartan to envelope the limbs of the higher classes in Edinburgh.

of their class, nor in the cumbrous belted plaid, but in a costly and fanciful version of that recent innovation, the philibeg or small kilt.

Two causes explain this remarkable change. One is general and European and can be briefly summarized. It was the romantic movement, the cult of the noble savage whom civilization threatened to destroy. Before 1745 the Highlanders had been despised as idle predatory barbarians. In 1745 they had been feared as dangerous rebels. But after 1746, when their distinct society crumbled so easily, they combined the romance of a primitive people with the charm of an endangered species. It was in this climate of opinion that Ossian enjoyed his easy triumph. The second cause was more particular and deserves closer examination. It was the formation, by the British government, of the Highland regiments.

The formation of the Highland regiments had begun before 1745 – indeed, the first such regiment, the Black Watch, afterwards the 43rd and then the 42nd line regiment, had fought at Fontenoy in 1745. But it was in the years 1757–60 that the elder Pitt systematically sought to divert the martial spirit of the Highlanders from Jacobite adventure to imperial war. As he would afterwards claim:

> I sought for merit wherever it was to be found; it is my boast that I was the first minister who looked for it, and found it, in the mountains of the North. I called it forth and drew into your service a hardy and intrepid race of men.

These Highland regiments would soon cover themselves with glory in India and America. They also established a new sartorial tradition. For by the 'Disarming Act' of 1747 they were explicitly exempted from the ban on Highland dress, and so, in the thirty-five years during which the Celtic peasantry took permanently to the Saxon trousers, and the Celtic Homer was portrayed in the bardic robe, it was the Highland regiments alone which kept the tartan industry alive and gave permanence to the most recent innovation of all, the Lancashire kilt.

Originally, the Highland regiments wore as their uniform the belted plaid; but once the kilt had been invented, and its convenience had made it popular, it was adopted by them. Moreover, it was probably their use of it which gave birth to the idea of differentiating tartan by clans; for as the Highland regiments were multiplied to meet the needs of war, so their tartan uniforms were differentiated; and when the wearing of tartan by civilians was resumed, and the romantic movement encouraged the cult of the clan, the same principle of differentiation was easily transferred from regiment to clan. That, however, was in the future. For the moment, we are concerned only with the kilt which, having been invented by an English Quaker industrialist, was saved from extinction by an English imperialist statesman. The next stage was the invention of a Scottish pedigree. This stage, at least, was undertaken by the Scots.

It began with an important step taken in 1778. This was the foundation, in London, of the Highland Society: a society whose main function was the encouragement of ancient Highland virtues and the preservation of ancient Highland traditions. Its members were mainly Highland noblemen and officers, but its secretary, 'to whose zeal for its success the society seems to have been peculiarly indebted', was John Mackenzie, a lawyer of the Temple who was the 'most intimate and confidential friend', the accomplice, general man of affairs, and afterwards executor of James Macpherson. Both James Macpherson and Sir John Macpherson were original members of the Society, one of whose expressed aims was the preservation of ancient Gaelic literature, and whose greatest achievement, in the eyes of its historian Sir John Sinclair, was the publication, in 1807, of the 'original' Gaelic text of Ossian. This text was supplied by Mackenzie from Macpherson's papers and edited, with a dissertation proving its authenticity (it is in fact a demonstrable fake), by Sinclair himself. In view of Mackenzie's double function and the Society's preoccupation with Gaelic literature (almost all of it produced or inspired by Macpherson), the whole venture can be seen as one of the operations of the Macpherson mafia in London.

A second and no less important aim of the Society was to secure the repeal of the law forbidding the wearing of the Highland dress in Scotland. For this purpose the members of the Society undertook themselves to meet (as they legally could in London)

> in that garb so celebrated as having been the dress of their Celtic ancestors, and on such occasions at least to speak the emphatic language, to listen to the delightful music, to recite the ancient poetry, and to observe the peculiar customs of their country.

But it may be observed that the Highland dress, even now, did not include the kilt: it was defined in the Society's rules as the trews and the belted plaid ('plaid and philibeg in one piece').[20] This aim was achieved in 1782, when the marquis of Graham, at the request of a

---

[20] Sir J. Sinclair, *An Account of the Highland Society of London* (1813).

committee of the Highland Society, successfully moved the repeal of the act in the house of commons. Its repeal occasioned great rejoicing in Scotland, and Gaelic poets celebrated the victory of the Celtic belted plaid over the Saxon trousers. From this date the triumph of the newly re-defined Highland dress can be said to have begun.

This triumph was not entirely unresisted. At least one Scotchman, from the beginning, raised his voice against the whole process whereby the Celtic Highlanders, so recently despised as outer barbarians, were claiming to be the sole representatives of Scottish history and culture. This was John Pinkerton, a man whose undoubted eccentricity and violent prejudices cannot rob him of his claim to be the greatest Scottish antiquary since Thomas Innes. For Pinkerton was the first scholar to establish something like the true history of Scotland in the Dark Ages. He was an implacable enemy of the historical and literary falsification of the two Macphersons. He was also the first scholar to document the history of the Highland dress. He did indeed make one grave error: he believed that the Picts were racially distinct from the Scots: that the Picts (whom he admired) were not Celts (whom he despised) but Goths. But this error did not invalidate his conclusions, which were that the early Caledonians had been distinguished by wearing not kilts, nor belted plaids, but trousers; that the tartan was an early modern importation; and that the kilt was more modern still.

Pinkerton had a ready listener in Sir John Sinclair himself. In 1794 Sinclair had raised a local military force – the Rothesay and Caithness Fencibles – to serve against France, and after careful research had decided to dress his troops not in the kilt (he knew all about the Quaker Rawlinson) but in tartan trews. Next year he decided to appear at court in Highland dress, including trousers of a tartan specially designed by himself. But before committing himself, he consulted Pinkerton. Pinkerton expressed his delight that Sinclair had substituted 'trousers or pantaloons for the philibeg', for that supposed ancient dress (he wrote) 'is in fact quite modern, and any improvement may be made without violating antiquity. Nay, the trousers are far more ancient than the philibeg'. Even the plaid and the tartan, he added, were not ancient. Having thus disposed of the antiquity of the whole outfit ascribed to 'our Celtic ancestors', Pinkerton turned to its intrinsic merit. The philibeg, he declared 'is not only grossly indecent, but is filthy, as it admits dust to the skin and emits the foetor of perspiration'; it is absurd, because while the breast is twice covered by vest and plaid, 'the parts concealed by all other nations are but loosely covered'; it is also effeminate, beggarly and ugly: for 'nothing can reconcile the tasteless regularity and vulgar glow of tartan to the eye of fashion, and every attempt to introduce it has failed'. Sir John's own private tartan, Pinkerton hastened to add, had 'avoided all such objections' and by using only two very mild colours had secured 'a very pleasing general effect'.[21]

So wrote 'the celebrated antiquary Mr Pinkerton'. He wrote in vain. For by now the Highland regiments had taken over the philibeg and their officers had easily convinced themselves that this short kilt had been the national dress of Scotland since time immemorial. Against a firm military order the tremulous voice of mere scholarship protests in vain, and any denial received short shrift. In 1804, the War Office – perhaps influenced by Sir John Sinclair – contemplated replacing the kilt by the trews, and duly sounded serving officers. Colonel Cameron, of the 79th regiment, was outraged. Was the High Command, he asked, really proposing to stop 'that free circulation of pure wholesome air' under the kilt which 'so peculiarly fitted the Highlander for *activity*'? 'I sincerely hope', protested the gallant colonel, 'that His Royal Highness will never acquiesce in so painful and degrading an idea...as to strip us of our native garb and stuff us into a harlequin tartan pantaloon.'[22] Before this spirited charge, the War Office retreated, and it was kilted Highlanders who, after the final victory of 1815, captured the imagination, and inspired the curiosity, of Paris. In the following years, the *Waverley Novels* combined with the Highland regiments to spread the fashion for kilts and tartans throughout Europe.

Meanwhile the myth of their antiquity was being pressed by another military man. Colonel David Stewart of Garth, who had joined the original 42nd Highlanders at the age of sixteen, had spent his entire adult life in the army, most of it abroad. As a half-pay officer after 1815, he devoted himself to the study first of the Highland regiments, then of Highland life and traditions: traditions which he had discovered more often, perhaps, in the officers' mess than in the straths and glens of Scotland. These traditions by now included the kilt and the clan tartans, both of which were accepted without question by the colonel. The notion that the kilt had been invented

---

[21] Pinkerton, *Literary Correspondence*, i, p. 404; Sir John Sinclair, *Correspondence* (1831), pp. 471–3.
[22] Dunbar, *op. cit.*, pp. 161–2.

by an Englishman had indeed come to his ears, but he declined to entertain it for a minute: it was, he said, refuted by 'the universal belief of the people that the philibeg had been part of their garb as far back as tradition reaches'. He also declared, with equal assurance, that tartans had always been woven 'in distinctive patterns (or setts, as they were called) of the different clans, tribes, families and districts'. For neither of these statements did he give any evidence. They were published in 1822, in a book entitled *Sketches of the Character, Manners and Present State of the Highlanders of Scotland*. This book, we are told, became 'the foundation of all subsequent works on the clans'.[23]

It was not only through literature that Stewart pushed the new Highland cause. In January 1820 he founded the Celtic Society of Edinburgh: a society of young civilians whose first object was 'to promote the general use of the ancient Highland dress in the Highlands', and to do so by wearing it themselves in Edinburgh. The president of the Society was Sir Walter Scott, a Lowlander. The members dined together regularly, 'kilted and bonneted in the old fashion, and armed to the teeth'. Scott himself, on these occasions, wore trews, but he declared himself 'very much pleased with the extreme enthusiasm of the Gael when liberated from the thraldom of breeches'. 'Such jumping, skipping and screaming' he wrote after one such dinner, 'you never saw.'[24] Such was the effect, even in decorous Edinburgh, of the free circulation of wholesome air under the Highlander's kilt.

Thus by 1822, thanks largely to the work of Sir Walter Scott and Colonel Stewart, the Highland takeover had already begun. It was given emphatic publicity in that year by George IV's state visit to Edinburgh. This was the first time that a Hanoverian monarch had ever appeared in the capital of Scotland, and elaborate preparations were made to ensure that the occasion was a success. What interests us is the persons who were charged with these preparations. For the master of ceremonies entrusted with all practical arrangements was Sir Walter Scott; Scott named as his assistant – his 'dictator' in all matters of ceremony and dress – Colonel Stewart of Garth; and the guards of honour which Scott and Stewart assigned to the protection of the king, the officers of state, and the regalia of Scotland were drawn

---

[23] *D.N.B.*, *s.v.* Stewart, David 1772–1829.
[24] *Letters of Sir W. Scott*, ed. H. C. Grierson (1932–7), vi, pp. 338–43, 452; J. G. Lockhart, *Life of Scott* (1850), pp. 443, 481–2.

from those 'enthusiasts for the philibeg', the members of the Celtic Club, 'dressed in proper costume'. The result was a bizarre travesty of Scottish history, Scottish reality. Imprisoned by his fanatical Celtic friends, carried away by his own romantic Celtic fantasies, Scott seemed determined to forget historic Scotland, his own Lowland Scotland, altogether. The royal visit, he declared, was to be 'a gathering of the Gael'. So he pressed the Highland chiefs to come with their 'tail' of followers and pay homage to their king. 'Do come and bring half-a-dozen or half-a-score of clansmen', he wrote to one such chief, 'so as to look like an island chief, as you are ... Highlanders are what he will best like to see.'[25]

The Highlanders duly came. But what tartan should they wear? The idea of differentiated clan tartans, which had now been publicized by Stewart, seems to have originated with the resourceful manufacturers who, for thirty-five years, had had no clients except the Highland regiments but who now, since the repeal of 1782, saw the prospect of a far larger market. The greatest of these firms was that of William Wilson and Son of Bannockburn, whose vast records are an invaluable source for historians. Messrs Wilson and Son saw the advantage of building up a repertoire of differentiated clan tartans, and thus stimulating tribal competition, and for this purpose they entered into alliance with the Highland Society of London, which threw, over their commercial project, a cloak, or plaid, of historical respectability. In 1819, when the royal visit was first suggested, the firm prepared a 'Key Pattern Book' and sent samples of the various tartans up to London, where the Society duly 'certified' them as belonging to this or that clan. However, when the visit was confirmed, the time for such pedantic consistency had passed. The spate of orders was now such that 'every piece of tartan was sold as it came off the loom'. In these circumstances, the first duty of the firm was to keep up the supply and ensure that the Highland chiefs were able to buy what they needed. So Cluny Macpherson, heir to the chief of the discoverer of Ossian, was given a tartan from the peg. For him it was now labelled 'Macpherson', but previously, having been sold in bulk to a Mr Kidd to clothe his West Indian slaves, it had been labelled 'Kidd', and before that it had been simply 'No. 155'. Thanks to such mercantile resourcefulness, the chiefs were able to respond to Sir Walter's summons, and the citizens of Edinburgh were able to admire Sir Evan Macgregor of Macgregor 'in his proper

[25] *Letters of Sir W. Scott*, vii, p. 213.

Highland tartan, with his tail, banner and pipers', and Colonel MacDonell of Glengarry, heir – after Rawlinson – to the oldest kilt in Scotland, now doubtless sophisticated for the occasion.

Thus was the capital of Scotland 'tartanized' to receive its king, who himself came in the same costume, played his part in the Celtic pageant, and at the climax of the visit solemnly invited the assembled dignitaries to drink a toast not to the actual or historic élite but to 'the chieftains and clans of Scotland'. Even Scott's devoted son-in-law and biographer, J. G. Lockhart, was taken aback by this collective 'hallucination' in which, as he put it, 'the marking and crowning glory' of Scotland was identified with the Celtic tribes which 'always constituted a small and almost always an unimportant part of the Scottish population'. Lord Macaulay, himself a Highlander by origin, was more outspoken. Writing in the 1850s, he did not doubt the antiquity of the Highland dress, but his historical sense was outraged by the retrospective extension of these 'striped petticoats' to the civilized races of Scotland. At length, he wrote, this absurd modern fashion had

> reached a point beyond which it was not easy to proceed. The last British king who held a court in Holyrood thought that he could not give a more striking proof of his respect for the usages which had prevailed in Scotland before the Union, than by disguising himself in what, before the Union, was considered by nine Scotchmen out of ten as the dress of a thief.[26]

'Beyond which it was not easy to proceed...' Macaulay under-estimated the strength of an 'hallucination' which is sustained by an economic interest. Scott might regain his balance – he quickly did – but the farce of 1822 had given a new momentum to the tartan industry, and inspired a new fantasy to serve that industry. So we come to the last stage in the creation of the Highland myth: the reconstruction and extension, in ghostly and sartorial form, of that clan system whose reality had been destroyed after 1745. The essential figures in this episode were two of the most elusive and most seductive characters who have ever ridden the Celtic hobby-horse or aerial broomstick: the brothers Allen.

The brothers Allen came from a well-connected naval family. Their grandfather, John Carter Allen, had been Admiral of the White. His son, their father, had served briefly in the navy; their mother was the daughter of a learned clergyman in Surrey. Their father is a shadowy

---

[26] Macaulay, *History of England*, ch. XIII.

person, and his life is mysterious. He seems to have lived mainly abroad, especially in Italy. The early life of the two sons is undocumented. All that we can say of them is that they were both talented artists in many fields. They wrote romantic poems in the style of Scott; they were learned, though evidently self-taught, in many languages; they were skilful draughtsmen, wood-carvers, furniture makers. They had persuasive manners and great social charm, which enabled them to move at ease in the best society. Whatever they did, they did thoroughly and with flair. The exact occasion of their first appearance in Scotland is unknown, but they were evidently there with their father during the royal visit in 1822, and they may have been there as early as 1819. 1819–22 was the period of preparation for the Royal visit. It was also the period in which the firm of Wilson and Son of Bannockburn was contemplating a systematic plan of Highland clan tartans, and the Highland Society of London, no doubt in collusion with them, was considering the publication of a lavishly illustrated book on Highland clan tartans.[27] There is some reason to think that the Allen family was in touch with Wilson and Son at this time.

In the following years the brothers may have spent some time abroad, but they also appeared occasionally in great Scottish houses or at fashionable functions, dressed (as one English observer put it) 'in all the extravagance of which the Highland costume is capable – every kind of tag and rag, false orders and tinsel ornaments'.[28] A visiting Russian aristocrat observed them, resplendent with orders and knighthoods, at Altyre, the house of the Gordon Cuming family. They had now Scoticized their name, first as Allan, then, via Hay Allan, as Hay; and they encouraged the belief that they were descended from the last Hay, earl of Errol. As he had been a bachelor, they presumably credited him with a secret marriage; but their claims were never weakened by explicit assertion. Sir Walter Scott recalled seeing the elder of them wearing the badge of the high constable of Scotland – an office hereditary in the house of Errol – 'which he could have no more right to wear than the Crown'.[29] No more, the wearer might have replied, and no less.

[27] Part of the proposal is among the MSS. of the Highland Society of London, National Library of Scotland, Deposit 268, Box 15. Undated, but watermark of 1818.   [28] *Letters and Journals of Lady Eastlake* (1895), i, pp. 54–5.

[29] It is fair to say that the brothers did not themselves originate their claim to be the heirs of the Earls of Errol. When their grandfather, Admiral John Carter Allen, died in 1800, his obituarist wrote that 'he was not only related to the Marchioness

Much of the brothers' time was spent in the far north, where the earl of Moray gave them the run of Darnaway Forest, and they became expert deer hunters. They never lacked aristocratic patrons. Hard-headed Lowland 'improvers' fell for them too. Such was Sir Thomas Dick Lauder, whose wife had an estate in Elgin. To him, in 1829, they revealed that they had in their possession an important historical document. This was a manuscript which (they said) had once belonged to John Leslie, bishop of Ross, the confidant of Mary Queen of Scots, and which had been given to their father by none other than the Young Chevalier, Bonny Prince Charlie. The manuscript was entitled *Vestiarium Scoticum*, or *The Garde-robe of Scotland*, and was a depiction of the clan tartans of Scottish families, declaring itself to be the work of one Sir Richard Urquhart, knight. Bishop Leslie had inserted his date – 1571 – but the manuscript could of course be much earlier. The brothers explained that the original document was with their father in London, but they showed to Dick Lauder a 'crude copy' which they had acquired, and which had evidently come ultimately from the Urquhart family of Cromarty. Sir Thomas was very excited by this discovery. Not only was the document important in itself, it also provided an authentic ancient authority for distinct clan tartans, and it showed that such tartans had been used by Lowlanders as well as Highlanders: a fact very gratifying to Lowland families eager to scramble in on the act.[30] So Sir Thomas made a transcript of the text, which the younger brother obligingly illustrated for him. He then wrote to Sir Walter Scott, as the oracle on all such matters, urging that the document be published to correct the numerous 'uncouth, spurious, modern tartans which are every day manufactured, christened after particular names, and worn as genuine'.

Scott's Augustan self had now reasserted itself, and he was not taken in. The history and content of the manuscript, and the character of the brothers, all seemed to him suspicious. He did not believe that

of Salisbury and the Marquis of Devonshire [*recte* Downshire], but Lord Hillsborough gave it as his opinion that the title of Erroll belonged to him as being descended from the old Earl Hay in the male line.' (*Gentleman's Magazine* (1800), p. 1021). The Marchioness of Salisbury, Lord Downshire and Lord Hillsborough were all members of the Hill family.

30 Thus the marquis of Douglas, about 1800, applied to the Highland Society of London to discover whether his family had 'any particular kind of tartan'. He admitted that 'it is so long since they used any that it must now be difficult to discover'; but he had hopes...(MSS. of the Highland Society of London, Box 1, no. 10).

Lowlanders had ever worn clan tartans, and he suspected a tartan weavers' ramp. At the very least he insisted that the original manuscript be submitted to experts at the British Museum. Sir Thomas followed up this suggestion and the elder brother very readily agreed; but that line of research was blocked when he produced a letter from his father, signed 'J. T. Stuart Hay', firmly reprimanding him for even mentioning the document, which (he said) – apart from the futility of seeking to revive a world now irrecoverably lost – could never be exhibited to profane eyes on account of certain 'private memorandums on the blank leaves'. 'As to the opinion of Sir Walter Scott,' said the writer of the letter, 'inasmuch as I have never heard it respected among antiquaries as of the least value, it is quite indifferent to me'.[31] That put the oracle of Abbotsford in his place.

Defeated by the authority of Scott, the brothers retired again to the north and gradually perfected their image, their expertise and their manuscript. They had now found a new patron, Lord Lovat, the Catholic head of the Fraser family, whose ancestor had died on the scaffold in 1747. They also adopted a new religious loyalty, declaring themselves Roman Catholics, and a new and grander identity. They dropped the name of Hay and assumed the royal name of Stuart. The elder brother called himself John Sobieski Stuart (John Sobieski, the hero–king of Poland, was the maternal great-grandfather of the Young Chevalier); the younger became, like the Young Chevalier himself, Charles Edward Stuart. From Lord Lovat they now obtained the grant of Eilean Aigas, a romantic lodge in an islet of the Beauly River in Inverness, and there they set up a miniature court. They were known as 'the Princes', sat on thrones, maintained a rigorous etiquette, and received royal honours from visitors, to whom they showed Stuart relics and hinted at mysterious documents in their locked charter chest. The royal arms were set up above the doorway of the house; when they were rowed upstream to the Catholic church at Eskadale, the royal pennant flew above their boat; their seal was a crown.

It was from Eilean Aigas, in 1842, that the brothers at last

---

[31] The correspondence of Dick Lauder and Scott, together with Dick Lauder's transcript of the *Vestiarium*, is now in The Royal Archives at Windsor, having been presented to Queen Mary by its owner, Miss Greta Morritt, Dick Lauder's great-granddaughter, in 1936. It has been published partially in the *Journal of Sir Walter Scott*, ed. D. Douglas, 2nd edn (1891), pp. 710–13; more fully in Stewart, *Old and Rare Scottish Tartans*. The documents, and those cited below on p. 40, are quoted by gracious permission of H.M. the Queen.

published their famous manuscript, *Vestiarium Scoticum*. It appeared in a sumptuous edition limited to fifty copies. The series of coloured illustrations of tartans was the first ever to be published and was a triumph over technical difficulties. These illustrations were executed by a new process of 'machine printing' and, in the words of a scholar writing fifty years later, 'for beauty of execution and exactness of detail have not been excelled by any method of colour-printing subsequently invented'. John Sobieski Stuart, as editor, supplied a learned commentary and new proofs of the authenticity of the manuscript: a 'traced facsimile' of Bishop Leslie's autograph in it and a 'transcript' of his receipt for it. The manuscript itself, he said, had been 'carefully collated' with a second manuscript recently discovered by an unnamed Irish monk in a Spanish monastery, unfortunately since dissolved; and another manuscript, recently in the possession of Lord Lovat, was also cited, although it had unfortunately been carried to America and there lost; but it was being actively sought...

The *Vestiarium Scoticum*, being of such limited distribution, was little noticed on its publication. Scott was now dead, and Dick Lauder, though he had remained 'a believer', held his peace. Had he scrutinized the printed setts, he might have noted, with surprise, that they had been considerably revised since they had been copied by the younger brother into his own transcript. But the published *Vestiarium*, it soon appeared, was only a preliminary *pièce justificative* for a far more wide-ranging original work. Two years later, the two brothers published an even more sumptuous volume, the result, clearly, of years of study. This stupendous folio, lavishly illustrated by the authors, was dedicated to Ludwig I, king of Bavaria, as 'the restorer of the Catholic arts of Europe' and contained a high-flown address, in both Gaelic and English, to 'the Highlanders'. According to the title-page, it was published in Edinburgh, London, Paris and Prague. It was entitled *The Costume of the Clans*.

The Costume of the Clans is an extraordinary work. For sheer erudition it makes all previous work on the subject seem thin and trivial. It cites the most arcane sources, Scottish and European, written and oral, manuscript and printed. It draws on art and archaeology as well as on literature. Half a century later a careful and scholarly Scottish antiquary described it as 'a perfect marvel of industry and ability',[32] and the best modern writer on the subject

---

[32] Stewart, *Old and Rare Scottish Tartans*.

describes it as 'a monumental work...one of the foundation-stones on which any history of the Highland dress is built'.[33] It is intelligent and critical. The authors admit the modern invention of the kilt (they had, after all, stayed with the MacDonells of Glengarry). Nothing that they say can be immediately discounted. On the other hand, nothing can be taken on trust. The book is shot through with pure fantasy and bare-faced forgery. Literary ghosts are gravely called in evidence as authorities. The poems of Ossian are used as a source, and elusive manuscripts are cited. These include 'a large copy of the original poems of Ossian and many other valuable Gaelic manuscripts' obtained from Douay by the late chevalier Watson but now, alas, invisible; a Latin manuscript of the fourteenth century found, with other manuscripts, in that Spanish monastery now so unfortunately dissolved; and, of course, the *Vestiarium Scoticum* itself, now firmly ascribed, 'on internal evidence', to the end of the fifteenth century. The hand-coloured illustrations represented monumental sculpture and ancient portraits. A portrait of the Young Chevalier in Highland costume was taken from 'the original in the possession of the authors'.

The Costume of the Clans was not only a work of antiquarian erudition, it also had a thesis. That thesis is that the peculiar Highland dress was the fossil relic of the universal dress of the Middle Ages, which had been replaced throughout the rest of Europe in the sixteenth century but which had survived, debased indeed but still recognizable, in that forgotten corner of the world. For in the Middle Ages (according to these authors) Celtic Scotland had been a flourishing part of cosmopolitan Catholic Europe: a rich, polished society in which the splendid courts of the tribal chiefs were nourished – thanks to the advanced Hebridean manufactures – by the luxuries and the enlightenment of the continent. Unfortunately, that rich civilization had not lasted: by the close of the Middle Ages those humming Hebridean looms, those brilliant island courts, that 'high intellectual sophistication' of Mull, Islay and Skye had declined; the Highlands had been cut off from the world; their society had become impoverished and introverted and their costume drab and mean. Only the *Vestiarium* – that great discovery of the two brothers – by revealing the brilliance of the original tartan setts, opened a narrow window on to that splendid culture which had now gone for ever. For the authors professed no interest in the modern

---

[33] Dunbar, *History of the Highland Dress*, p. 111.

attempt to revive the costume alone, divorced from the Catholic Celtic culture of which it was a part. That was to convert it into mere fancy dress. The only true revival was one in which the whole past lived again – as it was lived by the Stuart brothers, writing poetry, hunting the deer, maintaining their own tribal court on an island in the Beauly river. Like Pugin, who sought to revive not merely Gothic architecture but a whole imaginary civilization behind it, so 'the Sobieski Stuarts' (as they were generally called) sought to revive not merely the Highland costume but a whole imaginary Highland civilization; and they did so by a fiction as bold, and an historical revision as outrageous, as that of 'Ossian'.

Unfortunately, *The Costume of the Clans* never received the criticism, or even the notice, of the learned world. Before that could happen, the authors had made a grave tactical error. In 1846 they went as near as they would ever go towards explicitly claiming royal blood. They did this in a series of short stories which, under romantic but transparent names, professed to reveal historical truth. The work was entitled *Tales of a Century*: the century from 1745 to 1845. The burden of these tales was that the Stuart line was not extinct; that a legitimate son had been born to the wife of the Young Chevalier in Florence; that this infant, through fear of assassination by Hanoverian agents, had been entrusted to the care of an English admiral who had brought him up as his own son; and that in due course he had become the legitimate father of two sons who, having fought for Napoleon at Dresden, Leipzig and Waterloo, and been personally decorated by him for bravery, had then retired to await their destiny in their ancestral country, and were now seeking to restore its ancient society, customs, costumes. Learned footnotes citing the still uncatalogued Stuart papers, unverifiable German and Polish documents, and 'manuscripts in our possession' supplied evidence to support this history.

At this point a hidden enemy struck. Under the cloak of a belated review of the *Vestiarium*, an anonymous writer published in the *Quarterly Review* a devastating exposure of the royal claims of the two brothers.[34] The elder brother attempted to reply. The reply was

---

[34] 'The Heirs of the Stuarts', *Quarterly Review*, lxxxii (1847). The article was ascribed at the time, and often confidently, to J. G. Lockhart, to J. W. Croker, to Lord Stanhope and to James Dennistoun; and perhaps to others. In fact it was by George Skene, Professor at Glasgow University, the elder brother of the Celtic scholar W. F. Skene.

olympian in tone, but weak in substance.[35] The scholarly work of
the two brothers was now fatally compromised; the household at
Eilean Aigas suddenly broke up; and for the next twenty years the
two brothers maintained abroad, in Prague and Pressburg, the royal
pretensions which had been fatally damaged at home. In the same
year Queen Victoria bought Balmoral, and the real Hanoverian court
replaced the vanished, illusory Jacobite court in the Highlands of
Scotland.

In economic history we often witness the ruin of the bold,
imaginative, sometimes fantastic pioneer whose work is then taken
over and carried to success by a more pedestrian entrepreneur. The
Sobieski Stuarts never recovered from the exposure of 1847. Although
their personal charm, their good nature and their dignified,
inoffensive behaviour ensured that they never lacked believers,
always that fatal article in the *Quarterly Review* was cited against
them. But their work was not wasted. The *Vestiarium* might be
discredited, *The Costume of the Clans* ignored, but the spurious clan
tartans devised by them were taken up, without their damaged
names, by the Highland Society of London, and became the means
of the continuing prosperity of the Scottish tartan industry. The
pedestrian successor of the high-flying Sobieski Stuarts who achieved
this more lasting triumph was James Logan.

James Logan was an Aberdonian who, in his youth, suffered what
he called an 'appalling wound' while attending Highland games. At
the throwing of the hammer, the missile, weighing 17 lb, accidentally
landed on his head, as a result of which, as he afterwards explained
(in order to extenuate some unspecified misconduct), 'my skull was
literally shattered', and four square inches of it had to be replaced
by a metal plate.[36] In spite of this discouragement, Logan became
an enthusiast for Highland traditions, and in 1831, after an extensive
walking tour through Scotland, he published a book entitled *The
Scottish Gael* which he dedicated to King William IV. In this work
he repeated all the recent Highland mythology: the authenticity of
the poems of Ossian, the antiquity of the kilt, the differentiation of
clan tartans; and he announced that he was himself 'preparing a

---

[35] The reply was published by Blackwood & Sons (Edinburgh, 1848). Both the
attack and the reply were afterwards republished together, without date, by
Lorimer and Gillies, Edinburgh. The volume was privately printed, apparently
by, or in the interest of, the Sobieski Stuarts.

[36] MSS. of the Highland Society of London, Box 5, Logan to the committee of
directors of the Society (n.d.).

work expressly on tartans and badges, with illustrative plates'. By this time Logan had established himself in London, and the Highland Society, in recognition of his book, promptly elected him as its president and undertook to sponsor his promised work on tartans. This work ultimately appeared in 1843 – the year after the publication of the *Vestiarium*. It was called the *Clans of the Scottish Highlands*, and was lavishly illustrated, with seventy-two paintings of clansmen in their distinctive tartans, by R. R. MacIan.

It is unlikely that there were any direct relations between the Sobieski Stuarts, with their genuine erudition and not altogether bogus aristocratic airs, and the uncritical, plebeian James Logan. But the Sobieski Stuarts were undoubtedly in touch with the tartan manufacturers and had been advising both them and the clan chieftains on their tartans, perhaps as early as 1819. We know, too, that the greatest of the manufacturers, Messrs Wilson and Son, were in touch with Logan, whom they treated as a mere agent, sometimes correcting his work from their own superior knowledge; so they evidently had at their disposal what they considered better authority. It seems likely therefore that Logan's work was nourished throughout, directly or indirectly, by the fantasies of the Sobieski Stuarts. In the event, the Sobieski Stuarts' *Vestiarium* was published first. In his text, Logan paid tribute to 'the recent splendid work of John Sobieski Stuart' on which it clearly drew – though with occasional differences of detail, sufficient to justify a separate publication. In fact, as a later scholar has written, many of Logan's tartans were 'unacknowledged reproductions from the designs in the *Vestiarium Scoticum*'.[37]

Logan was fortunate in his timing. The exposure of the royal claims of the Sobieski Stuarts – the real inventors of the clan tartans – destroyed the credit of his rivals just at the moment when Queen Victoria's cult of the Highlands gave a new impulse to clan tartans, as to Highland scenery, Highland cattle, Sir Edwin Landseer and the ghillie John Brown. In 1850 no less than three works on clan tartans were published, all of them visibly but silently indebted to the discredited *Vestiarium* whose 'editors' had vainly sought to publish a cheap edition. One of them – General James Browne's *History of the Highlands and the Highland Clans*, which became the standard work – contained twenty-two lithographic plates of tartan in colour, taken without commentary from the *Vestiarium*.[38] For the rest of the century, numerous books of clan tartans were regularly

---

[37] Stewart, *op. cit.*   [38] Stewart, *op. cit.*

published. All of them were heavily dependent – directly or indirectly – on the *Vestiarium*.

This must have been mortifying to the Sobieski Stuarts, who returned to Britain in 1868. They were now desperately poor, but as always they continued their chosen role. They lived in London, went into society wearing their questionable orders and decorations, and were well known in the British Museum reading room, where a table was reserved for their use, and 'their pens, paper-knives, paper-weights, etc. were surmounted with miniature coronets, in gold'.[39] In 1872 an appeal was made to Queen Victoria to relieve the poverty of these supposed kinsmen, but the review in the *Quarterly* was cited against them and it failed.[40] In 1877 the younger brother, who alone survived, sought anonymously to recall their titles, but was silenced, once again, by a reference to the *Quarterly*.[41] As of John Keats, it could be said of them that they were killed by the *Quarterly*: indeed, many thought that they were killed by the same hand.[42] But they never lacked believers; their friends championed them to the end; and after their death Lord Lovat caused them to be buried at Eskadale by the church which they had once attended from their romantic island home at Eilean Aigas. Their effects were then sold, and Queen Victoria showed an interest in the sale; but no Stuart relics, paintings, miniatures, title deeds or manuscripts were found among them. Nor has anyone ever seen the original text of the *Vestiarium Scoticum*, with its annotation by Bishop Leslie, and its interesting private memorandums – presumably inscribed by its previous owner, the Young Chevalier, when he passed it on to his son 'J. T. Stuart Hay', alias 'James Stuart, comte d'Albanie', the even more elusive father of our elusive heroes.[43]

This essay began with reference to James Macpherson. It ends with the Sobieski Stuarts. Between these makers of Highland tradition there are many resemblances. Both imagined a golden age

---

[39] *D.N.B.*, *art cit.*   [40] Windsor Castle MSS. P.P. 1/79.

[41] *Notes and Queries* (July–Dec. 1877), pp. 92, 158, 214, 351, 397. The letters signed 'RIP' and 'Requiescat in Pace' are clearly by Charles Edward Stuart.

[42] J. G. Lockhart, who had written the notorious attack on Keats, was supposed by some – but wrongly – to be the author of the exposure of the Sobieski Stuarts.

[43] Nothing seems discoverable about Thomas Allen, Lieut R.N. retired, the father of the Sobieski Stuarts. His later names and titles are recorded only in the writings or forgeries of his sons, to whom they were a genealogical necessity. It is not known whether the father played any part in the pretence. He was evidently a recluse. He died in Clerkenwell in 1839 (not, as stated in *D.N.B.*, 1852), after which the elder son (and after his death, the younger) called himself Comte d'Albanie.

in the past of the Celtic Highlands. Both declared that they possessed documentary evidence. Both created literary ghosts, forged texts and falsified history in support of their theories. Both began an industry which would thrive in Scotland long after their death. Both were soon exposed, but ignored their exposure and turned calmly to other pursuits: Macpherson to Indian politics, the Sobieski Stuarts to an unreal life abroad.

But there were also great differences. Macpherson was a sensual bully whose aim, whether in literature or in politics, was wealth and power and who pursued that aim with ruthless determination and ultimate success. The Sobieski Stuarts were amiable, scholarly men who won converts by their transpicuous innocence; they were *fantaisistes* rather than forgers. They were also genuine in the sense that they lived their own fantasies. Unlike Macpherson, they died poor. The wealth which they generated went to the manufacturers of the differentiated clan tartans now worn, with tribal enthusiasm, by Scots and supposed Scots from Texas to Tokyo.

3. *From a Death to a View: The Hunt for the Welsh Past in the Romantic Period*

PRYS MORGAN

MERRIE WALES AND ITS PASSING

When one looks at the cultural life of Wales in the eighteenth and early nineteenth centuries one is struck by a paradox; on the one hand the decay or demise of an ancient way of life, and on the other an unprecedented outburst of interest in things Welsh and highly self-conscious activity to preserve or develop them. The Welsh historian Peter Roberts[1] wrote a survey of the old way of life in 1815, in which he observed

> When, from political or other causes, the manners and customs of a nation have, in general, undergone a great change, an inquiry into what they have been in former ages becomes interesting.[2]

Nearly all Welsh picturesque customs were 'now wholly laid aside', and some druidic beliefs had never been held at all. The Hon. John Byng visited Bala in 1784 and again in 1793 and complained that 'Within ten years there seem'd an alteration in the manners of the people.' Signs of Welsh merriment were gone, the Welsh were becoming like the English, and all the curiosity of travel was undone.[3] Decay and revival are curiously intermixed, because very often those who bewailed the decay were the very ones who brought about the revival. R. T. Jenkins said that the eighteenth century was not so much the century of the Methodist Revival as the century of revivals: educational, agrarian, industrial and cultural; the Welsh Renaissance or antiquarian revival being if not the most massive certainly the most original.[4] In this period Welsh scholars and patriots rediscovered the

---

[1] Most of the people mentioned in this chapter are described in *The Dictionary of Welsh Biography down to 1940* (London, 1959), but Peter Roberts is found in the Welsh supplement to the dictionary (London, 1970).

[2] Peter Roberts, *Cambrian Popular Antiquities* (London, 1815), introd.

[3] C. Bruyn Andrews (ed.), *The Torrington Diaries* (London, 1936), iii, pp. 254–5.

[4] R. T. Jenkins, *Hanes Cymru yn y Ddeunawfed Ganrif* (History of Wales in the Eighteenth Century) (Cardiff, 1928), pp. 2, 104–34. Cf. E. D. Evans, *A History of Wales 1660–1815* (Cardiff, 1976), pp. 231–50.

43

past, historical, linguistic and literary traditions, and where those traditions were inadequate, they created a past which had never existed. Romantic mythologizing went to quite extraordinary lengths in Wales, leaving a permanent mark on its later history.

The fact that the scholars who noted the decay were the ones who recreated the past presents no serious difficulty. Edward Jones (1752–1824), the harpist to George IV as prince and king, lamented in his book on Welsh music, *The Bardic Museum*,

> The sudden decline of the national Minstrelsy, and Customs of Wales, is in a great degree to be attributed to the fanatick impostors, or illiterate plebeian preachers, who have too often been suffered to over-run the country, misleading the greater part of the common people from their lawful Church; and dissuading them from their innocent amusements, such as Singing, Dancing, and other rural Sports, and Games, which heretofore they had been accustomed to delight in, from the earliest time...the consequence is, Wales, which was formerly one of the merriest, and happiest countries in the World, is now become one of the dullest.[5]

By his various books on Welsh music published between 1784 and 1820 Edward Jones was one of those who turned Welsh culture from being one of decaying but unselfconscious survival into self-aware revival, and the result, though often bogus, was never dull.

A very small number of Welsh scholars had long been aware of the disappearance of a distinctive Welsh way of life. In the sixteenth century the native culture bound up with Catholicism largely disappeared without an especially Welsh Protestant culture coming fully to replace it, the native legal system was abolished, the bardic system atrophied, the old language was outlawed from administration, and, although the official classes still spoke Welsh, their attitudes became anglicized or they approximated to western European norms of behaviour. The decay continued through the seventeenth and eighteenth centuries, but the critical stage was not reached until the eighteenth century because up until then scholars might always comfort themselves with the thought that much of the old culture remained among the common people. The critical stage was marked at first by a loss of self-confidence. The Welsh almanacker and lexicographer Thomas Jones said in 1688

> To Languages as well as Dominions...there is an appointed time; they have had their infancy, foundations and beginning, their

---

[5] Edward Jones, *The Bardic Museum* (London, 1802), introd., p. xvi.

growth and increase in purity and perfection; as also in spreading, and propagation: their state of consistency; and their old age, declinings and decayes.

And thus it hath pleased the Almighty to deal with us the Brittains; for these many ages hath eclipsed our Power, and corrupted our Language, and almost blotted us out of the Books of Records.[6]

The last phrase was crucial, for central to the loss of self-confidence was the loss of a sense of history. Sir John Vanbrugh in *Aesop* (about 1697) brings Aesop into contact with an aptly named Welsh herald called Quaint, who explains his trade by saying that of course his mother was a 'Welch Woman'

Aesop   A Welch Woman? Prithee of what Country's that?
Quaint   That, Sir, is a Country in the World's back-side, where
             every Man is born a Gentleman, and a Genealogist.[7]

The image of Wales was of a quaint back-of-beyond where gentlemen with hardly a shirt to their backs reeled off endless family trees going back to Aeneas from Troy, a land of unchanging backwardness, whose people had plenty of ancestry but no national history.

This had not been the case in earlier centuries. To put a complicated matter briefly, the older Welsh vision of history had been threefold: it concerned their origins as a nation, their conversion to Christianity and their lives of native princes. The oldest part was a set of myths or fables proving the Welsh to be the earliest and prime people of the British Isles (hence Thomas Jones's 'Brittains'). The Welsh memorized the facts concerning their early heroes, and how they had fought off waves of invaders and then been defeated and fought back again, in sets of three linked sentences 'The Triads of the Isle of Britain'.[8] The second part of the vision concerned British Christianity, introduced in Roman times, and defended by the Welsh against the pagan Saxons with heroes like Ambrosius Aurelianus and Arthur. In each locality the church or the holy well would be connected to this central theme by saints such as David or the other Celtic saints. The third part of the vision was more conventional and it concerned lines of native princes descending from tribal leaders, or Roman

---

[6] Thomas Jones, *The British Language in its Lustre* (London, 1688), preface.

[7] B. Dobrée and G. Webb (eds.), *The Works of Sir John Vanbrugh* (London, 1927), ii, p. 33.

[8] Rachel Bromwich, *Trioedd Ynys Prydein, the Triads of the Isle of Britain* (Cardiff, 1961), and *Trioedd Ynys Prydein in Welsh Literature and Scholarship* (Cardiff, 1969).

foederati like Cunedda, or from Cadwaladr the Blessed, last Welsh king to claim over-lordship of Britain, in the seventh century, right down to the death of Llywelyn II in 1282. In the mid-eighteenth century the people of Builth were unjustly known as 'the traitors of Builth' because Llywelyn was slain nearby.

During the later Middle Ages the different parts had become jumbled and transformed. In the twelfth century Geoffrey of Monmouth adapted the old myths and invented a Welsh tradition; he emphasized the Trojan origins of the British, Britain taking its name from Brutus, and Wales (Cymru) from Camber; he also emphasized the heroic role of King Arthur. The Galfridian version of Welsh history was still stubbornly retained by the Welsh historians in the mid-eighteenth century, and one of the main aims of the patriots was to find and publish the Welsh original they thought must lie behind Geoffrey's history. Welsh scholars of the period were also aware of the other dimension of the Welsh tradition, the prophetic or messianic dimension, which projected the Welsh past into the future. Evan Evans, for example, makes something of this in his discussion of the Welsh bardic tradition in 1764.[9] In early Celtic society the *vates* or seers foretold the future, a function taken over by the bards, and after the loss of independence in 1282 the literature of *brud* or prophecy took on great importance.[10]

The threefold native historical tradition was gradually transformed in the sixteenth century. The prophetic element decayed, though the tradition was manipulated cleverly by Henry Tudor to drum up Welsh support by posing as the messianic figure of the 'Second Owain', and his descent from Cadwaladr was used to legitimize Tudor claims to the overlordship of Britain. For others, Henry seemed to symbolize the long-awaited return of Arthur. A little later, the Anglican Church took to itself the Welsh myths of the founding of the British Church by Joseph of Arimathea, and blame for the loss of its independence could be easily laid not at the door of the English but the Normans and the Pope.[11] The rest of the Welsh

[9] Evan Evans, *Some Specimens of Early Welsh Poetry* (London, 1764), especially his 'Dissertatio de bardis'.

[10] M. M. Griffiths, *Early Vaticination in Welsh with English Parallels* (Cardiff, 1937); and Glanmor Williams, 'Prophecy, Poetry and Politics in Medieval and Tudor Wales', in H. Hearder and H. R. Loyn (eds.), *British Government and Administration* (Cardiff, 1974), pp. 104–16.

[11] Sydney Anglo, 'The British History in early Tudor propaganda', *Bulletin of the John Rylands Library*, xliv (1961), pp. 17–48. Glanmor Williams, 'Some Protestant Views of Early British Church History', *History*, xxxviii (1953), reprinted in his *Welsh Reformation Essays* (Cardiff, 1967), pp. 207–19.

tradition was not so much absorbed as discredited as baseless myth because Polydore Vergil exploded so much of Geoffrey of Monmouth's history as fabulous. What remained, then, after these attacks or adaptations, was taken over by English scholars as early English–British history for they wished to identify England with British antiquity.[12] It is clear that as late as the end of the seventeenth century separate bits and pieces of very early tradition were memorized as fireside tales by the common folk, tales of Emrys (Ambrosius), Merlin, Arthur, Taliesin, and others, on the evidence of the correspondents of Edward Lhuyd in the 1690s.[13] They did not form part of a coherent whole, but were like the pearls which have rolled off a broken necklace string. In some cases early bits of Welsh history were memorized in ballads as in Matthew Owen's 'Hanes y Cymru' (History of the Welsh) wherein the Welsh went over their ancient defeats passively.[14]

The loss of Welsh history had a debilitating effect on other aspects of culture. It is true that the bulk of literary texts of Welsh lore and learning surviving today date from about 1550 to 1700; G. J. Williams has observed that this is because scribes and antiquaries realized their familiar world was coming to an end, and a heroic act of salvage was needed as the world became more and more bleak.[15] G. J. Williams also observed a gradual decline in the grasp that Welsh literati had of the traditional culture, its symbols, language, grammar, and many of the owners of manuscripts confessed that, although Welsh-speaking, they understood nothing about their property save that it might be valuable. Thomas Hearne found it impossible to persuade Welshmen to put old Welsh manuscript chronicles into print: 'they are all averse, and are utterly for the discouraging of their own history'.[16] English lyrical forms (albeit with consonantal alliteration or *cynghanedd*) came to dominate poetry, and Protestant theology took the place of traditional symbolism and allusion in what remained of traditional verse. In the early eighteenth century a good Welsh scholar, John Morgan of Matchin, wrote to Edward Lhuyd's

[12] T. D. Kendrick, *British Antiquity* (London, 1950), pp. 34–134.
[13] F. V. Emery, 'A New Account of Snowdonia 1693 Written for Edward Lhuyd', *National Library of Wales Journal*, xviii (1974), pp. 405–17.
[14] Dafydd Jones, *Blodeugerdd Cymry* (Shrewsbury, 1759), p. 150; and T. H. Parry-Williams (ed.), *Llawysgrif Richard Morris o Gerddi* (Cardiff, 1931), p. 125.
[15] For all aspects of Welsh scholarship I have depended heavily upon G. J. Williams (ed. A. Lewis), *Agweddau ar Hanes Dysg Gymraeg* (Aspects of the History of Welsh Scholarship) (*Cardiff, 1969*), *passim*, but here esp. pp. 83–4.
[16] Quoted in J. Davies, *Bywyd a Gwaith Moses Williams* (Life and Work of Moses Williams) (Cardiff, 1937), pp. 24–5.

assistant Moses Williams (for a time secretary of the Royal Society) to say that just as one could not read Greek and Roman classics without a dictionary to classical allusion, so a dictionary to Welsh lore was now needed, otherwise Welsh history and literature would remain a lock without a key.

Thomas Jones – and he was not alone – mentioned in 1688 that the Almighty had 'corrupted our Language', and more and more Welshmen were beginning to refer to Welsh as *heniaith*, the 'old language', as though it were in a geriatric home. The poet and drover Edward Morus praised Bishop Lloyd of St Asaph (one of the Seven Bishops of 1688) for learning Welsh, and made the Welsh language say that it was 'an old battered language that was once top', and was 'a delicate peacock now in his old age'.[17] English satirists such as W.R. in his *Wallography* (London, 1681) hoped the language would soon be dead; it was the 'gibberish' of 'Taphydom', spoken now only by the lower orders. Henry Rowlands of Llanidan in his history of Anglesey complained

> And of late when the neighbouring *English* hath so much encroach'd upon it, by becoming the genteel and fashionable Tongue among us, many more words lye by us obsolete and useless, which were before perhaps the Flowers and Ornaments of our Language.[18]

As with everything else Welsh, the language had no status, it was 'regardless' (Thomas Jones's word in 1688). About 1730 the poet and squireen Huw Hughes wrote to the great scholar Lewis Morris that all the defenders of the old language had gone to sleep.[19] Welsh survived and was prevented from dissolution into dialects by the Anglican liturgy, and the Welsh Bible and Protestant apologetic literature. But it had little mechanism for modernization or development, and seemed to have no real dynamic behind it. It appeared, as it is shown on the graphic titlepage of James Howell's dictionary of 1659, as a scared wild woodland warrior maiden, in comparison with the richly clad court ladies of England or France.[20]

The great work of the Elizabethan Welsh Protestant leaders was not fully matched by a modern Welsh secular culture, for example

---

[17] O. M. Edwards (ed.), *Gwaith Edward Morus* (Llanuwchllyn, 1904), pp. 21–4.

[18] Henry Rowlands, *Mona Antiqua Restaurata* (Dublin, 1723), p. 38.

[19] Hugh Owen (ed.), *Additional Letters of the Morrises of Anglesey*, 2 vols. (London, 1947–9), i, p. 13.

[20] James Howell, *Lexicon Tetraglotton* (London, 1659) contains a section on Welsh proverbs.

a modern secular literature. Welsh letters were still dominated by the backward looking bards (who had fulfilled the functions of historians, copyists, librarians, heralds, musicians, and so on), and bardistry gradually died away as their culture appeared to be less and less relevant to the times. Bardistry seemed to decay in neighbourhoods that were half Welsh and fully Welsh more or less at the same time; there were few professional bards in Glamorgan after 1660, few in Montgomeryshire after 1640, and even in the remote Lleyn peninsula, if we follow Myrddin Fardd's *Cynfeirdd Lleyn*, there is a gap between the last bard in 1640 and the next one who is an amateur aboard a man-o'-war in 1800.[21] In Merioneth the last household bard retained in the old manner was Sion Dafydd Las at Nannau (1690), but it must be remembered that the gentry of Nannau and the neighbourhood were still writing Welsh poetry (for themselves and for publication) as late as the early nineteenth century, as amateurs. The bards who were no longer able to find employment, or who were now unwelcome, in the early years of the eighteenth century complained bitterly at the recent change, some such as Sion Prichard Prys in his *Difyrrwch Crefyddol* giving vent to impotent rage at the way the 'columns had been felled'.[22] The Welsh grandees no longer supported the native culture so that 'the Art weakened, the Language grew aged, and all of this was because of their weakness, and are led astray on errant paths to the brink of their own destruction'.[23] That amateurs among the lesser gentry or common folk still practised, that poetry was being published in books did not count. The bards looked back to a recent past when they had sung for the whole society from grandee down to peasant, when all had taken part in a merry joyous life, when the whole way of life had been harmonious. The savage satirist Ellis Wynne, a cleric from the lesser gentry, had no love for bards, but hated the modern elements in society too, and like Sion Prichard Prys felt some sort of vacuum in society: he describes the 'huge gaping manor house' whose owners had gone to England or to France 'to seek there what would have been easier found at home',

[21] G. J. Williams, *Traddodiad Llenyddol Morgannwg* (Literary Tradition of Glamorgan) (Cardiff, 1948); Enid Pierce Roberts, *Braslun o Hanes Llên Powys* (Sketch of Powyss Literary History) (Denbigh, 1965); and Myrddin Fardd, *Cynfeirdd Lleyn* (Early Poets of Lleyn) (Pwllheli, 1905).

[22] Gwyn Thomas, 'A Study of the Change in Tradition in Welsh Poetry in North Wales in the Seventeenth Century' (Oxford D.Phil. thesis, 1966).

[23] Sion Prichard Prys, *Difyrrwch Crefyddol* (Religious Entertainment) (Shrewsbury, 1721), preface.

so that the old family had abandoned the house to the owl and the crows and magpies:

There was a mass of such abandoned manor houses, which could have been, but for Pride, as of yore the haunt of the best of men, the shelter of the weak, a very school of peace and all goodness, and a blessing to a thousand lesser houses around them.[24]

Even if they had stayed at home it is unlikely that the greater nobles and gentry would have seen themselves as part of a small unified harmonious local community. The traditional Welsh hall house was now coming to an end, the gentry no longer living in a great hall with servants, tenants, friends and bards.[25] They were living their lives in private, and as they redesigned their houses they adopted London fashions, and vernacular regional styles came to an end. By 1700 the Welsh were perhaps catching up with styles of living fashionable in England a century or two earlier.[26]

The cultural break was seen very clearly in the world of music. In the late eighteenth century the collector of Welsh folk dances, William Jones of Llangadfan, was amazed that in a short space of time the tradition of so many centuries should have disappeared. Lewis Morris sent a poem, together with some harpstrings, to the diarist William Bulkeley, the squire of Brynddu in Anglesey in 1726, and we might render his little stanza thus:

There is in Wales, one must lament,
No music and no merriment,
And yet there was, in days of old,
A harp in every household.[27]

John Roderick the almanacker and grammarian wrote in his embittered old age to Lewis Morris in 1729 to bewail the fact that he could find no one to understand old Welsh music, the lists of tunes and directions for tuning and playing old instruments to be found in many Welsh manuscripts. Some years later, the Morris brothers and their circle came across a huge album of ancient Welsh music written in a strange notation. It was written by Robert ap Huw, King James I's harpist, in 1613. He came from the same area of the island of Anglesey as the Morris brothers, and he died in 1665 only a

---

24 Ellis Wynne, *Gweledigaetheu y Bardd Cwsc* (Visions of the Sleeping Bard) (London, 1703), p. 13. Cf. Gwyn Thomas, *Y Bardd Cwsg a'i Gefndir* (The Sleeping Bard and its Background) (Cardiff, 1971).

25 Peter Smith, *Houses of the Welsh Countryside* (London, 1975).

26 Mark Girouard, *Life in the English Country House* (London, 1978), pp. 10, 138.

27 Hugh Owen (ed.), *Life and Works of Lewis Morris* (Anglesey Antiquarian Soc. and Field Club, 1951), p. 162.

generation before the Morris brothers were born. The Morris family were very musical, they gathered around the harp for sing-songs, they knew how to tune a *crwth* or crowd, they had farm servants who went out to call the cattle while playing old airs on the *pibgorn* (a primitive shawm), they delighted in the music of Vivaldi and Corelli, and they claimed to be authorities on Welsh music. But a closer examination of young Richard Morris's notebook, with large numbers of tunes for playing on the fiddle, shows that four-fifths of the tunes had English names.[28] The great album of Robert ap Huw (which represented a selection of medieval music) was utterly incomprehensible to them and to every other Welsh musician of the eighteenth century. In most parts of Wales the old music had been associated with the rites and rituals of the customary life, and as they went so the music went too. In the late seventeenth century one of Edward Lhuyd's correspondents wrote to him at the Ashmolean in Oxford to describe the old life at Llandrillo, a remote village near Bala:

> Dafydd Rowland the old crowder used every Easter Sunday in the afternoon to go with the parish youngsters to the top of Craig Dhinan to share out the white oxen. Then he would play the tune called *Ychen Bannog* and all the other old tunes, which died with him.[29]

If those white oxen were like those of Glamorgan, then they were garlanded with flowers, and surrounded by colourful dancers, it must have been a sight worthy to have been put on Keats's Grecian Urn. The *Ychen Bannog* were the great long-horned oxen of primitive Europe. When the old crowder died, the tradition that was broken was a long one indeed. The crowd was barely known at all in South Wales, and Daines Barrington reported to the Society of Antiquaries in 1770 that the last of the Welsh crowders was still alive in Anglesey, but he had no successors. Even the old simple Welsh harp had been replaced in the seventeenth century by a larger triple harp. Lyric songs and ballads on the English pattern had flooded in after 1660, and with them came a host of English melodies. The Morris circle were aware that the singing of verses to harp music was a dying tradition, virtually confined by 1738 to remote parts such as Caernarfonshire and Merioneth.[30]

[28] Parry-Williams, *op. cit.*

[29] Edward Lhuyd (ed. R. H. Morris), *Parochialia* (Archaeologia Cambrensis, ii, 1909–11), p. 59.

[30] For the Morrises and their circle J. H. Davies (ed.), *The Morris Letters*, 2 vols. (Aberystwyth, 1906–7), *The Letters of Goronwy Owen* (Aberystwyth, 1924); and Owen, *Additional Letters.*

Edward Lhuyd and his correspondents in the 1690s were already aware that a dull uniformity was beginning to creep over Welsh life. For example they lovingly noted the rare surviving native baptismal names such as Llywarch, Goleubryd, Tegwared, Tangwystl and so on, which had been ousted by the stereotyped names like John or William. The fixed surname, in place of a string of patronymics connected by the particle *ap* (son of), had become the norm in the sixteenth and seventeenth centuries amongst the upper classes, and the ancient system, which emphasized a man's genealogy and his connection with others in his community descended from a common ancestor, survived only in remoter areas and amongst the poor. There was everywhere a move towards polite and genteel behaviour, which tended to take its standards not from Wales but from England or France. The Society of Sea Serjeants, often accused of Jacobitism, was a gentry dining club in West Wales which had women members and had rules against swearing and bad behaviour. A surprising number of squires were concerned with antiquarian studies or with translating pious works into Welsh, and some of the major gentry were extremely devout, Sir John Philipps of Picton being among the founders of the Society for Promoting Christian Knowledge. William Bulkeley of Brynddu, who, as we have seen, owned a harp and was fond of collecting Welsh verse, was sober, methodical and devout, a total contrast with the feckless and drunken seventeenth-century squire Bulkeley of Dronwy, whose account book survives.[31] Thomas Pennant, one of the leading figures in the eighteenth-century historical revival, used to take afternoon tea in the summer house used by his ancestors for drunken orgies. Like other observers of Welsh society he noted that the old habit of 'terming', that is, going on periodic violent pub-crawls, was disappearing. Pennant's pen-portrait of the mountain squire Lloyd of Cwm Bychan in Merioneth, untouched by modern fashions, embedded in mountain fastnesses, living an almost medieval life, eating oat-meal and hung goat, drinking draughts of home brew from a bull's scrotum, and rehearsing his genealogy going back to the Welsh princes, was the portrait of a quaint survivor.[32] Lloyd's kinsman Henry Lloyd of Cwm Bychan was at that time wandering about Europe as a military expert, writing books on strategy which were to influence Napoleon.

[31] Hugh Owen (ed.), *The Diary of William Bulkeley of Brynddu* (Anglesey Antiquarian Society and Field Club Publications, 1931), pp. 22–102.
[32] Thomas Pennant, *Tours in Wales*, *Journey to Snowdon* (London, 1781), ii, pp. 114–16. For Henry Lloyd see *D.N.B.*, *s.n.*

The Morris brothers, Lewis, Richard and William, were friends of Thomas Pennant and their extensive correspondence gives a good picture of a world which was becoming increasingly more sober and earnest. The Morrises were unpuritanical, and their editors have always had to make excisions from their letters for the sake of decency, but they knew that things were changing. Their friend Thomas Ellis, parson of Holyhead, conducted a campaign of moral reform in Anglesey, tranforming old rituals, driving all the fortune tellers out of the island, stopping the wakes, preventing the common people going to interludes. He seems to have achieved this with little difficulty, as if the old life was already dying. William Bulkeley of Brynddu noted in his diary for 31 October 1741: 'I saw but few Coelcerths or Bonefires this night, so it seems that old superstitious pageantry is upon the decay.' This change is confirmed by two peasant autobiographies from eighteenth-century Anglesey which have survived, that of Rhys Cox,[33] and of Matthew Owen, the nephew of the drunken feckless poetic genius Goronwy Owen,[34] which show an island obsessed with sports often of a violent kind, with terrible football matches which would put today's terraces to shame, but it was an island which became sober, earnest and reformed by the early nineteenth century. This is the picture we have from Edmund Hyde Hall in his description of Caernarfonshire in about 1810, where the life of the common people was being transformed partly by fanatics, and partly by the 'rapacious spirit of the age' which allowed men little leisure any more. The happy life of the Welsh people had now come to an end; he felt

> Of these folleries and pastimes the greater part now lie buried in the grave dug for them partly perhaps by the growing intelligence of the people, but certainly with a more immediate effect by the sour spirit of Methodism.[35]

Methodism was itself (although it did not admit it) the child of a complicated movement to moralize and evangelize the Welsh people, organized by dissenters and evangelical Anglicans from about 1660 to 1730, as has recently been shown beyond doubt by the massive work of G. H. Jenkins.[36] Methodism was certainly a movement of self-conscious individuals concerned to save souls, but

---

[33] Printed in *Lleuad yr Oes* (Swansea, 1827), pp. 316–18, 374–6.

[34] Printed in *Cymru* (Caernarfon, 1908), xxxiv, pp. 253–7.

[35] Edmund Hyde Hall (ed. E. G. Jones), *A Description of Caernarvonshire in 1809–11* (Caernarfon, 1952), pp. 313–14.

[36] Geraint H. Jenkins, *Literature, Religion and Society in Wales 1660–1730* (Cardiff, 1978).

it inherited many of the concerns of the older moralistic movement to advance literacy, to preach and publish, and to transform the old ways of life. Methodist culture was extremely lively and vigorous and helped to fill a vacuum in the life of the common people that had already appeared. Robert Jones of Rhos-lan in his highly popular chronicle of the pioneer days of Methodism in North Wales always criticizes the old way of life as 'heedless' and 'empty',[37] but in destroying the old culture the Methodists and other dissenters devised a new Welsh way of life which cut the people away from the past. Welsh almanacks (of which there were a very large number) mention fewer and fewer saints' days, patronal festivals and fairs, as the century advanced. Rituals and customs gradually died away, Maypole dancing, for example, disappeared from Capel Hendre (Carmarthenshire) in 1725, lingered at Aberdare (Glamorgan) until 1798, and lingered until the mid-nineteenth century at Penderyn in the moors above Aberdare.

In the early eighteenth century there was a considerable literature in Wales against the Welsh addiction to magicians, fortune-tellers and witchcraft, long after such things were dying away in England.[38] Even so, by 1767 Edmund Jones, 'the Old Prophet', a veteran dissenting preacher from Pontypool, was attacking the growing disbelief in magic in Wales and the creeping Sadduceism it represented.[39] Funeral wakes were being turned into prayer meetings, patronal festivals were becoming preaching meetings, a famous football match between two Cardiganshire villages called *Y Bêl Ddu* (The Black Ball) was turned by a canny vicar into a catechizing festival, because of growing revulsion at the deaths caused by the football match. Elias Owen the great folklorist in his fascinating book on the old stone crosses of the Vale of Clwyd[40] shows how Victorian church restoration removed stairways connecting the chancels to local taverns, removed niches kept in the churches for the prize ale given by the parson to winners in the Sunday sports, removed ball courts from the churchyards, and placed huge marble graves in

[37] Robert Jones (ed. G. Ashton), *Drych yr Amseroedd* (Mirror of the Times) (Cardiff, 1958), p. 46. The original ed. is 1820.

[38] Geraint H. Jenkins, 'Popular Beliefs in Wales from the Restoration to Methodism', *Bulletin of the Board of Celtic Studies*, xxvii (1977), pp. 440–62.

[39] Edmund Jones, *A Relation of Apparitions of Spirits...in Wales* (London, 1767). Cf. Edgar Phillips, *Edmund Jones, the Old Prophet* (London, 1959).

[40] Elias Owen, *Old Stone Crosses of the Vale of Clwyd* (London, 1886). Owen was a cleric and leading Welsh Victorian folklorist.

churchyards formerly laid out for dances and sports meetings. All this would be of interest to folklorists only if it were not for the fact that the common people whose lives were now totally transformed were also the last repositories of Welsh lore, music, historical learning, poetry and language. The changes in folk life had a fundamental importance in the eyes of scholars and patriots, who saw that if Wales were to survive at all, it would have to find some new artificial supports.

The Methodist leaders were not uncultured philistines. Thomas Jones of Denbigh was an excellent poet in the traditional Welsh metres; his friend Thomas Charles of Bala was familiar with Welsh manuscripts, was friendly with the romantic mythologist William Owen (Pughe), and interested in the legend of Madoc. He was vehemently opposed to the old communal culture. He wrote to a friend from Bala in 1791:

> No harps but the *golden* harps of which St John speaks, have been played in this neighbourhood for several months past. The craft is not only in danger but entirely destroyed and abolished.[41]

And in the same year he wrote to another friend:

> This revival of religion has put an end to all the merry meetings for dancing, singing with the harp, and every kind of sinful mirth, which used to be so prevalent amongst young people here.[42]

The fair recently held was the most decent and sober he ever remembered. Camden in the sixteenth century had reported Llanrwst in Denbighshire as a centre of harp manufacture. Samuel Lewis in his *Topographical Dictionary of Wales* noted: 'Llanrwst was formerly noted for the making of harps; at present the spinning of woollen yarn, and the knitting of stockings, constitute the principal branches of trade.'[43]

Early-nineteenth-century writers such as Peter Roberts or William Howells describe a Welsh way of life which is on its last legs.[44] Even comparatively recent innovations (probably of seventeenth-century origins) such as the popular play, the interlude (*anterliwt*) or the lyric ballad, were dying away quickly. The witty and licentious popular plays – 'filthy interludes' for Thomas Ellis of Holyhead – gave way

41 W. Hughes, *Life and Letters of Thomas Charles of Bala* (Rhyl, 1881), p. 182.
42 D. E. Jenkins, *Life of Thomas Charles of Bala*, 3 vols. (Denbigh, 1908), ii, pp. 88–91.
43 Samuel Lewis, *Topographical Dictionary of Wales* (London, 1833), *s.n.* 'Llanrwst'.
44 William Howells, *Cambrian Superstitions* (Tipton, 1831).

more and more to interludes of moral and social comment as the century advanced during the lifetime of the greatest of the actors and playwrights Thomas Edwards 'Twm o'r Nant'. Even before Twm died in 1810 the plays had become unfashionable. The lyrical ballads, even if on moralistic themes, were being attacked as immoral rubbish in the 1820s, and they soon disappeared.[45]

In the eyes of scholars and patriots the new earnest way of life seemed alien, an English importation, that grew neither from the Welsh gentry nor from the Welsh *gwerin* or folk. William Jones of Llangadfan was an Anglican country doctor, much influenced by Voltaire, and had little in common with the royalist, loyalist politics of Edward Jones the great harpist. William was convinced that Edward was collecting his music and folklore at the eleventh hour, and Edward felt the same about William's collecting and describing old folk dances.[46] People like Edward Jones belonged to the ranks of the lesser gentry and the yeomanry, a few, like Pennant, to the major gentry; they were all self-aware, standing a little apart from the common herd, and they realized that the Welsh past must be hunted out, must be found and preserved, and recreated for the Welsh people under new circumstances, taking account of the culture of printed books, of sober moralism, of improved transport and communications, of the desire for clubs and societies to take the place of the old comprehensive neighbourhood. There were, however, so many common-sense rational factors telling the Welsh people that they should no longer support such a decayed and threadbare society, that extra-special efforts would have to be made to gain their support. Hence the importance in Wales of the deliberate invention of tradition.

THE EISTEDDFOD

The eisteddfod was not in any way a deliberate invention, the first recorded meeting having been held at Cardigan by the Lord Rhys (one of the last princes of South Wales) in 1176. The word means

---

[45] Thomas Parry, *Baledi'r Ddeunawfed Ganrif* (Ballads of the Eighteenth Century) (Cardiff, 1935), pp. 148–9. A. Watkin-Jones, 'Popular Literature of Wales in the Eighteenth Century', *Bulletin of the Board of Celtic Studies*, iii (1926), pp. 178–95, and 'The Interludes of Wales in the Eighteenth Century', *ibid.*, iv (1928), pp. 103–11.

[46] Tecwyn Ellis, *Edward Jones, Bardd y Brenin 1752–1824* (Cardiff, 1957) is the standard biography of Edward Jones.

simply a 'session', and it described a set of musical and poetic competitions, of which notice had been given a year beforehand, and at which adjudications and prizes were given. An eisteddfod would also be the occasion in the Middle Ages for the bards (organized in an order or gild) to set their house in order, to examine and license the reputable performers, and to cut out the bad. Just as Welsh lawyers claimed that their native law codes went back to the ancient (but genuine) King Hywel the Good, so the Welsh bards claimed their meetings were held according to 'The Statute of Gruffydd ap Cynan', who was supposed to have brought the bardic order into its state of good government about 1100. In the Carmarthen eisteddfod of 1450, the bardic tests were made more elaborate and difficult, the bards having to write, for example, in a combination of twenty-four elaborate metrical forms, all in complex controlled alliteration. Two important eisteddfodau were held in the sixteenth century, both at Caerwys in Flintshire (1523 and 1567), but these were a sunset glow before nightfall, and efforts to recall past glory came to nothing when an eisteddfod was again planned in the 1590s. The bardic order was soon at death's door, for a variety of reasons, but fundamentally because the bards were tied up with an ancient way of life which was itself disappearing.[47]

Even while the decay and decline of the old way of life was going on we observe the first signs of revival. The bardic meetings called 'eisteddfodau' were revived about 1700, the moving spirit being the grammarian and almanacker John Roderick, and since he publicized the meetings in the almanacks, they are called the 'Almanack Eisteddfodau'. There had been an enormous increase in the reading public since 1660, and at least a small number here and there of bookish amateurs wishing for a culture that was something other than high-minded moral tracts and wishing to enjoy the beauties and the glories of their own native arts. There is, after all, a difference between the best of sanatoria and one's own home. The last of the professional bards had virtually ceased activity in the 1690s, so the poets who attended the new eisteddfodau were amateurs, and the meetings can hardly have been much more than lesser squires and yeomen meeting to swap poems or just to hurl doggerel at one

[47] Gwyn Thomas, *Eisteddfodau Caerwys* (Cardiff, 1967) is bilingual, and a survey of the eisteddfod from the 1450s to the 1700s. Helen Ramage, 'Eisteddfodau'r Ddeunawfed Ganrif' (Eighteenth-Century Eisteddfodau), in Idris Foster (ed.),*Twf yr Eisteddfod* (Eisteddfod Court, 1968), pp. 9–29. H. Teifi Edwards, *Yr Eisteddfod* (Eisteddfod Court, 1976) is a general survey, in Welsh.

another in a kind of *rhyfel tafod* (verbal warfare) over cheese and ale in smoke-filled taverns. Sometimes they would be organized into county teams – Lewis Morris came to the fore in a contest between poets of Anglesey and Caernarfonshire. All the same, there was an element of traditionalism: the poets tried to stick to the elaborate poetic rules of the Middle Ages, and they knew about the Tudor eisteddfodau and even about the Statute of Gruffydd ap Cynan. John Roderick's grammar book of 1728 was much more than a simple grammar.[48] It was meant for the tavern bards and contained a good deal of bardic lore; it was meant to help them write better compositions for the little eisteddfodau, to correct *camgynghanedd* (incorrect alliteration), and self-consciously referred to the Caerwys Eisteddfod of 1567, and Gruffydd ap Cynan. An acquaintance of Edward Lhuyd's, Dafydd Lewys, the rector of Cadoxton near Neath (Glamorgan), had published in 1710 an older anthology of choice epigrams from medieval Welsh verse, and at 4d. a copy it must have been meant for the common folk. A neighbour of Dafydd Lewys's, though a dissenter, Rhys Morgan of the farm of Pencraig–Nedd, had come into contact with John Roderick either through the almanacks or the early eisteddfodau, and Roderick chose to print in 1728 an *awdl* (ode) by this Rhys Morgan as a specimen of how to write the twenty-four metres laid down for bards in 1450. Morgan was a man of the new age, one of a band of literary dissenters who would be the backbone of early political radicalism in the uplands of Glamorgan in the 1770s.

The so-called almanack eisteddfodau continued with some amount of success, but never with any great public impact, until the 1780s, and there then took place a great change in the nature of the revived institution because it became linked with that other new force of the eighteenth century, the 'Welsh society'. Societies specifically devoted to things Welsh would have been unthinkable in an earlier century, but they appeared in the eighteenth, and proliferated in the nineteenth and twentieth centuries. The first of these were set up amongst London Welshmen. They helped Welshmen visiting London, they organized celebrations for Saint David's Day (1 March) and organized charity for Welshmen in difficulties. The earliest was the Society of Ancient Britons set up in 1715. It spawned in 1751 the more famous Honourable Society of Cymmrodorion (the word means Aborigines, and refers to the Welsh as the primary people of Britain), which had

---

48 Sion Rhydderch (John Roderick), *Grammadeg Cymraeg* (Welsh Grammar) (Shrewsbury, 1728).

the convivial and charitable purposes of the Ancient Britons, but added to them all kinds of literary gatherings, concerning itself with history and antiquities and present-day questions. The Cymmrodorion attracted so many members, many of them grandees, and the common folk wanted something more informal, and so they founded in 1770 the Gwyneddigion (meaning the men of North Wales), which was highly convivial, and whose members delighted in poetry and literary criticism and a great deal of singing and harp music. These societies and clubs meeting in London alehouses had corresponding members in Wales, and the Welsh at home took considerable interest in their metropolitan activities.[49] In the late 1780s men of letters from North Wales asked the London Gwyneddigion if they could use their money and organization to set up eisteddfodau on a grand scale at home. The organizing ability in fact came from some professional Welshmen at home, men like Thomas Jones, the exciseman of Corwen and Bala, followed by a number of others. It was these which really set the pattern and created the tradition, for it was now that there developed plenty of advance notice, inns and boarding houses prepared to take visitors, printed public notice of the competitions, large crowds present to watch the proceedings over many days, interludes by Twm o'r Nant as evening entertainments, booksellers' stalls all around to sell Welsh books, substantial prizes for poetry, prose and music, finely engraved medals, adjudications and prize entries printed. It was a triumph of professional organization, and a perfect adaptation of a very ancient institution to modern circumstances. Clearly the amateur men of letters and musicians wished for a large audience. There was now a body of professional men who could organize things. Tourism had opened up a number of fairly tolerable roads through North Wales, and there was a body of rich London Welshmen (such as Owen Jones, 'Owain Myfyr', the hard-working London currier, and father of the Victorian designer Owen Jones) who longed to use their money to do something for Wales.

The pattern set in 1789 was followed until 1798 when holding large gatherings became difficult. After the war was over in 1815 the pattern was resumed and, with few changes, has been followed since. The musical competitions were an innovation compared with the almanack eisteddfodau, and these came more and more to dominate

---

[49] R. T. Jenkins and Helen Ramage, *A History of the Honourable Society of Cymmrodorion 1751–1951* (London, 1951).

the proceedings. In 1791 at St Asaph the *penillion* singing competition went on for thirteen hours without apparently exhausting the audience. The superb medals were designed by Dupré, who became at that time the chief official sculptor of the infant French Republic, and the Gwyneddigion (who had some interest in political radicalism) tried to get the homespun bards to write about political freedoms, without much success. Monsieur Dupré is as near as the eisteddfodau came to the Revolution. Eisteddfod prizes were sometimes given for poems or prose works on loyalist themes such as George III's recovery of health, or the defeat of the French invasion of Wales in 1797 (the atmosphere in Wales became very anti-revolutionary), but more interestingly they were often given for historical themes, Wales from Cadwaladr the Blessed to Llywelyn the Last, Edward I's massacre of the Welsh Bards in 1282, and so on, which had a profound effect in creating interest in Welsh traditions (sometimes quite bogus ones) amongst the people.

After 1815 the new eisteddfodau which were held were under the auspices of Cambrian societies in Wales, the initiative having passed from the old convivial London dining clubs to groups of patriots, often gentry and clerics, at home. Another great turning point came in the provincial eisteddfod held in 1819 at Carmarthen under the auspices of Bishop Burgess of St David's. It was at this eisteddfod that the Gorsedd of Bards of the Island of Britain was first introduced into what had hitherto been purely a set of musical and literary competitions. The Gorsedd (meaning 'throne') was the invention of one of the most astonishing Welshmen of the period, Edward Williams (1747–1826), a stonemason from Glamorgan, who took the bardic pseudonym Iolo Morganwg (Neddy of Glamorgan). We shall have cause to mention him often, because he was not only an able man of letters and antiquary, but also a romantic mythologist who rolled into one many eighteenth-century dreams and fashions, fads and fancies. Iolo was obsessively concerned with myth and history, and out of the eighteenth-century interest in Druidism he created the notion that the Welsh bards had been the heirs of the ancient Druids, and had inherited their rites and rituals, their religion and mythology (the religion being a mixture of Iolo's own Unitarianism and eighteenth-century Nature worship). He seems to have invented his neo-Druidism in London in 1790 or 1791, and, convinced that he and his friend Edward Evan (Unitarian minister, harpist and poet from Aberdare) were the last remaining bards who came from this druidic apostolic succession, he held a Bardic–Druidic moot in London, on Primrose Hill on 21 June 1792. This amusing confidence trick caught the imagination of many of the London Welsh (such as his friend Dr David Samwell, Captain Cook's doctor) and many Welshmen of letters at home. On his return to Wales, Iolo set up various cells of bards called 'Gorseddau' all over Wales, gave them a set of rituals, liturgy, ceremonial, and set about creating a druidic corpus of lore for them until his death in 1826. To be fair to Iolo he did not merely think of the fancy-dress side of the Gorsedd: it was to be the revival of the bardic order, to be a national cultural institution for Wales, a kind of supporters' club for the language, literature and history of the Welsh.

After 1815 the time was ripe for Iolo's heady inventions to take effect, in an atmosphere much more attuned to the romantic imagination, and Iolo did not have great difficulty in convincing his hearers (including his friend Dr Thomas Bowdler, who had invented 'bowdlerization') of his authenticity. From 1819 onwards the eisteddfodau called upon the help of the Gorsedd of Bards, and the Gorsedd ceremonials were incorporated into the proclamation and holding of eisteddfodau. Some provincial Gorseddau of Bards, such as those of Anglesey and Powys, still exist to this day, connected with provincial eisteddfodau. Other Gorseddau, such as the one conducted at Pontypridd in industrial Glamorgan in the nineteenth century, were active quite apart from holding eisteddfodau. During the nineteenth century some five hundred important ceremonial eisteddfodau were held in Wales, and there must have been thousands of lesser ones in chapels or workmen's halls which have never been counted. The intrusion of the Gorsedd in 1819 tended to increase the eisteddfod's concern for myth and legend, sometimes to the virtual exclusion of literature concerning modern life. The national eisteddfodau (which became more and more highly organized as the nineteenth century advanced) on the one hand created a tremendous interest in history (genuine and mythical) amongst the Welsh, and on the other hand owed much of their popular success to the myth of the Gorsedd, its colourful ceremonial and its grandiose mumbo-jumbo. It was Iolo who first envisaged the Gorsedd as something which would incorporate the eisteddfod competitions, and turn them into something far more permanent than mere ad hoc competitions, part of a larger whole, a national institution. Iolo of course was a wild dreamer, a lifelong addict to laudanum, a drug which caused hallucinations, but he was driven by historical myths, and in turn he used historical myths to create new traditions which had profound, far-reaching effects. The modern eisteddfod, then, appeared when the last of the professional bards had finished, and it became its colourful self at the time when the old manners and customs had died and when life had become (according to Edward Jones) insufferably dull.

DRUIDS ANCIENT AND MODERN

Once Renaissance schoolboys in England and France had been given a diet of Caesar's *Gallic Wars* and Tacitus's *Agricola*, the ancient Druids were sure to be rediscovered, for the Druids stood behind the resistance of the native peoples of Britain and Gaul to the Roman invaders. The English antiquaries Leland and Bale suggested in the sixteenth century that the Welsh bards might be successors to the Druids, partly because the holy of holies of the Druids had been on the island of Anglesey, partly because the bards, like the Druids, were figures of authority and, like the Druids again, had a vaticinatory function.[50] Milton in *Lycidas* identified the ancient Druids with Welsh bards, and the professor of history at Leyden, M. Z. Boxhorn, when he published a book on Gaulish origins in 1654, included not only a copy of Davies of Mallwyd's Welsh dictionary but also his collection of Welsh proverbs translated into Latin as the 'Wisdom of the Ancient Druids'.[51] The Druids were supposed to have built mysterious monuments such as Stonehenge, and so their rediscovery created a new interest in the monuments and in forwarding the science of archaeology. Edward Lhuyd, the great Welsh scientist and antiquary, was on occasion suspicious of the Druids because they were arcane and obscurantist, and practised human sacrifice; on other occasions he was fascinated by them, and was delighted to find snake stone amulets (*glain y neidr* or *maen magl*) in the Scottish Highlands, Cornwall and Wales, because they seemed to resemble the *ova anguina* attributed by Pliny to the Druids. Indeed in 1698 Lhuyd called them 'Druid stones'.[52] It was in Lhuyd's time around 1700 that

[50] T. D. Kendrick, *The Druids* (London, 1927); Stuart Piggott, *The Druids* (Harmondsworth, 1974), pp. 112–57; and Aneurin Lloyd Owen, *The Famous Druids* (Oxford, 1962).

[51] Prys Morgan, 'Boxhorn, Leibniz and the Celts', *Studia Celtica*, viii/ix (1973–4), pp. 270–8.

[52] R. T. Gunther (ed.), *The Life and Letters of Edward Lhwyd* [sic] (Oxford, 1945), p. 376.

scholars began more closely to identify the Druids with the Welsh, as one finds from the work of the erratic Deist from Ireland, John Toland, or in the history of Anglesey by Lhuyd's friend Henry Rowlands, who went so far as to identify prehistoric remains in Anglesey with druidic shrines, sacrificial altars and the like. The Druid underwent a sea-change in the early years of the eighteenth century from the arcane obscurantist, who indulged in human sacrifice, to the sage or intellectual defending his people's faith and honour, and the Welsh began to see that they had a special relationship with him that was different from Druidism in England. Druidism was in the air; when his neighbour Mr Meredith wished to congratulate William Gambold of Puncheston (Pembrokeshire) on publishing his book on Welsh grammar in 1727 he felt it appropriate to see Gambold in a succession from the ancient Druids. The Morris circle were fascinated by the Druids, though in a vague and imprecise way, and when Lewis Morris designed a banner for the Cymmrodorion in 1751, an Ancient Druid appeared as a supporter of the arms. The most exact and learned scholar of the Morris circle, Evan Evans, 'Ieuan Fardd', often referred to Druids and obviously identified them with Welsh bards – early Welsh poetry, he said, was difficult to understand because it was probably written in the 'Druids' Cabala'. In a long poem *The Love of Our Country* in 1772 he saw the Druids as the first in a long line of defenders of the Welsh nation, before Caradog, Hywel the Good and the others. He even saw the scholars of the sixteenth-century Renaissance Gruffydd Robert and Sion Dafydd Rhys (who were recusants, and had worked in Italy) as the Druids' successors:

> Great was your Country's love, ye studious few,
> Who brought to light what Bards initiate knew,
> Roberts and learned Rhys, who taught the rules
> Of ancient verse, first plann'd in Druid schools...[53]

If such a careful and cautious scholar as Evan Evans (who was much exercised by the need to show that Welsh tradition was genuine and unlike the confidence trickery of Macpherson and his Ossian) could delight in Druidism, then it is not surprising that less scrupulous minds turned it into a fashionable and uncritical cult. It is often said

---

[53] D. Silvan Evans (ed.), *Gwaith y Parchedig Evan Evans* (Caernarfon, 1876), pp. 129ff. prints Evan Evans's booklet *in extenso*. For Evans's long correspondence with Thomas Percy see A. Lewis (ed.), *The Correspondence of Thomas Percy and Evan Evans* (Louisiana, 1957).

that Edward Williams, 'Iolo Morganwg' created this cult in Wales, and it is undeniable that it was he who carried it to its greatest height in the Gorsedd of Bards, but he was only putting his own personal stamp on what was quite generally believed and commonly accepted in Wales.[54]

Iolo Morganwg was deeply interested in Stukeley and the early English archaeologists and loved megalithic remains. He came across in his visits to London the English 'Ancient Order of Druids', was influenced by the Deistic religion of his friend David Williams of Caerphilly (whose *Theophilanthropia* had impressed Voltaire and Frederick the Great) and was delighted by the idyllic picture given him of peaceful native life in Polynesia by David Samwell, 'Dafydd Ddu Feddyg', a Welsh bard who was also Captain Cook's doctor and witness of his death.[55] Iolo believed that he and his friend Edward Evan[56] were the last surviving members of the order of bards, and that the time had come to open the arcane secrets, received by apostolic succession from the Druids, to the general public. Much of Iolo's druidic lore and invention was circulated in magazines and in manuscript during his lifetime, and then after his death in 1826 his son Taliesin ab Iolo (a decent upright schoolmaster at the industrial town of Merthyr Tydfil) published some of his father's works, for example his *Cyfrinach y Beirdd* (Secret of the Bards), and his marvellous *Coelbren y Beirdd* (Alphabet of the Bards), which he claimed had been recorded by sixteenth-century Glamorgan druid–bards. The Coelbren was an Ogam-like alphabet suitable to be scored on stone or wood, and since the English conquerors forbade the Welsh bards pen and ink, they had to communicate with one another by scoring messages in the strange Ogam-like characters on mysterious tally-sticks which one twiddled about in a wooden frame like an abacus, which was called a 'peithynen'. After Taliesin ab Iolo's death more of Iolo's papers on bardism were published by one of his most zealous disciples, a clergyman from North Wales called John Williams, 'Ab Ithel'. Iolo's druidic theology bore a strong resemblance to his

---

[54] Elijah Waring, *Recollections and Anecdotes of Edward Williams* (London, 1850). G. J. Williams, *Iolo Morganwg: y Gyfrol Gyntaf* (Cardiff, 1956) is a great but incomplete biography in Welsh. For a short study of Iolo in English see Prys Morgan, *Iolo Morganwg* (Cardiff, 1975).

[55] E. G. Bowen, *David Samwell, Dafydd Du Feddyg 1751–98* (Cardiff, 1974) is a bilingual study.

[56] R. T. Jenkins, *Bardd a'i Gefndir* (A Bard and his Background) (Cardiff, 1949) is a study in Welsh of Edward Evan of Aberdare.

own Unitarianism, and with it was mixed a good deal of pacifism. Iolo's druidic ceremonies were elaborate but they were shorn of human sacrifice. Iolo told the bards who were assembled at his Gorsedd on top of the Garth mountain near Cardiff in 1797 that his purposes were to make the common people support their language (Iolo himself had been brought up English-speaking, it should be added, and preached with the zeal of a convert), to make them know their own history through songs, and to achieve a moral religion without denominational squabbles. The Glamorgan yeomanry suppressed this druidic moot for fear it might attract the attention of a French Revolutionary fleet in the Bristol Channel.

The soldiers were not Iolo's only enemies: a number of Welsh scholars, especially those antiquaries and historians who were quietly recovering the Welsh past in a scholarly way, were deeply suspicious of him, as indeed were some of the bards he had received into his order. Edward Davies of Bishopston – 'Celtic Davies' to his friends – was a clerical critic of Iolo, but it should be remembered that Davies published a number of works which showed a profound faith in Druidism. It was merely that he disagreed with Iolo's version of it. None of Iolo's contemporaries was able to disprove his inventions or his forgeries, and so general was the national delight in myth and legend at this period that few seem to have shown a desire to explode Ioloism. The Unitarians thought that Druidism was eminently sensible as a religion, the dissenters worked out a version which suited them, the Anglican clerics adapted it to their purposes. The Morris circle in the mid-eighteenth century had adopted bardic pseudonyms in a light-hearted rib-poking fashion – William Morris collected shells for his great friend Thomas Pennant, and so was called 'Gwilym Gregynnwr' (William Shell-Man). Iolo took such bardic names with intense seriousness, and his bards had to take bardic names equally seriously. William Owen (Pughe) became 'Idrison' to associate him with Cader Idris, for example. It was at this time when baptismal names in Wales had reached their very dullest, with thousands upon thousands of John Jones and the like, that there arose the fashion among a very large number of Welsh literary figures for bardic names of charm and fantasy, such as Eryron Gwyllt Walia (Eagleman of Wild Wales). Iolo was familiar with eighteenth-century gardens with their Druidic grottoes (at Piercefield Park near Chepstow, or the garden of his friend Richard Colt Hoare at Stourhead). Iolo adapted this garden conceit with his sublime intensity, and made the Gorsedd, and later on the eisteddfod, construct miniature Stonehenges all over Wales for holding open-air druidic ceremonies. There is a fine one standing in the Gorsedd Gardens in front of the National Museum in Cardiff, for instance. The point is that what had been a joke earlier in the eighteenth century was transformed into something sublimely serious by the romantic vision. The bards and neo-druids with strong stomachs were interested in sacrificial altars, and cromlechs were, they supposed, used for sacrifice. Indeed, some supposed that this was proof that the ancients had always cremated the bodies of the dead. One of Iolo's followers who took this conceit seriously was William Price of Llantrisant (1800–93), a doctor and radical freethinker who rejected marriage, had many of Iolo's health fads, and who was so convinced of his Druidism and of the evil of burying diseased bodies, that he cremated the corpse of his infant son. His action was vindicated at the end of a most celebrated court case, as a result of which the modern practice of cremation began. The myth of druidic sacrifice, then, influenced our modern way of life (or, more exactly, our way of death).

The extensive neo-druidic literature published by Welshmen in the romantic period in Welsh and English has never been properly studied, but has been dismissed with a patronizing smile in the way historians used to treat early modern beliefs in magic and witchcraft. Responsible antiquaries and historians of the late eighteenth and early nineteenth centuries took it seriously, men such as Samuel Rush Meyrick or Richard Colt Hoare, and many others. Jonathan Williams wrote, about 1818, a most interesting history of Radnorshire, careful and detailed although highly critical of the people for abandoning the Welsh tongue. Five years later he published a short book on druidic education called *Druopaedia* which is quite unable to distinguish between the Druids of the ancient world and those of Iolo's dreams.[57] The revival of Druidism was a movement of considerable significance, all in all, because it involved myths which showed the cultural tradition of Wales to be older than any other in western Europe, and it made the scholar or poet or teacher central to that culture. To some extent it restored the bard to his primary place in Welsh life.

[57] For Dr Price of Llantrisant see Roy Denning, 'Druidism at Pontypridd', in Stuart Williams (ed.), *Glamorgan Historian* (Barry, 1963), i, pp. 136–45. Jonathan Williams's *Druopaedia* was published at Leominster in 1823. For some aspects of Welsh Druidism see D. Moore, 'Cambrian Antiquity', in G. C. Boon and J. M. Lewis (eds.), *Welsh Antiquity* (Cardiff, 1976), pp. 193–222.

THE REDISCOVERY OF THE CELTS

The Welsh had in the Middle Ages been dimly aware that they were connected with the Cornish and the Bretons, and some scholars such as Buchanan in the sixteenth century even suggested links between modern Welsh and ancient Gaulish. The predominant idea during the seventeenth century was that Welsh was somehow linked with Hebrew, and this corresponded with the myth that the Welsh could be traced back to one of the grandsons of Noah. In the 1680s and 1690s, however, a number of scholars were looking for fresh light on the matter. In Oxford Edward Lhuyd, who first gained fame as a fossilist and geologist, turned his attention to his native Welsh language, and began to compare it carefully and rationally with Cornish (now at death's door) and Breton, and, what was more original, to Irish and Scottish Gaelic. Lhuyd longed to contact a Breton abbé, Paul-Yves Pezron, best known in France as a chronologist, because Pezron was thought to be writing a book on the common origins of the Welsh and the Bretons. Lhuyd failed to meet Pezron when he visited Brittany, and Pezron's book appeared in 1703.[58] Lhuyd hoped it would soon be translated into Welsh for it would make the gentry take more interest in their language and antiquities. In the event it was translated into English in 1706 by a Welsh hack historian called David Jones. Pezron compared Welsh and Breton, tracing their origins through classical sources to the Celtae or Keltoi of ancient writers, a barbarian people whose sway in antiquity stretched from Gaul to Galatia (Asia Minor), and who had been the scourge of the Greeks and Romans. Pezron went even further and traced the Celts from earlier eponymous heroes back to patriarchal times. Pezron's method was fairly unscientific, but he wrote a gripping story, which caught the imagination, and his book launched a fashion for the Celts which amounted at times to a mania. Pezron in his English translation was still being reprinted in the early nineteenth century. Henry Rowlands of Llanidan observed nicely that while Edward Lhuyd tentatively suggested that the Welsh language came from a hypothetical mother tongue called Celtick, Pezron was sure of it.[59]

[58] Prys Morgan, 'The Abbé Pezron and the Celts', *Transactions of the Honourable Society of Cymmrodorion* (1965), pp. 286–95.

[59] Victor Tourneur, *Esquisse d'une Histoire des Etudes Celtiques* (Liège, 1905), pp. 171–206; A. Rivoallan, *Présende des Celtes* (Paris, 1957), pp. 178–211; and Stuart Piggott, *Celts, Saxons and the Early Antiquaries* (Edinburgh, 1967).

Edward Lhuyd's tentative empirical examination of the languages he thought were related to Welsh (the great *Archaeologia Britannica*) appeared in 1707. It was a seminal work, which used, however, a detailed comparative method of reasoning that was most difficult for people to understand, asking them as it did to believe in gradual changes taking several thousand years. One great mind which immediately grasped Lhuyd's point was that of Leibniz. Leibniz was already interested in Welsh before he came across Lhuyd's work, and through his etymological writings helped to lay down lines of inquiry into Celtic studies in Germany which were far deeper than any inquiries in Britain, and which were eventually to have profound repercussions in Wales. The Welsh may have found the comparative part of Lhuyd's work impossible, but they could at least appreciate one simple conclusion which was that the Welsh stemmed from the British, who stemmed from the Celts, and that the ancient Celts had had a glorious history. Monoglot Welsh readers were given some inkling of Lhuyd's vision in the *Drych y Prif Oesoedd* (Mirror of Primitive Ages), a history of early Wales by Theophilus Evans, written in 1716. Evans tried to subordinate his information to Anglican aims and purposes, as befitted a young patriotic clergyman, but the more far-seeing Welshmen quickly realized that they had been given for the first time in two hundred years a vision of their own history which was autonomous and separate from England. Lhuyd himself was a most fiery Welsh patriot, despite the careful rationality and caution of his academic method, and Welsh scholars of the early eighteenth century, while not coming near his undoubted genius, seemed to catch sparks from its fire. Such were his friends William Gambold or Moses Williams, such were the Morris circle. Lewis Morris laboured all his life at a catalogue of ancient Celtic names in Britain and the continent, called *Celtic Remains*, to amplify some of the points of Edward Lhuyd. Thomas Pennant and most of the stately historians of the later eighteenth century read or copied Lhuyd's writings on topography. The great English scholar Thomas Percy tried to stop the chevalier Mallet, the historiographer royal of Denmark, from persisting in his belief (common up to that time) that the ancient Teutons were the same as the ancient Celts, and sent Mallet a copy of Edward Lhuyd to prove his case. Mallet simply could not understand it and repeated his old mistakes in his history of Switzerland published in 1803.[60]

The Celts in fact had never by name been associated with the

---

[60] Lewis, *Correspondence of Thomas Percy and Evan Evans*, p. 106n.

British Isles, but that did not really matter, for they were a magnificent race of conquerors who had thundered across Europe in their early history and archaeology. The Celts reflected the fantasies Celtic myth had a profound effect in making the French interested in their early history and archaeology. The Celts reflected the fantsies of the age, and in Wales they provided the constricted, pathetically small nation, which had little to commend it in its present state, with an unimaginably grandiose past, by way of consolation. The antiquarian revival in the eighteenth century took more from Lhuyd's delight in the ancient Celts than it did from his exact methods. Eisteddfodic essays of the early nineteenth century, written by craftsmen or clerics, teachers or tailors, seem to bubble over with ill-informed enthusiasm for what the French textbooks call 'nos ancêtres les Gaulois' and the Welsh, their forefathers the Celts. Linguistic arguments lay at the centre of the rediscovery of the Celts, and Celticism had important consequences for language. To language one must turn next.

FROM THE 'GIBBERISH OF TAPHYDOM' TO THE 'LANGUAGE OF HEAVEN'

For the English humorists and satirists who were, in the main, the only people writing about the Welsh in the seventeenth century, Welsh was a grotesquely ugly guttural tongue, still spoken everywhere as a patois, but lacking any kind of status – and probably soon to disappear. We have already seen how Welsh scholars and patriots bewailed this lack of regard for what was becoming 'the old language'. Eighteenth-century scholars could be virulently anti-English, but they tended to write to one another in English because all their polite and intellectual education was in that language. Even the Morris brothers tended to turn to English in their voluminous correspondence when they wished to discuss academic or intellectual affairs, even though they wrote most racy and lively Welsh for all other purposes. Welsh itself reflected the paradox of Welsh culture in this period, for although it lacked any status (save what was given it by the Anglican liturgy) the period from 1660 to 1730 saw an enormous increase in the number of books published in Welsh, publishers of Welsh books moved closer to Wales, and by 1718 books were being printed inside Wales.[61] During the eighteenth century this

---

[61] W. Rowlands (ed. D. S. Evans), *Cambrian Bibliography/Llyfryddiaeth y Cymry* (Llanidloes, 1869); Jenkins, *Literature, Religion and Society in Wales.*

trend was maintained, and the range of subjects covered in Welsh by printed books was enormously increased. Lewis Morris even published a book in Welsh to explain to craftsmen how to do elaborate polishing and *verre eglomisé* and other sophisticated crafts and skills. In the late seventeenth century the intelligent Welsh speaker, at least in South Wales (as can be seen from the Welsh of the indefatigable translator and publisher of Puritan books Stephen Hughes of Meidrim and Swansea), found it hard to grasp his own grammar and rules of style. As Mr Meredith told William Gambold in 1727, before reading the grammar book he had simply learned by rote 'as country fiddlers play'. By the second quarter of the eighteenth century there was not only a huge printed literature of moral and religious tracts in Welsh, but a small number of literary texts, a few historical works (which were enormously popular), and a few grammar books and dictionaries. The role of Welsh in the life of the Anglican Church seems to have diminished after 1714, but this was more than outweighed by the great vigour of dissenting and Methodist literature in the language. By the later eighteenth century the number of grammar books and dictionaries increased, and they showed a greater self-confidence and pride, and less of the snivelling defeatism of the earlier age. The squire Rice Jones of Blaenau near Dolgellau published a magnificent edition of medieval Welsh poetry in 1773, *Gorchestion Beirdd Cymru* (Triumphs of the Welsh bards). As one would expect of a squire his own poetry is full of wit and bonhomie, and his Welsh has about it a kind of swagger and panache. His preface is full of optimism that the language has at last reached a hopeful period, after so many disappointments, losses and defeats in the past. He liked to think that 'Parnassus is unshifting', that 'Helicon is inexhaustible' as far as Welsh is concerned, and drew his preface to a close thus (we translate):

> For now I see the great love that gentry and commonalty have for the British tongue, and for the works of the old bards too; and thus we shall soon see the Muse (in a very short time one hopes) bursting forth from the graves of the skilled bards in unalloyed spendour.[62]

Squire Jones certainly did not speak the 'Gibberish of Taphydom'. He was driven by the belief that his native tongue was the oldest language in Europe, perhaps in the world, that it was not a mongrel

---

[62] Rice Jones, *Gorchestion Beirdd Cymru* (Shrewsbury, 1773), preface. Jones's own verse was published by Rice Jones Owen in 1818.

tongue such as the English language, that it was infinitely copious, and that it could be defended against all its enemies. One sign of the gradual change which had come over the language was the growing size of the dictionaries: to take a few examples, that of Thomas Jones in 1688 is neat and compact, that of Thomas Richards of Coychurch in 1753 is quite solid, that of John Walters of Llandough (published in parts from 1770 to 1795) is hefty, and the astounding dictionary of William Owen (Pughe) (published from 1795 to 1803) is immense. In the meantime the scholars had come to see Welsh as a national asset, even a national monument. The writers on Welsh were much moved by the idea that Welsh was directly connected with very early history and somehow was pure and undefiled. Thomas Richards called his dictionary a *Thesaurus* and in his preface he preens himself:

> Yet our Name hath not been quite blotted out from under Heaven: We hitherto not only enjoy the true Name of our Ancestors, but have preserved entire and uncorrupted for the most Part (without any notable Change or Mixture with any other Tongue) that PRIMITIVE LANGUAGE, spoken as well by the ancient *Gauls* as *Britans* some Thousands of years ago.[63]

John Walters, another Glamorgan cleric, was a neighbour of Thomas Richards, and he not only started his great dictionary in 1770 but also published at Cowbridge in the same year a manifesto of the Welsh scholars, *A Dissertation on the Welsh Language*, which believes in the same myths and legends as does Richards, and turns all the necessities of poor Welsh into virtues. It was a sign of excellence in this pure and undefiled language that it was not used for fleshly novelettes or bawdy plays, and its harsh sound was masculine and unaffected, unlike the simpering lisping English tongue.

Welsh was subjected to much wilder and more fantastic mythologizing than this. The Morris circle, Lewis as a royal official, William as a customs official at Holyhead and Richard at the Navy Office in Whitehall, were envious of one of their friends the barrister Rowland Jones because he had married the heiress of Broom Hall in Lleyn, and with his income could afford to publish whatever poured from his pen. His *Origin of Language and Nations* appeared in 1764, followed a few years later with such effusions as *The Circles of Gomer*

---

[63] Thomas Richards, *Antiquae Linguae Britannicae Thesaurus* (Bristol, 1753), preface. Cf. T. J. Morgan, 'Geiriadurwyr y Ddeunawfed Ganrif' (Lexicographers of the Eighteenth Century), in *Llên Cymru*, xi (1966), pp. 3–18.

and *The Ten Triads*, Gomer being the eponymous founder of Cymru (Wales). These books went beyond Pezron and the Celtomaniacs, and dissected Welsh words indiscriminately and unscientifically so as to show that Welsh was the root of all languages. In one sense it was very important to understand how languages should be analysed: it was through a knowledge of how languages were constructed and how they developed that men like John Walters (assisted by his neighbour the young Iolo Morganwg) extended Welsh vocabulary to invent Welsh words for new things or actions, and it was thus they invented the word *geiriadur* for dictionary and *tanysgrifio* for to subscribe, two words still in common use. Rowland Jones used the same methods wildly and madly, and there were a number of others like him. One was the pornographer John Cleland, who turned from the adventures of Fanny Hill to the murkier depths of Celtic lexicography and wrote some pamphlets relating the particles of Welsh to many other languages. Cleland as an Englishman belonged to the non-Celtic fringe, but the same could not be said of the greatest and most effective of the language mythologists William Owen (Pughe).

Pughe was born William Owen in North Wales in 1759 but from 1776 onwards he was a schoolmaster in London, returning to Wales in 1806 when he inherited a country estate, where he lived until his death in 1835. He took the name Pughe on inheriting his estate, but his son, the editor of Welsh manuscripts, Aneurin Owen, retained the older name. Pughe was at the centre of London Welsh life and was a friend of many English men of letters such as William Blake and Robert Southey. A man of many gifts, immensely learned and hard-working, he was very kindhearted and gullible, erratic and eccentric in his religious beliefs, and ended in 1802 as an elder of the prophetess Joanna Southcott. Pughe was the organizing genius behind the publications of the London Welsh, but in 1789 when he brought out the superb edition of the poems of the fourteenth-century poet Dafydd ap Gwilym, he was gulled by Iolo Morganwg into publishing a number of Iolo's pastiche poems as the genuine works of the master. In 1792, when he published an edition of the early Welsh poems associated with Llywarch the Old, he was again gulled by Iolo into publishing Iolo's bardic fantasies in a long introduction to the poems. In 1800 he collaborated with Iolo in bringing out a vast edition of all sorts of works from Welsh medieval literature, the *Myvyrian Archaiology of Wales*, into the latter parts of which again

Iolo introduced quantities of his own fabrications. Pughe was unable to resist the charms of the mythologists like Rowland Jones, so consuming was the fire of his passion for things Welsh, and he was sure that if one analysed Welsh it would yield the secrets of mankind's primeval language. Further, if one dissected or dismantled Welsh words one could then reconstruct the language on rational lines, and extend its scope and use infinitely. Pughe attacked Welsh (a knobbly angular language full of irregularities and syntactical oddities) with the extreme rational zeal of an enlightened despot such as Joseph II. He took the language to bits and reassembled it in an orderly whole in his great dictionary and his grammar books and in his various literary compositions. In this way he found a Welsh word for every possible nuance in any language: he invented *gogoelgrevy-ddusedd* for 'some degree of superstition', *cyngrabad* for 'general plenty', *cynghron* for 'conglobateous', so that the dictionary published from 1795 to 1803 is quite conglobateous with a general plenty, at least one hundred thousand words, that is forty thousand more than Dr Johnson's English dictionary. He wished to recreate modern Welsh as if it were the unchanged language of the patriarchs, and he made a language which was as solid and sublime as a neo-classical mausoleum. Among Pughe's friends was the Methodist leader Thomas Charles, and Charles distributed Pughe's Welsh grammar as a set book for his Sunday schools all over Wales in 1808. It is notable, however, that the edition published at Bala was written in a normal Welsh orthography, while the edition published in London was in Pughe's own orthography, for Pughe (like so many of the language enthusiasts of the eighteenth century) tinkered with the orthography to make it more logical, with one letter for every single sound. Iolo Morganwg had by this time quarrelled with Pughe and although Iolo was circulating his nonsensical *Coelbren y Beirdd* he had the audacity to criticize Pughe's ideas as mere 'hobbyhorsisms'. Pughe's new grammar had considerable (and lamentable) effects on most Welsh writers in the nineteenth century, and it should be remembered that he was one among many who played around with the orthography of the small European languages. Even the great Edward Lhuyd, whom we have hitherto presented as a model of rationality and intellectual probity, so messed about with the orthography of Welsh as to make his Welsh preface to the *Archae-ologia Britannica* almost unreadable. The Anglican clerics fortunately put up a spirited resistance to any departure from the Welsh of the

Bible of 1588, and Pughisms were limited to grammar and style. Pughe in other ways of course created tremendous interest amongst Welshmen in their own language, for they warmed to his notion of its purity, patriarchal tradition, and 'infinite copiousness'. He showed them it was 'The Language of Heaven' handed down from the patriarchs, and this is a cliché still heard to this day. Without mythologists such as Pughe few men would have bothered their minds about the status-less gibberish of Wales at all. In a way Pughe and the others were like Victorian church restorers through whom so many ugly churches were built, but without whom the old buildings would have crumbled to dust.

'LAND OF SONG'

In the early eighteenth century Welsh scholars were much perplexed by their not being able to read the great Robert ap Huw musical codex, although its author had died as recently as 1665.[64] When anthologies of Welsh verse appeared in the mid-eighteenth century the editors printed above the lyrics the tunes to which they were usually sung by the common folk. Welsh patriots were embarrassed because so many of the tunes were English, and the English would mock the Welsh for their lack of initiative. In some cases the tunes were changed by the Welsh beyond recognition, and their titles Welshified to the same extent. Some scholars suggested the titles of English tunes should all be translated, but William Wynne, a poet and squarson, considered this sheer dishonesty. William Williams of Pantycelyn, the great Methodist leader and creator of modern Welsh hymnology, virtually launched the second Methodist revival in 1762 with his hymnbook, yet he complained that he could not bring out more hymns until he had obtained fresh tunes from England. His tunes were often versions of the popular hits of the day and one is very typically entitled 'Lovely Peggy – Moraliz'd'.

A century later the position was totally altered, for Wales was considered to be above all else a 'Land of Song', where the sound of music had rung out from the harps and throats of the people for centuries. There were song books, choirs, consorts of Welsh harps, prizes and medals for music, and a network of societies to further

[64] Brit. Mus. Add. MS. 14905 published in facsimile by the University of Wales Press (Cardiff, 1936).

national music.[65] Erasmus Saunders, in his view of the Diocese of Saint David's in 1721, had observed that Welshmen were naturally addicted to poetry, but writing later in the century Iolo Morganwg observed tht Welshmen were addicted to music as well as poetry, and he was expressing a widely held view.

Early-eighteenth-century scholars had admired the simple stanzas sung by the common folk in remote areas to the music of the harp. Often these stanzas (*penillion telyn*) were pithy epigrams of sixteenth- or seventeenth-century origins. Some peasants knew hundreds of these verses and could adapt them to any well-known harp melody. The Morris brothers suspected that the stanzas were proverbial and might even contain scraps of druidic lore. This custom of singer after singer offering various stanzas impromptu to the playing of a harpist was known to be peculiarly Welsh, but it was not so much singing as harpistry which led to the revival of Welsh music in the eighteenth century. The first Welsh airs to be published appeared around 1726 as part of a collection called *Aria di Camera*, but the epoch-making collection was that of Blind John Parry in 1742 called *Ancient British Music*. Parry was the harpist of Frederick Prince of Wales, a friend of Handel's and a composer of Handelian harp music himself, and it was he who largely inspired Thomas Gray to complete his poem *The Bard* in 1757 when he played to the people of Cambridge tunes he claimed were a thousand years old with, as Gray said, 'names enough to choak you'.[66] Blind Parry traced the Welsh musical tradition through the musical competitions of the bards back to the Druids. The melodies as written seem to be fairly recent, however. The Morris circle were friendly with Parry and with his amanuensis Evan William, and Evan wrote out in 1745 a large manuscript volume (meant for publication) on the singing of *penillion* (harp stanzas). Professor Osian Ellis has studied this manuscript and finds that the music described by Evan Wiliam is of a fairly conventional operatic

[65] For harpistry I have relied on Robert Griffith, *Llyfr Cerdd Dannau* (Book on Harpistry) (Caernarfon, 1913); for religious music of the period on R. D. Griffith, *Hanes Canu Cynulleidfaol Cymru* (History of Congregational Singing in Wales) (Cardiff, 1948); for details of the individual folk songs on *Journal of the Welsh Folk Song Society*; and, for some controversial criticism, on Osian Ellis, 'Welsh Music: History and Fancy', *Transactions of the Honourable Society of Cymmrodorion 1972–3* (1974), pp. 73–94.

[66] Arthur Johnston, *Thomas Gray and the Bard* (Cardiff, 1966); F. I. McCarthy, 'The Bard of Thoms Gray and its Importance and Use by Painters', *National Library of Wales Journal*, xiv (1965), pp. 105–13.

type of the period, the singer sings any stanza of his choice (and goes on as long as he can think of words), accompanied fairly decoratively by the harp. No mention at all is made of what would have been regarded as the uniquely Welsh art of *penillion* singing, or *canu gyda'r tannau* as it would have been recognized by Welsh musicians from the 1830s to the present day. The unique art which Welsh people find so thrilling today is extremely peculiar; the harp plays the melody over and over, the singer chimes in as he can with a false-burden or descant of his own composition, as an accompanist to the musical instrument, and if possible the words are chosen from highly elaborate alliterative metres of medieval origin. If Parry and Wiliam were trying to give a picture of all that was most Welsh in music they surely could not have failed to describe what is today called *penillion* singing. Even more mystifying are the views of Edward Jones (1752–1824), the royal harpist and great propagandist of Welsh native music and customs in works between 1784 and 1820. Edward Jones came from Merioneth, from an area where native customs were still well kept in the eighteenth century and where there are numerous soloists and groups performing *penillion* singing today. He pays much attention to the pithy stanzas as literature, and he gives a vague description of the peasantry gathering around the harpist, each with his stock of verses to sing to the harp music. Thomas Pennant in his *Tours* also gives a similar description of the Welsh peasantry gathering on the hills around a harpist with a vast repertoire of stanzas, competing one with another as to who could sing the largest number of stanzas, until the mountains were loud with music. Edwards Jones never described the art as having any great peculiarity as music; it was merely the extempore stanzas which called for comment.

Professor Osian Ellis concluded from this lack of a good eighteenth-century description of the art as we know it today that it probably did not exist, except in a most elementary form. He concluded that since the art as we know it did exist by the mid-nineteenth century then it had somehow been evolved by Welsh musicians in the early nineteenth century, probably by John Parry, 'Bardd Alaw', (1775–1851) director of music at Vauxhall Gardens, a composer and great organizer of Welsh musicians at concerts and eisteddfodau. Not long before 1809 George Thomson, the Edinburgh music publisher, came to Wales to collect authentic Welsh tunes for Haydn to arrange (which were published in 1809) and he says that he failed to find the *improvisatori* he had been led to expect from Thomas Pennant. The 1791 eisteddfod had had a most successful *penillion* competition, so the early eisteddfod organizers were aware of the art; what we do not know, however, is the exact musical nature of the competition. Certainly by the time Owain Alaw published his *Gems of Welsh Melody* in 1860 the art was fully-fledged (though much simpler in form than the art as practised in the twentieth century), and he had collected his specimens of false-burden from the singing of John Jones, 'Talhaearn', Paxton's assistant in building the great Rothschild *châteaux* in England and France, and from a Manchester cobbler called Idris Vychan, a brilliant performer who could out-sing and out-word everybody in the great mid-nineteenth-century eisteddfodau. By this time it was certainly believed that the art was of the hoariest antiquity.

By the time Edward Jones was publishing his influential books the triple harp was regarded as the Welsh national instrument *par excellence*, the other old Welsh instruments such as the *pibgorn* or *crwth* (crowd) having recently disappeared. Thomas Price, 'Carnhuanawc', a patriotic cleric and scholar, claimed that he had been taught in the late eighteenth century in Breconshire to play a small harp with one row of strings. Iolo Morganwg claimed that the triple harp was first made in Wales by Queen Anne's harpist Elis Sion Siamas. By 1800, however, patriots were certain that the triple harp (so called because it had three rows of strings, the middle row providing the sharps and flats) was the ancient national instrument, and national honour demanded that it should be defended against the newer pedal harps of Sebastien Erard of Paris. The triple harp had become fashionable in England in the seventeenth century, and was a version of the Italian baroque harp. It seems to have become immensely popular in North Wales around the 1690s or 1700s, and it was only gradually brought to South Wales. Its popularity in the south was only established by the brilliant playing of Thomas Blayney, and by the encouragement of an eccentric squire of Glanbrân (Carmarthen) Sackville Gwynne. In the early nineteenth century the triple harp was protected by the money and patronage of gentry like Lady Llanover who set up harp societies and gave prizes for harp playing, and even distributed triple harps as presents. Lady Llanover would never have done this had she thought it an Italian baroque instrument. Despite all this encouragement the triple harp became more and more the instrument of the gypsies, many of the finest performers being descended from the Romany-speaking family or tribe of Abram Wood.

By the 1780s another important change had also taken place, and the Welsh now supposed that they as a people possessed an inexhaustible wealth of native melody, often of the greatest antiquity. English song titles were now adapted or translated without apology – a seventeenth-century 'Cebell' became 'Yr Hen Sibyl' and was said to refer to an ancient witch, 'General Monck's March' became 'Ymdaith y Mwngc' and was thought to refer to the flight of an early medieval monk, Martin Parker's ballad of 1643 'When the King enjoys his own again' became 'Difyrrwch y Brenin' and was said to refer to the court of a medieval Welsh prince. The quite recent 'delight' of the composer D'Urfey became 'Difyrrwch Gwyr Dyfi' and was thought to refer to the men of the vale of Dovey. Airs with genuine Welsh titles were said to come from far distant historical events: the obviously Purcellian air 'Morfa Rhuddlan' was said to be the lament of the Welsh at their defeat at Rhuddlan by King Offa about 750 A.D. The Welsh were egged on by romantic tourists and English publishers to this kind of invention. George Thomson and Haydn were almost the first to fit English words to old Welsh airs, and with the help of Mrs Hemans, Sir Walter Scott and others they often turned to historical themes. The romantic Anglo-Welsh poet was a feature first found in literary life in the 1800s and one of the earliest was Richard Llwyd, 'Bard of Snowdon', who found the song books an excellent field of activity. Welsh-language poets in turn were forced to produce Welsh historical ballads to match the English inventions. One of the most prolific of these writers of Welsh historical ballads to fit Welsh airs was John Hughes, 'Ceiriog'. The songs whether sung to English or Welsh words were enormously popular and were one of the chief means by which historical mythologizing reached the Welsh public at large. They did not always take them seriously – the early-nineteenth-century theatre in Cardiff used to burlesque 'Ar Hyd y Nos' (the ever popular 'All Through the Night') as 'Ah! Hide your Nose!'[67] The change which took place as a result of the work of men like Blind Parry and Edward Jones was that the Welsh had gained self-confidence. A number of most able musicians had appeared in Wales in the eighteenth century, and they

---

[67] Cecil Price, *The English Theatre in Wales* (Cardiff, 1948), p. 114. *Passim* it has much on the spread of English culture through Wales in the later eighteenth century.

produced a large number of native melodies for concerts and revues and eisteddfodau, as well as producing excellent hymn tunes for the teeming hymnbooks of the period. This was all achieved before Wales became the land of choral singing in the mid-nineteenth century. The myth of the great antiquity of Welsh native music had a great deal to do with this outburst of activity and sense of national pride involved in it.

Thomas Jones, 'Glan Alun', a bard and journalist, complained in the magazine *Y Traethodydd* in 1848 that Wales, however musical as a country, lacked a national anthem, a stirring song which would unify the nation as did the anthems of France or Prussia.[68] This was a fairly general desire, and it was soon answered, for in 1856 at Pontypridd in Glamorgan the tune and words of 'Hen Wlad Fy Nhadau' ('Land of My Fathers') were composed by Evan and James James, father and son. The song was deeply patriotic, and it had become popular by 1858 when it was entered in a collection of patriotic songs at the great national eisteddfod of Llangollen, and after 1860 it was accepted very widely as a national anthem. The princely anthem 'Tywysog Gwlad y Bryniau' ('God Bless the Prince of Wales') appeared in 1863 on the occasion of the marriage of Edward Prince of Wales, but although popular it never at any time succeeded in matching 'Land of my Fathers'.[69] It is most striking with what speed the tradition grew up that 'Land of my Fathers' should be sung on all public occasions.

DAME WALES

The host of tourists coming into Wales in the late eighteenth century, sometimes with their pet artists like John 'Warwick' Smith or J. C. Ibbetson in train, noted that the Welsh peasantry were about sixty years behind the times in their dress, and that they had many distinctive fabrics, patterns and materials. They never mention a national dress, nothing like the kilts in the Scottish Highlands.[70] As one would expect of tourists, they tried to find poverty colourful, and

---

[68] *Traethodydd*, iv (1848), pp. 387–92. This was the leading Welsh intellectual review, edited by Dr Lewis Edwards.

[69] Percy Scholes, 'Hen Wlad Fy Nhadau', *National Library of Wales Journal*, iii (1943), pp. 1–10.

[70] F. Payne, *Welsh Peasant Costume* (Cardiff, 1964); M. Ellis, *Welsh Costumes and Customs* (Aberystwyth, 1951); K. Etheridge, *Welsh Costume* (Llandybie, 1958 and reissued since).

they noted that the women often wore large blue or red tweed cloaks and mannish black hats. The tall hat and the great cloak bore a resemblance to the image of a witch, for the simple reason that they were the characteristic dress of an English country woman of the 1620s, the time of witchcraft persecutions. What had been fashionable in lowland England in the 1620s still lingered amongst the poor of some Welsh mountain areas in the 1790s, or even longer. It was an entirely unselfconscious survival. It was not in any sense a national costume, but it was turned deliberately into a national costume for women in the 1830s as a result of the efforts of a number of people, the chief of whom was Augusta Waddington (1802–96),[71] wife of Benjamin Hall, a great Monmouthshire landowner and industrialist, and the minister in Palmerston's government responsible for completing the Palace of Westminster, after whom Big Ben is named. Benjamin was ennobled and his wife is usually known as Lady Llanover. She was one of the leaders of the picturesque romantic side of the Welsh revival in the early and mid-nineteenth century and a patron of innumerable Welsh causes. She studied and sketched female costumes of the Welsh and in 1834 at the Cardiff Royal Eisteddfod won the competition for an essay on the desirability of speaking Welsh and wearing Welsh costumes. Her original intent was to persuade Welshwomen to support home products, to stick to local tweeds instead of going over to cottons and calicoes, and she and her friends later gave prizes for collections of native tweed designs and patterns. In 1834 she was not even clear as to what a national costume was, but she was sure there ought to be a costume which would be distinctive and picturesque for artists and tourists to look at. Within a very short time she and her friends had evolved a homogenized national costume from the various Welsh peasant dresses, the most distinctive features of which were an enormous red cloak worn over an elegant petticoat and bedgown (*pais a betgwn*) and a very tall black beaver hat, in the style of Mother Goose. It was to be worn on 'national occasions' on Saint David's Day, at concerts of native music, especially by the female singers and harpists, or at the processions which opened and closed Lady Llanover's colourful eisteddfodau at Abergavenny. She invented a costume for her male servants at Llanover Court, the harpist being in a weird raiment, half-minstrel, half-Scottish Highlander. Lord

---

[71] Lady Llanover is in the *Dictionary of Welsh Biography*, *s.n.* 'Benjamin Hall'; for many biographical details of Lord and Lady Llanover see various articles on them by Maxwell Fraser in the *National Library of Wales Journal*, xii-xiv (1962–6).

Llanover was not interested in wearing fancy dress, and so the menfolk of Wales were spared. Lady Llanover presented a portrait of herself in national costume in 1862 to the public school which she helped to found to foster Welsh among the upper classes at Llandovery College, in which she wears a jewelled leek in the brim of her tall hat and holds a sprig of mistletoe in her hand to show her connection with the Druids (she was a bard with the name of Gwenynen Gwent, the Bee of Monmouthshire). The costume was soon adopted, for example in newspaper cartoons, as a caricature of Wales; it was reproduced on Victorian post-cards; thousands of pottery models of the Welshwoman in her costume were sold each year; schoolchildren all over Wales still don it on 1 March. It was a symbol of all that was good and homely. It appeared, for example, on 'Dame Wales' flour packets and on many other Welsh products. Meanwhile, the old native costumes in all their local varieties (even including here and there a tall beaver hat and a large cloak) died away as Wales became one of the most industrialized countries in the world.

THE NEW CAMBRIAN VALHALLA

One of the most interesting features of the period is the appearance of national heroes, and of these none is more truly characteristic than Owain Glyndŵr, Shakespeare's Glendower, who had risen against Henry IV and ruled Wales from 1400 until his mysterious disappearance in 1415.[72] Glyndŵr appeared usually as a usurper or misguided rebel in literature, and although Ben Jonson said in 1618 that he was informed by Welsh friends that Glyndŵr was not regarded as a rebel in Wales but as a great hero, there seems little corroborative evidence for this. In the early eighteenth century the Morris circle seem to have been barely aware of him, since they mention him only once, and that as a traitor. Glyndŵr seems to burst forth in splendour in the 1770s as a national hero. He appears in 1772 as part of the pageant of the defenders of Wales in Evan Evans's *The Love of Our Country*, and in 1775 he is given much attention by the *History of the Island of Anglesey*, attributed to John Thomas of Beaumaris, based apparently on a manuscript life of Glyndŵr composed in the mid-seventeenth century. In 1778 Glyndŵr was given a most favourable treatment by Thomas Pennant in his *Tours in Wales*.

Gilbert White sent his famous letters on the natural history of

[72] J. E. Lloyd, *Owen Glyndŵr* (Oxford, 1931); D. Rhys Phillips, *A Select Bibliography of Owen Glyndŵr* (Swansea, 1915).

Selborne to Thomas Pennant and Daines Barrington, both leaders of the Welsh historical revival in the 1770s. Pennant, from Downing in Flintshire, was an anglicized aristocrat with a passionate love for things Welsh. He described Caernarfon Castle as 'that most magnificent badge of our servitude' and his portrait of Glyndŵr is most favourable with a very keen sense of the tragedy of his decline and disappearance, which led to a second conquest of the Welsh by the English. It is possible that Pennant was reflecting the views of his travelling companion John Lloyd of Caerwys, who was the son of the squire of Bodidris, which stands very close to Glyndŵr's home base. It was probably Pennant who launched Glyndŵr as a national hero, and the books on him become a trickle, then a stream and then a flood, portraying him first as a tragic figure, then as the man who foresaw the need for Welsh national institutions (such as a national church and university) and then as the pioneer of modern nationalism.[73]

Daines Barrington in 1770 published the early-seventeenth-century manuscript of the history of the Gwedir family by Sir John Wynne. This manuscript had been used some years earlier by Carte in his history of England, from which he took the story that Edward I had slaughtered the Welsh bards in 1282. Thoms Gray took the story from Carte and then was inspired by the playing of Blind Parry to complete his famous poem *The Bard* in 1757.[74] Gray did not believe the story literally – did not Welsh poets still exist, proving that the bards of 1282 had successors? Carte's story had some foundation in Welsh fables that all old Welsh books had been burned in London, and that the bards somehow were proscribed. Soon after 1757 the Welsh themselves began to believe Gray's picture, as one can see from such an exact scholar as Evan Evans who quoted extensively from Gray in the 1760s. The Morris circle earlier on had seen the Welsh bard primarily as an entertainer. For them poetry was an amusing social pastime, and this had led to a rupture with Goronwy Owen, who saw poetry as the sublime or epic literature. Evan Evans belonged to the generation which saw the bard as a heroic creature,

[73] Silvan Evans, *Gwaith y Parchedig Evan Evans*, p. 142; Davies, *Morris Letters*, i, p. 432; Thomas Pennant, *Tours*, i (1778), pp. 302–69.

[74] P. Toynbee and L. Whibley, *Correspondence of Thomas Gray* (Oxford, 1935), ii, pp. 501–2. For the interaction of Welsh and English men of letters in this period see Saunders Lewis, *A School of Welsh Augustans* (London, 1924); W. J. Hughes, *Wales and the Welsh in English Literature from Shakespeare to Scott* (London and Wrexham, 1924); and E. D. Snyder, *The Celtic Revival in English Literature 1760–1800* (Harvard, 1923).

often driven into great hostility to his environment. He deeply admired the earlier Welsh poets who had been real warriors. Iolo Morganwg carried this idolizing of the figure of the bard to its greatest heights, partly because of the influence of Goronwy Owen and Evan Evans, partly because he suffered from a terrible persecution complex and wished to turn the tables on everybody who scorned or slighted poets or scholars. Iolo made the bard the central figure in the Welsh historical pageant, though in some ages the bard was a Druid and in another a historian or scholar, and his imagination was never fired more heatedly than when he talked of the bard under persecution.

Gray's bard was a famous figure by the 1770s and 1780s, and had by then become a well-known subject in painting. One of the earliest versions was by Paul Sandby, and there were others by Philip De Loutherbourg, Fuseli and John Martin. One of the best is by Richard Wilson's pupil, Thomas Jones of Pencerrig.[75] This was exhibited in 1774 and shows the last surviving bard holding his harp, fleeing from the encroaching troops, who draw near his fane, a kind of miniature Stonehenge, the sun is setting in the west on Snowdon's slopes, a bitter wind blows from the east, from England. The dramatic scene, the confrontation of the poet with the power of the state, was to be repeated many times. It was soon set as a subject for poems and essays in eisteddfodau, retold in many English and Welsh books, and it found its way into the famous Magyar poem *The Welsh Bards* by Janos Árány, where Edward I is like a ferocious Habsburg emperor entering the Balkans. Needless to say, the whole story is a fable or myth. At best one might say it is a gross exaggeration of the fact that from time to time medieval English kings licensed and controlled Welsh bards because they caused discord through their prophecies.

One of the most extraordinary of the new heroes was Madoc, the son of Prince Owain Gwynedd, who, disheartened by quarrels at home in North Wales, left on his ship *Gwennan Gorn* for uncharted western seas about the year 1170, and discovered America. He returned to Wales, gathered some companions, set sail again with them, and never returned. His descendants were assumed to have intermarried with the Indians and to be still alive in the Wild West.[76]

[75] McCarthy, 'The Bard of Thomas Gray'; and Ralph Edwards's introduction to the catalogue of the exhibition of Thomas Jones's works: *Thomas Jones* (London, 1970).

[76] David Williams, *John Evans and the Legend of Madoc* (Cardiff, 1963).

The legend was not of eighteenth-century origin, but had first been used by the Tudors to undermine Spanish claims to rule North America. It remained known, but dormant, for some two hundred years in Wales and only came to life in the 1770s when Welsh interest in America was kindled by the American Revolution. Not only was there interest in the Revolution for its own sake, but also there was a strong movement for Welsh emigration to America, to set up a Welsh-speaking colony in the new republic. The Madoc myth only caught the imagination of the public in 1790 when Dr John Williams, London minister and historian, and librarian of Dr Williams's library, published an account of the Madoc story. The London Welsh were all agog. Iolo Morganwg (in London at the time) forged all sorts of documents to prove that Madoc's descendants were alive and Welsh-speaking, somewhere in the Mid-West, so that Dr Williams had to bring out a second volume. William Owen (Pughe) started a 'Madogeion' society to organize an expedition, which Iolo offered to lead. He was abashed when a serious young man, John Evans of Waun Fawr (1770–99), presented himself and was ready to go. Iolo made excuses and stayed at home, but John Evans left for America, eventually reaching the Wild West. He became an explorer in the service of the king of Spain. He found his way eventually by a series of hair-raising adventures to the lands of the Mandan Indians (whom he considered might be the Madogians), but found they were not Welsh-speaking. After experiencing other adventures he died in the palace of the Spanish governor in New Orleans in 1799. The map of his journey to the Mandans became the basis for the explorations of Meriwether, Lewis and Clark. The fact that no Welsh Indians were found did not destroy the faith of Iolo Morganwg or his London Welsh friends. Iolo indeed persuaded Robert Southey to write a book-length poem called *Madoc*. The Madogian movement caused considerable Welsh emigration to America, and one of its great leaders was the Welsh radical journalist Morgan John Rhys, who previously had been working in Paris attempting to sell Protestant Bibles to evangelize the French revolutionaries. Gwyn A. Williams has studied the work of Morgan John Rhys and the Madogian movement and stresses that Madoc fever was part of a crisis of modernization of much of Welsh society in this period, and that the dream of rediscovering the lost Welsh Indians had much in common with the desire to recreate Druidism or the Patriarchal Language.[77]

---

[77] Gwyn A. Williams, 'John Evans's Mission to the Madogwys, 1792–1799', *Bulletin of the Board of Celtic Studies*, xxvii (1978), pp. 569–601. For Morgan

It was the dream of a more pure and free society, and had something in common with the myths of the Freeborn Saxons and the Norman Yoke amongst contemporary English workmen.

Iolo Morganwg was responsible for turning many obscure figures into national heroes. One example will suffice here. Iolo was farming in the 1780s in the marshland between Cardiff and Newport, where he came into contact with Evan Evans, then a drunken, threadbare curate at Bassaleg, and they both visited the ruins of the fourteenth-century hall of Ifor Hael (Ivor the Generous), who, tradition stated in a vague and uncertain way, had been the patron of the great fourteenth-century poet Dafydd ap Gwilym. Evans wrote a fine romantic poem about the ivy-clad ruins, and Iolo set about his first important forgeries, the imitation of the love poems of Dafydd ap Gwilym, which contained subtle little references to Glamorgan and to Ifor Hael. Iolo in his subsequent writings did much to make out Ifor as the greatest patron of Welsh literature.[78] Ivor became a popular name in Wales, a household word for generosity. The most Welsh of the workmen's benefit societies, the Order of Ivorites, took their name from him; the inns where many of their lodges met were called Ivor Arms, and many of these still survive to this day. By the 1820s and 1830s there were many of these myth-makers to be found in Wales besides Iolo. One such figure writing popular histories for the Welsh-speakers was a Caernarfon printer William Owen, 'Sefnyn', who was also known as 'Pab' (Pope) for his Roman Catholic sympathies. He wrote on Glyndŵr, Edward I and the Welsh bards, the Treason of the Long Knives, and many other dramatic events of Welsh history. A rather similar figure writing in English was T. J. Llewelyn Pritchard, an actor and journalist concerned with creating an illusion of Welshness for the gentry and middle classes who no longer spoke Welsh, and with the tourist market.[79] He did not originate, but was the chief begetter of another curious Welsh hero, Twm Sion Catti, about whom he wrote a novel in 1828. The real Twm Sion Catti was one Thomas Jones, a respectable squire and genealogist from Fountain Gate near Tregaron in Cardiganshire in

John Rhys and emigration see Gwyn A. Williams, 'Morgan John Rhees and his Beula', *Welsh History Review*, iii (1967), pp. 441–72; also Gwyn A. Williams's two recent books, *Madoc: The Making of a Myth* (London, 1979) and *In Search of Beulah Land* (London, 1980).

[78] David Greene, *Makers and Forgers* (Cardiff, 1975); and Morgan, *Iolo Morganwg*, pp. 75–91 for the forgeries.

[79] T. J. Ll. Pritchard, *Welsh Minstrelsy* (London and Aberystwyth, 1825), and *The Adventures and Vagaries of Twm Sion Catty* (Aberystwyth, 1828).

the late sixteenth century, but over the years various local tales had arisen which mixed him up with other obscure raiders and highwaymen in the district. Pritchard turned this obscure figure into a Till Eulenspiegel of pranks and jokes, and into a Robin-Hood figure of folk justice, robbing the rich to pay the poor. Pritchard's work became popular, was translated into Welsh and soon enough the Welsh began to believe the fables were true. By the present century (when his popularity as a hero or anti-hero shows no signs of diminishing) it seems as if he steps out of genuine folk legend. It is a very good example of the way story-book heroes came to take the place of the decayed and enfeebled tradition of story-telling around the fireside.

SPIRITS OF THE PLACE – LANDSCAPE AND MYTH

T. J. Ll. Pritchard was in fact part of a wide movement which tried to make the Welsh understand that their landscape must be cherished, and in order to make this clear to common folk gave each stick and stone historical and human interest.[80] One of Pritchard's poems was *The Land beneath the Sea*, about Cantre'r Gwaelod, the Lowland Hundred which lay under Cardigan Bay, a kind of Welsh Lyonesse drowned early in the Dark Ages through the negligence of the servants of the carousing loose-living King Seithennyn. Legends which were genuinely ancient connected the story of the Lowland Hundred with the saga of the poet and prophet Taliesin. Writers like Pritchard made the folk legend known all over Wales, and the song 'The Bells of Aberdovey' was adapted to prove that it was the *Cathédrale Engloutie* music of the bells of the drowned spires lying off Aberdovey, although the song was in reality a recent one by Dibdin. The story was a most useful one, which could be turned into a tract against drunkenness or irresponsible monarchs. Thomas Love Peacock knew of the efforts of William Maddox to recover large areas of land from the sea near his town of Portmadoc. In his novel *Headlong Hall* he satirized the Welsh squires and their English visitors for romanticizing the Welsh landscape and for their schemes of 'improvement', and in his later novel *The Misfortunes of Elphin* he wrote a most spirited prose version of the legend of Taliesin and the Lowland Hundred's destruction. Some of the landscape legends were unashamedly invented for the tourists, an excellent example

[80] F. J. North, *Sunken Cities* (Cardiff, 1957), esp. pp. 147ff.

being that of the grave of Gelert at Beddgelert in Caernarfonshire. It was one of the spots most visited by tourists in the late eighteenth century, and some time between 1784 and 1794 a South Walian hotelier of the Royal Goat Hotel, Beddgelert, invented the legend that the village took its name from a burial cairn (which the enterprising hotelier stealthily constructed) put up by Prince Llywelyn the Great in memory of his having most unjustly killed his favourite hound Gelert. The Prince had gone hunting, leaving Gelert as baby-sitter with his heir, and on his return found Gelert covered with blood, and the baby gone. Having killed the dog he then found the baby in a dark corner, and it was clear that Gelert had killed a wolf which had attacked the royal cradle. The cairn was a token of his remorse.[81] The hearts of pet-loving tourists were touched, the Hon. W. Spencer wrote a famous poem about the incident, which Joseph Haydn set to the tune of Eryri Wen, and within a few years the story returned in Welsh versions to the monoglot Welsh inhabitants of Snowdonia. It is of course all moonshine, or more exactly, a clever adaptation of a well-known international folk tale. It is a good instance of the kind of complex myth-making which went on in a thousand places, helping very gradually to make the Welsh appreciate the harsh landscape from which they had to scratch a living.

By the end of the eighteenth century tourists considered Wales to be a country of great beauty of landscape. By the middle decades of the nineteenth century the Welsh themselves came to appreciate its charms. The second verse of the national anthem runs (we translate):

> Old mountainous Wales, paradise of bards,
> Each cliff and each valley to my sight is fair,
> With patriotic sentiment, magic is the sound
> Of her rivers and brooks to me...

Such sentiments were unthinkable in the eighteenth century. We have few if any descriptions of landscape in the period, and those which survive, for example the verses by Dafydd Thomas about 1750 on each county in Wales, mention human activity, produce and skills, and never boast about the beauty of the land.[82] The patriotic circle of the Morris brothers thought mountains horrid, dreary and hostile;

[81] D. E. Jenkins, *Bedd Gelert, its Facts, Fairies and Folklore* (Portmadoc, 1899), pp. 56–73.
[82] Dafydd Thomas's verses were printed by S. Williams at Aberystwyth in 1816, but I have relied on a version printed in *Trysorfa'r Plant* (Children's Treasury) for 1893–4.

if anything they were seen as a punishment meted out by the Almighty to the Welsh for past sins. The native Welsh were very slow to learn from the hordes of English tourists who came to admire the wild landscape; the Reverend William Bingley said that they asked him had he no rocks or waterfalls in his own country? William Gambold's grammar book of 1727 was reprinted more than once in the early nineteenth century and the 1833 edition took account of the needs of tourists in the 'romantic hills of the Principality', by augmenting such useful phrases as 'Is not there a waterfall in this neighbourhood?' and 'I long to see the Monastery. I will take a gig to go there.' The appetite of the tourists had been whetted by the engravings of Welsh scenery sold in shops. John Byng complained when he was at Crogen that the engravers should sell sketch-maps as well, to help one get to the place of the picture. But the fashion for the Welsh view stemmed in the first place not from a tourist but from a Welshman, Richard Wilson.

Richard Wilson (1714–82) was a kinsman of Thomas Pennant, and although much of his work was done in Italy and England, he seems to have made an original and independent discovery of the Welsh landscape in the 1750s and 1760s. Before this time the Welsh view had been purely a topographical record.[83] The Welsh scene forced Wilson (a native of Penegoes near Machynlleth) to adopt two unfashionable styles, one an open air style where nature seems to dominate mankind, another a more romantic style where Welsh hills or castle ruins are turned into something sublimely grand. He could sell few of his landscapes to the fashionable public, and died a near-failure near Mold in 1782. Very soon after this his views were reproduced and imitated by the thousand. When Cornelius Varley visited Cader Idris in 1803 he actually noted down Llyn y Cau as 'Wilson's Pool' so famous had Wilson's picture of it become. The shift of the imagination towards appreciating wild mountain scenery of course took place all over Europe, but it particularly affected small mountain peoples such as the Welsh or the Swiss. The Welsh very gradually came to see their hills not as a punishment from the

[83] Iolo A. Williams, 'Notes on Paul Sandby and his Predecessors in Wales', *Transactions of the Honourable Society of Cymmrodorion* (1961), pp. 16–33; A. D. Fraser Jenkins, 'The Romantic Traveller in Wales', *Amgueddfa*, vi (1970), pp. 29–37; D. Moore, 'The Discovery of the Welsh Landscape', in D. Moore (ed.), *Wales in the Eighteenth Century* (Swansea, 1976), pp. 127–51. The standard work on Wilson is W. G. Constable, *Richard Wilson* (London, 1953).

Almighty who had driven them from the lush lowlands of England, but as a fastness or fortress for the nation. *Gwlad y Bryniau* (Mountain Land) soon became a Welsh cliché, even for those living in lowland Wales. The image had become fixed even when in reality the road improvements of Telford and the like had penetrated wildest Snowdonia, when tourists like William Wordsworth could scale the top of Snowdon without too much discomfort, and the native population was flowing away from the moors and hills to the valleys and industrial areas. As the Welsh became more and more industrialized, so they came to cherish the image of the Welshman as a sturdy tough hillman, free as mountain air.

A HERALDRY OF CULTURE

Merrie Wales with its colourful rites and customs was dying or dead, yet there emerged in this period an elaborate set of patriotic insignia which not only gave colour to life, but also helped the people of separate valleys or religious sects to see that they were part of a nation. They appeared most often amongst Welshmen abroad, in London, America or in the colonies, but not always. These insignia of nationhood first appeared in the elaborate Saint David's Day ceremonies held by London Welshmen after 1714.[84] The Welshmen processed through London to a church, wearing leeks in their hats, listened to Welsh sermons, then gathered for huge dinners (set for hundreds of guests), drank numerous toasts of loyalty to Wales and to the reigning dynasty, made collections to Welsh charities, and then dispersed for private carousals.

In the eighteenth century, in fact, the commonest symbol for Wales was not the leek but the three ostrich plumes of the Princes of Wales, which had originally belonged (together with the motto *Ich Dien*) to Ostrevant in Hainault, and were taken by the Black Prince because his mother was Queen Philippa of Hainault. They are the perfect specimen of borrowed plumage. London Welshmen made a display of them, as at the ceremonies of the Ancient Britons, to show the Hanoverians that the Welsh were loyal, unlike the dangerous Irish or Scots. The plumes and motto were adopted in 1751 by the Cymmrodorion as the crest of their arms, and throughout the period

---

[84] A description of the junketings of the Society of Ancient Britons in 1728 by Richard Morris is in Davies, *Morris Letters*, i, p. 3.

they are by far the most common ideogram or *logo* for Wales. They remain to this day a very common symbol and form the badge, for example, of the Welsh Rugby Union.[85]

By contrast the now well-known red dragon was hardly used at all. It had been considered a Welsh symbol during the Middle Ages, and was given wide currency between 1485 and 1603 by the Tudor dynasty as part of their arms, where it probably symbolized their descent from Cadwaladr the Blessed and represented their claim to the overlordship of all Britain. It was not considered to be a national symbol as much as the administrative symbol of the Council of Wales, but it did make its reappearance as the royal badge for Wales in 1807, and thereafter was used increasingly in the banners and badges of the eisteddfodau or Welsh clubs and societies in the early nineteenth century. It only replaced the three plumes in Welsh esteem in the twentieth century, the three plumes with their subservient motto being considered too deferential for radicals, liberals and socialists.

The leek had for centuries been used by the Welsh themselves as a badge, the colours of green and white being associated with the Welsh princes, and used as a primitive military uniform in the fourteenth century. Shakespeare imagined Henry V (Harry of Monmouth) and Fluellen wearing it on Saint David's Day for the memorable honour of Wales. The leek was worn also in England, for example by the court in London, as late as the eighteenth century, and it is possible that it was one of the subtle ways in which the Anglican Church wished to graft itself on to the memory of the early British Church. The leek was certainly worn much more self-consciously by Welshmen outside Wales. Although it could never be called an invented tradition, it did become a common part of the elaborate symbolic décor which draped the eisteddfod pavilions or concert halls for native music in the early nineteenth century. The substitution of the daffodil for the leek as a national symbol appeared as recently as 1907, and was based on a misunderstanding of the Welsh word for 'bulb'. The rather feminine delicacy of the daffodil appealed to Lloyd George, who used it in preference to the leek in the immense stage-managed Investiture ceremonial in Caernarfon in 1911, and on such things as government literature of the period.

---

[85] The only treatment of the subject is Francis Jones, *The Princes and Principality of Wales* (Cardiff, 1969), esp. pp. 86–7, and 158–204. Edwards, *Yr Eisteddfod*, illustrates medals and pavilion decorations.

One of the symbols most frequently used for Wales in the eighteenth century was the Druid, especially the druidic high priest hooded and mantled, with his sickle and golden bough of mistletoe. He was with Saint David a supporter of the Cymmrodorion arms in 1751, and after that he was used with increasing frequency as a title for societies, clubs, inns. He appeared on the title pages of books on Wales, added to which we find the cromlech (which was imagined to be a Druid altar) used to accompany him, perhaps as a vignette or tailpiece. The *Cambrian Register* (an excellent journal for Welsh history and literature) chose the cromlech as its titlepage decoration in 1795, as also did William Owen (Pughe) in a number of his books. The Druid was a symbol for the lodges of workmen's benefit societies a little later, and it was probably the onward march of nonconformity which gradually drove out the pagan priest from Welsh national heraldry, though he long remained, together with swags of oakleaves and mistletoe, as a decorative element on eisteddfod crowns, chairs and medals.

The harp, to be precise the triple harp, was used frequently as a symbol of Wales. The triple harps themselves were sometimes decorated with national symbols, leeks entwined about the foot, and princely plumes sprouting from the top. Harps were used on banners and in books, on scrolls and medals, often with fitting mottoes in Welsh that 'Wales is the land of the harp', 'the language of the soul is upon its strings' and so on. The Welsh mountain goat, still a most impressive sight in Snowdonia, was adopted by some as a Welsh symbol. Pennant used a goatherd with his hornpipe or *pibgorn* and his goats as a frontispiece to his *Tours*, Lady Llanover adopted a wild goat as one of her heraldic supporters, and some of the Welsh regiments adopted the goat as a regimental mascot. Not unnaturally the goat was also a useful symbolic caricature for Wales in lampoons and cartoons.

The eisteddfod, provincial and national, was the occasion in this period for a riotous display of insignia, and the national symbols we have mentioned were all mixed up with the special insignia of the Gorsedd of Bards. Thousands of eisteddfod crowns and chairs were produced, and a language of decoration was needed for these objects. Iolo Morganwg (a good journeyman mason and amateur artist) was a prolific manufacturer of symbols, the most famous being his *nod cyfrin* (mystic sign) of three bars, each bar representing past, present and future, and representing the name of God in the druidic theology, which is still used as a most impressive ideogram for the National Eisteddfod. The high point of eisteddfod rites and rituals was not reached until the late nineteenth century when elaborate costumes and regalia, replete with all the symbols we have mentioned above, were designed for the Gorsedd of Bards by Sir Hubert von Herkomer and Sir Goscombe John.

The new ceremonials and the symbols and insignia all served to help Welshmen visualize their own country, and they had an exceptional importance in a national community that was not a political state. They were a substitute for the lost customs and rites of the old society of patronal festivals, merry nights and calendar feasts.

A TURNING POINT: 'THE TREASON OF THE BLUE BOOKS'

In 1847 the royal commission into the state of education in Wales reported its findings to the government in its Blue Books. The inquiry was instigated for many reasons; the concern for the growing hold of dissent or nonconformity over the common people, the lack of provision of education in Wales and the growth of unrest over the past few decades culminating in the Merthyr Rising of 1831, the Chartist risings of 1839 and the Rebecca Riots from 1839 to 1843. The commissioners (all Englishmen) reported on much in Wales besides education, attributing the backwardness and immorality of the people (especially the women) to the influence of dissent and the Welsh language. The storm of protest which resulted in Wales at what many considered a gross libel of a nation, based upon the biased evidence given by an unrepresentative minority of Welshmen to the English commissioners, was called 'The Treason of the Blue Books' (*Brad y Llyfrau Gleision*). This was an elaborate historical pun on the words 'Treason of the Long Knives' which had been a favourite subject of the romantic mythologists. The leader of the Welsh (or British) in the late fifth century was Vortigern (Gwrtheyrn) who invited the Saxons under Hengist and Horsa to come to Britain to aid him against his enemies. The Saxons invited Vortigern to a banquet, according to the story, at which he fell in love with Hengist's daughter Alys Rhonwen or Rowena and asked to marry her. The Saxons, some time later in another banquet, at a special signal leapt upon the carousing Welsh chieftains who were at the table, and slaughtered them with their long knives, forcing Vortigern to hand over a large area of England to them. This Welsh Saint Bartholomew's Eve had been known as a fable by the Welsh in past centuries. It was taken in the seventeenth century by the balladist Matthew Owen as a punishment for sins, to be accepted humbly and passively. In the eighteenth century, the mythologists had seen its dramatic interest and it was illustrated by romantic artists such as Henry Fuseli and Angelica Kauffmann in the 1770s. After 1847, however, it was turned into a form of political propaganda to goad the Welsh into action.[86]

The action taken as a result of the brouhaha over the Blue Books was paradoxical and contradictory. On the one hand it made the Welsh more nationalistic and Anglophobe than they had ever been before, on the other it made the Welsh concerned to answer the criticisms of the commissioners by becoming more like the English, by turning themselves into practical, hard-headed, business-like English-speaking Britons. The brouhaha also caused new alliances and new divisions in Welsh society. The historical revival of the eighteenth century, of which we have been discussing the mythological part, had stayed aloof from the great forces of religious debate, political reform and the industrial revolution. The great antiquarians and scholars were in general hostile to the tremendous force of Methodism, which not only destroyed the old merry way of life but also filled most effectively any vacuum which might have been left. Iolo Morganwg, for instance, wrote to his patron Owain Myfyr in 1799 that the Gwyneddigion and other London Welsh patriots were being maligned as Painites at the Methodist Association at Bala by one of Iolo's enemies whom he always called Ginshop Jones. Ginshop Jones was a life-guard of George III who left to become an innkeeper and Methodist elder. 'North Wales', complained Iolo, 'is now as Methodistical as South Wales, and South Wales as Hell.'[87]

William Roberts, 'Nefydd', Baptist minister and organizer of schools wrote a collection of essays in 1852 *Crefydd yr Oesoedd Tywyll* (Religion of the Dark Ages) where he contrasts the semi-pagan folk culture of Wales with the new respectable Welsh culture of his day, that of the eisteddfod, the literary society, the debating club and the journals, and noted that until recently the harsh spirit of Geneva had kept the Methodists from enjoying this blossoming culture. The

---

[86] David Williams, *A History of Modern Wales* (London, 1950), pp. 246–68 on nonconformity, and pp. 269–85 on the growth of national consciousness, is excellent for the 1840s.

[87] G. J. Williams, 'Llythyrau Llenorion' (Letters of Authors), *Y Llenor*, vi (1927), p. 39.

old guard of the Methodists were dying off rapidly in the 1840s. The young could see to what extent Welsh culture had changed, and the Blue Books controversy finally drove them into the arms of the other dissenters and the Welsh patriots, because the commissioners lumped them all together and attacked Methodists, dissenters and the Welsh language as one.

The closing of the gap between Welsh patriots and the dissenters and Methodists unfortunately meant the opening of a gap between the patriots and the Anglicans, who had in various ways dominated the cultural revival since the eighteenth century, and had certainly been its most brilliant promoters from 1815 to 1847. The new wave of interest in things Welsh after 1815 was much encouraged by the movement known in Welsh as *Yr Hen Bersoniaid Llengar* (Old Literary Parsons), but which in fact involved many laymen and laywomen as well.[88] They were somewhat reactionary in politics and harked back to the less disturbed peaceful Wales of the eighteenth century. They wished to preserve what was left of Merrie Wales, and through dominating literature and history they hoped to prevent any further encroachments by dissent or Methodism upon Welsh life. They included the historian Angharad Llwyd (the daughter of John Lloyd, Pennant's companion); Lady Llanover; Lady Charlotte Guest, the editor of the famous edition of Welsh medieval tales which she called *The Mabinogion* (1849); John Jones, 'Tegid', precentor of Christ Church, Oxford; the folk song collector Maria Jane Williams of Aberpergwm; Thomas Price, 'Carnhuanawc', cleric, historian and Celticist; John Jenkins, 'Ifor Ceri', cleric, eisteddfod organizer and folk song collector; and the cleric John Williams, 'Ab Ithel', the unscrupulous editor of Iolo Morganwg's druidic papers, and one of the founders of the Cambrian Archaeological Association.

The Welsh Manuscripts Society and the Cambrian Archaeological Association, the public school at Llandovery and the Saint David's University College at Lampeter were all means by which this brilliant circle of people tried to affect Welsh life, but they reached the common people mainly through the eisteddfod. In 1819 the Swansea radical journal *Seren Gomer* approved of the Carmarthen eisteddfod,

[88] Bedwyr Lewis Jones, *Yr Hen Bersoniaid Llengar* (Old Literary Parsons) (Denbigh, 1963); R. T. Jenkins, *Hanes Cymru yn y Bedwaredd Ganrif ar Bymtheg* (History of Wales in the Nineteenth Century) *i. 1789–1843* (Cardiff, 1933) has much *passim* on the clerical patriots. For the general position of Celtic studies in the 1830s to the 1860s see Rachel Bromwich, *Matthew Arnold and Celtic Literature: a Retrospect 1865–1965* (Oxford, 1965).

but by 1832 the editor Joseph Harris was deeply suspicious of the Beaumaris eisteddfod on the grounds that it would deflect the Welsh from political reforms. Angharad Llwyd in an appendix to her history of Anglesey, which won the prize at the eisteddfod, printed a speech by another of the patriot clerics, the poet John Blackwell, 'Alun', in which he said that the Welsh peasant was cultured and literate, his books unsullied by immorality, and he did not bother with politics or government.[89] But things were changing even in the romantic world of the eisteddfod, for already in 1831 Arthur James Johnes (later a judge) won the prize for an essay 'The Causes of Dissent in Wales', a work of what would now be termed sociology. It was only some years later that attempts were made to turn the eisteddfod into a Welsh version of the British Association for the Advancement of Science. The patriot clerics with their concern for the remote and mythological past still dominated the eisteddfod until the late 1840s, but the controversy over the Blue Books placed them in an impossible position, and gradually the dissenters and Methodists turned on their fields of endeavour and took them over, claiming to stand for the Welsh nation and branding the Anglicans as foreign intruders. When the great leader of radical Wales, Henry Richard, published his *Letters and Essays on Wales* in 1866 he virtually equated being Welsh with being a nonconformist, and he brushed the Anglicans aside. The nonconformist take over of Welsh culture created a new image. It weakened Welsh interest in the far-distant national past, replacing it with an interest in the past of the Old Testament and with the early history of dissenting causes in the seventeenth and eighteenth centuries, and emphasized the new puritanical Sunday as 'The Welsh Sunday', the new 'Welsh way of life' being that of the chapel, the singing school (for hymns not ballads), the temperance assemblies, the *Cymanfa Ganu* (hymnsinging assemblies), the quarterly meetings and associations, the mutual improvement societies, and much else which is familiar to the twentieth century as the typical Wales. It is no wonder then that the historian Sir John Lloyd remarked that the Wales of Victoria differed from that of Queen Anne as much as that of Queen Anne had differed from that of Boadicea. John Thomas, 'Ieuan Ddu', published his

---

[89] Angharad Llwyd, *A History of the Island of Anglesey* (Ruthin, 1832), p. 39 of appendix. Cf. Mary Ellis, 'Angharad Llwyd', *Flintshire Historical Society Publications*, xxvi (1976), pp. 52–95, and xvii (1978), pp. 43–87.

lost touch with the songs of the past; young men even in remote Cardiganshire were forced to sing hymns at wedding banquets because they knew nothing else.[90]

The great forces of politics and industrialism which had been kept at bay by the scholars and patriots closed in on the charmed circle of the romantic mythologists in the 1840s and 1850s. Not that the eighteenth-century patriots were ignorant of either world; the Morris circle, for example, dabbled in industry and politics, as was inevitable since Lewis Morris was the controversial head of the royal mines in Cardiganshire and Richard Morris was at the Navy Office. Thomas Pennant came from the Greenfield valley of Flintshire where there was much early industry, and as a leading squire concerned himself with the government reforms in the 1780s. Patriots such as Iolo Morganwg or Morgan John Rhys and their friends were involved in radical politics in the 1780s and 1790s, when there was a considerable literature on political matters in Welsh.[91] Owain Myfyr considered that the Gwyneddigion society should be a debating society for radical discussion of reform in church and state, and the same was true of some of the other London Welsh societies. Men like Iolo and Morgan John Rhys belonged to a tradition of political discussion amongst the dissenting craftsmen of the hill country of Glamorgan, but they were a small minority, and the repression of the long years of war deadened the reform movement, while strengthening the anti-revolutionary feeling in Wales.

Henry Richard writing in 1866 referred back to the culture of his childhood and he recalled the large number of Welsh journals read by his father, observing that they were concerned with poetry and religion, with barely a mention of politics or commerce, save in a small appendix in the back.[92] This would have gained the approval of Lady Llanover and the clerical patriots, for their zestful cultural renaissance took place against a background of grinding poverty and seething discontent. Angharad Llwyd bought the stock of books of Willaim Owen, 'Sefnyn', to destroy them, because he supported

---

[90] John Thomas, 'Ieuan Ddu', *The Cambrian Minstrel* (Merthyr, 1845), p. 29n. The tradition of hymn singing at football matches is a late nineteenth-century phenomenon, arising from the same causes.

[91] David Davies, *The Influence of the French Revolution on Welsh Life and Literature* (Carmarthen, 1926); J. J. Evans, *Dylanwad y Chwyldro Ffrengig ar Lenyddiaeth Cymru* (Influence of the French Revolution on Welsh Literature) (Liverpool, 1928), and *Morgan John Rhys a'i Amserau* (M. J. Rhys and his Times) (Cardiff, 1935).

[92] Henry Richard, *Letters and Essays on Wales*, 2nd edn (London, 1884), p. 93.

Catholic emancipation, and Lady Llanover would have nothing to do with Llywelyn Williams (1822–72), a brilliant triple harpist, because his father Sephaniah Williams was the leader of the Chartist rising of 1839. Just as the controversy of the Blue Books brought the Methodists to the point of involving themselves in Welsh politics and culture, so it strengthened the hand of the Welshmen who wished their countrymen to involve themselves in business and politics. Even without the Blue Books controversy, the general circumstances of Welsh society were forcing men to play a more and more active part in controlling their own affairs. Edwin Chadwick observed that the extraordinary rites and rituals associated with the Rebecca Riots from 1839 to 1843 had grown out of the custom of *Ceffyl Pren* (Horseplay).[93] The customary society had long punished sexual misdemeanours with nocturnal processions of men in female garb and effigy-burning and mock trials. But in 1839 they were transformed for a violent social and political purpose. Thomas Jones, 'Glan Alun', who appealed for a national anthem in 1848, also appealed in the same number of the *Traethodydd* against the current Welsh concern for dry factual rational English practicality. The turning point had been reached, and from 1848 onwards the invention of tradition, which had been so long dominant in Welsh culture, began to decay.

The poets and mythologists and dreamers found themselves subjected to harsher criticism, sometimes of a general nature, from those who believed that Wales must now progress from a lower stage of human evolution where poetry and history were important to a higher stage of evolution where practical things must dominate; at other times the harsh criticism was particular. John Williams, 'Ab Ithel', hoped to make the Llangollen Eisteddfod in 1858 a revival of the great days of the patriot clerics of the 1820s and 1830s. He himself hoped to win the prize for the history essay by proving the truth of the Madoc story. He won the prize but the real victor was Thomas Stephens, from Merthyr Tidfil who had already published a history of Welsh literature, and who exploded Madoc as a baseless myth. The change was observable right through the proceedings at Llangollen; for example William Roos of Amlwch gained one of the painting prizes, one painting being of the death of Owain Glyndŵr,

---

[93] David Williams, *The Rebecca Riots* (Cardiff, 1955), pp. 53–6, 104, 128, 185, 191, 241, 290. For unrest from the 1790s to 1835 see D. J. V. Jones, *Before Rebecca* (London, 1973).

but another being of the recent death of Captain Wynn at the Alma. Within a few years the Welsh began to learn through their periodicals of the great advances of German philology, and of the work of Bopp and Zeuss setting Welsh scientifically in its true philological context, making it more and more difficult for the Welsh to believe in the irrational historical myth-making of the eighteenth century.[94] The chickens of Lhuyd and Leibniz long before had at last come home to roost. The sprites and phantoms of remote centuries of Welsh history and literature which had so entertained and inspired the previous generations were dispelled as they were brought out into the light of common day.

Just as this was happening, and the survivors of the older world such as the clerics 'Ab Ithel' and 'Glasynys', or Lady Llanover, were withdrawing into disgruntled isolation or silence, the new world of radical and nonconformist Wales began to turn itself into a myth, the fogs and mists descended upon recent history, and people were entertained by a host of fresh legends about themselves, about the persecution of the early Methodists (which they read in Robert Jones of Rhos-Lan's *Drych yr Amseroedd*, a book which R. T. Jenkins called 'The apocrypha of the Revival'), or about Dic Penderyn and the Merthyr Rising of 1831, or the fight against the oppressive landlords and captains of industry.

CONCLUSION: THE ELUSIVE QUARRY

What, in conclusion, had been achieved by this extraordinary movement? The Wales we have been describing was not a political state, and for want of such a state the people were driven to give a disproportionate amount of their energies to cultural matters, to the recovery of the past and, where the past was found wanting, to its invention. The old way of life decayed and disappeared, the past was very often tattered and threadbare, and so a great deal of invention was needed. The romantic mythologists had succeeded so well, in some ways, that they made things Welsh appear charmingly and appealingly quaint. While things antique had authority this was good, but when an age of progress arrived it was bad. Welshness, then, was preserved and handed on to the future by the crucial efforts

---

[94] Bromwich, *Matthew Arnold and Celtic Literature*; Francis Shaw, 'The Background to the *Grammatica Celtica*', *Celtica*, iii (1953), pp. 1–17 on the work of Bopp in 1839 and of Zeuss in 1853.

of the patriots we have been describing. But Welshness was rejected by a large number because it was associated with quaintness and with a rather discredited mythology. The Welshness of Victoria's reign could be very fierce and passionate, but this is because it had to contend with so many enemies. To survive, Welshness had, in the 1860s and 1870s, to transfer itself subtly to the new world of radicalism and nonconformity.

The historical revival and the invention of tradition had an effect in Wales more far-reaching than anything comparable in England, though it did resemble what was happening in small European countries. Wales in the eighteenth century did not have an unbroken or a fortunate historical tradition; it did not have a glorious or heroic recent past. Hence the rediscovery of the remote past, the Druids and the Celts and the others, had an astounding effect on the Welsh. Wales did not have a network of learned or academic institutions to check and balance myths and inventions with criticism. The reader and the writer could not hunt for the past systematically together. The manuscripts for instance were nearly all locked up in private libraries, and few texts were published; hence it was easy for a forger of genius like Iolo Morganwg to bamboozle the Welsh (and English) public. It was precisely this lack of scholarly institutions and criticism which made it possible for Macpherson to defend his Ossian poems in Scotland, Baron Hersart de la Villemarqué (Kervarker) to compose his bogus ancient Breton poetry in *Barzaz Breiz*, or Vaclav Hanka to publish his bogus medieval Czech manuscript the *Kralodvorsky Rukopis*. Hanka wrote this only two years after Ossian was translated into Czech, and it was only revealed as a forgery a half century or more later by Thomas Masaryk. The English, on the other hand, were not slow to detect the forgeries of Chatterton.

In Wales the movement of revival and myth-making grew out of a crisis in Welsh life, when the very lifeblood of the nation seemed to be ebbing away. Common sense and reason dictated that Welshmen should regard the past as closed and finished, and that since they were 'blotted out of the books of records' they should be happy with their lot. It required a superhuman effort by a small number of patriots to force their fellow-countrymen to appreciate their heritage, to value what was their own. They felt that the only way to bring this about was to ransack the past and transform it with imagination, to create a new Welshness which would instruct, entertain, amuse and educate the people. The mythical and romantic Wales which they created allowed the Welsh to lose their immediate past, and to gain a version of it in the arts and literature; they could, as it were, have their cake and eat it. The art and artifice which we have described here had a great healing function at this difficult juncture in Welsh history. Welsh life went on changing, and as it changed so the process we have described recurred. As soon as the romantics fell from their steeds, their place was taken by fresh myth-makers and creators of traditions, those of radical and nonconformist Wales. The huntsmen had changed, but the hunt went on.[95]

[95] For an extended treatment of the subject of this chapter, see Prys Morgan, *The Eighteenth-Century Renaissance* (Llandybie, 1981).

4. *The Context, Performance and Meaning of Ritual: The British Monarchy and the 'Invention of Tradition', c. 1820–1977*[1]

DAVID CANNADINE

In 1820, *The Black Book*, a radical critique of the corruption and power of the English Establishment, made this comment on royal ritual:

Pageantry and show, the parade of crowns and coronets, of gold keys, sticks, white wands and black rods; of ermine and lawn, maces and wigs, are ridiculous when men become enlightened, when they have learned that the real object of government is to confer the greatest happiness on the people at the least expense.[2]

Forty years later, Lord Robert Cecil, the future third marquess of Salisbury, having watched Queen Victoria open parliament, wrote with scarcely more approval:

Some nations have a gift for ceremonial. No poverty of means or absence of splendour inhibits them from making any pageant in which they take part both real and impressive. Everybody falls naturally into his proper place, throws himself without effort into the spirit of the little drama he is enacting, and instinctively represses all appearance of constraint or distracted attention.

But, he went on to explain:

This aptitude is generally confined to the people of a southern climate and of non-Teutonic parentage. In England the case is exactly the reverse. We can afford to be more splendid than most nations; but some malignant spell broods over all our most solemn

[1] An earlier draft of this paper was presented to the Social History Seminar at Cambridge University and to a joint student-faculty seminar at Princeton University. I am most grateful to the participants for their comments and criticisms, to Dr S. D. Banfield and Mr C. J. Babbs for help with two particular problems, and to Mr J. Whaley for sharing with me his incomparable knowledge of ritual and ceremony in early modern Europe. Some preliminary thoughts on this subject were outlined in my article, 'The Not-So-Ancient Traditions of Monarchy', *New Society* (2 June 1977), pp. 438–40. This final version was completed in 1979.
[2] Quoted in D. Sutherland, *The Landowners* (London, 1968), p. 158.

ceremonials, and inserts into them some feature which makes them all ridiculous...Something always breaks down, somebody contrives to escape doing his part, or some bye-motive is suffered to interfere and ruin it all.[3]

Taken together, these quotations exemplify contemporary attitudes towards the ceremonial of the British monarchy during the first three-quarters of the nineteenth century. The first argued that as the population was becoming better educated, royal ritual would soon be exposed as nothing more than primitive magic, a hollow sham. And the second suggested, on the basis of impeccable inside knowledge, that in any case the pageantry centred on the monarchy was conspicuous for its ineptitude rather than for its grandeur.

Today in England the situation is the exact reverse. With the possible exception of the papacy, no head of state is surrounded by more popular ritual than Queen Elizabeth II. The mass of the population may indeed have become better educated, as the authors of *The Black Book* had hoped; but they have not, as a result, lost their liking for the secular magic of monarchy. On the contrary, as Ian Gilmour has noted, 'Modern societies still need myth and ritual. A monarch and his family supply it.'[4] And, in additional contrast to this earlier period, the ceremonial is now splendidly performed, so much so that observers have assumed that this has always been the case. 'All the pageantry and grandeur of a thousand-year-old tradition'; 'a pageantry that has gone on for hundreds of years'; 'all the precision that comes from centuries of precedent'; 'the English are particularly good at ceremonial': these are the phrases of contemporary commentators and journalists as they describe the great royal ceremonials.[5] However accurate may have been the accounts of *The Black Book* and of Cecil in their time, they have ceased to be valid today. The purpose of this chapter is to describe and explain the subsequent changes in the context and nature of English royal ceremonial which have rendered their comments irrelevant and confounded their predictions.

[3] *The Saturday Review*, 9 Feb. 1861, pp. 140–1. The article was published anonymously.

[4] I. Gilmour, *The Body Politic* (London, 1969), p. 313.

[5] J. Dimbleby, *Richard Dimbleby* (London, 1977), p. 329; Sir J. Wheeler-Bennett, *King George VI: His Life and Reign* (London, 1965), p. 310; H. Vickers, 'Twenty Five Years a Queen', in H. Montgomery-Massingberd (ed.), *Burke's Guide to the British Monarchy* (London, 1977), p. 42; *Illustrated London News*, 6 Feb. 1965.

I

Despite the continued centrality of the monarchy in British political, social and cultural life, the changing nature of its public image during the last two hundred years has received remarkably little attention from historians. The 'theatre of power' of Tudor and Stuart courts – the manner by which royal and republican prestige was enhanced by elaborate ceremonial – has been extensively investigated, not only for Britain but for Europe as a whole.[6] For the late nineteenth and early twentieth centuries, a second efflorescence of 'invented' ritual and tradition in Wilhelmine Germany and the French Third Republic has been the subject of a number of studies, which throw out suggestive hints as far as contemporary British ceremonial is concerned.[7] And, in inter-war Europe, the elaborate rituals of the new Fascist and Communist régimes have recently begun to attract extensive scholarly attention.[8] By comparison, English royal ritual has been almost entirely ignored for the period since the late seventeenth century. Although biographies of kings and

---

[6] R. E. Giesey, *The Royal Funeral Ceremony in Renaissance France* (Geneva, 1960); R. Strong, *Splendour at Court: Renaissance Spectacle and Illusion* (London, 1973); S. Anglo, *Spectacle, Pageantry and Early Tudor Policy* (Oxford, 1969); D. M. Bergeron, *English Civic Pageantry, 1558–1642* (London, 1971); F. A. Yates, *The Valois Tapestries* (London, 1959); E. Muir, 'Images of Power: Art and Pageantry in Renaissance Venice', *Am. Hist. Rev.*, lxxxix (1979), pp. 16–52; G. Reedy, 'Mystical Politics: The Imagery of Charles II's Coronation', in P. J. Korshin (ed.), *Studies in Culture and Revolution: Aspects of English Intellectual History, 1640–1800* (London, 1972), pp. 21–42; C. Geertz, 'Centers, Kings and Charisma: Reflections on the Symbolics of Power', in J. Ben-David and T. N. Clark (eds.), *Culture and its Creators: Essays in Honor of E. Shils* (Chicago and London, 1977), esp. pp. 153–7.

[7] G. L. Mosse, 'Caesarism, Circuses and Monuments', *Journal of Contemporary History*, vi (1971), pp. 167–82; C. Rearick, 'Festivals and Politics: the Michelet Centennial of 1898', in W. Laqueur and G. L. Mosse (eds.), *Historians in Politics* (London, 1974), pp. 59–78; C. Rearick, 'Festivals in Modern France: The Experience of the Third Republic', *Journal of Contemporary History*, xii (1977), pp. 435–60; R. Samson, 'La Fête de Jeanne d'Arc en 1894: Controverse et Célébration', *Revue d'Histoire Moderne et Contemporaire*, xx (1973), pp. 444–63; M. Agulhon, 'Esquisse pour une Archéologie de la République: l'Allegorie Civique Féminine', *Annales: Economies, Sociétés, Civilisations*, xxviii (1973), pp. 5–34; E. J. Hobsbawm, 'Inventing Traditions in Nineteenth-Century Europe' (Past and Present Conference Paper, 1977), pp. 1–25. My debt to Prof. Hobsbawm's work will be apparent throughout this chapter.

[8] G. L. Mosse, 'Mass Politics and the Political Liturgy of Nationalism', in E. Kamenka (ed.), *Nationalism: The Nature and Evolution of an Ideal* (London, 1976), pp. 39–54; H. T. Barden, *The Nuremberg Party Rallies, 1929–39* (London, 1967).

queens contain appropriate accounts of weddings, coronations and funerals, there has been no systematic attempt to analyse such ceremonial in a long-term, comparative, contextual perspective.

Accordingly, the pioneer work on the ceremonial aspect of the British monarchy has been almost entirely undertaken by sociologists, with regard to both the provision and the interpretation of the evidence. Since the establishment of Mass Observation in 1937, there has been a continuous stream of surveys assessing popular responses to successive royal ceremonial occasions, from the coronation of George VI to the Silver Jubilee of Queen Elizabeth.[9] Some sociologists have attempted to analyse their 'meaning' within a Durkheimian, functionalist framework, stressing the integrative force of such ceremonial, and the way in which it embodies and reflects, upholds and reinforces, deeply rooted, widely held popular values.[10] In another tradition, the same ritual has been seen, not as expressing a publicly articulated expression of consensus, but as embodying the 'mobilization of bias' – an example of the ruling élite consolidating its ideological dominance by exploiting pageantry as propaganda.[11] Either way, for the sociologist, the 'meaning' of ceremonial in industrial society is inferred from an essentially decontextualized analysis of the ritual itself, evaluated within the relatively historical framework of Marxist or functionalist theory.

This chapter seeks to rediscover the 'meaning' of such royal ceremonial by employing a rather different methodology, namely that of setting it more comprehensively within its historical context. The central idea underlying this approach is that ceremonial occasions, like works of art or of political theory, cannot be interpreted merely 'in terms of their internal structure, *indépendant de tout sujet, de tout*

---

[9] H. Jennings and C. Madge, *May the Twelfth* (London, 1937); L. Harris, *Long to Reign Over Us?* (London, 1966); J. G. Blumler, J. R. Brown, A. J. Ewbank and T. J. Nossiter, 'Attitudes to the Monarchy: Their Structure and Development during a Ceremonial Occasion', *Political Studies*, xix (1971), pp. 149–71; R. Rose and D. Kavanagh, 'The Monarchy in Contemporary British Culture', *Comparative Politics*, viii (1976), pp. 548–76. For the most recent analysis, using such material, see P. Ziegler, *Crown and People* (London, 1978).

[10] E. Durkheim, *The Elementary Forms of the Religious Life* (trans. J. W. Swain, London, 1915), pp. 220, 225, 358, 375, 379; E. Shils and M. Young, 'The Meaning of the Coronation', *Sociological Review*, new ser., i (1953), pp. 63–81; Blumler *et al.*, 'Attitudes to the Monarchy', pp. 170–1.

[11] S. Lukes, 'Political Ritual and Social Integration', in S. Lukes, *Essays in Social Theory* (London, 1977), pp. 62–73; N. Birnbaum, 'Monarchies and Sociologists: A Reply to Professor Shils and Mr Young', *Sociological Review*, new ser., iii (1955), pp. 5–23; R. Bocock, *Ritual in Industrial Society* (London, 1974), pp. 102–4.

objet, et de toute contexte'. Like all cultural forms which may be treated as texts, or all texts which may be treated as cultural forms, 'thick' rather than 'thin' description is required.[12] For ceremonial occasions as much as for great works of political theory, 'to study the context...is not merely to gain additional information...; it is also to equip ourselves...with a way of gaining a greater insight into...its meaning than we can ever hope to achieve simply from reading the text itself".[13] So, in order to rediscover the 'meaning' of royal ritual during the modern period, it is necessary to relate it to the specific social, political, economic and cultural milieu within which it was actually performed. With ceremonial, as with political theory, the very act of locating the occasion or the text in its appropriate context is not merely to provide the historical background, but actually to begin the process of interpretation.[14]

For clearly, even if the text of a repeated ritual like a coronation remains unaltered over time, its 'meaning' may change profoundly depending on the nature of the context. In an essentially static age, unchanging ritual might be a genuine reflection of, and reinforcement to, stability and consensus. But in a period of change, conflict or crisis, it might be deliberately unaltered so as to give an impression of continuity, community and comfort, despite overwhelming contextual evidence to the contrary. Under certain circumstances, a coronation might be seen by participants and contemporaries as a symbolic reaffirmation of national greatness. But in a different context, the same ceremony might assume the characteristics of collective longing for past glories. In the same way, a royal funeral might be a service of thanksgiving and celebration for a monarch who had made his nation great. Or, with the same format and text, it could be interpreted as a requiem, not only for the monarch himself, but for the country as a great power. Just as the 'meaning' of the Statue of Liberty has altered profoundly during the last century as a result of changes in 'the historical tissue of circumstance', so the same argument may be made with regard to the texts of ritual events.[15]

[12] C. Geertz, *The Interpretation of Cultures* (London, 1975), pp. 7, 14, 449.
[13] Q. Skinner, *The Foundations of Modern Political Thought*, 2 vols. (Cambridge, 1978), i, pp. xii–xiv.
[14] Cf. D. M. Schneider, 'Notes Towards a Theory of Culture', in K. H. Basso and H. A. Selby (eds.), *Meaning in Anthropology*, (Albuquerque, New Mexico, 1976), pp. 214–15: 'all meaning is to some degree context-defined or context-determined'.
[15] M. Trachtenberg, *The Statue of Liberty* (Harmondsworth, 1977), pp. 15–19, 186–96. For a similar analysis of the changed 'meaning' of the famous railway bridge over the Zambezi at Victoria Falls, see: J. Morris, *Farewell the Trumpets: An Imperial Retreat* (London, 1978), pp. 347–8.

However, a work of art such as a statue is, by definition, static: insofar as its 'meaning' alters over time, that can only be as a result of changes in the context. But in the case of ritual and ceremonial, the performance itself is also elastic and dynamic. While the basic text of a repeated ritual may remain essentially unaltered – such as the crowning, anointing and recognition of an English coronation – the precise manner in which the ceremonial is produced may differ, which in itself only serves to give a further dimension to changes in 'meaning'. The ceremonial might be performed well or badly. It might be carefully rehearsed or blundered through with little prior preparation. The participants might be bored, indifferent, interested, or even passionately assured of the historical importance of the pageant in which they were participating. And so, depending both on the nature of the performance and the context within which it is set, the 'meaning' of what is ostensibly the same ceremony might fundamentally alter. No analysis restricted to the text, which ignores both the nature of the performance and the 'thick' description of context, can hope to offer a historically convincing explanation of the 'meaning' of royal ritual and ceremonial in modern Britain.[16]

Viewed in this light, there are at least ten aspects of ritual, performance and context which need to be investigated. The first is the political power of the monarch: was it great or small, growing or declining? The second is the personal character and standing of the monarch: was he loved or loathed, respected or reviled? The third is the nature of the economic and social structure of the country over which he ruled: was it localized, provincial and pre-industrial, or urban, industrial and class-dominated? The fourth is the type, extent and attitude of the media: how vividly did it describe royal events, and what picture of the monarchy did it convey? The fifth is the prevailing state of technology and fashion: was it possible for the monarchy to benefit from using anachronistic modes of transport or dress to enhance its mystery and magic? The sixth is the self-image

[16] This seems to me, as a historian, to be the chief problem in the textualist approach in anthropology, exemplified in E. Leach, *Culture and Communication: The Logic by which Symbols are Connected: an Introduction to the Use of Structuralist Analysis in Social Anthropology* (London, 1976), pp. 84–93, where he analyses the biblical story of the consecration of Aaron as High Priest. For an even better example of this genre, see the same author's unpublished lecture, 'Once a Knight is Quite Enough', where he compares the investiture of knighthood with pig sacrifice in Borneo in the 1940s, a comparison which, from a historian's standpoint, says almost nothing of interest about the 'meaning' of the ceremony of investiture in the context of the present.

of the nation over which the monarch ruled: was it confident of its position in the international hierarchy, or worried and threatened by foreign challengers? Was it opposed to formal empire, or self-consciously imperialist? The seventh is the condition of the capital city in which most royal ceremonials took place: was it squalid and unimpressive, or endowed with splendid buildings and triumphal thoroughfares as a fitting backdrop for ritual and pageantry? The eighth is the attitude of those responsible for liturgy, music and organization: were they indifferent to the ceremonial and inept in organization, or eager and able to make the display a success? The ninth is the nature of the ceremonial as actually performed: was it shabby and slovenly, or splendid and spectacular? Finally, there is the question of commercial exploitation: how far did manufacturers of pottery, medals and other artefacts feel that there was money to be made from the sale of commemorative pieces?

If the ritual and ceremonial of the British monarchy is context-ualized and evaluated in this way, it becomes possible to rediscover its 'meaning' in a more historically convincing manner than sociol-ogists have so far been able to do. For them, England from the 1800s is assumed to be a 'modern', 'industrial', 'contemporary' society, the structure of which is taken as given.[17] But, as is so often the case, for the historian it is the *changes* and discontinuities which are of major interest rather than the unifying aspects. To suppose, for instance, as many sociologists do, that Walter Bagehot's description of the mid-Victorian monarchy was valid for its time in the same way that it is assumed to have been valid since, is to show a profound ignorance, not only of the very peculiar context within which he wrote *The English Constitution* and his articles in *The Economist*, but also of the exact way in which both the context and performance of royal ritual have changed and developed since that time.[18]

Set in this 'thick' descriptive context, four distinct phases in the development of the ceremonial image of the British monarchy

[17] E. g. Lukes, 'Political Ritual and Social Integration', pp. 62, 64.
[18] Shils and Young, 'The Meaning of the Coronation', p. 64; Bocock, *Ritual in Industrial Society*, p. 103; Rose and Kavanagh, 'The Monarchy in Contemporary British Culture', pp. 553, 557. In fact, the most important point about Bagehot's complex and occasionally contradictory picture of the power and pomp of the monarchy was that it was not so much *de*scription as *pre*scriptive. For the fullest analysis along these lines, see: N. St John-Stevas (ed.), *The Collected Works of Walter Bagehot*, 12 vols. so far (London, 1965–78), v, pp. 81–3. But see also: R. H. S. Crossman, introduction to W. Bagehot, *The English Constitution* (London, 1963), p. 36.

emerge. The first period, extending from the 1820s, and before, to the 1870s, is a period of ineptly managed ritual, performed in what was still preponderantly a localized, provincial, pre-industrial society. The second, beginning in 1877, when Victoria was made empress of India, and extending until the outbreak of the First World War was, in Britain as in much of Europe, the heyday of 'invented tradition', a time when old ceremonials were staged with an expertise and appeal which had been lacking before, and when new rituals were self-consciously invented to accentuate this development. Then, from 1918 until Queen Elizabeth's coronation in 1953 came the period in which the British persuaded themselves that they were good at ceremonial because they always had been – a belief in large part made possible because Britain's former rivals in royal ritual – Germany, Austria and Russia – had dispensed with their monarchies, leaving Britain alone in the field. Finally, since 1953, the decline of Britain as a great power, combined with the massive impact of television, suggests that the 'meaning' of royal ceremonial has once again changed profoundly, although as yet the outlines of this new period of change can only be dimly discerned. Each of these successive phases will now be examined in turn.

II

The period lasting to the 1870s saw the British monarchy at its most significant in terms of the real, effective political power which it wielded. And, with the experience of the seventeenth century still strong in the English corporate memory, it followed that there remained hostility to the further aggrandizement of royal influence by re-opening of the theatre of power which had been happily closed down by the end of the seventeenth century. In 1807, for example, George III dissolved a parliament less than one year old so as to increase the strength of a ministry hostile to Catholic Emancipation. Four years later, when the Prince of Wales assumed the regency, it was generally supposed that, if he had so wished, he could have removed the Tory administration and put in the Whigs in their place.[19] Thereafter, he remained an exasperating and important figure in the political firmament, a constant irritant to Canning, Liverpool and Wellington alike. And his successor, William IV, was even more energetic, as Professor Gash explains:

[19] C. Hibbert, *George IV* (Harmondsworth, 1976), pp. 379–83, 675–86, 694.

In his short reign of seven years, he thrice dismissed a ministry; twice dissolved Parliament for political purposes before its time; three times made formal proposals to his ministers for a coalition with their political opponents; and on one celebrated occasion allowed his name to be used, independently of his political advisers, to influence a crucial vote in the House of Lords.[20]

Nor was Victoria, in her early years as queen, exactly quiescent. In 1839, by refusing to accept Ladies of the Bedchamber who were agreeable to Peel, she succeeded in artificially prolonging the life of Melbourne's government. In 1851, she all but sacked Palmerston from the Foreign Office and, after Albert's death, remained 'a shrewd, persistent and opinionated adviser and critic of her governments'. Even as late as 1879 the Commons once more debated Dunning's famous motion 'that the influence of the Crown has increased, is increasing, and ought to be diminished'.[21]

If continuing royal power made grand royal ceremonial unacceptable, then renewed royal unpopularity made it impossible. For the public character and reputation of successive generations of the royal family during the first three-quarters of the nineteenth century meant that they were almost without exception viewed with indifference or hostility. The lives, loves and morals of George III's children were such as to make them arguably the most unloved royal generation in English history. In particular, George IV's extravagance and womanizing brought the monarchy to a low ebb, the nadir of which was reached in 1821 when his marriage to Queen Caroline became both public politics and public scandal. 'There never was an individual less regretted by his fellow creatures than this deceased king', noted *The Times* in its damning editorial on his death. 'What eye has wept for him? What heart has heaved one throb of unmercenary sorrow?'[22] In the same way, William IV's short honeymoon of popularity vanished as a result of his hostility to the Whig reforming government, so that *The Spectator* could castigate him for his 'feebleness of purpose and littleness of mind, his ignorance and his prejudices'.[23] Nor, initially, did Victoria fare any

---

[20] N. Gash, *Reaction and Reconstruction in English Politics, 1832–1852* (Oxford, 1965), p. 5.

[21] D. Beales, *From Castlereagh to Gladstone, 1815–1885* (London, 1971), pp. iii, 163, 166; J. Ridley, *Palmerston* (London, 1972), pp. 529–40; K. Martin, *The Crown and the Establishment* (London, 1962), p. 52.

[22] Hibbert, *George IV*, pp. 782–3.

[23] Martin, *op. cit.*, p. 27.

better. Her partiality for her first prime minister earned her the sobriquets 'Mrs Melbourne' and 'Queen of the Whigs', and Albert's Germanic intensity was generally frowned upon – 'a Prince who has breathed from childhood the air of courts tainted by the imaginative servility of Goethe'.[24] And the new Prince of Wales, ensnared successively in the Mordaunt Scandal and the Aylesford Case, damningly described by Bagehot as an 'unemployed youth', was hardly able to add any lustre to this dowdy and unpopular crown.

In short, the monarchy was neither impartial and above politics nor Olympian and above society, as it was later to become, but was actively part of both. And, because both politics and society were quintessentially London-based, metropolitan activities, the ceremonial appeal of the monarchy was only further circumscribed. For between the age of Wilkes and the age of Chamberlain, the national influence of London was relatively restricted as provincial England reasserted itself. Local loyalties and rivalries remained strong; the county community was still a cohesive and realistic unit.[25] Moreover, the uneven development of the economy and slow adoption of steam power meant that while Britain may have been the 'workshop of the world', the workshops were both small in size and relatively few in number. Engels's Manchester, with its massive mills and segregated suburbs, was the exception rather than the rule. In 1851, agriculture remained the largest employer of labour. 'The England of the rectory and the modest mansion house and the farm house' was preponderant. 'Country towns, both large and small...were the norm, so far as urbanization in the mid nineteenth century was concerned.'[26] In such a localized, provincial, face-to-face world, the scope for presenting a ceremoniously enhanced monarch, Olympian, aloof and detached, as the father figure of the nation and focus of all loyalties, was distinctly limited.

[24] R. Fulford, *The Prince Consort* (London, 1966), pp. 156–9.
[25] A. Briggs, *Victorian Cities* (Harmondsworth, 1968), pp. 312, 357–9; H. Pelling, *A History of British Trade Unionism* (Harmondsworth, 1963), pp. 14–15.
[26] W. L. Burn, *The Age of Equipoise: A Study of the Mid-Victoria Generation* (London, 1968), p. 7; Briggs, *op. cit.*, p. 32; W. A. Armstrong, *Stability and Change in an English County Town: A Social Study of York, 1801–1851* (Cambridge, 1974), pp. 10–11; P. Mathias, *The First Industrial Nation: An Economic History of Britain, 1700–1914* (London, 1969), pp. 259–73; C. Chamberlain, 'The Growth of Support for the Labour Party in Britain', *British Journal of Sociology*, xxiv (1973), pp. 482–4; A. E. Musson, *British Trade Unions, 1800–1875* (London, 1972), pp. 16–21; A. Reid, 'Politics and Economics in the Formation of the British Working Class: A Response to H. F. Moorhouse', *Social History*, iii (1978), p. 359.

The condition and attitude of the press was a further barrier to such a development. For while the great royal ceremonies were fully reported in provincial as well as metropolitan newspapers, the press as a whole remained hostile to the monarchy. In the early decades of the nineteenth century, the attacks in the London press of Gillray, Rowlandson and the Cruickshanks made the monarchy 'without doubt the most regular topic and target for the cartoonists'.[27] From the 1850s to the 1870s, Victoria was constantly the object of criticism in newspaper editorials. Sensational scandals and murders had a more significant effect in boosting circulation than did the lavishly reproduced commemorative editions of *The Times* and *The Observer* on the occasions of William IV's and Victoria's coronations.[28] And the provincial press, Liberal, intellectual, rational, middle-class, opposed to display as much as to emotion, was in general no more favourable to the monarchy than its metropolitan counterparts.[29] In addition, the lack of pictures made even the greatest of royal ceremonial something of a mystery to all except the most literate and wealthy. For there was no cheap, pictorial press, and the *Illustrated London News*, begun in 1842, sold at a shilling a copy, and was restricted to the 'rectory' public.[30] Under these circumstances, great royal ceremonies were not so much shared, corporate events as remote, inaccessible group rites, performed for the benefit of the few rather than the edification of the many.[31]

The prevailing state of transport technology served further to contain the monarchy within society rather than elevate it above. For there was nothing particularly anachronistic, romantic or splendid about the way in which English royalty travelled. Victorian England was, as Professor Thompson reminds us, a horse-drawn society, in which there were 120,000 privately owned large carriages and 250,000

---

[27] M. Wynn Jones, *A Cartoon History of the Monarchy* (London, 1978), pp. 40–5, 68–77; M. Walker, *Daily Sketches: A Cartoon History of British Twentieth-Century Politics* (London, 1978), p. 23.

[28] R. D. Altick, *The English Common Reader* (Chicago, 1957), pp. 343–4.

[29] A. J. Lee, *The Origins of the Popular Press, 1855–1914* (London, 1976), pp. 38, 45, 74, 120–1.

[30] C. Fox, 'The Development of Social Reportage in English Periodical Illustration during the 1840s and Early 1850s', *Past and Present*, no. 74 (1977), pp. 92–3, 100–2, 111; J. D. Symon, *The Press and its Story* (London, 1914), p. 213.

[31] It is also noteworthy that few volumes were produced commemorating great royal occasions during this period, and those which were, such as Sir George Naylor, *The Coronation of His Most Sacred Majesty King George IV*, 2 vols. (London, 1839), were so lavish that their sale was restricted to a very small audience.

light two wheelers by 1870.[32] Indeed, the carriages which members of the royal family drove today were in widespread use tomorrow. The Phaeton, for example, was introduced by George IV, the Wagonette by the Prince Consort, and the Victoria by the Prince of Wales.[33] Stimulated by such royal patronage, there was a massive proliferation in the range of carriages available by the mid-Victorian period. As W. B. Adams noted as early as 1837, 'the varieties of shape and make have become so numerous that it is difficult even for the practised observer to be familiar with them all'.[34] As a result, the monarchy's carriages were no more grand than those of lesser mortals. At William IV's coronation, for instance, the most outstanding coach was that of Prince Esterhazy. And at Victoria's coronation seven years later, the carriage of Marshal Soult, the French ambassador, rather than that of the queen herself, was regarded as the most splendid.[35]

This lack of concern about successful foreign rivalry in trivial matters was the obverse side of supreme confidence in international competition in important affairs. The defeat of Napoleon left Britain without a rival in continental Europe, and in North America the United States, racked by civil war, seemed determined to pass from infancy to disintegration without going through great-power status on the way. Palmerston's 'Don Pacifico' speech embodied this self-confidence perfectly, combining as it did a panegyric on Britain's unique social and constitutional stability with a strident and popular assertion of her unchallenged role as policeman of the world.[36] The early and mid-Victorians saw themselves as the leaders of progress and pioneers of civilization, and prided themselves on the limited nature of their government, their lack of interest in formal empire, their hatred of show, extravagance, ceremonial and ostentation.[37] The certainty of power and the assured confidence of success meant that there was no need to show off. Little Belgium might spend more

[32] F. M. L. Thompson, *Victorian England: The Horse-Drawn Society* (London, 1970), p. 16.

[33] Sir W. Gilbey, *Modern Carriages* (London, 1905), pp. 46–53, 63–4; G. A. Thrupp, *The History of Coaches* (London, 1877), pp. 87–90.

[34] W. B. Adams, *English Pleasure Carriages* (London, 1837), p. 220.

[35] Thrupp, *op. cit.*, pp. 89–90; P. Ziegler, *King William IV* (London, 1971), p. 193.

[36] Burn, *Age of Equipoise*, p. 103; Ridley, *Palmerston*, pp. 523–4; A. Briggs, *Victorian People* (Harmondsworth, 1965), pp. 10–11, 24, 51.

[37] R. Robinson and J. Gallagher, *Africa and the Victorians: The Official Mind of Imperialism* (London, 1961), pp. 1–4.

than Great Britain on its metropolitan law courts, but the reality of power and religion of parsimony meant that the English regarded such petty one-upmanship with disdain or indifference.[38]

This attitude goes far in explaining why London was ill-suited to be the setting for grand royal ceremonial, and why the English positively made a virtue of it. Even the most ardent champion of the 'infernal wen' conceded that it could not rival the careful planning of L'Enfant's Washington, the venerable ruins of Rome, the magnificence of Haussmann's Paris, the grand schemes for the reconstruction of Vienna instituted by Francis Joseph in 1854, or the splendid constellation of five squares constructed in St Petersburg during the first half of the nineteenth century.[39] In these great capitals, the grand buildings and splendid thoroughfares were monuments to the power of the state or the influence of the monarch. In London, by contrast, the squares and suburbs, railway stations and hotels, were monuments to the power and wealth of the *private* individual. Mid-Victorian London, as Donald Olsen has argued, was a statement against absolutism, a proud expression of the energies and values of a free people.[40] Grandeur in the style of Paris or St Petersburg spelt despotism: for how else could enough power be wielded or funds mobilized to make it possible to complete such mammoth schemes? London, by contrast, might be slovenly, but at least its people were not enslaved. As one contemporary explained: 'The public buildings are few, and for the most part mean... But what of all this? How

[38] Sir J. Summerson, *Victorian Architecture in England: Four Studies in Evaluation* (New York, 1971), p. 115: 'English governments in the mid-nineteenth century were parsimonious to an almost unbelievable degree; their parsimony being part of a national philosophy which expressed itself from time to time in a horrified contempt for architects and for architecture.' Poelaert's Brussels Law Courts cost £1,760,000; Street's first design for those in London was only £1,500,000.

[39] E. J. Hobsbawm, *The Age of Capital, 1848–1875* (1977), pp. 326, 328, 329, 334, 337; E. N. Bacon, *Design of Cities*, rev. edn (London, 1978), pp. 196–9, 220–3; J. W. Reps, *Monumental Washington: The Planning and Development of the Capital Center* (Princeton, N.J., 1967), pp. 5, 20, 21; A. Sutcliffe, *The Autumn of Central Paris: The Defeat of Town Planning, 1850–1970* (London, 1970), ch. 2; D. H. Pinkney, *Napoleon III and the Rebuilding of Paris* (Princeton, 1958), *passim*; P. Abercrombie, 'Vienna', *Town Planning Review*, i (1910–11), pp. 221, 226–7; G. R. Marek, *The Eagles Die* (London, 1975), pp. 171–2; I. A. Egorov, *The Architectural Planning of St Petersburg* (Athens, Ohio, 1969), pp. 104–5, 182, 192; J. H. Bater, *St Petersburg: Industrialisation and Change* (London, 1976), pp. 17–40.

[40] D. Olsen, *The Growth of Victorian London* (London, 1976), pp. 51–3, 61, 329. For some general comments on the value-structures of spatial systems, see: D. Harvey, *Social Justice and the City* (London, 1973), pp. 31–2.

impressively do you feel that you are in the metropolis of a free people?[41]

Such love of freedom and economy and hatred of ostentation was the kiss of death for grand royal ceremonial, and the ineptitude with which the musical arrangements were made only further darkened the picture. The first seventy years of the nineteenth century were among the bleakest in England's musical history: no major work by any English composer has survived; still less the relatively trivial ephemera of ceremonial music.[42] The national anthem was far from being the venerated patriotic hymn it was later to become: it was not even sung at Victoria's coronation; new choral arrangements were relatively infrequent; and during the reign of George IV,[43] alternative versions criticizing the king and praising his queen proliferated. Successive Masters of the King's Musick were men of no distinction, whose duties were limited to conducting the royal orchestra.[44] And Sir George Smart, organist of the Chapel Royal, to whom the musical arrangements for all great royal ceremonies from the funeral of George IV to the coronation of Victoria were entrusted, was singularly inept. At Victoria's coronation, for instance, it was claimed that he would play the organ and give the beat to the orchestra simultaneously, a prediction which *The Musical World* regarded with scorn on the grounds that he was unable to do either singly.[45] And this lack of inspiration and leadership at the top was reflected in the sad state of English cathedral choirs, especially those of the Abbey and St Paul's. Rehearsals were unknown; surplices were not worn; choirs did not process; absenteeism, indiscipline and irreverent behaviour were endemic; services were long and badly planned. At Westminster Abbey, most of the minor canons and lay clerks were old and incompetent, and those few of real ability were usually members of other London church choirs, so that their attendance could not be relied upon.[46]

---

[41] Quoted in Olsen, *op. cit.*, pp. 55–6.

[42] M. Kennedy, *The Works of Ralph Vaughan Williams* (London, 1964), p. 1.

[43] P. A. Scholes, '*God Save the Queen*': *The History and Romance of the World's First National Anthem* (London, 1954), pp. 147–8, 165, 203–4, 209. See also app., table 3.

[44] They were: Sir William Parsons (1786–1817), William Shield (1817–29), Christian Kramer (1829–34), François Cramer (1834–8), George Anderson (1848–70), Sir William Cusins (1870–93). See: E. Blom (ed.), *Grove's Dictionary of Music and Musicians*, 5th edn, 10 vols. (London 1954), v, p. 627.

[45] Anon., 'Music at the Last Coronation', *Musical Times*, xliii (1902), pp. 18–20.

[46] B. Rainbow, *The Choral Revival in the Anglican Church (1839–1872)* (London,

Part of the problem derived from a lack of interest in ritual on the part of the clergy, who were either indifferent or hostile. As one authority noted as early as 1763, 'the higher ranks of the church do not think themselves concerned' in the performance of services.[47] The combination of poverty of means and absence of taste made the first three-quarters of the nineteenth century a low point in ecclesiastical ritual and ecclesiological concern.[48] At Westminster Abbey, Wren's incomparable Altar Piece was removed at the time of George IV's coronation, and was replaced by an undignified, mock-Gothic structure. Thereafter, the choir was remodelled, and the stalls were placed so close together, with accommodation for some of the congregation between, that choral singing of any merit was impossible – even if the choir had been competent. James Turle, organist from 1831 to 1882, was unable to bring any discipline to the choir, and the organ he played was old and inaudible. In 1847–8, Dean Buckland again reorganized the choir, and placed most of the congregation in the transepts where they could neither hear nor see the clergy. And when, finally, the congregation was restored to the nave, they were obliged to sing the hymns 'from large posters placed on the columns'. With good cause, Jebb castigated the 'coldness, meagreness and irreverence in the performance of the divine offices'. Even as late as the time of Dean Stanley (1870–91), the administration of the Abbey was marked by 'ignorance of finance and incapacity for business'.[49] If the efficient stage managing of routine services was more than the clergy could cope with, then effective planning and execution of the great royal ceremonial which took place in the Abbey was quite beyond them.

III

It is in this context that the actual performance and popularity of royal ritual and ceremonial during the first three-quarters of the

1970), ch. 13; Sir F. Bridge, *A Westminster Pilgrim* (London, 1919), pp. 72–5, 196–201. For contemporary comment, see: J. Pearce, *Apology for Cathedral Service* (London, 1839); J. Jebb, *The Choral Service of the Church* (London, 1843); S. S. Wesley, *A Few Words on Cathedral Music* (London, 1849).

[47] Quoted in Pearce, *op. cit.*, pp. 18–19.

[48] W. O. Chadwick, *The Victorian Church*, 2nd edn (London, 1972), pt 2, pp. 366–74.

[49] J. Perkins, *Westminster Abbey: Its Worship and Ornaments*, 3 vols. (London, 1938–52), i, pp. 89–94, 106–9, 144, 153–63; ii, p. 16; iii, pp. 141, 149, 152, 155, 160, 163–4; R. E. Prothero, *The Life and Correspondence of Arthur Penrhyn Stanley, D.D., late Dean of Westminster*, 2 vols. (London, 1893), ii, pp. 282–3.

nineteenth century needs to be understood. Clearly, in this first period, ceremonial did not exist to exalt the crown above the political battle, to that Olympus of decorative, integrative impotence which it was later to occupy, or to that earlier peak of picturesque power which it had once scaled. The abiding political influence which the monarch wielded made it dangerous; the real power of the nation made it unnecessary; and the localized nature of society, reinforced by the provincial press, combined with the lack of a sufficiently splendid metropolitan setting, made it impossible. For the majority of inhabitants, local loyalties still took precedence over national allegiance. And, at rare moments when ceremonial did rivet national attention, it was not connected with the monarchy, but with heroes like Nelson or Wellington, whose funerals, significantly, far surpassed those of George III, George IV, William IV and Albert in splendour and popularity.[50]

Monarchs who were politically energetic but personally unpopular, trundling through the miserable streets of London by the conventional mode of transport, were more the head of society than the head of the nation. So, the royal ritual which accompanied them was not so much a jamboree to delight the masses, but a group rite in which the aristocracy, the church and royal family corporately re-affirmed their solidarity (or animosity) behind closed doors. To put it in the language of the anthropologist, these London-based displays in this early period did not articulate a coherent ceremonial language, as had been the case in Tudor and Stuart times, and as was to happen again towards the end of the nineteenth century. There was little self-conscious attempt by the promoters, participants or spectators to see them as parts of a cumulative, inter-related ceremonial series. There was, as it were, no vocabulary of pageantry, no syntax of spectacle, no ritualistic idiom. The whole was not greater than the sum of its parts.

Under these circumstances, the ineptitude of British ritual during this first period becomes more readily explicable. Indeed, the future third marquess of Salisbury was not alone in finding British ceremonial unimpressive. 'The English', noted the *Illustrated London News* in 1852 on the occasion of Wellington's state funeral,

---

[50] R. Davey, *A History of Mourning* (London, n.d.), pp. 75–7, 81–3; J. S. Curl, *The Victorian Celebration of Death* (Newton Abbot, 1972), pp. 4–5; C. Oman, *Nelson* (London, 1947), pp. 563–6; E. Longford, *Wellington*, 2 vols. (St Albans, 1971–5), ii, pp. 489–95.

are said to be a people who do not understand shows and celebrations, or the proper mode of conducting them. It is alleged that they flock to and applaud the rudest attempts of the kind; and that, unlike the French, and other nations of the continent, they have no real taste for ceremonial. There is, doubtless, something in the charge.[51]

Six years later, on the occasion of a royal wedding, the same journal added that 'in this country we have few if any public pageants; and the materials of their composition are as invariably the same as they are sparse and ineffective'.[52] Indeed, even as late as 1883, William Jones could still observe that 'it must be admitted that the present age is not favourable to the perpetuation of elaborate ceremonies'.[53]

And he was quite correct. For the majority of the great royal pageants staged during the first three-quarters of the nineteenth century oscillated between farce and fiasco. In 1817, at the funeral of Princess Charlotte, the daughter of the Prince Regent, the undertakers were drunk. When the duke of York died, ten years later, the chapel at Windsor was so damp that most of the mourners caught cold, Canning contracted rheumatic fever and the bishop of London died.[54] George IV's coronation, although conceived in the grandest manner possible, in a desperate and unsuccessful attempt to win some popularity, was so overblown that grandeur merged into farce. It was necessary to employ prize-fighters in Westminster Hall to keep the peace between the distinguished but belligerent guests. George himself, although sumptuously clad, 'looked too large for effect, indeed he was more like an elephant than a man'. And the pathetic, unsuccessful attempt made by Queen Caroline to gain access to the Abbey marred the whole proceedings. At George III's coronation, the deputy earl marshal, in reply to the monarch's well-merited criticisms of the arrangements, had observed: 'it is true, sir, that there has been some neglect, but I have taken care that the next coronation shall be regulated in the exactest manner possible'. But circumstances had confounded his prediction.[55]

---

[51] *Illustrated London News*, 25 Sept. 1852.

[52] *Ibid.*, 30 Jan. 1858.

[53] W. Jones, *Crowns and Coronation* (London, 1883), p. viii.

[54] C. Hibbert, *The Court at Windsor: A Domestic History* (London, 1964), pp. 171–2.

[55] J. Perkins, *The Coronation Book* (London, 1902), pp. 97, 115, 175, 258; Hibbert, *George IV*, pp. 597–604. It is important to stress that there is much about George IV's public style that anticipates subsequent developments: grandeur in London (Regent Street), royal visits (to Scotland and Ireland), and an expensive

George IV's flirtation with grandeur was so unsuccessful that it was not repeated for the next half century. At George's own funeral at Windsor, William IV talked constantly and walked out early. 'We never saw so motley, so rude, so ill-managed a body of persons', noted *The Times* in its description of the mourners.[56] William, for his part, loathed ceremonial and ostentation, and tried to dispense with his coronation altogether. Eventually, he allowed it to proceed, but it was so truncated that it became mockingly known as the 'Half-Crownation'. His funeral was equally squalid – 'a wretched mockery', Greville described it. The ceremony was long and tedious, and mourners loitered, laughed, gossipped and sniggered within sight of the coffin.[57] Nor was Victoria's coronation any more impressive. It was completely unrehearsed; the clergy lost their place in the order of service; the choir was pitifully inadequate; the archbishop of Canterbury put the ring on a finger that was too big for it; and two of the trainbearers talked throughout the entire ceremony.[58] Albert's funeral was almost a private affair at Windsor, as was the wedding of the Prince of Wales. In London, where Alexandra was greeted, commentators noted 'the poor taste of the decorations, the absence of outriders, and the extraordinary shabbiness of the royal equipages'. *Punch*, in turn, protested that the wedding should take place at Windsor – 'an obscure Berkshire village, noted only for an old castle with no sanitary arrangements'. And, once again, the planning and organization were woefully inadequate. Palmerston had to travel back from Windsor third class on the special train, and Disraeli was obliged to sit on his wife's lap.[59]

But the nadir of royal grandeur and ceremonial presence was reached in those two decades following Albert's death, when the queen's reclusive widowhood and the public scandals involving the Prince of Wales 'provided the matter for innumerable denunciations'.[60] Between 1861 and 1886, the queen, now known in the popular press as 'Mrs Brown', only opened parliament six times. Even *The Times* felt 'regret' at her continued absence at Windsor,

coronation (see app., table 1). My point is that, despite all this, without the appropriate concatenation of contextual circumstance (as was to occur later), it simply did not work.
[56] Hibbert, *George IV*, pp. 777–9.
[57] Ziegler, *William IV*, 152–3, 291.
[58] E. Longford, *Victoria, R.I.* (London, 1966), pp. 99–104.
[59] *Ibid.*, p. 395; G. Battiscombe, *Queen Alexandra* (London, 1972), pp. 45–6.
[60] Ziegler, *Crown and People*, p. 21.

Balmoral and Osborne.[61] In 1864 a notice was pinned to the rails of Buckingham Palace in the manner of an advertisement: 'These commanding premises to be let or sold, in consequence of the late occupant's declining business.'[62] Between 1871 and 1874, eighty-four republican clubs were founded, and radicals such as Dilke and Chamberlain were loud in their demands for investigations into the Civil List. Walter Bagehot, although in favour of a grand and splendid monarchy, constantly stressed that such was not, in fact, the case. 'To be invisible', he noted, 'is to be forgotten...To be a symbol, and an effective symbol, you must be vividly and often seen.' Or, as he put it even more stridently, 'From causes which it is not difficult to define, the Queen has done almost as much to injure the popularity of the monarchy by her long retirement from public life as the most unworthy of her predecessors did by his profligacy and frivolity.'[63]

But Victoria was adamant. In 1863, for example, she refused to open parliament, stressing her 'total inability, without serious injury to her health, to perform these functions of her high position which are accompanied by state ceremonials, and which necessitate the appearance in full dress in public'.[64] For, as she later explained, even in her husband's presence, she 'was always terribly nervous on all public occasions', and the absence of Albert's support now made such appearances unbearable.[65] But for Gladstone, during his first prime ministership, such a state of affairs could not be allowed to continue. 'To speak in rude and general terms', he noted, 'the Queen is invisible and the Prince of Wales is not respected.' Time and again, between 1870 and 1872, with all the energy but tactlessness at his command, Gladstone reminded the queen of the 'vast importance' of the 'social and visible functions of the monarchy', for both 'the social well-being of the country' and the 'stability of the throne'.[66] But, however energetically he sought solutions to this 'great crisis of Royalty', either

[61]   *The Times*, 9 Nov. 1871.
[62]   Longford, *Victoria, R.I.*, p. 401.
[63]   W. Bagehot, 'The Monarchy and the People', *The Economist*, 22 July 1871; *idem*, 'The Income of the Prince of Wales', *The Economist*, 10 October 1874. Both articles are reprinted in St John-Stevas, *The Collected Works of Walter Bagehot*, v, pp. 419, 431.
[64]   G. E. Buckle (ed.), *The Letters of Queen Victoria*, 2nd ser., *1862–1885*, 3 vols. (London, 1926–8), i, p. 133.
[65]   *Ibid.*, i, p. 244.
[66]   P. Guedalla, *The Queen and Mr Gladstone, 1845–1879*, 2 vols. (London, 1933–4), ii, p. 357.

by urging the queen to appear more frequently in public or by establishing the Prince of Wales as viceroy of Ireland, Victoria would not be moved. As Disraeli explained in the Commons, she was 'physically and morally incapacitated' from performing her duties.[67]

This picture of ineptly managed ritual, with only limited appeal, is corroborated by the restricted scale of commercial exploitation which these ceremonials stimulated during this first period. Commemorative pottery, for example, had been a recognized genre since the 1780s. But the monarchy was much less often depicted than other contemporary figures. Frederick the Great was far more popular than George II, and Nelson and Wellington were more frequently commemorated than George III. And, during the reign of George IV, more pottery was produced in support of Queen Caroline than in favour of the king himself. The coronations of William IV and Victoria received little attention, and between 1861 and 1886, despite numerous royal marriages, there was virtually no royal commemorative pottery produced at all. The private production of medals for sale tells a similar story. Once again, more medals were issued in support of Queen Caroline than in commemoration of the coronation of her husband, and the coronations of William and Victoria were scarcely noticed.[68] During this early period, the royal family was so unpopular, and the appeal of its ceremonial was so limited, that it was not deemed worthy of large-scale commercial exploitation.

IV

Between the late 1870s and 1914, however, there was a fundamental change in the public image of the British monarchy, as its ritual, hitherto inept, private and of limited appeal, became splendid, public and popular. To some extent, this was facilitated by the gradual retirement of the monarchs from active politics. Victoria, however obstinate and obstructive she had been at the beginning of her reign, wielded much less effective power by the end. The growing size and importance of the electorate, combined with increased party consciousness, meant that assertions of the royal prerogative of the

[67] P. Magnus, *Gladstone: A Biography* (London, 1963), pp. 207–17.

[68] J. and J. May, *Commemorative Pottery, 1780–1900* (London, 1972), pp. 22, 40–5, 51, 58–9, 73; D. Rogers, *Coronation Souvenirs and Commemoratives* (London, 1975), pp. 25–30, 31–3, 36; J. Edmundson, *Collecting Modern Commemorative Medals* (London, 1972), pp. 39–42. See also app., table 2.

kind which had precipitated the Bedchamber crisis were much less in evidence. Once the electorate had spoken in 1880, for example, the Queen Empress could no more keep Disraeli in than Gladstone out.[69] And Edward VII came to the throne old and inexperienced, had little taste for desk work, spent three months of the year abroad and, apart from occasional interference in matters of foreign policy and the award of honours and decorations, played only a minimal role in political life.[70] And so, as the real power of the monarchy waned, the way was open for it to become the centre of grand ceremonial once more. In other countries, such as Germany, Austria and Russia, ritualistic aggrandizement was employed, as of old, to exalt royal *influence*. In Britain, by contrast, similar ritual was made possible because of growing royal *weakness*. In England, unlike other countries, it was not so much the re-opening of the theatre of power as the première of the cavalcade of impotence.

At the same time, the growth in popular veneration for the monarchy made such enhanced ceremonial convincing in a manner that had not been possible before, as power was exchanged for popularity. Victoria's longevity, probity, sense of duty and unrivalled position as matriarch of Europe and mother-figure of empire came to outweigh, and then eclipse, the earlier hostile attitude towards her. At her death, she was no longer 'Mrs Guelph', the 'Queen of the Whigs', but the 'most excellent of sovereigns', who 'bequeathed a name eternally to be revered'.[71] Nor was time any less generous to Edward VII. His extravagant life; the zest and style with which he travelled; his notable racing successes; and the incomparable beauty, charm and appeal of his consort: all these advantages were his during the brief years of his reign. Bagehot's 'unemployed youth' had become, in regnal old age, a grand, august, patriarchal figure, father to the empire and uncle of Europe. As one rhymester put it at his death:

> Greatest sorrow England ever had
> When death took away our dear old Dad.[72]

[69] Longford, *Victoria, R.I.*, pp. 537–8.
[70] P. Magnus, *King Edward VII* (Harmondsworth, 1967), pp. 342, 348, 373–7.
[71] R. Davey, *The Pageant of London*, 2 vols. (London, 1906), ii, p. 623. Within a month, 3,000 elegies were published in the United Kingdom and colonies, subsequently reprinted in J. A. Hammerton, *The Passing of Victoria* (London, 1902). As Hynes noted, 'The most striking thing about them is the frequency with which they apostrophise the old Queen as Mother.' See: S. Hynes, *The Edwardian Turn of Mind* (Princeton, N.J., 1968), p. 15.
[72] Magnus, *Edward VII*, p. 526; Martin, *Crown and the Establishment*, p. 68; Ziegler, *Crown and People*, p. 28.

This change in the position of the monarch, placing both Victoria and Edward above politics as patriarchal figures for the whole of the nation, was rendered increasingly urgent by economic and social developments during the last quarter of the nineteenth century. Once more, London re-asserted its national dominance, as provincial identity and loyalties markedly weakened.[73] It was at the end, rather than the beginning, of the nineteenth century that Britain became a preponderantly urban, industrial, mass society, with class loyalties and class conflicts set in a genuinely national framework for the first time. The New Unionism, the controversies surrounding Taff Vale and the Osborne Judgement, and the growing, unprecedented industrial unrest in the years immediately before the First World War, all betokened a harsher social and economic climate.[74] Moreover, as was stressed at the time of Edward's coronation, the 'antique character of many of the material circumstances of life at the date when Queen Victoria was crowned' contrasted markedly with the dramatic, disorienting developments which had taken place in the subsequent sixty years – a widening franchise, the railway, the steamship, the telegraph, electricity, the tram.[75] In such an age of change, crisis and dislocation, the 'preservation of anachronism', the deliberate, ceremonial presentation of an impotent but venerated monarch as a unifying symbol of permanence and national community became both possible and necessary. In the 1860s, Walter Bagehot had predicted that 'the more democratic we get, the more we shall get to like state and show, which have ever pleased the vulgar'. And he was proved to be correct.[76]

Of particular importance in promoting this new picture of the monarch as head of the nation were developments in the media from the 1880s. For with the advent of the yellow press, news became increasingly nationalized and sensationalized as the old, rational, intellectual, middle-class, provincial Liberal press was gradually superseded by the great national dailies: London-based, increasingly

---

[73] Briggs, *Victorian Cities*, pp. 312–13, 327, 330, 356–9.

[74] Chamberlain, 'The Growth of Support for the Labour Party', pp. 481, 485; Pelling, *History of British Trade Unions*, p. 89; Musson, *British Trade Unionism*, p. 65; J. Lovell, *British Trade Unions, 1875–1933* (London, 1977), pp. 9, 21–3, 30–3, 41–6.

[75] J. E. C. Bodley, *The Coronation of King Edward the Seventh: A Chapter in European and Imperial History* (London, 1903), pp. 203–6.

[76] W. Bagehot, 'The Cost of Public Dignity', *The Economist*, 20 July 1867; reprinted in St John-Stevas, *The Collected Works of Walter Bagehot*, v, p. 413.

Conservative, strident, vulgar and working-class in their appeal.[77] In 1896, Harmsworth launched the *Daily Mail*, which sold for one half-penny, and achieved a daily circulation of 700,000 within four years. The *Mirror*, the *Sketch* and the *Daily Express* soon followed. At the same time, the savage cartoons and editorials of the earlier period disappeared almost entirely. Edward VII's liaisons were discreetly ignored, and cartoonists such as Partridge and Carruthers Gould depicted great occasions in the lives and deaths of monarchs in a restrained and respectful way. Only in the foreign press was criticism of the British monarchy still to be found. But in English papers it had already become virtually sacrosanct.[78] A third major change concerned the development of new techniques in photography and printing, which meant that illustrations were no longer confined to expensive, middle-class weeklies. As a result, by the end of the nineteenth century the great royal ceremonies were described with unprecedented immediacy and vividness in a sentimental, emotional, admiring way, which appealed to a broader cross section of the public than ever before.[79]

If the press was one major agent in exalting the monarchy to venerated Olympus, then changes in transport technology produced a similar effect, as developments served to render the monarchs' coaches increasingly anachronistic and splendid. From the 1870s, the carriage trade received a severe check in its hitherto spectacular growth rate.[80] The invention of the pneumatic tyre by Dunlop in 1888 led to the cycling boom of the next decade. By 1898 there were more

---

[77] Briggs, *Victorian Cities*, pp. 356–8.

[78] Walker, *Daily Sketches*, pp. 7–8, 13; Wynn Jones, *Cartoon History of the Monarchy*, pp. 130, 138–9; Lee, *The Origins of the Popular Press*, pp. 120–30, 190–6; Symon, *The Press and its Story*, pp. 229–32; H. Herd, *The March of Journalism* (London, 1952), pp. 233–40.

[79] Symon, *op. cit.*, pp. 235–9. It is noteworthy that this is also the period which sees a massive proliferation in popular works explaining, describing and commemorating great royal occasions. For the coronations of Edward VII and George V, see, for example: J. H. Pemberton, *The Coronation Service according to the Use of the Church of England* (London, 1902, 1911); D. Macleane, *The Great Solemnity of the Coronation of the King and Queen of England* (London, 1902, 1911); W. H. Stackpole, *The Coronation Regalia* (London, 1911); E. Metallinos, *Imperial and Royal Coronations* (London, 1902); L. G. Wickham Legg, *English Coronation Records* (London, 1901); H. F. Burke, *The Historical Records of the Coronation* (London, 1904); Bodley, *Coronation of Edward the Seventh;* Perkins, *The Coronation Book.* The upsurge in popular, laudatory royal biographies also dates from this time.

[80] Thompson, *Victorian England*, pp. 16–18.

than one thousand miles of tramways in English cities, and by 1914 that figure had trebled.[81] For town dwellers in particular (who were by now the majority of the population), the horse ceased to be part of their way of life as it had previously been. In London, for example, in 1903, there were 3,623 horse buses and only thirteen motor buses. By 1913 there were only 142 horse buses left, compared with 3,522 motor buses. And the shift from hansom cabs to taxis was equally pronounced. In 1908, 10,500 cars and commercial vehicles were produced; in 1913 the figure was 34,000.[82] Under these circumstances, the royal carriages, previously commonplace, became endowed with a romantic splendour which had never been attainable before. So, while coachmakers like Mulliner were obliged to turn to motor cars because of the decline in demand for their more traditional products, Edward VII actually commissioned a new state landau in which he drove back from the Abbey after his coronation. Described as being 'in its build, proportions and adornment probably the most graceful and regal vehicle ever built', it was emphatic proof of the monarchy's new and unique capacity to call in the old world to redress the balance of the new.[83]

Internationally, the same trends were in evidence. For the novelty of a mass society at home was reflected in the newness of formal empire abroad. And, once more, the originality of the development was concealed and rendered acceptable by associating it with the oldest national institution, the monarchy. During the first three-quarters of the nineteenth century, no royal ceremonial occasion could plausibly have been called an imperial event. But, from 1877, when Disraeli made Victoria empress of India, and 1897, when Joseph Chamberlain brought the colonial premiers and troops to parade in the Diamond Jubilee procession, every great royal occasion was also an *imperial* occasion.[84] As Bodley noted, during the final decades of Victoria's reign, her crown became 'the emblem of the British race, to encourage its expansion over the face of the globe'.[85] Edward, while Prince of Wales, visited Canada and India, and in the 1900s the

---

[81] P. S. Bagwell, *The Transport Revolution from 1770* (London, 1974), pp. 150, 155.

[82] F. M. L. Thompson, 'Nineteenth-Century Horse Sense', *Economic History Review*, 2nd ser., xxix (1976), p. 61; S. B. Saul, 'The Motor Industry in Britain to 1914', *Business History*, v (1962), pp. 24–5.

[83] Gilbey, *Modern Carriages*, pp. 36–8; M. Watney, *The Elegant Carriage* (London, 1961), p. 81.

[84] J. L. Garvin and Julian Amery, *The Life of Joseph Chamberlain*, 6 vols. (London, 1932–69), iii, pp. 185–95.

[85] Bodley, *Coronation of Edward the Seventh*, p. 19.

duke of York followed in his footsteps with an imperial world tour, and additional visits to Canada and India.[86] Significantly, his father was the first British monarch to be crowned emperor of India and ruler 'of the British Dominions beyond the seas'. Even Edward's illness at the time of his coronation worked to imperial advantage. For while the European delegations departed, those from the empire remained, making the coronation – when it finally happened – 'a family festival for the British Empire'. There were the 'unprecedented circumstances' under which the 'immemorial tradition' was celebrated. Or, as another commentator put it more eloquently:

> The great ceremony... possessed a further quality all its own, with which none of its predecessors at Westminster could attempt to compete... For the first time in the history of our land, did the Imperial idea blaze forth into prominence, as the sons and daughters of the Empire gathered together from the ends of the earth to take their part. The archaic traditions of the Middle Ages were enlarged in their scope so as to include the modern splendour of a mighty empire.[87]

'In this regard', as Sir Sidney Lee later noted, 'the precedent of the Diamond Jubilee of 1897 was improved upon.'[88]

Whether these royal ceremonials, in part reflecting a novel consciousness of formal imperial possession, were an expression of national self-confidence or of doubt is not altogether clear. It remains a widely held view that Victoria's jubilees and Edward's coronation mark the high noon of empire, confidence and splendour.[89] But others, following the mood of Kipling's 'Recessional', regard them in a very different light – as an assertion of show and grandeur, bombast and bravado, at a time when real power was already on the

---

[86] Magnus, *Edward VII*, pp. 52–8, 131–2, 238–41; H. Nicolson, *King George the Fifth: His Life and Reign* (London, 1967), pp. 106–10, 128–33, 228–37.

[87] J. Perkins, *The Coronation Book* (London, 1911), p. 329; Ziegler, *Crown and People*, pp. 56, 66; P. E. Schramm, *A History of the English Coronation* (Oxford, 1937), p. 104.

[88] Sir S. Lee, *King Edward the Seventh: A Biography*, 2 vols. (London, 1925–7), ii, p. 100. It is also noteworthy that the national anthem was increasingly treated as an imperial anthem in these years. In 1892, S. G. R. Coles wrote an imperial verse beginning, 'God Save our Empress Queen', and five years later, H. A. Salmone produced *The Imperial Sun*, 'a translation of the third verse of the National Anthem metrically rendered into fifty of the most important languages spoken in the Queen's Empire'. See Scholes, *'God Save the Queen'*, p. 141.

[89] For two recent works which take this view, see: J. Morris, *Pax Britannica: The Climax of an Empire* (London, 1968); C. Chapman and P. Raben, *Debrett's Queen Victoria's Jubilees, 1887 and 1897* (London, 1977).

wane.[90] For there can be no doubt that during this period, Britain was increasingly challenged by new, rival world powers, economically, colonially and politically. The unification of Italy and Germany, the recovery of the United States from the traumas of the Civil War, the Scramble for Africa, the tariffs adopted by the continental powers, the decision by Britain to abandon 'Splendid Isolation' and seek alliance and support in Europe, the Boer War, and the crises of Fashoda, Agadir and Morocco, all betokened a world of fear, tension and rivalry which had not existed in the balmy days of Palmerston. The freedom of diplomatic manoeuvre which foreign secretaries had possessed in the past had vanished by the time of Salisbury.

This growing international competitiveness was mirrored in the large-scale rebuilding of capital cities, as the great powers bolstered their self-esteem in the most visible, ostentatious manner. In Rome, the Master Plan of 1883 sought to create a capital city worthy of a new nation, with grand avenues and boulevards on the Parisian model. And the completion of the massive Victor Emmanuel Monument in 1911 was a further emphatic assertion of national grandeur and pride.[91] In Vienna, that clutch of grand buildings facing the Ringstrasse, most of which were constructed in the 1870s and 1880s, was specifically intended to reflect 'the greatness of Empire'.[92] In Berlin, German unification was expressed visually in 'magnificent spacious streets, tree-planted squares, monuments and decorations', including the Column of Victory, the Reichstag, the Siegesalle and the Cathedral, all buildings conceived in a spirit of chauvinistic ostentation, 'the silent sentinels of national glory'.[93] In Paris, the

[90] Hynes, *Edwardian Turn of Mind*, pp. 19–20.

[91] S. Kostof, 'The Drafting of a Master Plan for *Roma Capitale*: An Exordium', *Journal of the Society of Architectural Historians*, xxxv (1976), p. 8; A. Robertson, *Victor Emmanuel III: King of Italy* (London, 1925), pp. 104–6; R. C. Fried, *Planning the Eternal City: Roman Politics and Planning Since World War II* (London, 1973), pp. 19–29; C. Meeks, *Italian Architecture, 1750–1914* (New Haven, 1966), pp. 189ff. For one specific episode, see: E. Schroeter, 'Rome's First National State Architecture: *The Palazzo della Finanze*, in H. A. Millon and L. Nochlin (eds.), *Art and Architecture in the Service of Politics* (Cambridge, Mass., 1978), pp. 128–49.

[92] Marek, *The Eagles Die*, pp. 173–7.

[93] P. Abercrombie, 'Berlin: Its Growth and Present Day Function – II – The Nineteenth Century', *Town Planning Review*, iv (1914), pp. 308, 311; D. J. Hill, *Impressions of the Kaiser* (London, 1919), pp. 59–62; Prince von Bülow, *Memoirs, 1897–1903* (London, 1931), p. 543.

Eiffel Tower, constructed for the Exhibition of 1889, was designed to '*frapper le monde*', to stand as 'a triumphal arch as striking as those which earlier generations have raised to honour conquerors'.[94] And in Washington, too, the Park Commission, which recommended the completion and extension of L'Enfant's original grand plan, was in part motivated by similar aims. For, as Olmstead explained, the objective was to enhance 'the effect of grandeur, power and dignified magnificence which should mark the seat of government of a great and intensely active people'. The completion of the Washington Memorial, the White House extension, the Union Station, the Lincoln Monument and the scheme for grand government buildings surrounding the Capitol all date from this period. And, as the commission explained, when these offices were completed, 'the resulting architectural composition will be unparalleled in magnitude and monumental character by any similar group of legislative buildings in the modern world'.[95]

In this environment of extreme international competition, the smugness and pride with which Londoners of a previous generation had venerated their shabby capital city was no longer tenable. Indeed, as early as 1868, *The Builder* had urged that, since 'the stately magnificence of a capital city is one of the elements of national prestige, and therefore of national power and influence', it was imperative that London's architecture should become 'worthy of the capital of the richest nation in the world'.[96] But it was not until the closing decades of the nineteenth century, when national prestige was seen to be threatened, that action was taken, converting the squalid, fog-bound city of Dickens into an imperial capital. The establishment of the L.C.C. in 1888 finally provided London with a single administrative authority, beholden neither to royal despotism nor state power, visibly embodied in the construction of a grand County Hall begun in 1908.[97] The War Office in Whitehall, the Government Buildings at the corner of Parliament Square, the

[94] Trachtenberg, *The Statue of Liberty*, p. 129.

[95] C. M. Green, *Washington*, 2 vols. (Princeton, N.J., 1962–3), ii, ch. 7; Reps, *Monumental Washington*, pp. 91, 115; L. Craig *et al.*, *The Federal Presence: Architecture, Politics and Symbols in U.S. Government Building* (Cambridge, Mass., n.d.), esp. pp. 244–65. Cf. the observations of the American architect Cass Gilbert that public building should inspire 'just pride in the state', and be 'a symbol of the civilisation, culture and ideals of our country'.

[96] Quoted in Olsen, *Growth of Victorian London*, p. 53.

[97] Briggs, *Victorian Cities*, pp. 325, 332–3.

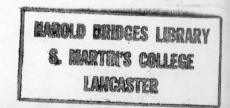

Methodist Central Hall and Westminster Cathedral all added to the feeling of grandeur and magnificence.[98] In London, as in other great cities, monumental, commemorative statues proliferated.[99] But the most significant, coherent piece of rebuilding was the widening of the Mall, the building of Admiralty Arch, the re-fronting of Buckingham Palace and the construction of the Victoria Monument in front. This grand, monumental, imperial ensemble, which gave London its only triumphal, ceremonial way, was accomplished between 1906 and 1913 under the auspices of the Queen Victoria Memorial Committee, whose chairman was Lord Esher.[100] And, in London as in Washington or Rome or Paris, the element of international competition was strongly present. For, as Balfour explained when setting up the committee, its aim was to produce a grand, stately, monumental ensemble, 'of the kind which other nations have shown examples, which we may well imitate and can easily surpass'.[101]

Such developments, in London as elsewhere, provided the setting for ceremonial which was itself a further aspect of international rivalry. For the *parvenu* monarchies of Germany and Italy not only sought to rival the more venerable dynasties of Europe in their court ritual, yachts and trains; they also, self-consciously, competed in grand public displays of royal pageantry.[102] Thus in Austria, the six hundredth anniversary of the Habsburg monarchy, the millennium of the kingdom of Hungary, the Golden and Diamond Jubilees of Francis Joseph and the emperor's eightieth birthday were all celebrated with unprecedented pomp and grandeur.[103] Italy retali-

---

[98] A. Service, *Edwardian Architecture: A Handbook to Building Design in Britain, 1890–1914* (London, 1977), ch. 10; M. H. Port, 'Imperial Victorian', *Geographical Magazine*, xlix (1977), pp. 553–62.

[99] See app., table 4. See also Trachtenberg, *The Statue of Liberty*, p. 100: 'As the mid century became the late century, the momentum of colossus building increased, topping out a thickening forest of monuments of more ordinary scale that almost threatened to choke the city squares and picturesque sites of Europe.'

[100] G. Stamp, *London, 1900* (London, 1978), p. 305.

[101] E. and M. Darby, 'The Nation's Monument to Queen Victoria', *Country Life*, clxiv (1978), p. 1647.

[102] For court ritual in late nineteenth-century Europe, see: Baron von Margutti, *The Emperor Francis Joseph and His Times* (London, 1921), pp. 166–85; Princess Fugger, *The Glory of the Habsburgs* (London, 1932), pp. 100–40; A. Topham, *Memories of the Kaiser's Court* (London, 1914), pp. 85–6, 123, 184–202; Hill, *Impressions of the Kaiser*, ch. 3; Count R. Zedlitz-Trützschler, *Twelve Years at the Imperial German Court* (London, 1924), pp. 46–60, 70–1, 95, 117, 165; M. Buchanan, *Recollections of Imperial Russian Court* (London, 1913), p. 143.

[103] K. Tschuppik, *The Reign of the Emperor Francis Joseph, 1848–1916* (London, 1930), pp. 272, 354, 400.

ated with an extravagant funeral for Victor Emmanuel II in 1878, and the unveiling of his monument in 1911, which was also the jubilee of Italian Unification.[104] In Russia, the funeral accorded to Alexander III in 1894 was without precedent in splendour and magnificence, and the tercentenary celebration of the Romanov dynasty in 1913 was conceived on the grandest possible scale. And in Germany, the funeral of Kaiser Wilhelm I and the Silver Jubilee of his grandson were similarly magnificent.[105] Even republican régimes joined in. In France, Bastille Day was invented in 1880, and was repeated annually thereafter. The funeral of Victor Hugo in 1885 and the centennial of the revolution four years later were further pageants in the grand manner.[106] Likewise, in the United States, the centennial of the revolution and the four hundredth anniversary of Columbus's discovery of America were lavishly commemorated. At the same time, President Chester Arthur began to improve the ritual and ceremonial associated with the White House, and, significantly, Gilbert's plan for Washington in 1900 included provision for 'a great receiving ground for pageants and official ceremonies'.[107]

Once more, the element of competition was noteworthy. An English reporter in Moscow and St Petersburg, covering the funeral of Alexander III for *The Times*, recalled that 'rarely or never, perhaps, in all history, had a more gorgeous open-air pageant been seen. It was only rivalled, though not, perhaps, outshone, by Victoria's jubilee procession to Westminster Abbey'.[108] In the same

104 G. S. Godkin, *Life of Victor Emmanuel II, First King of Italy*, 2 vols. (London, 1879), ii, pp. 233–44; Robertson, *Victor Emmanuel III*, pp. 103–6.

105 C. Lowe, *Alexander III of Russia* (London, 1895), pp. 65–76, 289–303; R. K. Massie, *Nicholas and Alexandra* (London, 1968), pp. 42–5, 224–7; B. Tuchman, *The Proud Tower: A Portrait of the World before the War, 1890–1914* (New York, 1978), p. 403.

106 Mosse, 'Caesarism, Circuses and Monuments', p. 172; Rearick, 'Festivals in Modern France', pp. 447–8.

107 Reps, *Monumental Washington*, pp. 72–3, 85; S. M. Alsop, *Lady Sackville: A Biography* (London, 1978), pp. 27–30. One consequence of making powerful monarchs and presidents more grand (and therefore more public) was an increase in the number of assassinations during this period: President Garfield of the United States, 1881; Alexander II of Russia, 1881; President Carnot of France, 1894; Prime Minister Canovas of Spain, 1897; Empress Elizabeth of Austria, 1898; King Humbert of Italy, 1900; President McKinley of the United States, 1901; Prime Minister Stolypin of Russia, 1911; Prime Minister Canalejas of Spain, 1912; Archduke Francis Ferdinand of Austria, 1914. In England, by constrast, all the attempts on Victoria's life took place between 1840 and 1882. Pomp without power was far safer than pomp and absolutism. See: Tuchman, *The Proud Tower*, pp. 72, 76; Longford, *Victoria, R.I.*, pp. 188–9, 211–12, 490, 560–1.   108 Lowe, *Alexander III*, pp. 66–7.

way, when King Edward VII visited Germany in 1909, the Kaiser
was determined to dazzle the English king with a display of
ceremonial grandeur. And, despite the occasional hitch, he succeeded.
'The Emperor', the Comptroller of the Household later confided to
his diary,

> was delighted with the visit of King Edward, and said: 'The
> English cannot come up to us in this sort of thing', meaning the
> splendour of the procession, the royal apartments in the Castle,
> the Banquet, the Court Ball and so forth.[109]

Even Americans, however much they prided themselves on the
egalitarianism of their society, were not immune to such competition.
At the turn of the century, when attempts were made to enlarge the
White House, the main concern was that its cramped quarters were
inadequate for receptions, which resulted in 'a consequent loss of that
order and dignity which should characterise them'.[110]

  In such competitive circumstances, it was perhaps fortunate – if
largely accidental – that there coincided with this upsurge of interest
in ritual and ceremony the English musical renaissance, instigated by
Parry, promoted by the entrepreneurial zeal of Stanford and presided
over by the genius of Elgar, the first English composer of international renown since Purcell.[111] One aspect of this was a growth of
interest in musical history and patriotic hymns, well illustrated by
the fact that there were more histories and choral settings of the
national anthem in the decades 1890–1910 than in any period before
or since.[112] More importantly, such an efflorescence made it possible
for the great royal occasions to be presented, not as embarrassing
indictments of the dearth of music in England, but as festivals of
native talent. Accordingly, the coronations of Edward VII and
George V were adorned with specially commissioned works by
Stanford, Parry, Elgar, German and Sullivan.[113] At the same time,

---

[109] Zedlitz-Trützschler, *Twelve Years at the Imperial German Court*, p. 257.

[110] Reps, *Monumental Washington*, p. 131.

[111] F. Howes, *The English Musical Renaissance* (London, 1966), chaps. 7–9; Kennedy,
   Ralph Vaughan Williams, ch. 1.

[112] For historical accounts, see: *Musical Times*, xix (1878), pp. 129–30, 196–7, 260–2,
   315–18, 379–81, 438–9; F. K. Harford, *God Save the Queen*, (London, 1882);
   A. C. Bunten, '*God Save the King': Facsimiles of the Earliest Prints of our
   National Anthem* (London, 1902); W. H. Cummings, '*God Save the King': The
   Origins and History of the National Anthem* (London, 1902); S. Bateman, *Our
   Illiterate National Anthem: A Jacobite Hymn and a Rebel Song* (London, 1911).
   For choral settings, see app., table 3.

[113] For full accounts of the music at these two coronations, see *Musical Times*, xliii
   (1902), pp. 387–8, 577–84; lii (1911), pp. 433–7. See also: Sir A. C. Mackenzie,

the improvement in the standards of choirs and orchestras meant that they were also well performed. In this development, the key figures were Sir George Stainer, organist at St Paul's from 1872 to 1888, and Sir Frederick Bridge, his opposite number at Westminster Abbey from 1882 to 1918. Under their firm, efficient guidance, choirs became expertly drilled and trained, processed and behaved in a dignified manner, and were dressed in surplices.[114] As a result, the standard of performance at the early-twentieth-century coronations was incomparably better than at those which had gone before. Finally, the work of Sir Walter Parratt, who was Master of the King's Musick from 1893 to 1924, meant that the overall organization was also improved. For during his tenure of the post, it ceased to be a sinecure, as he became the supreme authority in arranging the music of great royal events.[115] As a result of these developments, it was possible for Bridge and Parratt to collaborate triumphantly in the musical arrangements of the coronations of Edward VII and George V.

During the same period, the attitude of the Established Church towards ritual and ceremony changed markedly. Unconsciously echoing Bagehot, Samuel Wilberforce had noted as early as 1865 that 'there is, I believe, in the English mind a great move towards a higher ritual', and in ensuing decades his prediction was borne out. Bishops began to wear purple cassocks and carry pastoral staffs.[116] Vestments, surplices, incense and altar candles became increasingly common in cathedrals and city churches. In 1887 and again in 1897, the officiating clergy at Victoria's jubilee services dressed in copes and coloured stoles, a novel and picturesque innovation. And, as with the secular side of royal ritual, the motive was in part a wish to appeal to the working-classes. As E. W. Benson, archbishop of Canterbury, noted after the Golden Jubilee, 'days afterwards, everyone feels that

A Musician's Narrative (London, 1927), p. 155; C. L. Graves, *Hubert Parry: His Life and Work*, 2 vols. (London, 1926), ii, pp. 28–31, 56–7; W. H. Scott, *Edward German: An Intimate Biography* (London, 1932), pp. 152–4; P. M. Young, *Sir Arthur Sullivan* (London, 1971), pp. 248, 261; H. P. Greene, *Charles Villiers Stanford* (London, 1935), pp. 223–4.

[114] Chadwick, *Victorian Church*, pp. 385–7; Rainbow, *Choral Revival in the Anglican Church*, pp. 286–9; W. Sinclair, *Memorials of St Paul's Cathedral* (London, 1909), pp. 411–12; Bridge, *Westminster Pilgrim*, pp. 65–77, 172–8, 182–6, 222–34.

[115] Sir D. Tovey and G. Parratt, *Walter Parratt: Master of the Music* (London, 1941), pp. 90–1, 96–102, 119. Parratt was also organist at St George's Chapel, Windsor, from 1882 to 1924, and in 1897 had arranged a volume of 'Choral songs in honour of Her Majesty Queen Victoria', which included compositions by Stanford, Bridge, Parry and Elgar.

[116] Chadwick, *Victorian Church*, p. 311.

the socialist movement has had a check'.[117] Significantly, the biographies and reminiscences of late Victorian and Edwardian prelates contain full accounts of elaborate preparations for the great royal ceremonials – something conspicuously lacking in similar books by and about their predecessors. In particular, Randall Davidson became an unrivalled ecclesiastical authority on royal ritual, participating in Victoria's Golden Jubilee as dean of Windsor, her Diamond Jubilee and Edward's coronation as bishop of Winchester, and that of George V as archbishop of Canterbury.[118] At the same time, Westminster Abbey itself was transformed into a more colourful and dignified setting for great ceremonial. The organ was rebuilt in 1884 and 1894; the choir was remodelled and lit with electricity; the choristers were provided with red cassocks in 1897; and Lord Rosebery presented a new cross for the High Altar in 1899.[119] So, by the coronation of Edward VII, the attitude of the church towards ritual had changed markedly since the early days of Victoria. As Jocelyn Perkins the sacrist of the Abbey (and himself responsible for much of the improvement there) explained:

> Anything even remotely suggestive of such brilliant muddling was unthinkable...Things accepted without question in 1838 could not fail to meet with stern condemnation in 1902...The attainment of a lofty standard of worship and ceremonial at the solemn sacring of Edward VII was felt on all sides to be imperative.[120]

And, for someone as well-disposed towards ecclesiastical grandeur as Perkins, the result was a complete success:

> From end to end did the altar blaze with a display of alms dishes, flagons, chalices...Upon the amateur ritualists of the nineteenth century, with his tailor made vases, his feeble floral decorations, the scene bestowed a sorely needed lesson.[121]

---

[117] A. C. Benson, *The Life of Edward White Benson, sometime Archbishop of Canterbury* (London, 1899), p. 133.

[118] G. K. A. Bell, *Randall Davidson: Archbishop of Canterbury*, 3rd. edn (London, 1952), pp. 118–19, 307–11, 351–7, 367–72, 608–11, 1,300–1.

[119] Perkins, *Westminster Abbey: Its Worship and Ornaments*, i, pp. 112, 187, 189; ii, pp. 16–17, 111; iii, pp. 163, 169, 179.

[120] *Ibid.*, ii, p. 111. Perkins was sacrist at Westminster from 1899 to 1958.

[121] Perkins, *Coronation Book*, pp. 336–7.

V

It is in this significantly changed context, both domestic and international, that the more elaborate and more appealing royal ritual of this second phase must be set. From the 1870s onwards, in England as in other western countries, the position of the head of state was ceremonially enhanced. A venerated monarch, conveyed in a splendid state coach along triumphal throughfares was no longer, as his predecessors had been, just the head of society, but was now seen to be the head of the nation as well.[122] In England, as elsewhere in Europe, the unprecedented developments in industry and in social relationships, and the massive expansion of the yellow press, made it both necessary and possible to present the monarch, in all the splendour of his ritual, in this essentially new way, as a symbol of consensus and continuity to which all might defer.[123] And, as international relations became increasingly tense, this added a further inducement to the 'invention of tradition', as national rivalry was both expressed and sublimated in ceremonial competition. Only in one major regard did the English experience differ from that of other western nations: in Russia, Germany, Italy, America and Austria, this efflorescence of ceremonial was centred on a head of state who still exercised real power. But in England, while the ceremonial shadow of power was cast over the monarch, the substance increasingly lay elsewhere.

In retrospect, these developments in context and circumstance seem a helpful way of explaining the changes in the performance and 'meaning' of ritual. But at the time, it was not, perhaps, as deliberate as this might imply. For it was only slowly, as one ceremony followed another, that this coherent syntax and language of symbols and meanings emerged. In 1887, after fifty years on the throne, the Widow at Windsor was persuaded – although only with the greatest reluctance – to participate in a grand state pageant in London. It was, indeed, a risk, for her recent unpopularity made it impossible to predict what sort of reception she would receive. And Victoria's emphatic refusal to wear the crown and robes of state only seemed to give substance to such forebodings. Even Princess Alexandra,

---

[122] See the letter from Professor Norman Cohn to Professor Terence Ranger quoted in T. Ranger, 'The Invention of Tradition in Colonial Africa' (Past and Present Conference Paper, 1977), p. 85, n. 31.
[123] Hobsbawm, 'Inventing Traditions', p. 15.

whose powers of persuasion over the queen were unrivalled, failed in her attempts to get Victoria to change her mind.[124] Nevertheless, the resulting Golden Jubilee, with its procession and service of thanksgiving in the Abbey, was a great success: 'Pageantry such as this generation never saw...The grandest state ceremony of this generation'.[125] The Diamond Jubilee, planned with more confidence and certainty ten years later, was even more splendid. As the queen herself noted, with delighted surprise:

> No one, ever, I believe, has met with such an ovation as was given to me passing through these six miles of streets...The crowds were quite indescribable, and their enthusiasm truly marvellous and deeply touching.[126]

Thereafter came Victoria's funeral, the coronation and funeral of Edward VII, the coronation and durbar of George V, and the investiture of his son as Prince of Wales at Carnarvon Castle. Indeed, by this time, departments of state and of the royal household, which had been woefully ignorant of precedent and ceremonial in 1887, had become expert. Hitches might still occur, as when the horses bolted at Victoria's funeral. But such mishaps were rare and, in this particular instance, were themselves immediately incorporated in 'tradition'.[127] Meticulous planning, popular enthusiasm, widespread reporting and unprecedented splendour were successfully allied. Significantly, while the funerals of Nelson and Wellington were both more grand and more popular than those accorded to the early-nineteenth-century monarchs, the last rites of Victoria and Edward far outshone the state funeral accorded to Gladstone.[128]

Insofar as the success of these pageants depended on improved performance, three people in particular were of major significance. The first was Reginald Brett, Viscount Esher, the *éminence grise* in British governing circles at the turn of the century, friend of Victoria, Edward VII and George V, secretary of the Office of Works from 1895 to 1902, and deputy constable and lieutenant governor of Windsor Castle from 1901–28. He was responsible, not only for the

---

[124] Battiscombe, *Queen Alexandra*, p. 174.
[125] *Illustrated London News*, 25 June 1887; Longford, *Victoria, R.I.*, p. 626.
[126] Ziegler, *Crown and People*, p. 23; Longford, *Victoria, R.I.*, pp. 685–91.
[127] Sir F. Ponsonby, *Recollections of Three Reigns* (London, 1951), pp. 32–3, 83–94, 271–2.
[128] P. Cunnington and S. Lucas, *Costume for Births, Marriages and Deaths* (London, 1971), p. 240.

redecoration of the royal palaces and the sorting of the royal archives after Victoria's death, but also for the overall planning of every great state pageant from the Diamond Jubilee of Victoria to the funeral of Edward VII.[129] In theory, responsibility for such occasions lay with the duke of Norfolk as hereditary earl marshal, the master of the horse, the lord steward and the lord chamberlain. But Esher's charm, tact, historical sense, flair for organization and love of ceremonial ensured that the lion's share of the work was done by him. And there was much to do. For it was so long since there had last been a major royal event that no one could remember what to do. 'The ignorance of historical precedent', Esher once noted in exasperation, 'in men whose business it is to know, is wonderful'. But despite such obstacles, his carefully rehearsed and meticulously researched pageants were triumphantly successful, bringing him 'scores of congratulatory letters' from the royal family and politicians alike. Although Victoria did feel, true to her lifelong antipathy to the Grand Old Man, that Esher's careful and tactful arrangements for Gladstone's state funeral in Westminster Abbey smacked of 'misdirected enthusiasm'.[130]

Esher's interest in royal ritual was matched by that of Edward VII himself. For while his mother had been a reluctant participant in public ceremonial, who loathed splendid costume and public appearances, Edward was eager to 'show himself to his subjects, clothed in his attributes of sovereignty'.[131] He had been a constant critic of his mother's mournful gloom, and had also bitterly resented the way in which his nephew, the Kaiser, had outshone him in splendour. So, as king, there was a double incentive for him to enhance the grandeur of monarchy. And, with the assistance of Esher, he succeeded spectacularly. Indeed, it was Esher himself who paid tribute to his master's 'curious power of visualising a pageant', his 'promptness, imagination and *invention*', which were, he noted, significantly, 'the primary gifts without which *improvisation* is hopeless' (my italics).[132] Sensing more acutely the competitive element in the new ceremonial, another courtier noted, with evident

[129] P. Fraser, *Lord Esher: A Political Biography* (London, 1973), pp. 68–71, 80–3.
[130] M. V. Brett and Oliver, Viscount Esher (eds.), *Journals and Letters of Reginald, Viscount Esher*, 4 vols (London, 1934–8), i, pp. 204–7, 214–17, 331–2, 274–87, 304, 322, 333, 337; iii, p. 5.
[131] Bodley, *Coronation of King Edward the Seventh*, p. 205.
[132] Lord Esher, *Cloud Capp'd Towers* (London, 1927), pp. 182–3.

approval: 'Our King makes a better show than William. He has more graciousness and dignity. William is ungracious, nervous and plain'.[133]

So it was entirely characteristic that one of Edward's earliest acts as king was to revive the state opening of parliament as a full-dress ceremonial occasion, with a procession in the state coach through the streets of London, and with the king, clad in his full regalia, personally reading the speech from the throne – something which Victoria had not done in forty years.[134] And, ironically, it was Edward's funeral, in which the ubiquitous Esher once more had a hand, which was 'the grandest state pageant in which he was to take part'. Of especial significance was the lying-in-state at Westminster Hall – 'an innovation which proved extremely popular'. One quarter of a million people filed past the coffin: never before had so many ordinary people, personally, individually, paid their last respects to a British monarch. And it was this novel precedent, combined with the long procession through the streets of London, with the coffin placed on a gun carriage pulled by naval ratings, followed by the more private interment at Windsor, which was emulated at the funerals of both George V and VI.[135]

If Esher provided the expertise and organizing flair, and Edward himself supplied the enthusiasm and support, it was Elgar whose compositions raised ceremonial music from mere trivial ephemera to works of art in their own right. His 'Imperial March' of 1897 was the smash hit of the Diamond Jubilee, and successfully established him as the nation's unofficial musical laureate. Five years later, he composed the 'Coronation Ode' to commemorate the accession of Edward VII, which included, at the king's request, the choral setting of the broad and soaring melody of 'Pomp and Circumstance Number One' which has since gone round the world as 'Land of Hope and Glory'. Then, for the accession of George V, came the 'Coronation March', and the masque, 'The Crown of India' for the Delhi durbar. Such works, which reflected Elgar's genuine love of colour, pageantry, precision and splendour, provided the ideal martial, musical background to the great royal ceremonies.[136] At the same time, they should not be seen as the embodiment of Edwardian

---

[133] Quoted in J. Elliott, *Fall of Eagles* (London, 1974), p. 137.
[134] Lee, *King Edward the Seventh*, ii, pp. 21–3.
[135] *Ibid.*, ii, p. 720.
[136] I. Parrott, *Elgar* (London, 1971), pp. 7, 18, 65; P. M. Young, *Elgar, O. M.: A Study of a Musician* (London, 1955), pp. 7ᶜ, 97, 222, 288.

bombast, pride, smugness and self-assurance.[137] For his great melodies are more often than not funereal, melancholy, wistful, ruminative and introspective. Even the great motto theme of his first symphony, gloriously ennobled and triumphant as it appears towards the end of the last movement, never fully banishes the forces of doubt and darkness, diffidence and despair, which stalk through that work.[138] But, even though the real tenderness of his music was often forgotten in the expansive brashness of the words fitted to his tunes, his marches and melodies nevertheless established themselves as the indispensable accompaniment of all great royal occasions – and have since so remained.

Assisted by the strong personal contribution of these three men, the public image of the British monarchy was fundamentally transformed in the years before the First World War, as the old ceremonial was successfully adapted in response to the changed domestic and international situation, and new ceremonial was invented and added. And such changes are well reflected in the unprecedented manner in which these royal occasions were commercially exploited. For, although no precise figures are available, it is clear that the massive outpouring of royal commemorative pottery dates from this time, as manufacturers cashed in on the appeal of royal ceremonial to a mass market which had never existed before.[139] Likewise, new, consumer-oriented firms such as Rowntree, Cadbury and Oxo exploited royal events to help their advertising campaigns, and local authorities began to distribute beakers, mugs and other gifts in commemoration. In the same way, there were more private commemorative medals produced for sale for Victoria's Golden Jubilee than for the previous four great events combined, and the coronation of Edward VII was another medal-maker's paradise. In addition, in 1887, commemorative medals in the manner of campaign medals, to be worn on the left breast, were first issued, another novelty which was emulated at all subsequent coronations and jubilees in this period.[140] So, in mugs

---

[137] For this interpretation of Elgar, see: A. J. Sheldon, *Edward Elgar* (London, 1932), pp. 16, 33, 48; C. Lambert, *Music Ho!*, 3rd edn (London, 1966), p. 240; D. M. McVeagh, *Edward Elgar: His Life and Music* (London, 1955), p. 181; B. Maine, *Elgar: His Life and Works* (London, 1933), ii, pp. 196–7, 297–300.

[138] For the most eloquent presentation of this interpretation, see: M. Kennedy, *Portrait of Elgar* (London, 1968), pp. 132–53, 202–9.

[139] May, *Commemorative Pottery*, pp. 73–4; D. Seekers, *Popular Staffordshire Pottery* (London, 1977), pp. 30–1.

[140] Official medals were also produced by the Royal Mint – a further innovation – in 1887, 1897, 1902 and 1911. See Rodgers, *Coronation Souvenirs*, pp. 38–41; Edmundson, *Collecting Modern Commemorative Medals*, pp. 54–61; H. N. Cole,

and medals, as in music and magnificence, the last quarter of the
nineteenth century and the first decade of the twentieth was a golden
age of 'invented traditions', as the appeal of the monarchy to the
mass of the people in an industrialized society was broadened in a
manner unattainable only half a century before.

Nor was this greater stress on ritual limited to the royal family.
In many other spheres of activity, too, venerable and decayed
ceremonials were revived, and new institutions were clothed with all
the anachronistic allure of archaic but invented spectacle. In London
the Lord Mayor's Show was revived as a grand pageant, and in
provincial cities, the new baroque town halls and the enhanced
concept of civic dignity were further evidence of an efflorescence in
civic ritual. In the same way, the new generation of redbrick
universities, with their deliberately anachronistic styles of architecture, their aristocratic chancellors, their antique gowns and lavish
degree ceremonies, were part of a similar trend.[141] In the Dominions,
the grand vice-regal régime introduced by Lord Dufferin to Ottawa
when he was governor general of Canada (1872–8) set a precedent
which was later emulated in Australia, New Zealand and South
Africa.[142] And in India, the three Delhi durbars of 1877, 1902 and
1911 marked a high point in the public face – although not the
private power – of the Raj. At the same time, the honours system was
greatly enlarged, with the creation of the Indian Orders, the Royal
Victorian Order, the Orders of Merit and of Companions of Honour,
and grand ceremonies of installation were revived for Knights of the
Garter and of the Bath.[143] In short, the enhanced and ritualized
public face of the British monarchy was but one example of a more
general proliferation of new or revived ceremonial during this period,
which characterized English, European and American public life, not
only at the level of the head of state, but in a more widespread manner
as well.

Coronation and Commemoration Medals, 1887–1953 (Aldershot, 1953), p. 5. See
also app., table 2.
[141] D. Cannadine, 'From "Feudal" Lords to Figureheads: Urban Landownership
and Aristocratic Influence in Nineteenth-Century Towns', *Urban History Yearbook*, v (1978), pp. 26–7, 31–2; M. Sanderson, *The Universities and British
Industry, 1850–1970* (London, 1972), p. 81.
[142] R. H. Hubbard, *Rideau Hall: An Illustrated History of Government House,
Ottawa, from Victorian Times to the Present Day* (London, 1977), pp. 20–38.
[143] *Sir. I. de la Bere, The Queen's Orders of Chivalry* (London, 1964), pp. 129, 143,
144, 149, 168, 171, 177, 178; Perkins, *Westminster Abbey: Its Worship and
Ornaments*, ii, p. 202.

VI

During the third period, from 1914 to 1953, the context once again shifts profoundly, so that the ritual of the British monarchy ceased to be merely one aspect of widespread competitive inventiveness, and became instead a unique expression of continuity in a period of unprecedented change. To begin with, the late-Victorian and Edwardian formula of a monarchy ceremonially grand but politically impartial was repeated in an even more strictly constitutional manner. For the limited power which Edward VII wielded was further eroded during the reigns of his three successors. Although, for example, George V was obliged to play some part in the constitutional crisis which he inherited on his accession, in the choice of a Conservative prime minister in 1923, and in the formation of the National Government in 1931, and although his private preferences were for the Conservatives, he maintained in his public, constitutional duties scrupulous rectitude and impartiality.[144] He was a figurehead in politics, aptly reflecting his position as a figurehead in ceremonial, realizing the prediction of one radical in 1913 who observed: 'In England the king does what the people want. He will be a Socialist king'.[145] The abdication of Edward VIII was further emphatic proof that it was parliament which made and unmade kings, and George VI was his father's son, not only in terms of his private preference for the Conservatives, but also in terms of his public impartiality. Even his rights to be consulted, to warn and to encourage were relatively attenuated. In 1940, he would have preferred Halifax as prime minister, and in 1945 was sorry to see Churchill depart. But on neither occasion did he have any power to influence events.[146] The evolution of constitutional monarchy was complete.

From impotence to aloofness to veneration to grandeur the line ran unbroken, reinforced by the high reputation of the monarchs as individuals. In particular, George V, by allying the private probity

---

[144] Nicolson, *King George the Fifth*, pp. 98–101, 218, 486–90, 597–601; E. Longford, *The Royal House of Windsor* (London, 1976), pp. 65, 91; R. Rhodes James (ed.), *Memoirs of a Conservative: J. C. C. Davidson's Memoirs and Papers, 1910–37* (London, 1969), pp. 177–8.

[145] Quoted in J. A. Thompson, 'Labour and the Modern British Monarchy', *South Atlantic Quarterly*, lxx (1971), p. 341.

[146] Wheeler-Bennett, *King George VI*, pp. 636–7, 649–50; Longford, *House of Windsor*, p. 91.

of his grandmother with the public grandeur of his father, created a synthesis which both his long-serving successors have emulated.[147] On the one hand, like his father, he was assiduous in attention to public ritual and ceremonial, and obsessed with matters such as the correct dress and manner of wearing decorations; but at the same time, his private life combined the unpretentiousness of the country gentleman with the respectability of the middle class.[148] Perhaps accidentally, but certainly with great success, George V contrived to be both grand and domestic, a father-figure to the whole empire, yet also in his own right the head of a family with which all could identify. (Significantly, Edward VIII overrode both elements of the Georgian synthesis, caring not at all for ceremony, and living an eventful and indiscreet private life.)[149] George VI, by contrast, deliberately took that name to emphasize the return to the style of his father. Indeed, on his accession, Baldwin noted that 'what will endear him to the people is that more than any of his brothers he resembles in character and mind his father'.[150] Once again, the monarch assiduously carried out public, ceremonial duties, while at the same time enjoying a domestic life which was the very antithesis of his elder brother's.[151] Like his father, his qualities were those of 'courage, endurance, kindliness, devotion': the man who conquered his stammer and resolutely refused to leave London during the Second World War.[152] If his father was 'George the Well-beloved', he in turn was 'George the Faithful'.

Under these circumstances, the monarchy appeared, particularly on grand, ceremonial occasions, as the embodiment of consensus, stability and community. Indeed, the great royal rituals, the Armistice Day ceremonial, and the ever-expanding cult of Christmas (in both of which latter events the royal family figured strongly) were the three greatest celebrations of consensus, in which the royal family, individual families and the national family were all conflated. During the years 1914–53, Britain experienced a series of internal changes

---

[147] J. A. Thompson and A. Mejia, Jr., *The Modern British Monarchy* (New York, 1971), p. 38.

[148] Longford, *House of Windsor*, p. 63.

[149] Thompson and Mejia, *op. cit.*, pp. 73, 79.

[150] Quoted in R. Lacey, *Majesty: Elizabeth II and the House of Windsor* (London, 1977), p. 109.

[151] For the iconography of the royal family in the twentieth century, see: R. Strong, 'The Royal Image', in Montgomery-Massingberd (ed.), *Burke's Guide to the British Monarchy*, p. 112.

[152] Ziegler, *Crown and People*, pp. 76–7.

which far surpassed those of the preceding period in magnitude. Between 1910 and 1928, Britain moved from being a nation with one of the narrowest electoral franchises in Europe to full adult suffrage, with what was feared as 'a war-worn and hungry proletariat endowed with a huge preponderance of voting power'.[153] The Liberal Party was eclipsed by Labour as the second party in the state and, especially after the Second World War, the demise of the great aristocratic families left the crown increasingly isolated in London society. The General Strike and the Great Depression brought with them animosity and distress on an unprecedented scale, as did the two world wars. Accordingly, a politically neutral and personally admirable monarchy was presented, with great success, as 'the rallying-point of stability in a distracted age', the most effective aspect of which was its restrained, anachronistic, ceremonial grandeur.[154]

In part, this was greatly facilitated by the continuing obsequiousness of the media, which continued to report the great ceremonies of state in an awed and hushed manner. Indeed, how else was it possible to treat an institution which combined political neutrality with personal integrity: there was nothing to criticize or caricature after the manner of Rowlandson or Gillray. From Partridge to Shepherd and Illingworth, royal cartoons were restricted to tableaux, congratulating members of the royal family on successful imperial tours, hailing the House of Windsor, or mourning the death of a sovereign. Significantly, when Low tried to publish a cartoon in 1936 which was critical of the monarchy at the time of the abdication, no newspapers in London would accept it.[155] For editors and reporters, like cartoonists, remained deferential, as the gentleman's agreement among the press lords at the time of the abdication eloquently illustrated. In the same way, newspaper photographs, like newsreel films, were carefully edited. After the coronation of George VI, the earl marshal and the archbishop of Canterbury were empowered to edit 'anything which

---

[153] Wheeler-Bennett, *King George VI*, p. 160.

[154] Longford, *House of Windsor*, p. 91.

[155] Walker, *Daily Sketches*, pp. 13, 23, 126–7; Wynn Jones, *Cartoon History of the Monarchy*, pp. 132, 157–64, 174–9. There were, of course, exceptions which tended to prove the rule. In 1937, Tom Driberg, then a reporter for the *Daily Express*, reported the coronation in a tone hostile to the 'hushed awe considered appropriate in most of the press', which provoked 'a storm of shocked rage' among the readers. See: T. Driberg, *Ruling Passions* (New York, 1978), pp. 107–9. The flood of commemorative and biographical literature also continued unabated during this period.

may be considered unsuitable for the public at large to see'. Likewise, in 1948, when Harold Nicolson was invited to write the public life of George V, he was explicitly asked to 'omit things and incidents which were discreditable to the royal family'.[156]

But the most important development during this period was the advent of the B.B.C., which was of profound significance in conveying the dual image of the monarchy so successfully built up by George V. On the one hand, the Christmas broadcasts, instituted in 1932 and immediately adopted as 'traditional', enhanced the image of the monarch as the father-figure of his people, speaking to his subjects in the comfort and privacy of their homes.[157] So successful a broadcaster was George V that his second son, although handicapped with a stammer, was obliged to continue the 'tradition'. At the same time, the B.B.C.'s first director general, Sir John Reith, himself a romantic devotee of pageantry and the monarchy, rapidly recognized the power of the new medium to convey a sense of participation in ceremonial which had never been possible before.[158] So, from the time of the duke of York's wedding in 1923, 'audible pageants' became a permanent feature of the B.B.C.'s programmes, as each great state occasion was broadcast live on the radio, with special microphones positioned so that the listener could hear the sound of bells, horses, carriages and cheering. In a very real sense, it was this technical development which made possible the successful presentation of state pageants as national, family events, in which everyone could take part. And, if the evidence of Mass Observation is any guide, they did: record audiences were a constant feature of the outside broadcasts of great royal occasions.[159]

The combination of the novelty of the media and the anachronism of the ceremonial rendered royal ritual both comforting and popular in an age of change. For by now, the monarchs' mode of conveyance, already unusual and grand in the preceding period, had become positively fairytale. At the coronation of George VI, for example, even the majority of peers attending arrived in cars. Henry Channon,

[156] Lacey, *Majesty*, p. 333; Jennings and Madge, *May the Twelfth*, p. 16.
[157] Ziegler, *Crown and People*, p. 31; Nicolson, *King George the Fifth*, pp. 670–1.
[158] A. Boyle, *Only the Wind Will Listen: Reith of the B.B.C.* (London, 1972), pp. 18, 161, 281.
[159] J. C. W. Reith, *Into the Wind* (London, 1949), pp. 94, 168–9, 221, 238–41, 279–82; A. Briggs, *The History of Broadcasting in the United Kingdom*, 4 vols. so far (Oxford and London, 1961–79), i, pp. 290–1; ii, pp. 11, 81, 100–1, 112–13, 157, 266, 272, 396, 505.

whose eye for colour and romance was unerring, counted only three in coaches.[160] Indeed, by then, the horse-drawn society of the mid-nineteenth century was so long forgotten that the scavengers who cleared up the horse droppings after the main procession had passed by received some of the loudest cheers of the day.[161] In the world of the aeroplane, the tank and the atomic bomb, the anachronistic grandeur of horses, carriages, swords and plumed hats was further enhanced. As one book on coaches noted in 1948, even great families had ceased to use state carriages; they were now limited to 'such purely ceremonial, walking-pace vehicles as the carved and gilded Royal State Coach, the coach of the Lord Mayor of London' and the 'rarely used Speaker's coach'. Indeed, by the time of Elizabeth's coronation, even the royal household possessed insufficient coaches to accommodate all the visiting royalty and heads of state, and it proved necessary to borrow seven extra carriages from a film company.[162]

The advanced organization involved in acquiring these extra carriages was evidence that the tradition of administrative expertise initiated by Esher was fully maintained. The sixteenth duke of Norfolk, Hereditary Earl Marshal, although only twenty-nine at the time of the coronation of George VI, soon acquired a reputation for punctuality, showmanship and theatrical flair which rivalled that of Esher. Indeed, by 1969, when his last great pageant was produced, the investiture of the Prince of Wales, his experience of royal ritual spanned forty years. At the 1937 coronation, he was prepared to pay a colleague £1 for every minute that the actual crowning was too late or too early, and he lost only £5.[163] For that ceremony, Norfolk was assisted by the archbishop of Canterbury, Cosmo Gordon Lang, himself described by Hensley Henson as 'a born actor', and by his biographer as displaying great 'attention to the minutest details of an occasion which called for all the drama and pageantry which, with him, were so strong an impression of religious feeling'. Like Norfolk, the archbishop thought in 'the language of the theatre', and it was these representatives of church and state who dominated the three committees and superintended the eight rehearsals in preparation for

---

[160] R. Rhodes James (ed.), '*Chips*': *The Diaries of Sir Henry Channon* (London, 1967), p. 123.
[161] Jennings and Madge, *May the Twelfth*, pp. 112, 120.
[162] H. McCansland, *The English Carriage* (London, 1948), p. 85; C. Frost, *Coronation: June 2 1953* (London, 1978), pp. 57–8.
[163] *Ibid.*, p. 39.

the coronation.[164] Moreover, by this time, largely as a result of the efforts of Dean Ryle and the sacrist, Jocelyn Perkins, Westminster Abbey itself was a more fitting setting for ceremonial. The choir was improved and the stalls gilded; the bells were restored in the towers; and processions with banners and copes were revived. Indeed, during the years of Ryle's decanate (1914–25), no fewer than eighty-six special services were held, including the interment of the Unknown Warrior. The 'development of stateliness and colour in the services of the Abbey' meant that the additional demands of the great royal ceremonials could be met with unprecedented ease, experience and expertise.[165]

Likewise, as far as music was concerned, the innovations of the previous period were consolidated and further extended. In 1924, on the death of Parratt, Elgar himself was made Master of the King's Musick, the first composer of distinction to occupy the position for over a century, thus giving emphatic recognition of the importance of his music in royal ritual.[166] Thereafter, the post has continued to be filled by composers of merit, and the incumbent has retained control of the musical arrangements of royal ceremonies. By the time Elgar was appointed, his creative passion was spent, and no more great works or popular music came from his pen. But other composers assumed his mantle, and continued the recently established tradition that each great royal occasion was also to be a festival of contemporary British music.[167] Bax, Bliss, Holst, Bantock, Walton and Vaughan Williams all wrote music to command for the coronations of George VI and Elizabeth II. Indeed, Walton's two coronation marches, 'Crown Imperial' (1937) and 'Orb and Sceptre' (1953), rivalled Elgar himself, not only in their melodic richness and

---

[164] H. Henson, *Retrospect of an Unimportant Life*, 3 vols. (London, 1942–50), i, pp. 380–5; J. G. Lockhart, *Cosmo Gordon Lang* (London, 1949), pp. 408–23.

[165] Perkins, *Westminster Abbey: Its Services and Ornaments*, i, pp. 113–17, 193–4; ii, p. 207; iii, pp. 180–7; M. H. Fitzgerald, *A Memoir of Herbert E. Ryle* (London, 1928), pp. 290–2, 307–10; L. E. Tanner, *Recollections of a Westminster Antiquary* (London, 1969), pp. 65–8, 144–52.

[166] Since 1924, the incumbents have been as follows: Sir Edward Elgar (1924–34), Sir Walford Davies (1934–41), Sir Arnold Bax (1941–52), Sir Arthur Bliss (1953–75), Malcolm Williamson (1975–). See: Blom, *Grove's Dictionary of Music and Musicians*, v, p. 627. For the work of one particular incumbent, see: H. C. Coles, *Walford Davies: A Biography* (London, 1942), pp. 157–61.

[167] For the music performed at the coronations of George VI and Elizabeth II, see: *Musical Times*, lxxviii (1937), pp. 320, 497; xciv (1953), pp. 305–6.

colourful orchestration, but also in that they have both become regular, established concert-hall pieces.[168]

These developments in the domestic context of royal ritual were accompanied by even greater changes in the international sphere. In the previous period, British ceremony, however much improved on the mid- and early-Victorian era, was of a piece with other nations' grand pageants. But in this third phase, it ceased to be one instance of competitive inventiveness, and became instead unique, by default. For during the reign of George V, the majority of great royal dynasties were replaced by republican régimes. In 1910, the German emperor, eight kings and five crown princes attended the funeral of Edward VII as representatives of their respective nations. But during the next quarter of a century, 'the world witnessed the disappearance of five emperors, eight kings and eighteen minor dynasties – one of the most spectacular political landslides in history'.[169] And again, at the end of the Second World War, the Italian and Yugoslavian dynasties were vanquished, and the Japanese emperor was discredited. In this spectacularly changed international context, the ritual of the British monarchy could be presented as the unique embodiment of a long and continuing tradition in a way that had not been possible before.

In 1937, for example, one commentator on the forthcoming coronation noted that 'an English Coronation is a thing apart from all other ceremonies: there is in fact no other spectacle of any kind so impressive, so awe-inspiring, to be witnessed anywhere else in the world'.[170] By then, such words were, indeed, true. But only twenty-five years before, with similar ceremonial to be found in Moscow, Berlin, Vienna and Rome, they would have been demonstrably false. Of itself, survival had rendered venerable in an age of change that which had recently been novel in an era of competition. Percy Schramm, in his *History of the Coronation*, made the same point, with greater rhetorical luxuriance:

Everything at Westminster remains as of yore, while Aachen and Rheims are desolate. There is no longer an *Imperator Romanorum*. Even the Habsburgs and Hohenzollerns have had to lay aside their

[168] I. Holst, *The Music of Gustav Holst*, 2nd edn (London, 1968), pp. 46, 162; C. Scott-Sutherland, *Arnold Bax* (London, 1973), pp. 181–2; S. Pakenham, *Ralph Vaughan Williams: A Discovery of his Music* (London, 1957), pp. 118, 164–5; F. Howes, *The Music of William Walton*, 2nd edn (London, 1974), pp. 119–21.
[169] Nicolson, *King George the Fifth*, p. 154.
[170] W. J. Passingham, *A History of the Coronation* (London, 1937), p. vii.

imperial titles, and the Crown, sceptre and robes of the old imperial treasury are gazed at as exhibits in a museum. In France, not even this memory of the past survives... If we look more wisely about us, we shall see on every side old state traditions flung on the rubbish heap. There is hardly a country that has succeeded in so continually adapting her medieval institutions as to avoid their complete overthrow or their entire re-construction. Indeed, it is one of the symptoms of our age that countries, in the enjoyment of newly-awakened powers, create an entirely new form of state, and consciously throw the past aside. In the midst of these scenes of construction and destruction, no tokens of the past as symbols of the present remain in existence save the Cathedral Sancti Petri at Rome and the choir of King Edward at Westminster.[171]

The contrast between adaption and reconstruction was not only metaphorical; what was true of constitutions was true of capital cities as well. For while the rebuilding of London had largely been completed before the First World War, the capitals of other new, or newly assertive, powers were constantly being reconstructed as further expressions of national greatness. In Italy, for example, it was Mussolini's wish that Rome 'must appear marvellous to all the peoples of the world – vast, orderly, powerful, as in the time of the Empire of Augustus', and the 1931 Master Plan had as its first objective the creation of a splendid monumental capital, including the making of the Piazza Venezia, and the great, monumental access roads, such as the Via dell'Imperio, which led to the Coliseum.[172] In Germany, too, the massive, monumental, megalomanic buildings of the Third Reich, the fruits of collaboration between Hitler and Albert Speer, embodied a similar view. The House of German Art, the Berlin Chancellery, and the buildings and parade grounds of Nuremberg, to say nothing of the later, and unrealized schemes for triumphal ways and arches in Berlin, all reflected Hitler's abiding belief that a civilization was judged by the great buildings it left behind.[173] Nor was such innovative neo-classicism confined to Fascist powers. In Moscow, the making of Red Square as a ceremonial centre may be

---

[171] Schramm, *History of the English Coronation*, pp. 104–5.

[172] Fried, *Planning the Eternal City*, pp. 31–3; E. R. Tannenbaum, *Fascism in Italy: Society and Culture, 1922–1945* (London, 1973), p. 314; S. Kostof, 'The Emperor and the Duce: the Planning of *Piazzale Augusto Imperatore* in Rome', in Millon and Nochlin (eds.), *Art and Architecture in the Service of Politics*, pp. 270–325.

[173] A. Speer, *Inside the Third Reich* (New York, 1970) chaps. 5, 6, 10, 11; B. M. Lane, *Architecture and Politics in Germany, 1918–1945* (Cambridge, Mass., 1968), pp. 185–95; Barden, *Nuremberg Party Rallies*, ch. 6.

seen as part of a similar expression, as was the massive (and unrealized) plan for the Palace of the Soviets in stupendous, neo-classical style.[174] And in Washington, the completion of the Lincoln Memorial, the building of the Jefferson Monument and the Arlington Bridge, as well as a clutch of administrative offices on Constitution Avenue, showed the force of the same influence on the other side of the Atlantic.[175]

But, in buildings as in constitutional arrangements, London was once more the exception. For while other countries completed or rebuilt the theatres in which the ruling élite performed its pageants, in London the stage remained largely unaltered after the Buckingham Palace–Admiralty Arch *ensemble* was inaugurated. In the inter-war years, only County Hall was added to the great public buildings, and that had been begun before 1914. Even the Cenotaph, for all its symbolic connotations, was a relatively insignificant addition to London's architectural heritage. So, buildings which had been novel in 1910 became, compared with the rush of construction in other capitals, venerable within two decades. Instead of smugly accepting chaos, as in the first phase, or belatedly seeking to catch up and compete, as in the second, Londoners now viewed their city as the most stable capital architecturally – a physical stability which aptly reflected the stability of its politics. As Harold Clunn, surveying the changes which had taken place between 1897 and 1914, put it:

> Taking into consideration the enormous improvements which have been carried out all over Central London..., it would seem that the London of the present day probably eclipses Paris in magnificence. While opinions regarding the merits of different cities vary enormously, London undoubtedly has an almost undisputed claim to be considered the finest capital city in the world.[176]

In building, as in constitutional arrangements, survival rendered venerable in an age of change that which had recently been novel in an era of competition.

These contrasts are exactly reflected in the ceremonial itself. In

---

[174] M. F. Parkins, *City Planning in Soviet Russia* (Chicago, 1953), pp. 33–43; A. Kopp, *Town and Revolution: Soviet Architecture and City Planning, 1917–1935* (London, 1970), pp. 219–26; J. E. Bowlt, 'Russian Sculpture and Lenin's Plan of Monumental Propaganda', in Millon and Nochlin (eds.), *Art and Architecture in the Service of Politics*, pp. 182–93.

[175] Reps, *Monumental Washington*, pp. 167, 170–4; Craig, *Federal Presence*, pp. 309–27.

[176] H. Clunn, *London Rebuilt, 1897–1927* (London, 1927), p. 10.

Italy, as in Russia, the new political order brought with it strident, emotional, technologically sophisticated forms of ritual, the very antithesis of those prevalent in England. In Germany, in particular, the use of tanks, planes and searchlights implied a commitment to technology and an impatience with anachronism at odds with state coaches and ceremonial swords. Instead of lining the streets, cheering but orderly, as was the case with Londoners, one quarter of a million Germans participated annually in the Nuremberg rallies, where they listened with 'delirious rapture' to the 'unbridled emotionalism' of Hitler's oratory. The semi-liturgical chanting and intercession between speaker and audience; the manner in which the words seemed to erupt through the body of the Führer; the state of almost sexual exhaustion in which he was left after his speeches: all this contrasted strongly with the 'unassailable dignity' of George V and his queen.[177]

However backward-looking and derivative much Fascist ritual (and building) has subsequently been discovered to be, to contemporaries in England, it was its strident, hysterical novelty that was noted, and compared with the more obvious traditionalism of the monarchy. As Bronislaw Malinowski explained, at the time of the coronation of George VI, the dictators:

create in a hurry, from all kinds of ill-assorted odds and ends, their own symbolism and ritual, their own mythologies, and their directly religious and even magical creeds. One of them becomes the Aryan godhead incarnate; the other, blatantly, places the bays of the ancient Roman emperors on his own head... Pomp and ritual, legend and magical ceremonies, are enacted round them with an *eclat* which outshines the time-honoured, historically-founded institutions of traditional monarchy.[178]

Of course, insofar as the traditions of British monarchy related to ritual, they were 'time-honoured' and 'historically-founded' in a relative sense; it was only when compared with recent rival rituals that they could plausibly be described in this way. But, in the inter-war years, this is exactly the viewpoint which was taken. In 1936, for example, the *New Statesman* compared the 'kind and fatherly common sense of the king's Christmas broadcast' with the Nazi

[177] J. P. Stern, *Hitler: The Fuhrer and the People* (London, 1975), pp. 39, 82, 85–6, 88–91; Sir N. Henderson, *Failure of a Mission: Berlin, 1937–1939* (London, 1940), pp. 70–1; Barden, *Nuremberg Party Rallies*, pp. 113–20, 125, 133–4; S. Morley, '*A Talent to Amuse': A Biography of Noel Coward* (Harmondsworth, 1974), p. 193.

[178] B. Malinowski, 'A Nation-wide Intelligence Service', in C. Madge and T. Harrison, *First Year's Work, 1937–38* (London, 1938), p. 112.

official who 'ended by asking his audience all to join with him in offering the Nazi Christmas greeting to the leader – "Heil Hitler"'. Or, as Kingsley Martin put it even more pithily in the same year, 'if we drop the trappings of monarchy in the gutter..., Germany has taught us some guttersnipe will pick them up'.[179]

In these diverse and disorienting national and international circumstances, the appeal of Empire, and the ceremonial association of the crown with it, only increased – partly as a distraction from internal problems, and partly as an expression of the comforting belief that, in a newly competitive world of great power politics, Britain and her empire remained at the forefront. The Irish treaty, the independence of Egypt, the end of the Raj in India and the departure of Ireland and Burma may have implied that it was already on the wane. But the outstandingly successful tours of the Prince of Wales and the duke of York to the Dominions and India only cemented the bonds between crown and empire the more closely, so that each royal ritual remained an imperial, as well as a domestic occasion.[180] Here, for example, is Professor Malinowski's interpretation of the 'meaning' of the coronation of George VI:

The Coronation was, among other things, a large-scale ceremonial display of the greatness, power and wealth of Britain. It was also an occasion on which the unity of the Empire, the strength of its bonds, was publicly enacted... Psychologically, I think, there was no doubt that the Coronation generated an increased feeling of security, of stability, and the permanence of the British Empire.[181]

Or, as George VI himself put it more succinctly in his own coronation broadcast: 'I felt this morning that the whole Empire was in very truth gathered within the walls of Westminster Abbey'.[182] And the coronation of his daughter was seen in the same broad, ample perspective. As Philip Ziegler has explained:

The Empire was already crumbling, but the Commonwealth still seemed a powerful reality. Bound together by its common monarchy, it would grow in strength and cohesion. Britain, still clinging valiantly to the trappings of a great power, would regain her proper place in the world.[183]

[179] *New Statesman*, 25 Jan. 1936; K. Martin, 'The Evolution of Popular Monarchy', *Political Quarterly*, vii (1936), pp. 155–6.
[180] Wheeler-Bennett, *King George VI*, pp. 199, 215, 254, 302–4, 371–81; F. Donaldson, *Edward VIII* (London, 1976), chaps. 6–8.
[181] Malinowski, 'A Nation-Wide Intelligence Service', pp. 114–15.
[182] The Times, *Crown and Empire* (London, 1937), p. 184.
[183] Ziegler, *Crown and People*, p. 97.

Indeed, it is in this context that Elizabeth's own words must be set: 'I am sure that this, my Coronation, is not a symbol of a power and a splendour that are gone, but a declaration of our hopes in the future'.[184]

VII

Under these circumstances, the 'meaning' of royal ritual was further developed and extended. Assuredly, the political power and personal appeal of the monarch, the attitude of the media, the condition of London and the state of technology, all of which had changed profoundly during the previous period, remained unaltered. As before, the monarch was the father of his people, and the patriarch of Empire, and the royal ceremonial was as splendid and successful as in the days of Esher. Yet, paradoxically, it is such very real elements of *continuity* which both disguise and explain *changes* in 'meaning'. For it was the very fact of continuity, at a time of internal unrest and international revolution, which imparted to royal ritual in England those attributes of uniqueness, tradition and permanence which, in the previous period, they had so conspicuously lacked. It was not so much despite, as because of, the continuity in style and circumstance, that the 'meaning' of royal ritual altered once more.

Moreover, the impression of continuity and stability was further enhanced by innovation, as new ceremonials were invented. One such series of innovations was centred on Queens Consort. During the period from the 1870s to the 1910s, no spouse of a monarch had died: Albert predeceased Victoria, and Alexandra outlived Edward. In this third phase, however, the role of the Queen Consort and Queen Dowager became important, and this was reflected in royal ritual. At her death in 1925, Queen Alexandra was accorded a state funeral which owed more to the precedent of her late husband than to Prince Albert.[185] Again, there was a lying-in-state (this time in Westminster Abbey), followed by the procession through the streets of London and then the private interment at Windsor. And, in the case of Queen Mary in 1953, the ceremonial resembled that of the monarchs themselves even more closely, for she actually lay in state in Westminster Hall. Equally new was the fact that, so as to give

---

[184] Frost, *Coronation*, p. 136.
[185] Battiscombe, *Queen Alexandra*, p. 302; Tanner, *Recollections of a Westminster Antiquary*, p. 67.

maximum proof of family solidarity, Queen Mary attended the coronation of her son as George VI, another novel precedent which was followed by Queen Elizabeth the Queen Mother in 1953.[186]

The two public funerals of dowager queens were not the only new royal occasions invented during this period. Because of the age of Victoria and Edward, there were few weddings of the monarch's children during the second period, the last being in 1885 when Princess Beatrice married Prince Louis of Battenberg. But with two relatively young kings on the throne between 1910 and 1953, the potential for ceremonial derived more from the rites of passage of the earlier stages of the family life cycle was enhanced. In 1922, Princess Mary married Viscount Lascelles, and George V took the occasion to transfer royal marriages back from the privacy of Windsor or the Chapel Royal to the streets of London, by staging the ceremony in the Abbey, with a full procession beforehand.[187] As the duke of York explained, the result was a great public success: 'it is now no longer Mary's wedding, but (this from the papers) it is the "Abbey Wedding" or the "Royal Wedding" or the "National Wedding" or even the "People's Wedding"'.[188] This was followed in 1923 by the marriage of the duke of York, the first time a prince of the royal house had been wed in the Abbey for five hundred years. In 1934, the duke of Kent was also married there, and in 1947 so was Princess Elizabeth. But, significantly, the wedding of the duke of Gloucester, which took place in 1935, was staged in the relative seclusion of the Chapel Royal at Buckingham Palace, for fear that, in jubilee year, there might be too much royal ceremonial, and that its scarcity value might be eroded.[189]

But the novelty of Abbey weddings for royal children and state funerals for dowager queens was far surpassed by the Silver Jubilee of George V, for which, again, there was no exact precedent, the twenty-fifth anniversary of Victoria's accession having fallen at exactly the time of Albert's death and her seclusion. Once more, the innovation was a great success, arousing widespread feelings of enthusiasm and support. In Lord Salisbury's opinion, the occasion represented 'an astonishing testimony to the deeply founded stability and solidarity of this country and empire under Your Majesty's

[186] Lacey, *Majesty*, p. 116.
[187] *Ibid.*, pp. 76–8; Nicolson, *King George the Fifth*, p. 92.
[188] J. Pope-Hennessy, *Queen Mary, 1867–1953* (London, 1959), pp. 519–20.
[189] Lacey, *Majesty*, p. 78; Wheeler-Bennett, *King George VI*, p. 151.

authority'.[190] And Ramsay Macdonald, who described the service on jubilee day as 'glowing with emotion', was even more moved by a reception for the Dominion prime ministers: 'Here the Empire was a great family, the gathering of a family reunion, the King a paternal head. We all went away feeling that we had taken part in something very much like a Holy Communion'.[191] The idea of the monarchy as secular religion could not be more explicitly articulated. But the most extensive and, it seems, realistic appraisal of the popular feeling which the jubilee evoked is summarized in Harold Nicolson's biography:

> There was pride in the first place, pride in the fact, that, whereas the other thrones had fallen, our own monarchy, unimpaired in dignity, had survived for more than a thousand years. Reverence in the thought that in the Crown we possessed a symbol of patriotism, a focus of unison, an emblem of continuity in a rapidly dissolving world. Satisfaction in feeling that the sovereign stood above all class animosities, all political ambitions, all sectional interests. Comfort in the realisation that here was a strong, benevolent patriarch, personifying the highest standards of the race. Gratitude to a man who by his probity had earned the esteem of the whole world. King George represented and enhanced those domestic and public virtues which the British regarded as specifically their own. In him, they saw, reflected and magnified, what they cherished as their own individual ideals – faith, duty, honesty, courage, common sense, tolerance, decency and truth.[192]

Whether such sentiments, expressed on this occasion, should be seen as evidence of the success of mobilizing bias or as a genuine efflorescence of collective opinion, or whether, indeed, they were some combination of the two, will no doubt remain a matter for debate. But that such feelings existed cannot be contested.

The remainder of the pageants of this period were of the type already established in the preceding phase of development. George V's funeral was an act of thanksgiving for the king who had survived the war and weathered the peace.[193] George VI's coronation was an extravagant, imperial re-affirmation of the stability of monarchy after the interruption of the abdication. And, again, his funeral was

[190] Longford, *House of Windsor*, p. 94.
[191] D. Marquand, *Ramsay Macdonald* (London, 1977), p. 774.
[192] Nicolson, *King George the Fifth*, pp. 671–2.
[193] The fullest account of this is given in The Times, *Hail and Farewell: The Passing of King George the Fifth* (London, 1936).

a further expression of national appreciation for a man who had not wished to be king, but had triumphed over war and a stammer by a strong sense of duty. The records of Mass Observation record widespread grief, shock and sympathy, so much so, indeed, that it seems likely that Richard Dimbleby's famous radio commentary describing the lying-in-state at Westminster Hall did in fact embody the feelings of the majority of his audience:

The oak of Sandringham, hidden beneath the rich, golden folds of the Standard. The slow flicker of the candles touches gently the gems of the Imperial Crown, even that ruby that Henry wore at Agincourt. It touches the deep, velvet purple of the cushion, and the cool, white flowers of the only wreath that lies upon the flag. How moving can such simplicity be. How real the tears of those who pass by and see it, and come out again, as they do at this moment in unbroken stream, to the cold, dark night and a little privacy for their thoughts...Never safer, better guarded, lay a sleeping king than this, with a golden candlelight to warm his resting place, and the muffled footsteps of his devoted subjects to keep him company...How true tonight of George the Faithful is that single sentence spoken by an unknown man of his beloved father: 'The sunset of his death tinged the whole world's sky.'[194] The contrast between this proud, loyal, reverential, popular broadcast, and the savage *Times* editorial on the occasion of the death of George IV, well illustrates the extent to which popular attitude towards royal ceremony and royal occasions had altered.

The last great ceremony in this sequence, successfully conflating monarchy and empire, stressing stability in an age of change, and celebrating the continuity of Britain as a great power, was the coronation of Elizabeth II in 1953. For it was still avowedly an *imperial* occasion, with the queen's dress containing embroidered emblems of the dominions, with regiments of Commonwealth and colonial troops marching in procession, with the prime ministers of the Dominions and India present in the Abbey, and an assortment of heads of state from various exotic colonial protectorates.[195] At the time, it seemed as though the threats and challenges of the war and austerity period had been surmounted: the empire was still largely

[194] Dimbleby, *Richard Dimbleby*, pp. 227–9; L. Miall (ed.), *Richard Dimbleby: Broadcaster* (London, 1966), pp. 75–6. For popular reaction to the death of the king, see: Ziegler, *Crown and People*, pp. 84–96.
[195] Morris, *Farewell the Trumpets*, p. 498.

intact; the problem of Indian independence and republican status within the Commonwealth had been triumphantly resolved; Churchill was back at 10 Downing Street; Britain had once more asserted her place as a great power; there was a new Elizabethan age around the corner. All this was not only implicit, but was self-consciously articulated at the time of the coronation. According to the *Delhi Express*,

> the second Elizabethan era begins on a note of spiritual buoyancy which Britain has never experienced before. At no time in British history has she enjoyed the moral prestige which the Commonwealth, including Britain, now commands.

In this excessively euphoric context, it is not entirely surprising that the archbishop of Canterbury should feel that Britain was close to the Kingdom of Heaven on Coronation Day, or that Elizabeth herself should make her ringing declaration of faith in the future.[196]

The appeal of this sequence of ceremonies is well gauged by the high level of commercial exploitation and commemoration. Once more, at jubilees and coronations, commemorative pottery proliferated. Indeed, so anxious were domestic manufacturers to profit from the coronation in 1937 that a 100 per cent import duty was imposed on all foreign, imported souvenirs. In 1953, Birmingham Corporation offered local children a choice between a Bible, *Elizabeth Our Queen* by Richard Dimbleby, a spoon and fork, two commemorative mugs, a tin of chocolate, propelling pencils, a pen knife or a dish with a portrait of the queen.[197] Commemorative medals in the manner of campaign badges were once more awarded, and collectors' medals were again privately produced.[198] But these were in smaller numbers than before, largely because two new modes of commemoration were appearing. The first was the planting, throughout the empire, of trees, an innovation particularly noteworthy at the coronations of George

[196] Briggs, *History of Broadcasting*, iv, p. 470; Martin, *Crown and the Establishment*, p. 15. The best accounts of all the great royal ceremonials, from the Silver Jubilee of George V to the coronation of his granddaughter, are those by Sir Henry Channon. See: Rhodes James, ' *Chips*', pp. 32–3, 54–7, 123–6, 464–5, 472–4, 275–7.
[197] Rodgers, *Commemorative Souvenirs*, pp. 38–43.
[198] See app., table 2. Official medals were again produced at the Royal Mint for George V's jubilee and George VI's coronation, in the manner customary since 1887. But in 1953, there was no official Coronation Medal from the Royal Mint, only a Crown. Edmundson's comment is instructive: 'It was argued by collectors that not to produce such a medal was a serious break with tradition, but it was pointed out that in modern times, the 'tradition' had only existed since the Coronation of Edward VII.' Edmundson, *Collecting Modern Commemorative Medals*, pp. 65–6.

VI and Elizabeth II.[199] The second, dating from the time of George V's Silver Jubilee, was the issuing by the Post Office of specially designed commemorative stamps. Previously, the issuing of royal commemoratives had been limited to the empire, and in England only such secular festivals as the Empire Exhibition at Wembley had received notice. But from 1935, every royal jubilee, coronation, major wedding and wedding anniversary (but not, significantly, births or funerals) has been the subject of a special issue.[200] Once more, it was an innovation; but well within 'traditional' moulds.

VIII

By definition, the period since the coronation in 1953 is too recent for detailed or satisfactory historical analysis. While it seems clear that the 'meaning' of royal ritual has entered a new phase, in which many of the presuppositions of the previous period have ceased to be valid, it is not as yet entirely clear how, positively, it might be described. But, in the interest of completeness, here are some observations consistent with the analysis employed thus far. To begin with, the political power of the monarch remains limited, or at least is exercised so discreetly that it seems not to matter. In a recent poll, 86 per cent of those asked felt that the queen 'was a figurehead, signing laws and doing what the government directs her to do'.[201] At the same time, the queen has carried on those traditions of 'extreme consciousness and dutifulness' which have characterized the British monarchy since the reign of her grandfather, and remained loyal to the Georgian synthesis of private probity and public grandeur. Above all, in a period when large parts of London

[199] E.g., Coronation Planting Committee, *The Royal Record of Tree Planting, the Provision of Open Spaces, Recreation Grounds and Other Schemes Undertaken in the British Empire and Elsewhere, Especially in the United States of America, in Honour of the Coronation of His Majesty King George VI* (Cambridge, 1939).

[200] L. N. and M. Williams, *Commemorative Postage Stamps of Great Britain, 1890–1966* (London, 1967), pp. 9, 25–40; T. Todd, *A History of British Postage Stamps, 1660–1940* (London, 1941), pp. 211, 214, 215, 217; H. D. S. Haverbeck, *The Commemorative Stamps of the British Commonwealth* (London, 1955), pp. 89–94. See also app., table 5. It is noteworthy that Britain was slow to adopt commemorative stamps in comparison with both Europe and the empire. In most European countries, special stamps had been issued for anniversaries and jubilees in the period 1890–1914, and in the empire, Newfoundland had issued special stamps to commemorate the coronation of George V. See: Hobsbawm, 'Inventing Traditions', p. 19.

[201] Rose and Kavanagh, 'The Monarchy in Contemporary British Culture', p. 551.

have been rebuilt, men have been put on the moon, and Concorde has brought New York within commuting distance, the romantic glamour of anachronistic ceremony has become all the more appealing. As Sir Charles Petrie explains, 'the modern world has been so mechanised that its inhabitants are clutching at every chance which presents itself to escape from its monotony', and the monarchy, whose 'pageantry and ceremonial' brings 'glamour, mystery and excitement' into the lives of millions, is especially well equipped to do this.[202] If, for example, the queen had travelled to St Paul's Cathedral in a limousine for her Jubilee Thanksgiving Service, much of the splendour of the occasion would have been lost.

Of greater significance has been the way in which royal ceremony has been an antidote to, or legitimation of, social change domestically, in a manner closely reminiscent of the previous period. As the lengthening perspective makes clear, the effect of the Second World War was in many ways far greater, socially and economically, than that of the First. The aristocracy has virtually vanished as part of government. There has been a decline in public conformity to Christian ethics. Problems of race, colour, violence, crime and drug addiction have proliferated. Opinion, and legislation, has changed markedly on issues such as the death penalty, abortion, pre-marital sex and homosexuality. Wealth and income have been redistributed, not drastically, but certainly more than ever before this century. So, in an 'egalitarian, sexually permissive and multi-racial society', the monarchy remains true to that public, ceremonial role identified by Harold Nicolson when describing the Silver Jubilee of George V: 'a guarantee of stability, security, continuity – the preservation of tradition values'.[203] Or, as a recent opinion poll put it, more fully:

> Its existence means safety, stability and continued national prestige: it promises religious sanction and moral leadership; it is 'above party' focus for group identification; it means gaiety, excitement and the satisfaction of ceremonial pageantry; it is an important, and perhaps an increasingly important, symbol of national prestige.[204]

As those concluding words suggest, the role of royal ritual has also acquired a new meaning in an international context, as Britain's

---

[202] Sir Charles Petrie, *The Modern British Monarchy* (London, 1957), p. 215; Harris, *Long to Reign Over Us?*, pp. 27, 55.

[203] Lacey, *Majesty*, p. 245; Ziegler, *Crown and People*, p. 198; A. Duncan, *The Reality of Monarchy* (London, 1970), p. 95.

[204] Harris, *Long to Reign Over Us?*, p. 137.

world position has declined profoundly. The fond, euphoric hopes of the coronation – that there was a new Elizabethan age ahead – have proved vain. Indeed, to perceptive observers at that ceremony, the writing was already on the wall. One American commentator, not taken in by the buoyancy of the occasion, suggested that 'this show' was in part 'put on by the British for a psychological boost to their somewhat shaky empire'.[205] And, significantly, Elizabeth's title was much less grandly imperial than that of her three predecessors. For she was neither empress of India, nor ruler of 'the British Dominions beyond the Sea', but merely 'Head of the Commonwealth'.[206] Since then, the slide into impotence has only accelerated, with the break up of the colonial empire, the disappearance of the last generation of imperial statesmen like Smuts and Menzies, the fiasco of Suez, the problems of Biafra and Northern Ireland, recurrent economic crises and the entry of Britain into the Common Market. Indeed, the state funeral of Sir Winston Churchill in 1965, poised exactly half way between Elizabeth's coronation and Silver Jubilee, was not only the last rites of the great man himself, but was also self-consciously recognized at the time as being the requiem for Britain as a great power.[207]

So, 'as the power of Britain waned..., pride grew in the Royal family as something which was uniquely ours and which no country could match'.[208] Just as, in previous periods of international change, the ritual of monarchy was of importance in legitimating the novelty of formal empire and in giving an impression of stability at a time of international bewilderment, so in the post-war world it has provided a comfortable palliative to the loss of world-power status. When watching a great royal occasion, impeccably planned, faultlessly executed, and with a commentary stressing (however mistakenly) the historic continuity with those former days of Britain's greatness, it is almost possible to believe that they have not entirely vanished. As Richard Dimbleby noted condescendingly at the time of the coronation, the Americans might be 'a race of such vitality', but they were so 'lacking in tradition' that 'they must wait a thousand years before they can show the world anything so significant

---

[205] Briggs, *Sound and Vision*, p. 471.
[206] Longford, *House of Windsor*, p. 196; Morris, *Farewell the Trumpets*, pp. 498–9.
[207] *Ibid.*, pp. 545–57; Dimbleby, *Richard Dimbleby*, pp. 370–5; B. Levin, *The Pendulum Years: Britain in the Sixties* (London, 1972), pp. 399–407; R. Crossman, *The Diaries of a Cabinet Minister*, 3 vols. (London, 1975–7), i, pp. 141–3, 145.
[208] Ziegler, *Crown and People*, p. 84.

or so lovely'.[209] And, since 1953, this attitude has become more widespread, as evidence of decline has proved inescapable. In the words of D. C. Cooper, 'while people can see the gloved hand waving from the golden coach, they feel assured that all is well with the nation, whatever its true state'. The 'tendency to elevate royalty as national prestige declines', to stress as never before the grandeur and uniqueness of its ceremonial in particular, has been especially marked in post-war Britain.[210]

As such, it has been greatly facilitated by the impact of television, which has made the royal pageants accessible in a vivid and immediate manner which neither the radio nor newsreels could achieve. Here, as in other ways, the coronation of Elizabeth was a bridge between an older era and a new phase of development. For while the tone of Richard Dimbleby's commentary placed it in a world which had more in common with 1935 (or even 1897) than 1977, the fact that it was a television commentary, and that more people *watched* the ceremony on television than *listened* to it on radio, made it clear that a new way of reporting the great occasions of state had been perfected.[211] Largely as a result of television, Elizabeth was, indeed, the 'first British sovereign truly to be crowned, as the rubric requires, "in the sight of the people"'. Hence the comment of Shils and Young, who regarded the whole occasion as an 'act of national communion'.[212] For never before had it been possible for the population as a whole to see the ceremonial as it happened, thereby obtaining an unprecedented sense of active participation.

But, as with the press or radio, the medium of television also contained a message. And, significantly, while television has cut politicians down to size, so that the grand manner in parliament or Whitehall is now no longer effective, it has continued to adopt the same reverential attitude towards the monarchy which radio pioneered in the days of Reith. On the one hand, such programmes as the film 'Royal Family' have successfully perpetuated the picture of the queen and her family as quintessentially middle-class.[213] On

[209] Miall, *Richard Dimbleby*, p. 83.
[210] D. C. Cooper, 'Looking Back in Anger', in V. Bogdanor and R. Skidelsky (eds.), *The Age of Affluence, 1951–64* (London, 1970), p. 260; Harris, *Long to Reign Over Us?*, pp. 18, 52.
[211] Briggs, *Sound and Vision*, pp. 457–73; Dimbleby, *Richard Dimbleby*, pp. 223–39.
[212] Lacey, *Majesty*, p. 208; Shils and Young, 'The Meaning of the Coronation', p. 80.
[213] Ziegler, *Crown and People*, pp. 131–7.

the other, the coverage of the great state ceremonials has enhanced the picture of grandeur and fairytale splendour which Reith and B.B.C. Radio did so much to promote. Of special significance in this regard were the commentaries of Richard Dimbleby, who covered every major royal occasion for the B.B.C. between the coronation and his death in 1965. For his eloquent, emotional commentaries, lit up by profound devotion to the monarchy and a romantic feeling for history and tradition, described royal ritual in the most fulsome, obsequious terms. By explaining the ceremonial and expressing a sense of history in the manner he did, Dimbleby's commentaries were of the greatest significance in presenting the ritual of monarchy as a festival of freedom and celebration of continuity in a worried and distracted age. As his biographer notes, in the 1950s and early 1960s, Richard Dimbleby, by his commentaries, 'did more than any other individual to secure the position of the monarch in the affections of the British people'.[214]

So, despite the initial misgivings about the live broadcast of the coronation, it proved to be so successful that all subsequent royal ceremonial occasions have been primarily television spectaculars. Indeed, this element has brooked so large that it has even influenced the nature of the rituals themselves. At the Prince of Wales's investiture at Carnarvon, for instance, the canopy above the dais was deliberately made transparent so that the television cameras might see through it.[215] As for the ceremonies themselves, they have again had more in common with the monarchies of George V and VI than with Victoria or Edward: they have been the rites of passage of a relatively young family, rather than the jubilees, funerals and coronations of venerable monarchs. The weddings of Princess Margaret (1960), the duke of Kent (1961), Princess Alexandra (1963) and Princess Anne (1973), the investiture of the Prince of Wales (1969) and the Queen's Silver Jubilee (1977), as well as the state opening of parliament since 1958 have all been essays in television ritual.

It is in this 'traditional' but changed context that the Silver Jubilee of 1977 may most usefully be set. At one level, that of public reaction, that occasion may be seen as part of a tradition harking back to the

---

[214] Miall, *Richard Dimbleby*, pp. 145–6, 157, 161, 167; Dimbleby, *Richard Dimbleby*, pp. 225–52, 326–30.

[215] For an account of television coverage of royal ceremonial, see: R. Baker, 'Royal Occasions', in Mary Wilson *et al.*, *The Queen: A Penguin Special* (Harmondsworth, 1977), pp. 105–27.

Silver Jubilee of George V and the more venerable celebrations of Victoria: a popular piece of well-planned pageantry which the public enjoyed. At another level, however, the grand, unrivalled pomp and circumstance of the occasion was seen as a perfect tonic to Britain's declining self-esteem:

> We were all sharing a rich piece of history...Somebody said that Britain may have lost out on a number of things, but we can still show the world a clean pair of heels when it comes to ceremonial. Yesterday's pageantry was a superb example...It proves there is something to be said for doing things the old-fashioned way.[216]

But, at the same time, the experts also recognized that the diminished scale of the ceremonial placed the event emphatically in a new, post-imperial age:

> Only a few members of the Royal Family would accompany the queen on her drive to St Paul's; there would only be a handful of troops from overseas to supplement the anyway modest British contingent; no foreign potentates...would lend exotic glamour to the proceedings.[217]

In different ways, then, the jubilee ceremonial was an expression of national and imperial decline, an attempt to persuade, by pomp and circumstance, that no such decline had really taken place, or to argue that, even if it had, it really did not matter.

IX

The account of the evolution of royal ritual which has been sketched in here would certainly surprise both those nineteenth- and twentieth-century authorities quoted at the beginning of this article. Ceremonial which was badly performed has now become so well stage-managed that the British have been able to persuade themselves (despite overwhelming historical evidence to the contrary) that they are good at ritual because they always have been. And, however much literacy and education have increased, the liking which the British public has for royal pageant and display has grown rather than lessened. Old ceremonies have been adapted and new rituals invented, the combined effect of which has been, paradoxically, to give an impression of stability in periods of domestic change, and of continuity and comfort in times of international tension and decline. While there may be a sense in which the British monarchy legitimates the status quo, the fact remains that during the last two hundred years or so,

[216] *Daily Mirror*, 8 June 1977.   [217] Ziegler, *Crown and People*, p. 176.

the status quo has itself changed profoundly, and the public, ceremonial image of the monarchy has changed along with it. If, as seems possible, the next coronation takes place without a house of lords, a Commonwealth or an Established Church, the role of the ceremonial in creating the comforting picture of stability, tradition and continuity will only be further enhanced. The dynamic dialogue between ritual and society, between text and context, will continue.

At the same time, the picture of evolution, development and change which has been presented here may surprise those commentators and journalists who, on every great royal ceremonial occasion, talk glibly of a 'thousand-year-old tradition'. Of course it is true that the monarchy and some of its ceremonies are, genuinely, thus antique. Nor can it be denied that in England, as in much of Europe, there was a previous period in the sixteenth and seventeenth centuries when lavish and splendid royal ceremony abounded. But, as Professor Hobsbawm has argued, the continuity which the invented traditions of the late nineteenth century seek to establish with this earlier phase is largely illusory.[218] For while the materials out of which they were forged may have been on occasions genuinely venerable, their 'meaning' was specifically related to the social, political, economic and cultural circumstances of the time.

In Britain, as in Europe generally, there seem to have been two great phases of royal ceremonial efflorescence. The first was in the sixteenth and seventeenth centuries, and was centred on absolutism in pre-industrial society. By the early nineteenth century, after a last gasp under Napoleon, this phase of development was past, and was succeeded by a second period of invented, ceremonial splendour which began in the 1870s or 1880s, and lasted until 1914. In Austria, Russia and Germany, it was once more centred on royal power, however much it might be declining. But in England, it was centred on royal weakness, and in France and the United States it was centred, perhaps less successfully, on republican loyalties. Moreover, this second major phase of ritualistic efflorescence took place in societies whose economic and social structures differed profoundly from those which had existed in the previous period of ceremonial inventiveness, with the result that the motives of those who promoted and invented such new 'traditions', and the manner in which contemporaries interpreted and understood them, had also changed profoundly.

It is, then, in this second period of international, competitive,

---

[218] Hobsbawm, 'Inventing Traditions', pp. 1, 11.

ceremonial inventiveness that can most immediately be located the *origins* of those grand and splendid rituals which English comment-ators assume go back for a thousand years. But at the same time, the most important element in the *survival* of these 'traditions' to the present day lies in the unique continuity preserved between pre- and post-First World War royal ritual. In Austria, Germany and Russia, the rituals invented in the period from the 1870s to the First World War were swept away in the years 1917–19 along with the monarchies whose image they were designed to enhance. So the new ruling élites which replaced them in the inter-war years were obliged to begin again. In Britain, by contrast, the monarchy survived, and the 'invented traditions' along with it. So, to the extent that innovation did take place in the ceremonial image of the British monarchy in the inter-war years, it was within, not outside, the formula which had been evolved in the years before the First World War.

Of necessity, this is a limited account of a broad and complex subject, and even in a chapter of this length, it has been impossible to pursue all the themes and ramifications in the detail which they merit. All that has been attempted here is a description of the changing nature, performance and context of royal ritual, in the hope that this offers some explanation of how it is that similar ceremonies have meant different things to different people at different times. Of course, the phases of evolution are more easily (and, no doubt, too crudely) identified than the dynamics of change are explained. But at least this approach seems to make more sense of the evidence, at the level of meaning, than the approach of those anthropologists who look at ritual *indépendant de tout sujet, de tout objet, et de toute contexte,* or of those sociologists who see the context as static and unchanging. And if, in such an essay in 'thick' description, the text of ceremony has on occasions disappeared in the context of circumstance, that only serves to demonstrate just how 'thick' the description needs to be. For if, indeed, cultural forms are to be treated as texts, as imaginative works built out of social materials, then it is to an investigation of those social materials and of the people who – consciously or unawares – do the building, that our attention needs to be directed, rather than to an intricate and decontextualized analysis of the texts themselves.[219] Using the example of British royal ceremonial during the last two hundred years, this essay is one tentative step in that direction.

[219] Geertz, *Interpretation of Cultures,* p. 449.

Appendix: statistical tables

Table 1. *Expenditure on coronations*

Coronation	Cost (£)
George IV, 1821	238,238
William IV, 1831	42,298
Victoria, 1838	69,421
Edward VII, 1902	193,000
George V, 1911	185,000
George VI, 1937	454,000
Elizabeth II, 1953	912,000

Sources: H. Jennings and C. Madge, *May the Twelfth* (London, 1937), pp. 4–5; C. Frost, *Coronation, June 2 1953* (London, 1978), p. 24.

Note: In the case of Elizabeth's coronation, the parliamentary estimates for 1952–3 came to £1,560,000; but £648,000 was recovered from the sale of seats.

Table 2. *Commemorative medals struck to celebrate royal events*

Reign	Occasion	Date	Number
George IV	Coronation	1821	40
William IV	Coronation	1831	15
Victoria	Coronation	1838	30
Victoria	Golden Jubilee	1887	113
Victoria	Diamond Jubilee	1897	80
Edward VII	Coronation	1902	100
George V	Coronation	1911	42
George V	Silver Jubilee	1935	12
Edward VIII	Coronation	1937	36

Source: J. A. Mackay, *Commemorative Medals* (London, 1970), pp. 75–8, revising M. H. Grant, 'British Medals since 1760', *British Numismatic Journal*, xxii (1936–7), pp. 269–93, xxiii (1938–41), pp. 119–52, 321–62, 449–80.

Table 3. *Choral settings of the national anthem*

Decade	Number	Decade	Number
1801–10	2	1871–80	4
1811–20	2	1881–90	3
1821–30	3	1891–1900	7
1831–40	6	1901–10	14
1841–50	3	1911–20	3
1851–60	4	1921–30	1
1861–70	1	1931–7	3

Source: P. A. Scholes, '*God Save the Queen*'!: *The History and Romance of the World's First National Anthem* (London, 1954), pp. 274–9.

Table 4. *Commemorative statues erected in London and Washington*

Decade	London	Washington	Decade	London	Washington
1801–10	3	0	1871–80	13	7
1811–20	1	0	1881–90	14	8
1821–30	2	0	1891–1900	11	6
1831–40	5	0	1901–10	18	14
1841–50	8	0	1911–20	13	7
1851–60	7	2	1921–8	7	8
1861–70	10	1			

Sources: Lord Edward Gleichen, *London's Open Air Statuary* (London, 1973 edn), *passim*; J. M. Goode, *The Outdoor Sculpture of Washington, D.C.: A Comprehensive Historical Guide* (Washington, 1974), *passim*.

Note: This list is confined to commemorative, free-standing or equestrian statues, and excludes reliefs, allegorical, fountain, animal, abstract and cemetery sculpture. But if all these were added, the same trend would still be apparent.

Table 5. *Issues of royal commemorative stamps*

Reign	Occasion	Date	Stamps issued	Total sold
George V	Silver Jubilee	1935	$\frac{1}{2}d.$, $1d.$, $1\frac{1}{2}d.$, $2\frac{1}{2}d.$	1,008,000,000
George VI	Coronation	1937	$\frac{1}{2}d.$	388,731,000
George VI	Silver Wedding	1948	$2\frac{1}{2}d.$, £1	147,919,628
Elizabeth II	Coronation	1953	$2\frac{1}{2}d.$, $4d.$, $1s.3d.$, $1s.6d.$	448,849,000
Elizabeth II	Investiture of Prince of Wales	1969	$5d.$, $9d.$, $1s.$	125,825,604
Elizabeth II	Silver Wedding	1972	3p, 20p	66,389,100
Elizabeth II	Silver Jubilee	1977	$8\frac{1}{2}$p, 9p, 10p, 11p, 13p	159,000,000

Sources: A. G. Rigo de Righi, *The Stamp of Royalty: British Commemorative Issues for Royal Occasions, 1935–1972* (London, 1973), pp. 14, 19, 26, 33, 41, 48; S. Gibbons, *Great Britain: Specialised Stamp Catalogue*, ii, *King Edward VII to George V*, 3rd edn (London, 1974), pp. 172, 207, 211; *idem*, *Great Britain: Specialised Stamp Catalogue*, iii, *Queen Elizabeth II: Pre-Decimal Issues* (London, 1976), pp. 148–9, 254–6; H. D. S. Haverbeck, *The Commemorative Stamps of the British Commonwealth* (London, 1955), pp. 91, 92, 94.

Note: Haverbeck gives the figure of 450,000,000 for the 1937 coronation issue. I have taken the lower figure from Gibbons.

5. *Representing Authority in Victorian India*

BERNARD S. COHN

CULTURAL CONTRADICTIONS IN THE CONSTRUCTION OF A RITUAL IDIOM

By the middle of the nineteenth century, India's colonial society was marked by a sharp disjunction between a small, alien ruling group, British in culture, and a quarter of a billion Indians whom the British effectively controlled. The military superiority of these aliens had just been successfully demonstrated in the brutal suppression of a widespread military and civil revolt which had spread through much of Upper India in 1857 and 1858. In the two decades that followed this military action, a theory of authority became codified, based on ideas and assumptions about the proper ordering of groups in Indian society, and their relationship to their British rulers. In conceptual terms, the British, who had started their rule as 'outsiders', became 'insiders' by vesting in their monarch the sovereignty of India through the Government of India Act of 2 August 1858. This new relationship between the British monarch, her Indian subjects and the native princes of India was proclaimed in all principal centres of British rule in India on 8 November 1858. In the proclamation Queen Victoria assured the Indian princes that 'their rights, dignity and honour' as well as their control over their territorial possessions would be respected, and that the queen 'was bound to the natives of Our Indian territories by the same obligations of duty which bind us to all our other subjects'. All her Indian subjects were to be secure in the practice of their religions. They were to enjoy 'the equal and impartial protection of the law', and in the framing and administration of this law: 'due regard would be paid to the ancient rights, usages and customs of India'. The princes and her Indian subjects were informed by the queen that all would be done to stimulate 'the peaceful industry of India, to promote works of public utility and improvement', and that they 'should enjoy that social advancement

which can only be secured by internal peace and good government'.[1]

The proclamation was based on two main assumptions: firstly that
there was an indigenous diversity in culture, society and religion in
India, and secondly that the foreign rulers had a responsibility for
the maintenance of an equitable form of government which would
be directed not only to protecting the integrity inherent in this
diversity, but also to social and material progress which would benefit
the ruled.

The proclamation can be viewed as a cultural statement which
encompasses two divergent or even contradictory theories of rule:
one which sought to maintain India as a feudal order, and the other
looking towards changes which would inevitably lead to the
destruction of this feudal order. Each of these theories about British
rule incorporated ideas about the sociology of India, and the
relationship of the rulers to individuals and groups in Indian society.
If India were to be ruled in a feudal mode, then an Indian aristocracy
had to be recognized and/or created, which could play the part of
'loyal feudatories' to their British queen. If India were to be ruled
by the British in a 'modernist' mode, then principles which looked
to a new kind of civic or public order had to be developed. Those
adhering to this view desired a representational mode of government
based sociologically on communities and interests with individuals
representing these entities.

British adherents of both the feudal and the representational mode
of colonial government shared a number of assumptions about the
past and present of India, and the continued necessity and desirability
of monarchical rule for India. In both modes, although Indians might
become associated with their white rulers as feudatories or as
representatives of communities and interests, effective system-wide
decisions would be made by the British colonial rulers. The British
rulers assumed that Indians had lost their right to self-rule through
their own weakness, which led to their subjugation by a succession
of 'foreign' rulers, stretching back to the Aryan invasions, and, in
the more recent past, to the British conquest of the preceding
imperial rulers of India, the Mughals. The apparent fact of Indian
incompetence for self-rule was accepted by all the British concerned

---

[1] 'Queen Victoria's Proclamation, 1 November 1858', in C. H. Phillips, H. L. Singh
and B. N. Pandey (eds.), *The Evolution of India and Pakistan 1858–1947: Select
Documents* (London, 1962), pp. 10–11.

with ruling India. What arguments there were among the British were related to whether this incompetence was inherent and permanent, or whether under proper tutelage Indians could become effective enough to rule themselves. The feudal theory could encompass the representational theory and the possibility of evolution of competence, since the British had lived through a feudal stage in their own history, and in analytical terms the Indian present could be seen as the British past. The British polity, society and economy had evolved into its modern form from this past; hence theoretically the present feudal society of India could also evolve into a modern one in the distant future. In policy terms the members of the ruling group could argue about the political efficacy of supporting landlords, princes, the peasants or the rising urban-based western-educated Indians in terms of a general agreement on the nature of Indian society and the accomplishment of ultimate goals for India, without questioning the existing institutions of colonial rule.

In the 1860s and 1870s, the notion that 'authority once achieved must have a secure and usable past'[2] was also becoming established. The past, which was being codified and required representation to both the British in India and at home, and the Indians, had a British and an Indian component, and a theory of the relationship of the two parts. The queen was the monarch of both India and Great Britain, an authoritative centre of both societies. The head of the British government in India after 1858 had a dual title and office. As governor general, he was responsible ultimately to the parliament and as 'viceroy', he represented the monarch and her relationship to the princes and peoples of India.

Starting in 1858, as part of the re-establishment of political order, Lord Canning, the first viceroy of India, undertook a series of extensive tours through North India to make manifest the new relationship proclaimed by the queen. These tours had as one of their main features durbars, meetings, with large numbers of Indian princes, notables and Indian and British officials, at which honours and rewards were presented to Indians who had demonstrated loyalty to their foreign rulers during the uprisings of 1857–8. At these durbars Indians were granted titles such as Raja, Nawab, Rai Sahib, Rai Bahadur, and Khan Bahadur, presented with special clothes and emblems (*khelats*), granted special privileges and some exemptions from normal administrative procedures, and given rewards in the

[2] J. H. Plumb, *The Death of the Past* (Boston, 1971), p. 41.

form of pensions and land grants for various actions such as the protection of Europeans during the uprising and the provision of troops and supplies to the British armies. The form of these durbars was a model derived from court rituals of the Mughal emperors and utilized by eighteenth-century Indian rulers, Hindu and Muslim, and then adapted by the British in the early nineteenth century with English officials acting as Indian rulers.

The central ritual which took place in the Mughal's durbar was an act of incorporation. The person to be thus honoured offered *nazar*, gold coins, and/or *peshkash*, valuables such as elephants, horses, jewels and other precious objects. The amount of gold coins offered, or the nature and amount of *peshkash* presented, were carefully graded and related to the rank and status of the person making the prestation. The Mughal would present a *khelat* which, narrowly construed, consisted of specific and ordered sets of clothes, including a cloak, turban, shawls, various turban ornaments, a necklace and other jewels, arms and shields, but could also include horses and elephants with various accoutrements as signs of authority and lordship. The number of such items and their value was also graded. Some insignia, clothes and rights, such as the use of drums and certain banners, were restricted to members of a ruling family. Under the Mughals and other Indian rulers, these ritual prestations constituted a relationship between the giver and receiver, and were not understood as simply an exchange of goods and valuables. The *khelat* was a symbol 'of the idea of continuity or succession... and that continuity rests on a physical basis, depending on contact of the body of recipient with the body of the donor through the medium of the clothing'.[3] The recipient was incorporated through the medium of the clothing into the body of the donor. This incorporation, according to F. W. Buckler, rests on the idea that the king stands for a 'system of rule of which he is the incarnation... incorporating into his body... the persons of those who share his rule'.[4] Those thus incorporated were not just servants of the king, but part of him, 'just as the eye is the main function of sight, and the ear in the realm of hearing'. *Nazar*, the term applied to gold coins offered by the subordinate, comes from an Arabic and Persian word for 'vow'. In its typical form it is offered in the coin of the ruler, and is the officer's acknowledgement that the ruler is the source of wealth and well-being.

---

[3] F. W. Buckler, 'The Oriental Despot', *Anglican Theological Review*, (1927–8), p. 241.   [4] *Ibid.*, p. 239.

The offering of *nazar* is the reciprocal of the receipt of the *khelat* and part of the act of incorporation. These acts, seen from the perspective of the giver of *nazar* and the acceptor of the *khelats*, were acts of obedience, pledges of loyalty, and the acceptance of the superiority of the giver of the *khelats*.

In durbars there were well-estabished rules for the relative placement of people and objects. The spatial order of a durbar fixed, created and represented relationships with the ruler. The closer to the person of the ruler or his representative one stood, the higher one's status. In a durbar, traditionally, the royal personage sat on cushions or a low throne placed on a slightly raised platform; all others stood in rows ordered vertically from the left and right down the audience hall or tent. In other durbars the rows might be horizontally ordered and separated by railings, but in either case the closer one stood to the person of the royal figure, the more one shared his authority. On entering the durbar, each person made obeisance to the person of the ruler, usually by prostrating himself and saluting by touching his head in various manners. In Mughal terms the saluter 'has placed his head (which is the seat of the senses and mind) into the hand of humility, giving it to the royal assembly as a present'.[5] If *nazar* or *peshkash* were to be offered, and *khelats* or other honours to be received, the person would step forward, and the prestations seen and/or touched by the royal personage; then he would be robed by an official or the ruler and receive other valuables. If horses or elephants were being presented, these would be led to the entrance of the audience hall for viewing.

The British in the seventeenth and eighteenth centuries tended to misconstrue these acts by seeing them as economic in nature and function. The offering of *nazar* and *peshkash* were seen as paying for favours, which the British then translated into 'rights' relating to their trading activities. In the case of the subordinates of Indian rulers, the rights established privileges which were the source of wealth and status. The objects which formed the basis of the relationship through incorporation – cloth, clothes, gold and silver coins, animals, weapons, jewels and jewelry, and other objects – were construed by the British to be utilitarian goods which were part of their system of trade. To the Indians, the value of the objects was not set in a market, but by the ritual act of incorporation. A sword

---

[5] Abu Al Fazl, *The Ain-i-Akbari*, trans. by H. Blochman, ed. D. C. Phillot, 2nd edn (Calcutta, 1927), clxvii.

received from the hand of the Mughal or with a long lineage, having been held by various persons, had value far transcending its 'market' value. The cloth and clothes which were key elements in a *khelat* took on the character of heirlooms. They were to be stored, maintained from generation to generation, and displayed on special occasions. They were not for ordinary use and wear. The British glossed the offering of *nazar* as bribery and *peshkash* as tribute, following their own cultural codes, and assumed there was a direct *quid pro quo* involved.

In the second half of the eighteenth century, the East India Company emerged after a series of struggles with their French competitors as the most militarily powerful of the Indian states, by defeating successively the Nawab of Bengal (1757), the Nawab Vizier of Awadh and the Mughal emperor (1764), Tipu, the Sultan of Mysore (1799) and the Marathas under Scindhia (1803). Their position as a national power *within* the state system of eighteenth-century India was derived from their appointment as Diwan (chief civil officer) of Bengal by the Mughal Emperor in 1765, and establishment of their role of 'protector' of the Mughal emperor in 1803, after Lord Lake had captured Delhi, the Mughal 'capital'. Rather than deposing the Mughal and proclaiming themselves rulers of India in succession to the Mughal empire, the British were content, on the instructions of Lord Wellesley, their governor general, to offer the Mughal 'every demonstration of reverence, respect, and attention'.[6] Creating the East India Company as what Wellesley and other officials of the time thought of as the 'protector' of the Mughal emperor, they thought they would come into 'possession of the nominal authority of the Mughal'.[7] The acquisition of 'nominal authority' was thought by the British to be useful, for even though the Mughal in European terms had 'no real power, dominion and authority, almost every state and class of people in India continue to acknowledge his nominal authority'.[8] Sir John Kaye, whose *History of the Indian Mutiny*, was and in many regards still is the standard work on the 'causes' of the Great Uprising, commented on the relationship between the East India Company and the Mughal

---

[6] Wellesley to Lake, 27 July 1803, in Montgomery Martin (ed.), *The Despatches, Minutes and Correspondence of the Marquess of Wellesley During His Administration in India* (London, 1837), iii, p. 232.

[7] *Ibid.*, p. 208.

[8] Wellesley to the Court of Directors, 13 July 1804, in Martin, *Despatches*, iv, p. 153.

from 1803 to 1857, that a 'political paradox' had been created as the Mughal was 'to become a pensioner, a pageant, and a puppet. He was to be a King, yet no King – a something and yet a nothing – a reality and a sham at the same time'.[9]

After the East India Company gained military control of Bengal in 1757, its influence grew and employees of the Company began to return to England with great wealth; this wealth and influence was beginning to be exerted in the home political system. The question of the relation of the Company to the crown and the parliament became a crucial political issue. A compromise was affected in the India Bill of 1784, which made parliament ultimately responsible for the governance of India, but retained the Company as the instrumentality for commercial activity and the governance of those territories in India over which the Company came to be the ruler. Parliament and the directors of the Company also began to limit the acquisition of private fortunes by their employees, through reducing and then eliminating private trading activities and to define as 'corruption' the incorporation of officials of the Company into the ruling native groups through the acceptance of *nazar*, *khelats*, and *peshkash*, which were declared to be forms of bribery.

With this definition of 'corruption', and with the maintenance of the Mughal emperor as the symbolic centre of the Indian political order, another political paradox was established. The British crown was not the crown of India; the British in India were subjects of their own kings, but the Indians were not. The Mughal continued to be the 'fountain of honour' for Indians. The English could not be incorporated through symbolic acts to a foreign ruler, and perhaps more importantly they could not incorporate Indians into their rulership through symbolic means.

In the late eighteenth century, as officers of the East India Company came more and more to fill the function of tax assessors and collectors, judges and magistrates, legislators and executives in the Indian political order, they were prohibited by their employers and their parliament from participating in rituals and constituting proper relationships with Indians who were their subordinates. Yet in relationships with territorial rulers allied with the British who were their subordinates, officers of the East India Company realized that loyalty had to be symbolized to be effective in the eyes of subordinates and followers. The British therefore began the practice of presenting

[9] John W. Kaye and George B. Malleson, *Kaye's and Malleson's History of the Indian Mutiny of 1857–8*, 2nd edn (London, 1892), ii, p. 4.

khelats and accepting *nazar* and *peshkash* in formal meetings that could be recognized by Indians as durbars.

Although the British, as 'Indian rulers' in the first half of the nineteenth century, continued the practice of accepting *nazar* and *peshkash* and giving *khelats*, they tried to restrict the occasions for such rituals. For example, when a prince or notable visited the Government House in Calcutta, or when the governor general, governors, commissioners and lower British officials went on tour, a durbar would be held. *Khelats* were always granted in the name, and by permission, of the governors of presidencies or the governor general. What was offered by the Indians as *nazar* and *peshkash* was never kept by the official to whom it was given. Rather, valuations and minute listings were made of the objects presented, which were ultimately deposited in the Toshakhana, a special government treasury for the receipt and disbursement of presents. Unlike the Indians, the British recycled presents which they received, either directly, by giving one Indian what had been received from another, or indirectly, by selling at auction in Calcutta what they received and then using the funds realized to buy objects to be given as presents. The British always tried to equalize in economic terms what they gave and received by instructing Indians of the exact worth of objects or cash they would be allowed to give. So if a person was to give 101 rupees as *nazar*, he would receive a shawl or robe worth that much as his *khelat*.

Mughal ritual might seem to have been retained but the meanings had been changed. What had been, under Indian rulers, a ritual of incorporation now became a ritual marking subordination, with no mystical bonding between royal figure and the chosen friend and servant who was becoming part of the ruler. By converting what was a form of present-giving and prestation into a kind of 'economic exchange', the relationship between British official and Indian subject or ruler became contractual. In the first half of the nineteenth century the British, as they expanded their rule, rested their authority on the idea of contract and 'good government'. They created a mercenary army in which the contract was metaphorically expressed as 'having eaten the Company's salt'. Loyalty between Indian soldiers and their European officers was maintained on the basis of regular pay, 'fair' treatment and observation of the rule of non-interference with indigenous religious beliefs and customs. When there was rebellion, it was based on the belief, on the part of the soldiers, that their 'contract', explicit or implicit, had been violated, by being made to wear leather hats, or having to travel over 'the black waters', or having to ingest forbidden substances in the form of fat from pigs or bullocks. The state became the creator and guarantor of contractual relations between Indians in relation to the use of the basic resources of labour and land, through the introduction of European ideas of property, rent and revenue. Local lords who were the upholders of a social order based on cosmological concepts, and who maintained right order through ritual action, were converted into 'landlords'. Indian 'kings' who were allowed internal autonomy over their domains were reduced to the status of 'chiefs and princes'. They were controlled through treaties which were contractual in nature, as they guaranteed the boundaries of the states, pledged the support of the Company to a royal family and its descendants, in return for giving up the capacity for making war, and effective as long as they 'practised good government' and accepted the supervision of an English official.

I would argue that in the first half of the nineteenth century there was an incompleteness and contradiction in the cultural–symbolic constitution of India. 'A cultural symbolic constitution', to quote Ronald Inden,

> embraces such things as classificatory schema, assumptions about how things are, cosmologies, world views, ethical systems, legal codes, definitions of governmental units and social groups, ideologies, religious doctrines, myths, rituals, procedures, and rules of etiquette.[10]

The elements within a cultural–symbolic constitution are not a mere assemblage of items or things, but are ordered into a pattern which asserts the relationship of the elements to each other and constructs their value.

The indigenous theory of rulership in India was based on ideas of incorporation, and a theory of hierarchy in which rulers not only outranked everyone but could also encompass those they ruled. Hence the continuing significance of the Mughal emperor, even as a 'pensioner', as both Indian subjects of the East India Company and rulers of the allied states still bore titles of honour which he alone could grant. The *khutba* in mosques, even in British India, continued to be read in his name, coins of the East India Company until 1835

---

[10] Ronald Inden, 'Cultural Symbolic Constitutions in Ancient India', mimeograph (1976), pp. 6–8.

bore his name, and many of the Indian states continued to mint coins until 1859–60 with the regnal year of the Mughal emperor on them. Although the British referred to the Mughal emperor in English as the 'King of Delhi', they continued to use his full imperial titles when they addressed him in Persian. As the monarch of Great Britain was not the monarch of India until 1858, the governor generals had difficulty in honouring Indians with medals and titles. When a governor general went on tour and held durbars for Indian rulers, they were usually with only one ruler at a time, avoiding the question of ranking one chief above another in terms of placement vis-à-vis the body of the governor general. It was not until the 1850s that the British began to try to regularize the practice of firing gun salutes as marks of respect for Indian rulers. The rank system which the gun salutes signified was not fixed until 1867. Efforts on the part of governor generals to symbolize a new order or to eliminate some of the contradictions and lacunae in the cultural–symbolic constitution met with scepticism and even rebuke on the part of the directors of the East India Company and the president of the Board of Control in London. Lord William Bentinck, governor general 1828–35, was the first to perceive the desirability of locating an 'Imperial' capital away from Calcutta, and suggested to his employees in London the 'need for a Cardinal point' for their seat of government.[11] Agra became his choice for such a 'Cardinal point', as he believed it was Akbar's capital, and he thought there was little difference between the political conditions of Akbar's time and his own as both rulers were concerned with 'preservation of empire',[12] Agra was seen as 'the brightest jewel' of the governor general's 'crown',[13] as it was located 'amid all the scenes of past and future glory, where the empire is to be saved or lost'.[14]

When Bentinck raised the question of the possibility of moving the capital in 1829, the court of directors forbade the consideration of such a move by pointing out that their rule was not the rule of a single independent sovereign, but that India 'is governed by a distant Maritime power, and the position of the seat of Government must be considered with reference to that peculiar circumstance'. It was

[11] 'Bentinck Minute 2 January 1834', I.O.L.R., Board's Collection, 1551/62/250, p. 83.
[12] Ibid., p. 94.
[13] John Rosselli, Lord William Bentinck (Berkeley, 1974), p. 192.
[14] 'Extract Political Letter to Bengal 3 July 1829', I.O.L.R., Board's Collection, 1370/54/508, p. 12.

precisely this maritime/mercantile past which Bentinck sought to change, as he believed the character of British rule was 'no longer the inconsistent one of Merchant and Sovereign',[15] but rather that of an imperial power. Lord Ellenborough, who had been president of the Board of Control, 1828–30, at the time of periodic investigation of the state of the East India Company's territories prior to the renewal of its twenty-year charter by parliament, suggested to the then prime minister, the duke of Wellington, that the government of India should be transferred to the crown.[16] The suggestion was turned down by the duke who, Ellenborough thought, was 'anxious not to estrange the London commercial interests'.[17]

Ellenborough became the governor general of India after the great defeat of the Company's army by the Afghans in 1842, and was determined to restore the prestige of British rule in India. He directed an invasion of Afghanistan, which resulted in the sacks of Ghazni and Kabul as an act of retribution. Ellenborough conceived of symbolizing the defeat of the Muslim Afghans by having what were thought to be the Gates of Somnath, a famous Hindu temple in Gujarat (which had been plundered and desecrated six hundred years earlier by Muslims, and the gates carried off to Afghanistan), returned in triumph to India and placed in a newly built temple in Gujarat. He issued instructions that the sandalwood gates be carried on a cart through the city of Punjab and brought to Delhi, accompanied by a honour guard, and with due ceremony. Ellenborough signalized his intention by issuing a proclamation 'to all the Princes and Chiefs and the People of India'. The return of the gates was to be, Ellenborough proclaimed, the 'proudest record of your national glory; the proof of your superiority in arms over the nations beyond the Indus'. He went on to identify himself with peoples and princes of India 'in interest and feeling', stated that the 'heroic army' reflected 'immortal honour upon my native and adopted country', and promised that he would preserve and improve 'the happiness of our two countries'.[18] He wrote in a similar vein to the young Queen Victoria about the victory and that the 'recollections of the imperial authority [were] now... transferred to the British Government', and

[15] 'Bentinck to Ct Director, Minute, 2 January 1884', *ibid.*, p. 83.
[16] Albert H. Imlah, *Lord Ellenborough: A Biography of Edward Law, Earl of Ellenborough, Governor General of India* (Cambridge, 1939), p. 41.
[17] *Ibid.*, p. 42.
[18] John William Kaye, *History of the War in Afghanistan* (London, 1851), ii, pp. 646–7.

all that remained to be done was to make the princes of India 'feudatories of an Empress', if 'your Majesty were to become the nominal head of the Empire'.[19]

Ellenborough had a special medal struck to honour those British and Indian soldiers in the Company's army who served in China during the Opium War. The duke of Wellington felt that Ellenborough, through this action, had usurped the prerogatives of the crown.[20] Ellenborough's action and his proclamation concerning the return of the Gates of Somnath led to vicious criticism and ridicule amongst the British in India as well as in England. Although Ellenborough's concerns with symbolic representations of the imperial role for the British in India were not the cause of his recall in 1844, they were taken as indicative of a view of the relationship between India and England which found little support either in England or in India.

The contradictions and difficulties in defining a symbolic–cultural constitution are traceable in the efforts made during the first half of the nineteenth century to construct a ritual idiom through and by which British authority was to be represented to Indians. The continued use of the Mughal idiom caused continuing difficulties, such as arduous negotiations between British officials and Indian subjects over questions of precedence, forms of address, the continued rights to use Mughal titles, the Mughal's continued receipt of the *nazar* from both Indians and British officials, and his granting of *khelats* and issuance of *sanads* (royal charters) at the succession to the *masnad* in Indian states. This latter practice the British referred to as the 'traffic in *sanads*'.

The conflict was not only amongst the nobles and élites and British officials, but found its way into the daily practice of East India's courts and local offices, in what became known as the 'shoe controversy'. The British in India followed a metonymical logic in their relations with their Indian subjects, and the wearing of shoes by Indians in the presence of the British was seen as an effort to establish relationships of equality between the ruled and their rulers. Hence, Indians were always forced to remove their shoes or sandals when entering what the British defined as their space – their offices and homes. On the other hand, the British always insisted on wearing shoes when entering Indian spaces, including mosques and temples.

---

[19] Lord Colchester (ed.), *The History of the Indian Administration of Lord Ellenborough* (London, n.d.), p. 64.   [20] *Ibid.*, pp. 324–38.

The one significant exception that was allowed was if an Indian habitually wore European clothes in public, then he would be allowed to wear shoes in the presence of his English masters on such occasions of western-style rituals such as the governor general's levee, a drawing room, conversazione or a ball.

The British experimented with varying forms of ritual to mark public occasions. The laying of the corner stones for the Hindu College building and the Muhammadan College in 1824 in Calcutta was celebrated 'with the usual imposing ceremonies of Masonry'.[21] The colleges were established under the auspices of the Committee on Public Instruction, which was made up of Indians and Europeans who raised funds largely from private sources for these institutions. The colleges were to instruct Indians on the 'fundamental principles of the Moral and Physical Sciences'.[22] The members of the Free Mason lodges of Calcutta, of which there were several, marched in procession through the streets of Calcutta led by a band and each lodge's insignia and banner, and assembled in the square in which the building was to be constructed.

> The Cups, Square, and other implements of the Craft were then placed on the Pedestal... The Reverend Brother Bryce... offered up a solemn prayer to the great Architect of the Universe... As far as the eye could reach, it met Tiers above Tiers of human faces, the house tops in every direction being crowded to cramming by the natives anxious to have a view of the imposing scene.[23]

After the prayer, coins and a silver plate with the dedicatory inscription were deposited in the hole over which the foundation stone was to be placed. The stone was then lowered and anointed with corn, oil and wine. There then followed a speech by the Provincial Grand Master, and the conclusion of the ceremony was marked by the playing of the national anthem, 'God Save the King'. Not only is the idiom of the ritual a European one, but so is the institution being celebrated and its underlying public/civic ideal. The education to be offered at these two institutions was to be a secular one, not involved with the transmission of sacred knowledge as in the indigenous educational institutions. Although one institution was for Hindus and the other for Muslims, admission was not restricted to particular groups of Hindus or Muslims as was the normal

---

[21] A. C. Das Gupta (ed.), *The Days of John Company: Selections from The Calcutta Gazette, 1824–1832* (Calcutta, 1959), p. 23.
[22] *Ibid.*, p. 26.   [23] *Ibid.*, p. 3.

practice. The fact that funds were raised by public subscription, seen as a European-style charitable act, as well as the use of funds raised by public lotteries, marked the occasion as, if not unique, certainly quite novel.

The first decades of the nineteenth century were rich in the celebrations of British victories in India and Europe, the arrivals and departures of governor generals and military heroes, the deaths and coronations of English kings and royal birthdays. The idiom of these occasions would appear to be the same as in England, with fireworks, military parades, illuminations, dinners with their cere-monial toasts, music accompaniments, Christian prayers and, above all, frequent speeches. Indians participated marginally as soldiers in the parades, as servants or as audiences for the public parts of the celebrations.

EVENTS INTO STRUCTURE: THE MEANING OF THE UPRISING OF 1857

The contradictions in the cultural–symbolic constitution of British India were resolved in the rising of 1857, traditionally described as the Indian Mutiny, which led to the desacralization of the person of the Mughal emperor, a brutal demonstration of the power which the British had to coerce Indians, and the establishment of a myth of the superiority of the British character over that of the disloyal Indians.

The trial of the emperor, following the defeat of the rebellion, formally announced a transformation of rule.[24] The bringing of a king to trial means those doing so believe this is an act of justice and 'an explicit denial of the King's claim to rule'. Its meaning, according to Michael Walzer, is that it severs the past from the present and future and establishes new political principles marking the triumph of a new kind of government.[25]

The trial of the emperor has to be seen in relation to the Government of India Act of 1858, and the Queen's Proclamation of 1 November 1858. The trial and judicial exiling of the emperor and the end of Mughal rule was accomplished by completely desanctifying the previous political order of the society. The parliamentary act and

[24] Punjab Government Records: *Correspondence*, vii, pt 2, p. 39; H. L. O. Garrett, 'The Trial of Bahadur Shah II', *Journal of the Punjab University Historical Society*, i, pt 1 (April, 1932), pp. 3–18; F. W. Buckler, 'The Political Theory of the Indian Mutiny', *Transactions of the Royal Historical Society*, 4th ser., v (1922), pp. 71–100.

[25] Michael Walzer, *Regicide and Revolution* (Cambridge, 1974), p. 6.

the queen's proclamation declare the beginning of a new order. This new order required a centre, required a means by which Indians now could relate to this centre, and the development of the ritual expression of British authority in India.

In the cultural system of Anglo–India the Great Rebellion of 1857–8 can be viewed as demarcating crucial changes. For the British ruling élites, at home and in India, the meanings attached to the events of 1857–8, and the resulting constitutional changes, were increasingly the pivot around which their theory of colonial rule rotated. The war led to redefinitions of the nature of Indian society, the necessary and proper relationships of the rulers to the ruled, and a reassessment of the goals of the government of India, which in turn led to continued changes in the institutional arrangements required to implement these goals. For the Englishmen in the latter half of the nineteenth century, travelling in India as visitors or in the course of their duties, there was a regular Mutiny pilgrimage to visit the sites of the great events – the Delhi Ridge, the Memorial Well and the Gardens in Kanpur, capped by a large marble statue of the Angel of Resurrection, and the Residency in Lucknow. Tombs, memorials, stones and their inscriptions, and tablets which are affixed to the walls of European churches marked for the English the martyrdom, sacrifice and ultimate triumphs of military and civilians whose death made sacred, to the Victorian Englishmen, their rule in India.

To the English from 1859 to the early part of the twentieth century, the Mutiny was seen as a heroic myth embodying and expressing their central values which explained their rule in India to themselves – sacrifice, duty, fortitude; above all it symbolized the ultimate triumph over those Indians who had threatened properly constituted authority and order.

THE FORMALIZATION AND REPRESENTATION OF THE RITUAL IDIOM: THE IMPERIAL ASSEMBLAGE OF 1877

The twenty years after the desacralization of Delhi and the final suppression of the uprising of 1858 were marked by the completion of the symbolic–cultural constitution of British India. I will only briefly list the components of the content of this constitution, and then go on to describe how these components were represented in a ritual event, the Imperial Assemblage of 1877, which was held to proclaim Queen Victoria empress of India.

The central political fact was the end of the Company's rule and the establishment of the monarch of Great Britain as the monarch of India in 1858. This act may be seen as the reciprocal of the final desacralization of the Mughal empire. It ended the ambiguity in the position of the British in India as now the British monarchy encompassed both Britain and India. A social order was established with the British crown seen as the centre of authority, and capable of ordering into a single hierarchy all its subjects, Indian and British. The Indian princes now were Queen Victoria's 'loyal Indian Feudatories', who owed deference and allegiance to her through her viceroy. The governor general and the viceroy, being the same person, was unequivocally the locus of authority in India, and all the British and Indians could be ranked in relation to him, whether it be by office held, or membership in various status groups. The British operated in India with an ordinal theory of hierarchy, in which individuals could be ranked by precedence – this precedence being based on fixed and known criteria, established by ascription and succession, or achievement and office. For the allied princes an effort had been made by 1876 to group them by region, with a fixed assignment of rank vis-à-vis other rulers in their region. The size of a prince's state, the amount of their revenue, the date at which they had become allies of the East India Company, the history of their families, their standing in relation to the Mughal empire and their acts of loyalty towards the British could all be weighed, and an index established to determine the rank of any ruler. This status was then represented at durbars held by governors or lieutenant governors of the region, or when the viceroy–governor general went on a progress. A code of conduct was established for princes and chiefs for their attendance at the durbar. The clothes they wore, the weapons they could carry, the number of retainers and soldiers that could accompany them to the viceroy's camp, where they were met by British officials in relation to the camp, the number of gun salutes fired in their honour, the time of the entry into the durbar hall or tent, whether the viceroy would rise and come forward to greet them, where on the viceregal rug they would be saluted by the viceroy, where they would be seated, how much *nazar* they could give, whether they would be entitled to a visit from the viceroy, were all markers of rank and could be changed by the viceroy to raise or lower their rank. In correspondence with the viceroy, the forms of salutation, the kinds of Indian titles which the British would use and the phrases used in the conclusion of a letter were all graded, and were seen as marks of approval or approbation.

Similarly, the Indians who were under direct British rule were ordinarily ranked in their towns, districts, and provinces in the durbar books of various officials. The leading men of district were ranked on the basis of revenue paid, land held, ancestry of their families, acts of loyalty or disloyalty to the British government. Indian officials and employees of the imperial or provincial government were ranked by office, length of service and honours achieved, and the masses, by caste, community and religion.

Immediately after the suppression of the rebellion, and the establishment of the queen of England as the 'fountain of honour' for India, investigations were made into the system of Indian royal titles, with the goal of ordering them in a hierarchy. Not only was the system organized, but holders of titles had to 'prove' by criteria established by the British that their titles were legitimate. Henceforth only the viceroy could grant Indian titles, based on the recommendation of local or provincial officials. The basis of entitlement became specified by acts of loyalty, outstanding and long-term service in the government, special acts of charity such as endowing schools and hospitals, contributions to special funds and 'good' management of resources leading to the improvement of agricultural production. Indian entitlements were for the length of the life of the holder, although in some of the leading families there was the presumption that with demonstrated good behaviour by the successor to the headship of the family, he would in due course be rewarded by the renewal in the next generation of a title previously held. Honour and titles by the 1870s were closely tied to the expressed goals of the new governmental order, 'progress with stability'.

In 1861 a new royal order of Indian knights was established, the Star of India. At first this order, which included both Indian and British knights, was restricted to twenty-five members who were the most important Indian princes and senior and distinguished British civil and military officers. In 1866 the order was expanded by the addition of two lower ranks, and by 1877 there were several hundred holders of knighthoods in the order, which were personal, and granted by the queen. The investiture and holding of chapters of the order added an important European component to the ritual idiom which the British were establishing in India. The accoutrements of the order were English and 'feudal': a robe or mantle, a collar, a medallion with the effigy of the queen (the wearing of such a human effigy was anathema to Muslims) and a jewelled pendant. The investiture was in the European style, with the reading of the warrant and a presentation of the insignia, the newly entitled knight kneeling before the monarch or her representative. The contractual aspect of the entitlement was painfully clear to the Indian recipients as the accoutrements given had to be returned at the death of the holder. Unlike prestations received from Indian rulers in the past which were kept as sacred objects in treasure rooms to be viewed and used on special occasions, these had to be returned. The statutes of the order required the recipients to sign a bond that the valuables would be returned by their heirs. Indians also objected to one of the statutes which specified the conditions under which the knighthood could be rescinded for acts of disloyalty. The knighthoods became rewards for 'good service'.

The relationship between the crown and India was beginning to be marked by tours of India by members of the royal family, the first of these being the Duke of Edinburgh in 1869. The Prince of Wales went on a six month tour of India in 1875–6. The royal tours were not only significant in India in terms of the representation of the bond between the princes and peoples of India and their monarch, but were extensively reported in the British press. On the return of the Prince of Wales, exhibitions were held in major English cities of the exotic and expensive presents which he had received. Ironically, one of the major gifts which the Prince of Wales gave in return was an English translation of the Vedas by Max Müller.

The period of 1860 to 1877 saw a rapid expansion of what might be thought of as the definition and expropriation of Indian civilization by the imperial rulers. Colonial rule is based on forms of knowledge as much as it is based on institutions of direct control. From the founding by Sir William Jones and other European scholars in 1784 of the Asiatic Society of Bengal, there had been a steady development in the accumulation of knowledge about the history of India, its systems of thoughts, its religious beliefs and practices and its society and institutions. Much of this accumulation was the result of practical experience in law courts, in the assessment and collection of revenue and the attendant English imperative to order and classify information. Through this period more and more Europeans came to define what they thought of as the uniqueness of Indian civilization. This definition included the development of an apparatus for the study of Indian languages and texts, which had the effect of standardizing and making authoritative, not only for Europeans but for Indians themselves, what were thought to be the 'classics' of

Indian thought and literature. Through the encouragement of the production by Indians of school books, Indians began to write history in the European mode, often borrowing European ideas about the past of India. In the 1860s an archaeological survey was established, with Europeans deciding what were the great monuments of India, which monuments were fit for preservation or for description as part of the Indian 'heritage'. Census operations and the establishment of an ethnographic survey were to describe 'the peoples and cultures of India', to make them available in monographs, photographs and through statistical tabulations not only to their own officials but to social scientists so that India could be part of the laboratory of mankind. The British believed that Indian arts and crafts had entered a period of sharp decline in the face of western technology and machine-made products, hence their arts and crafts had to be collected, preserved and placed in museums. In addition, art schools were founded in major cities where Indians could be taught how to produce sculptures, paintings and craft products, Indian in content but appealing and acceptable to western tastes. Indian architectural builders began to construct European-style buildings, but with 'Oriental' decorative motifs. The imperial government established committees to search for and preserve Sanskrit, Persian, Arabic and vernacular language manuscripts. Educated Indians increasingly were to learn about their own culture through the mediation of European ideas and scholarship. The British rulers were increasingly defining what was Indian in an official and 'objective' sense. Indians had to look like Indians: before 1860 Indian soldiers as well as their European officers wore western-style uniforms; now the dress uniforms of Indians and English included turbans, sashes and tunics thought to be Mughal or Indian.

The reified and objectified vision of India, its life, thought, sociology and history were to be brought together to celebrate the completion of the political constitution of India, through the establishment of Victoria as empress of India.

THE ROYAL TITLES ACT OF 1876

On 8 February 1876, for the first time since the death of her husband in 1861, Queen Victoria opened parliament. Much to the surprise of the Liberal opposition, she announced in her speech that a bill would be introduced in parliament to add to her Royal Style and Titles. In her speech she referred to the 'hearty affection' with which her son, the Prince of Wales, then touring in India, was being received 'by My Indian Subjects'. This assured her that 'they are happy under My rule, and loyal to My throne'.[26] She therefore deemed it an appropriate time to make an addition to her Royal Style and Titles.

In a speech on 17 February 1876, the prime minister, Disraeli, reviewed the discussions of 1858 concerning the declaration of Victoria as empress of India. At that time it had been considered premature to make Victoria empress because of unsettled conditions in India. But, he continued, in the subsequent twenty years there had been growing interest about India in Great Britain. The Prince's visit had stimulated a mutual feeling of sympathy in these two countries, and Disraeli had been assured that an imperial title, the exact nature of which was unspecified, 'will give great satisfaction not merely to the Princes, but to the nations of India'.[27] It would signify 'the unanimous determination of the people of this country to retain our connection with the Indian Empire'.[28] Disraeli, in this speech, stressed the diversity of India, describing it as 'an ancient country of many nations', varying peoples and races, 'differing in religion, in manners and in laws – some of them highly gifted and civilized, and many of them of rare antiquity'. 'And this vast community is governed', he continued, 'under the authority of the Queen, by many Sovereign Princes, some of whom occupy Thrones which were filled by their ancestors when England was a Roman Province'.[29] The hyperbolic historical fantasy voiced by Disraeli was part of the myth later acted out in the Imperial Assemblage. India was diversity – it had no coherent communality except that given by British rule under the integrating system of the imperial crown.

Thus at the base of the Conservative defence of the bill was the idea that Indians were a different kind of people from the British. The Indians were more susceptible to high-sounding phrases, and would be better ruled by appeal to their Oriental imaginations, as 'they attach enormous value to very slight distinctions'.[30] It was argued that, given the constitutional relations between India and Great Britain, the Indian princes were indeed feudatories, and the ambiguity existing in the relationship of the princes to the British paramountcy would be reduced if the British monarch had a title of

---

[26] Hansard's *Parliamentary Debates* (3rd ser., ccxxvii, 1876), p. 4.
[27] *Ibid.*, p. 409.   [28] *Ibid.*, p. 410.
[29] *Ibid.*, p. 409.   [30] *Ibid.*, p. 1750.

'Emperor'. Although some Indian rulers were called 'Prince' in English, their titles in Indian languages were those of kings, for example Maharaja. With the imperial title, the hierarchic order would be clear cut and unequivocal. It was pointed out that Queen Elizabeth had used an imperial title, and that in practice, from Canning's time in India onwards, imperial titles were used to refer to the queen by princes and independent Asian rulers such as the Amirs of Central Asia. The claim was reiterated that the British were successors to the Mughals, who had an imperial crown which Indians of all status understood. The British, the Conservatives argued, were the successors of the Mughal; hence it was right and proper that India's monarch, Queen Victoria, should be declared empress.

The Royal Titles Act was passed, and received the royal assent on 27 April 1876. The need to overcome the acrimonious debate, the adverse newspaper coverage, especially as it found its way into Indian newspapers and was discussed by western-educated Indians, became part of the rationale for planning the Imperial Assemblage. The three principal designers of the assemblage, Disraeli, Salisbury (secretary of state for India) and Lord Lytton (the newly appointed viceroy), realized that the Imperial Assemblage must be designed to make an impact upon the British at home as well as upon Indians.

THE INTENTIONS OF THE PLANNERS OF THE IMPERIAL ASSEMBLAGE

Lord Lytton, the newly appointed viceroy and governor general, returned to England from Portugal, where he had been serving as ambassador, and by January 1876 had begun his effort to overcome his 'absolute ignorance...concerning India'. This effort included meetings in February with members of the Indian Office staff and others in London considered 'experts' on India. The most influential was O. T. Burne, who later accompanied Lytton to India as his private secretary and was regarded by Lytton as the originator of the plan for the assemblage.[31]

Lytton chose Burne to be his private secretary to 'help restore friendly and sound relations between India and Afghanistan and at the same time to proclaim the Indian Imperial title, both of which questions', Burne wrote, 'I was recognized as having a special

[31] Lytton to Salisbury, 12 Aug. 1876, I.O.L.R., E218/518/1, p. 367.

knowledge'.[32] As was true of most viceroys, Lytton came to India
with little knowledge of India or, perhaps more importantly, about
the workings of the government of the colony. Most of the highest
officials of the Raj rose through the ranks of the civil service, which
meant twenty to thirty years of experience and well-entrenched
relationships throughout the bureaucracy, as well as a highly developed capacity for political intrigue. Viceroys complained bitterly
about the frustrations in implementing their plans and policies,
dictated by political position in England. It fell to the viceroy's
private secretary to articulate the viceroy's office with the bureaucracy.
Questions of appointments, promotions, postings and honours
initially went through his hands. Viceroys were dependent on the
private secretary's knowledge of personal relationships and factions
within the bureaucracy, and their capacity to utilize viceregal power
effectively in relation to the civil service. After twenty years of
experience in various staff positions, Burne had a wide acquaintance
with officials in India, and because of his service in Ireland and
London was well-acquainted with leading politicians at home.

The planning of the Imperial Assemblage was started in secrecy
soon after the arrival of Lytton and of Burne in Calcutta in April
1876. A committee was established which included T. H. Thornton,
acting foreign secretary of the government of India who was to be
responsible for relations with the Indian princes and chiefs, and
Major General (later Field Marshal) Lord Roberts, quartermaster
general of the Indian army, who was in charge of the military
planning of the assemblage. Also on the committee was Colonel
George Colley, Lytton's military secretary, and Major Edward
Bradford of the political department, head of the recently established
secret police.

The president of the committee was Thomas Thornton, who had
served mainly in positions in the secretariat, having been secretary
to the Punjab government for twelve years before acting briefly as
foreign secretary. Major General Roberts, who had made a reputation
for himself as a logistics specialist, was in charge of planning the
camps in Delhi.[33] Lord Lytton was much impressed with Roberts's
abilities. It was because of his performance in planning the assemblage

---

[32] Major General Sir Owen Tudor Burne, *Memories* (London, 1907), p. 204, and
      passim for his career.
[33] Field-Marshal Lord Roberts of Kandahar, *Forty-one Years in India* (New York,
      1900), ii, pp. 91–2.

that he was selected for command of the British forces in Afghanistan, the keystone to Roberts's later career in India and England.[34]

The committee drew on the ideas and suggestions of a small and influential group of political officers, men who had served for many years as residents or agents of governor generals in the principal Indian courts. In the earliest stages of the work Major General Sir Henry Dermot Daly, about whom Lytton wrote 'there is universal consensus of opinion that there is no man in India who knows how to manage Native Princes as well as Daly',[35] seems to have been part of the group. Daly argued that holding a durbar with all the major princes represented would be impossible because of the jealousies and susceptibilities of the chiefs.[36] The view held by most of the political experts was that 'Questions of precedence and slumbering claims of various kinds would infallibly arise, and heart burnings and umbrage and even more serious difficulties would ensue'.[37] Lytton tried to dissolve the opposition of the political officers by quietly ignoring them, and by insisting that the meeting in Delhi was not to be a durbar but rather an 'Imperial Assemblage'. Thus in particular, he hoped that the question of precedence would not arise, and, by carefully controlling the visits with the princes, to avoid discussing various territorial claims.[38]

By the end of July 1876, the committee had finished its preliminary planning. The plan was divulged to the viceroy's council, and an outline forwarded to London for the approval of Salisbury and of Disraeli. At this stage, and into August, strict secrecy was maintained, for Lytton feared that early announcement of the plan would lead to an outcry in the Indian press – European and Indian – about details of the plan, and that there would follow a debate as 'unseemly' as that which had marked the Royal Titles Act.

Lytton expected to accomplish a great deal with the assemblage. He hoped it would conspicuously 'place the Queen's authority upon the ancient throne of the Moguls, with which the imagination and tradition of [our] Indian subjects associate the splendour of supreme

---

[34] O. T. Burne, 'The Empress of India', *Asiatic Quarterly Review*, iii (1887), p. 22.
[35] Lytton to Salisbury, 11 May 1875, I.O.L.R., E218/518/1, p. 147.
[36] *Ibid.*, p. 149.
[37] L. A. Knight, in his article, 'The Royal Titles Act and India', *Historical Journal* xi, no. 3 (1968), pp. 488–507, details many of the current claims to territories and grievances which were felt might surface at the durbar; T. H. Thornton, *General Sir Richard Meade* (London, 1898), p. 310.
[38] Lytton to Salisbury, 11 May 1876, I.O.L.R., E218/518/1, p. 149.

power!'[39] Hence the decision was made to hold the assemblage at Delhi, the Mughal capital, rather than in Calcutta. At this time Delhi was a relatively small city recovering from the destruction of the rebellion of 1857. The population of the city was treated as a conquered people. One of the 'concessions' announced on behalf of the queen at the assemblage was the reopening of Zinat ul Musajid, long closed on 'military grounds' for public worship, and the restoration to the Muslims of Delhi of the Fatepuri Mosque in Chandi Chowk, which had been confiscated in 1857.[40]

The selection of Delhi as the site also avoided associating the crown with a distinctly regional centre such as Calcutta or Bombay. Delhi had the advantage of being in a relatively central location, even though the facilities available for a gathering of large numbers were limited. The location of the assemblage was related to British rather than Mughal Delhi, as the site selected was not the large Maidan in front of the Red Fort (which had been cleared and which today is the political ritual centre of India), but one near the ridge on sparsely settled ground which had been the scene of the great British victory of the Mutiny. The British camp was located on the ridge and to the east going down to the Jamuna river.

The assemblage was to be an occasion to raise the enthusiasm of 'the native aristocracy of the country, whose sympathy and cordial allegiance is no inconsiderable guarantee for the stability...of the Indian Empire'.[41] Lytton was striving to develop strong ties between this 'aristocracy' and the crown. He believed that India would never be held by 'good government' alone, that is, by improving the condition of the *ryot* (agriculturalist), strictly administering justice, and spending huge sums on irrigation works.

The assumed special susceptibility of the Indian to parade and show and the key position of the aristocracy were the defining themes of the assemblage, which was, Lytton wrote, to have an effect also on 'public opinion' in Great Britain, and would act as a support for the Conservative government in England. Lytton hoped that a successful assemblage, well reported in the press, and displaying the loyalty of the Indian princes and peoples, would be evidence of the wisdom of the Royal Titles Act.

[39] Lytton to Queen Victoria, 21 April 1876, I.O.L.R., E218/518/1.
[40] I.O.L.R., Political and Secret Letters from India, Jan. and Feb. 1877, no. 24, para. 20.
[41] Lytton to Queen Victoria, 4 May 1876, I.O.L.R., E218/518/1.

Lytton wanted the assemblage to bind the British official and unofficial communities in India closer together in support of the government. This expectation was not achieved by the assemblage. The governors of both Madras and Bombay advised against holding the assemblage, and for a time it appeared that the governor of Bombay might not even attend. He argued that there was a famine in Bombay and he was needed there; any cost to the central government or the presidency attendant upon participation would be better spent to alleviate the famine. Both governors complained about the disruption caused by having to leave their governments for two weeks with large numbers of their staff to attend the assemblage.

Many British in India, official and unofficial, and several influential British papers saw the assemblage as part of a policy of elevating the 'blacks', and paying too much attention to the Indians, because most concessions and acts of grace were directed towards Indians. Lytton wrote that he faced 'practical difficulties of satisfying the European element, which is disposed to be querlesome and avoiding the difficulty of favouring the conquered more than the conquering race'.[42]

The opposition to the plans in London and India was so strong that Lytton wrote to Queen Victoria,

If the Crown of England should ever have the misfortune to lose the great and magnificent empire of India, it will not be through the disaffection of your Majesty's native subjects, but through party spirit at home, and the disloyalty and insubordination of those members of Your Majesty's Indian Service, whose duty it is to cooperate with the Government... in the disciplined and loyal execution of its orders.[43]

COLONIAL SOCIOLOGY AND THE ASSEMBLAGE

In analytical terms the goal of the assemblage was to make manifest and compelling the sociology of India. The invitees were selected in relation to ideas which the British rulers had about the proper social order in India. Although emphasis was placed on the princes as feudal rulers and 'the natural aristocracy', the assemblage was also to include other categories of Indians, 'native gentlemen', 'landlords', 'editors and journalists' and 'representative men' of various kinds.

[42] Lytton to Salisbury, 30 Oct. 1876, *ibid.*
[43] Lytton to Queen Victoria, 15 Nov. 1876, *ibid.*

In the 1870s a contradiction in the British theory of Indian sociology had become apparent. Some members of the British ruling group viewed India in historical terms as a feudal society consisting of lords, chiefs and peasants. Other British saw India as a changing society which was composed of communities. These communities could be large and somewhat amorphous, such as Hindu/Muslim/Sikh/ Christian/Animist; they could be vaguely regional, such as Bengali or Gujarati; they could be castes such as Brahmans, Rajputs, Baniyas; or communities could be based on educational and occupational criteria, that is, westernized Indians. Those English rulers who saw India as made up of communities sought to control them through identifying the 'representative men', leaders who were thought to speak for, and who could shape responses from, their communities.

According to the feudal theory, there was a 'native aristocracy' in India. Lytton, in order to define and regulate this aristocracy, planned the establishment of a privy council and a College of Arms in Calcutta. The privy council was to be purely consultative, summoned by the viceroy 'who would keep the machinery completely under his own control'.[44] Lytton's intention was to arrange the constitution of the privy council 'to enable the Viceroy, whilst making parade of consulting native opinion to swamp the native members, and still secure the prestige of their presence and assent'.[45] The plan for a privy council for India quickly encountered constitutional problems and opposition from the council of India in London. A parliamentary act was necessary to establish such a body, and parliament was not sitting through the summer and autumn of 1876. The result, announced at the assemblage, was the naming of twenty 'Counsellors of the Empress', for the purpose of 'seeking from time to time, in matters of importance, the counsel and advice of Princes and Chiefs of India, and thus associating them with the Paramount Power'.[46]

The College of Arms in Calcutta was to be the Indian equivalent of the British College of Arms in London, which would in effect establish and order a 'peerage' for India. Indian titles had been a vexing question for the British rulers of India since the early nineteenth century. There appeared to the English to be no fixed lineally ordered hierarchy or any common system of titles, such as

---

[44] Lytton to Salisbury, 30 July 1876, *ibid.*, p. 318.
[45] *Ibid.*, p. 319.
[46] *Gazette of India*, Extraordinary, 1 Jan. 1877, p. 11.

the British were familiar with in their own society. What were thought to be royal titles, such as Raja, Maharaja, Nawab or Bahadur, seemed to be used randomly by Indians, and were not attached to actual control of territory or office, or a hierarchical system of status distinctions.

Coordinated with the establishment of the College of Arms was a plan to present at the Imperial Assemblage ninety of the leading Indian princes and chiefs with large banners emblazoned with their coats of arms. These banners were shield-shaped in the European mode. The crests were also European, with the heraldic devices derived from the history of the particular royal house. The representations of 'history' on the crests included the mythic origins of the families, events connecting the houses to Mughal rule and, particularly, aspects of the past which tied the Indian princes and chiefs to English rule.

The banners were presented at the Imperial Assemblage to attending Indian princes. These presentations were substituted for the former Mughal practice of exchange of *nazar* (gold coins) and *peshkash* (precious possessions) for *khelats* (robes of honour) which marked previous British durbar practice. By eliminating what had been rituals of incorporation, the British completed the process of redefinition of the relationship between ruler and ruled begun in the middle of the eighteenth century. What had been a system of authority based upon the incorporation of subordinates to the person of the emperor now was an expression of linear hierarchic order in which the presentation of a silk banner made the Indian princes the legal subjects of Queen Victoria. In the British conception of the relationship, Indian princes became English knights and should be obedient and offer fealty to the empress.

Lytton was aware that some of the more experienced and hard-headed officials, who had served in India and were now members of the secretary of state for India's council, would see the presentation of the banners and the establishment of the College of Arms as 'trivial and silly'.[47] Lytton thought this response would be a great mistake. 'Politically speaking', Lytton wrote, 'the Indian peasantry is an inert mass. If it ever moves at all it will move in obedience, not to its British benefactors, but to its native chiefs and princes, however tyrannical they may be'.[48]

[47] Lytton to Salisbury, 11 May 1876, I.O.L.R., E218/518/1, p. 149.
[48] *Ibid.*

The other possible political representatives of 'native opinion' were what Lytton scornfully referred to as the 'Baboos', who had been taught to write 'semi-seditious articles in the Native Press, and who represent nothing but the social anomaly of own position'.[49] He felt that the Indian chiefs and princes were no mere noblesse, but 'a powerful aristocracy', whose complicity could be secured and efficiently utilized by the British in India. In addition to their power over the masses, the Indian aristocracy could be easily directed, if appealed to properly, as 'they are easily affected by sentiment and susceptible to the influence of symbols to which facts inadequately correspond'.[50] The British, Lytton continued, could gain 'their allegiance without giving up any of our power'.[51] To buttress his argument, Lytton referred to the British position in Ireland and especially the recent experience with Ionian Greeks, who, not withstanding the 'good government' which British rule gave them, enthusiastically surrendered all these advantages for what he termed 'a bit of bunting with the Greek colours on it'. He added, to underline his argument about the Indian aristocracy, 'the further East you go, the greater becomes the importance of a bit of bunting'.[52]

THE ENACTMENT OF THE COLONIAL SOCIOLOGY OF INDIA: THE INVITEES TO THE IMPERIAL ASSEMBLAGE

At centre stage, according to the designers of the assemblage, were the sixty-three ruling princes who appeared in Delhi. They were described by Lytton as ruling forty million people and holding territories larger than France, England and Italy.[53] The ruling chiefs and the three hundred 'titular chiefs and native gentlemen' who attended were seen as the 'flower of Indian Nobility'. Lord Lytton wrote:

Among them were the Prince of Arcot and the Princes of Tanjore from the Madras Presidency; the Maharajah Sir Jai Mangal Singh, and some of the principle Talukdars of Oudh; forty representatives of the most distinguished families of the North-Western Province, scions of the ex-Royal family of Delhi; descendants of the Saddozai of Cabul, and the Alora Chiefs of Sindh, Sikh Sardars

[49] *Ibid.*
[50] *Ibid.*, p. 150.
[51] *Ibid.*
[52] *Ibid.*
[53] I.O.L.R., Political and Secret Letters from India, Feb. 1877, no. 24, para. 5.

from Amritsar and Lahore, Rajputs from the Kangra Hills; the semi-independent Chief of Amb, on the Hazara border, envoys from Chitral and Yassin, who attended in the train of the Maharaja of Jammu and Chasmere; Arabs from Peshawar, Pata chiefs from Kohat and Derajat; Biluch Tommduis from Dera Ghazi Khan; leading citizens from Bombay; Gond and Mahratha nobles from the Central Provinces; Rajputs from Ajmere and natives of Burma, Central India, Mysore and Baroda.[54]

This litany of names, titles and places was for Lytton and the English the embodiment of the assemblage. The exotic names, the 'barbaric' titles and, above all, the elaborate variation in dress and appearance were constantly noted by English observers of the assemblage. The list of invitees included representatives of many of the dispossessed Indian royal families, such as the eldest son of the 'ex-King of Oudh', the grandson of Tipu Sultan, and members of the 'ex-Royal family of Delhi' (the House of the Mughal emperor). The presence of these descendants of the former great ruling houses of India imparted some of the flavour of a Roman triumph to the assemblage. The British conception of Indian history thereby was realized as a kind of 'living museum', with the descendants of both the enemies and the allies of the English displaying the period of the conquest of India. The 'rulers' and 'ex-rulers' were fossilized embodiments of a past which the British conquerors had created in the late eighteenth and early nineteenth centuries. All of this 'history' was brought together in Delhi, to announce, enhance and glorify British authority as represented by the person of their monarch.[55]

The conjunction of past and present was proclaimed in the first official announcement of the Imperial Assemblage, when it was stated that among those to be invited would be 'those Princes, chiefest and nobles in whose persons the *ambiguity of the past* is associated with the prosperity of the present'.[56] Indians from all parts of the empire and even some Asians from beyond the boundaries were seen in their diversity as a statement of the need for British imperial rule. The Viceroy, standing for the empress, represented the only authority which could hold together the great diversity inherent in the 'colonial sociology'. The unity of empire was literally seen as

[54] *Ibid.*
[55] For a listing of the major invitees, see *ibid.*, encs. 1 and 2.
[56] *Gazette of India*, Extraordinary, 18 Aug. 1876.

that provided by the super-ordinate and heaven-blessed British rulers of India. The diversity was mentioned frequently in the speeches which were a feature of the ten days of assemblage activities. At the state Banquet before the assemblage, with a mixed audience of Indians in their 'native costumes' and British in their frock coats and uniforms, Lytton proclaimed that if one wanted to know the meaning of the imperial title, all they had to do was 'to look around' and see an empire 'multitudinous in its traditions, as well as in its inhabitants, almost infinite in the variety of races which populate it, and of the creeds which have shaped their character'.[57]

The colonial sociology of India was by no means fixed and rigidly ranked and ordered. The classificatory system was based on multiple criteria, which varied through time and from region to region of India. At the base of the classification were two kinds of criteria, one which the English rulers believed was 'natural', such as caste, race and religion, and the other, social criteria which could include achievement, education – both western and Indian, the financing of works of public utility, acts of loyalty performed on behalf of their English rulers and the family history seen as descent and genealogy. What the English thought of as the 'natural aristocracy' of India were at times contrasted with the category of 'native gentlemen' whose status was based on their actions (social criteria) rather than their descent (natural criteria).

Most of the twenty-two Indians who were invited by the Bengal government as 'native gentlemen' were large landholders, controlling extensive estates, such as Hatwa, Darbangha and Dumroan in Bihar, or men such as Jai Mangal Singh of Monghyr who had performed loyal service during the Santhal 'Rebellion' and the Sepoy 'Mutiny'.[58]

The Madras contingent of 'nobles and native gentlemen' was led by descendants of two deposed rulers: the prince of Arcot and the daughter of the last Maharaja of Tanjore. In addition to large landholders of Madras presidency, the Indian members of the Madras legislative council and two Indian lower civil servants were among the official guests. The Bombay contingent of 'nobles and native gentlemen' was the most diverse, and was apparently selected

[57] I.O.L.R., Political and Secret Letters from India, Feb. 1877, no. 24, enc. 11, 'Speech of Lord Lytton at State Banquet'.
[58] I.O.L.R., Political and Secret Letters from India, Jan. and Feb. 1877, no. 24, enc. 2.

for representative qualities. The city of Bombay sent two Parsis, one of whom, Sir Jamesetji Jajeebhoy, was the only Indian at the time to have an hereditary English knighthood, and had been declared by the English government head of the Bombay Parsi community. In addition, there was a leading merchant, thought to be the 'representative member of the Mahommedan community', a government pleader from the Bombay high court, and another successful lawyer. In terms of the 'communities' of cosmopolitan Bombay, there were two Parsis, two Marathas, a Gujarati and a Muslim. From the rest of the presidency came several large landholders, a judge of small claims court, a deputy collector, a professor of mathematics from the Deccan college, and the oriental translator to the Bombay government.[59]

LOGISTICS AND THE PHYSICAL PLANNING: THE CAMPS, THE AMPHITHEATRE AND DECORATIVE MOTIFS

By the end of September 1876 guest lists were drawn up and official invitations were sent. Planning now shifted to the actual physical arrangements for the assemblage, the location and preparation of the sites of the camps, which were to provide living accommodation for over 84,000 people, who were to converge on Delhi late in December. The camps were spread in a semi-circle of five miles, taking the Delhi railway station as the starting point. Preparation of the site required the clearing of one hundred villages, whose lands were rented and whose cultivators were prevented from planting their winter crops. Considerable work was involved in developing a road network, water supplies, establishing several bazaars and proper sanitary facilities. As always with a large gathering of Indians in the nineteenth century, the British were greatly concerned about the possibility of an epidemic breaking out, and extensive medical precautions were taken. Labour had to be recruited, much of which came from the peasants in the villages which were dislocated by the utilization of their fields for the camps. Actual preparation for the building of the camp sites began on 15 October, with Major General Roberts in overall charge.

The Indian rulers who were invited were instructed to bring their tents and equipage; railway schedules had to be worked out to transport the thousands of retainers and animals that accompanied

[59] *Ibid.*

the rulers. Strict limits were put on the number of followers who could accompany their masters. The number of retainers allowed to each chief was based on their gun salutes, with those honoured by seventeen and above being allowed five hundred; those with fifteen allowed four hundred; eleven, three hundred; nine, two hundred and those 'feudatories' without salutes were allowed one hundred.[60] The planners estimated that the Indian rulers and their retinues would total 25,600, but, after the event, it was estimated that there were 50,741 Indians in their own camps, 9,741 Indians in the imperial camps, as clerks, servants and followers, and another 6,438 in the 'miscellaneous camps', such as those of the police, post and telegraph, the imperial bazaar, and visitors.[61] Excluding the camps of the troops – approximately fourteen thousand in number – attending the assemblage, there were eight thousand tents erected in and around Delhi to house the guests. Overall, there were at least eighty-four thousand people attending the assemblage, of whom 1,169 were Europeans.

The central imperial camp stretched for a mile and a half, by half a mile wide, on the flats abutting the north-eastern side of the Delhi ridge and covered the grounds of the pre-Mutiny military cantonment. The viceroy's canvas camp complex faced the main road, so that there would be easy access for the great numbers of visitors, European and Indian, whom he would receive in audience. Wheeler, the official historian of the assemblage, described the viceroy's tents as 'canvas houses' and 'the pavilion' – the enormous Durbar tent – as 'a Palace'.[62] In this tent the viceroy held court, sitting on the viceregal chair on a raised platform, at the back of which was hung a painting of a stern visaged, black attired Queen Victoria, surveying the proceedings. In front of him stretched the huge viceregal rug, with the coat of arms of the imperial Indian government. Chairs were arranged on the rug in a rough semi-circle for members of his staff, and the important retainers of the chief who were to come to pay homage to the newly proclaimed Empress and her viceroy. In ranks around the wall of the viceregal tent stood mare and yak tail whisk bearers, dressed in the livery of the viceregal household, and down

---

[60] I.O.L.R., Imperial Assemblage Proceedings 8, 15 Sept. 1876, Temple Papers, Euro. MSS. F86/166.

[61] Figures are given in I.O.L.R., Political and Secret Letters from India, 6 Aug. 1877, no. 140, enc. 8.

[62] J. Talboys Wheeler, *The History of the Imperial Assemblage at Delhi* (London, 1877), p. 47.

the sides of the tent behind the chairs were European and Indian troopers. The whole scene was brilliantly lit by gas lamps.

Camped immediately to the right of the viceroy was the governor of Bombay, and to his left the governor of Madras; there then followed the camps of the lieutenant governors. At the south-east end of the imperial camp, adjoining those of the viceroy and the governor of Madras, were the camps of the commander-in-chief of the Indian army and the commanders of the Madras and Bombay armies. These had their own entrances and were almost as large as the camps of the viceroy. At the back of the camps of the viceroy, the governors and lieutenant governors were those of the chief commissioners, the resident of Hyderabad and the agents to the governor general for Central India, Baroda and Rajputtana. Access to these latter was by internal roads as they did not face outwards on to the plains.

Scattered around the plains from a distance of one to five miles were the camps of the Indians, organized regionally. On the eastern side of the ridge, on the flood plain of the Jumna river and closest to the imperial camp, were those of the Nizam of Hyderabad, the Gaekwar of Baroda and the Maharajah of Mysore. These were the 'Special Native Camps'. To the front of the imperial camp were those of the Central Indian chiefs, with the camp of Maharajah Sindhia of Gwalior closest to that of the viceroy. Two and a half miles to the south were the camps of the chiefs of Bombay Northwest Province and the Central Province. Strung along the west and the south walls of the city of Delhi were the Punjab chiefs, with pride of place being given to the Maharajah of Kashmir, who, at a distance of two miles, was the closest to the imperial camp. The Rajputana chiefs were camped five miles along the Gurgoan Road, due south of the imperial camp. Five and a half miles along the Kootub Road were the camps of the Oudh Talukdars. The Bengal and the Madras nobles were within a mile of the main camp.

There was a marked contrast between the layouts of the European and the Indian camps. The European camps were well ordered, with straight streets and neat rows of tents on each side. Grass and flowers were laid out to impart the touch of England which the British carried with them all over India. The plants were supplied by the Botanical Gardens at Saharanpur and Delhi. In the Indian camps, spaces were provided for each ruler who was then left to arrange his camp in his own fashion. To the European eye, the Indian camps were cluttered and disorganized, with cooking fires seemingly placed at random, and with a jumble of people, animals and carts impeding easy movement. Nonetheless, most European observers commented on how vibrant and colourful the Indian camps were.[63]

The contrast between the imperial camp and the other camps was not lost on some of the Indians. Sir Dinkar Rao, who was Sindhia's *dewan* (prime minister), commented to one of Lytton's aides:

> If any man would understand why it is that the English are, and must necessarily remain the master of India he need only go up to Flagstaff Tower [highest point overlooking the camps] and look down upon this marvellous camp. Let him notice the method, the order, the cleanliness, the discipline, the perfection of the whole organization and he will recognize at once the epitome of every title to command and govern which one race can possess over others.[64]

There is much hyperbole, and perhaps some self interest, in Sir Dinkar Rao's statement; however, it effectively points to one of the main things which Lytton and his associates wanted to accomplish through the assemblage, which was to represent the nature of British rule as they conceived it, and this was what the camp represented in their own ruling theory: order and discipline, which was in their ideology part of the whole system of colonial control.

THE AMPHITHEATRE AND PRECEDENCE

From the inception of the planning, the question of the seating arrangements for the Indian rulers was seen as the most crucial single question on which the success of the Imperial Assemblage would rest. As we have seen, the problems of precedence which, in the opinion of experts like Daly, bedevilled a durbar had to be avoided. Its terminological transformation into an assemblage allowed Lytton to do this. He insisted that the assemblage would not resemble a durbar 'in its arrangements or ceremonies, of any of the meetings customarily so called',[65] as the actual ritual to proclaim the new title would not be 'under canvas' but in 'the open plain thereby freeing it from questions of precedence, exchange of presents and other impedimentia of an ordinary durbar'.[66] The planners of the assemblage hit

---

[63] Wheeler, *op. cit.*, p. 47.

[64] Quoted in Lady Betty Balfour, *The History of Lord Lytton's Administration, 1876–1880* (London, 1899), p. 123.

[65] Lytton, 'Memorandum', I.O.L.R., Imperial Assemblage Proceedings 8, 15 Sept. 1876, Temple Papers, Euro. MSS. F86/166, para. 16.   [66] *Ibid.*

upon a unique solution to the seating arangements for the Imperial Assemblage. It was decided that the princes would be seated in a semi-circular grandstand, by their regional groupings from north to south. The viceroy would be seated on a dais, on his viceregal chair, and with only members of his immediate staff and family group around him. The dais was placed in such a fashion that all the Indians, at least in the first row, would be equidistant from the person of the viceroy. Hence none could claim to have superiority over their fellow chiefs. The grandstand was to be divided by province or agency, with the exception of the Gaekwar of Baroda, the Nizam of Hyderabad and the Maharaja of Mysore, who would be in a special section in the centre of the seats. Each of the major geographic sections had a separate entrance, and as the precedence for each of the geographic units was fairly well worked out, there wouldn't arise, the planners thought, the question of cross-regional precedence. There was a separate road providing access to the entrances, and timing of the entries prescribed. European officials were to sit intermixed amongst the Indians, for example the lieutenant governor of Punjab with the Punjab princes and notables, the agent general for Rajputana and the various residents amongst the chiefs from that region. Lytton wrote

> the Chiefs do not so much object to be seated in groups of their own nationalities and province, as to be mixed up and classified with those of other provinces, as in a Durbar. Each chief would proceed from his camp to the Dais assigned to him in a separate elephant procession, in time to receive the Viceroy.[67]

In addition to the pavilion for the seating of the grandees, two large grandstands were erected obliquely facing it for retainers and other visitors. Large numbers of soldiers from the Indian army and princes' armies stood in semi-circular ranks facing the pavilion, as did servants and other Indians. Interspersed with the onlookers were large numbers of elephants and horses with their grooms and *mahouts* (riders).

To emphasize the uniqueness of the event the planners developed an overall design motif which could be termed 'Victorian Feudal'. Lockridge Kipling, Rudyard Kipling's father and director of the Lahore Art School, a minor pre-Raphaelite and to use his own

---

[67] *Ibid.*, para. 18; See also Thornton, *op. cit.*, app. to ch. 21, 'Note on the Arrangement of the Imperial Assemblage'.

description, a 'monumental ceramicist', was in overall charge of the designing of the uniforms and decorations for the assemblage.

A large dais for the viceroy was built facing the pavilion in the shape of a hexagon, each side being 40 feet long for a total of 220 feet around; its masonry base was 10 feet high. There was a broad flight of stairs leading to the platform on which was placed the viceregal throne. Over the dais was a large canopy. The shafts holding the canopy were festooned with laurel wreaths, imperial crowns, gargoyle-like eagles, banners displaying the Cross of St George and the Union Jack. There was a embroidered frieze hanging from the canopy displaying the Rose, Shamrock and Thistle with the Lotus of India. Also hanging from the shafts supporting the canopy were shields with the Irish Harp, the Lion Rampant of Scotland and the Three Lions of England. The 800 foot semi-circular pavilion in which the chiefs and high government officials were seated was decorated with fleurs-de-lis and gilded lances, the supporters of the canvas, displaying the imperial crown. Along the back posts were mounted the large silken banners with the coats of arms of the princes and chiefs. Not all observers of the scene were impressed. Val Prinsep, a painter who had been commissioned to paint a picture of the scene, which was to be a collective present from the princes to their new empress, was aghast by what was thought to be a display of bad taste. On seeing the site he wrote:

Oh Horror! What have I to paint? A kind of thing that out does the Crystal Palace in hideosity... [it] is all iron, gold, red, blue and white... The Viceroy's dais is a kind of scarlet temple 80 feet high. Never was such a brummagem ornament, or more atrocious taste.[68]

He continued:

They have been heaping ornament on ornament, colour on colour. [The viceregal dais] is like the top of a twelfth cake. They have stuck pieces of needlework into stone panels and tin shields and battle axes all over the place. The size [of the whole collection of structures] gives it a vast appearance like a gigantic circus and the decorations are in keeping.[69]

[68] Val C. Prinsep, *Imperial India: An Artist's Journal* (London, 1879), p. 20.
[69] *Ibid.*, p. 29.

THE IMPERIAL ASSEMBLAGE

On 23 December, all was in readiness for the arrival of the central figure of the Imperial Assemblage, the viceroy, Lord Lytton. The eighty-four thousand Indians and Europeans had occupied their far-flung camps, the roads were laid out and the site was complete. The activities of the assemblage were to last for two weeks; the purpose being to mark Queen Victoria's accession to her imperial title as 'Kaiser-i-Hind'. The title was suggested by G. W. Leitner, professor of Oriental Languages and principal of the Government College in Lahore. Leitner was a Hungarian by birth and began his career as an Orientalist, linguist and interpreter with the English army during the Crimean War. He was educated at Constantinople, Malta, King's College, London, obtained a Ph.D. from the University of Fribourg and was a lecturer in Arabic and Turkish, professor of Arabic and Muhammadan Law at King's College, London before going to Lahore in 1864.[70] Leitner argued that the term 'Kaiser' was well known to the natives of India, having been used by Muhammadan writers in relation to the Roman Caesar, and therefore the ruler of the Byzantine empire should be known as 'Kaiser-i-Rum'. In the present circumstance of the British ruler in India it was appropriate, Leitner thought, as it neatly combined the Roman 'Caesar', German 'Kaiser' and Russian 'Czar' imperial titles. In the Indian context it would be unique, and would not run the risk of being mispronounced by Indians as would the title empress, nor would it associate British rule with such exhausted titles as 'Shah', 'Padishah' or 'Sultan'. It avoided the overt association of the title with either Hindu or Muslim titles.[71]

Lord Lytton had suggested to Lord Salisbury in late July 1876, on either his or Burne's reading of Leitner's pamphlet, that 'Kaiser-i-Hind', was 'thoroughly familiar to the Oriental mind', and 'widely recognized' in India and Central Asia as 'the symbol of Imperial power'. In addition, the title was the same in Sanskrit and Arabic, 'sonorous' and not 'hackneyed or monopolized by any Crown since the Roman Caesars'. Lytton left it to Salisbury to make the final decision on the question of the queen's Indian title.[72] Salisbury agreed

[70] G. W. Leitner, *Kaiser-i-Hind: The Only Appropriate Translation of the Title of the Empress of India* (Lahore, 1876), pp. 11–12.

[71] *Ibid.*, p. 9.

[72] Lytton to Salisbury, 30 July 1876, I.O.L.R., E218/515, pp. 321–2.

to the use of Kaiser-i-Hind and it was duly announced officially in *The Times* of 7 October 1876. The title drew criticism as being obscure from the distinguished Orientalist R. C. Caldwell, and Mir Aulad Ali, professor of Arabic and Urdu at Trinity College, Dublin, thought it was 'preposterous' as it formed 'the picture of a European lady, attired partly in the Arab, partly in the Persian garment peculiar to men, and wearing upon her head an Indian turban'.[73]

Lytton's arrival in the Delhi railway station was the official commencement of the assemblage. He descended with his wife and two young daughters and his immediate official party from the railway car, gave a brief speech of welcome to assembled Indian rulers and high government officials, briskly shook hands with some of those assembled, and then moved off to mount a train of waiting elephants.

Lord and Lady Lytton rode in a silver houdah, created for the Prince of Wales's visit the year before, mounted on the back of what was purported to be the largest elephant in India, owned by the Rajah of Banaras.

The procession, led by troops of cavalry, moved through the city of Delhi to the Red Fort, circled around the Jama Masjid and then proceeded towards the north-west to the camps on the ridge. The procession route was lined by Indian army soldiers, Indian and British, interspersed between whom were contingents from the princely state armies, outfitted in their 'medieval' armour and bearing Indian weapons. Lytton commented that these native soldiers present 'a most striking and peculiar appearance...a vivid and varied display of strange arms, strange uniforms, and strange figures'.[74]

The procession took three hours to move through the city to the camps. As the viceroy, his party and other British officials passed, some of the retainers of the Indian princes fell in behind the official party. However, none of the attending princes or Indian notables rode in the procession. As was to be their role throughout, they were there as recipients of largesse and honour given them by their empress, and to be spectators to the British acting on her behalf as the Indian monarch.

---

[73] *Athenaeum*, no. 2559 (11 Nov. 1876), pp. 624–5; no. 2561 (25 Nov. 1876), pp. 688–9.

[74] Lytton to Queen Victoria, I.O.L.R., Letters Despatched to the Queen, 12 Dec. 1876 to 1 Jan. 1877, E218/515/2.

The week between Lord Lytton's arrival and grand entry and the day of the assembly held for the reading of the actual proclamation of Victoria's ascension to the imperial throne on 1 January 1877, was taken up with audiences given by Lytton to leading chiefs, various receptions and dinners for distinguished visitors and participants. In all Lytton gave 120 audiences in his time in Delhi, including return visits to many of the princes, and received several delegations offering petitions and loyal addresses for the new empress.[75]

The most important of these meetings were the ones held for the princes in the viceroy's reception tent. A prince would appear at an appointed time accompanied by some of his retinue. On entry, depending on his precise status, he would be greeted by the viceroy, who would then present him with 'his' coat of arms embroidered and fixed on a large silken standard. The armorial bearings of the Indian rulers were designed by Robert Taylor, a Bengal civil servant and amateur heraldist. Taylor had first designed coats of arms for Indian rulers on the occasions of the visits of the Duke of Edinburgh in 1869 and the Prince of Wales in 1876. Lord Lytton now decided that in addition to those which Taylor had already created, another eighty were to be created.

The devices which Taylor created related to his conception of the mythic origins of the various ruling houses, their identification with particular gods or goddesses, events in their history, topographic features of their territories, or they incorporated some ancestral emblem associated with a ruling house or even a group of houses. Most of the arms of the Rajputs bore the sun to symbolize their descent from Rama. The Sikh chiefs of the Punjab all had a boar on their banners. The background colour of the device could also be used to denote regional groups of chiefs, some had particular trees or plants which had sacred significance for a particular house. Even events of the Mutiny were represented if they indicated loyalty to the British. At times Taylor's imagination seemed to run out. Kashmir, a buffer state created by the British in 1854 by the installation of a Maharaja over territories held previously by a number of other rulers, had to be satisfied by three wavy lines representing the three ranges of the Himalayas, and three roses to represent the beauty of the Vale of Kashmir. The armorial bearings were embroidered on large silk standards, 5 ft by 5 ft, in the Roman style; Indian banners, which are silk streamers, were not thought to be the right shape to

[75] Thornton, *op. cit.*, p. 305.

bear the arms of the new feudal nobility.[76] In addition to the gift of the banner and the coat of arms, the most important of the Indian rulers were presented with a large gold medallion which was worn from a ribbon around their necks. Lesser chiefs received silver medallions as did hundreds of lower civil servants and soldiers, Indian and British.

Not all went smoothly with the presentation of the banners and medallions; the banners proved to be very awkward and hard to handle because of the weight of the brass poles and the fixtures on them, and it wasn't clear to the Indians what should be done with them. It was thought they might be used in processions by fixing them to the backs of elephants. One British Army officer, who was presenting the silver medallions to several of his Indian troopers in Urdu, was not up to the task of conveying their significance to his men. He addressed his troops as follows 'Suwars [pigs – he meant sowar, the Urdu word for trooper], your Empress has sent you a billi [cats – he meant billa, a medallion] for you to wear around your necks'.[77] The presentations which were from the empress were meant to replace the giving of khelats and obviate the presentation of nazar, the gold coins. It is significant that the major present was a representation of the British version of the Indian rulers' pasts as represented in their coats of arms.

At noon on 1 January 1877, all was in readiness for the entry of the viceroy into the amphitheatre. The princes and other notables were all seated in their sections, the spectators' grandstand filled, and thousands of Indian and European troops were drawn up in ranks. The viceroy and his small party, including his wife, rode into the amphitheatre to the 'March from Tannhäuser'. As they got down from the carriage six trumpeters, attired in medieval costume, blew a fanfare. The viceroy then mounted to his throne to the strains of the National Anthem. The chief herald, described as the tallest English officer in the Indian army, read the queen's proclamation which announced that henceforth there would be the addition of 'Empress of India' to her Royal Styles and Titles.

A translation of the proclamation of the new title was read in Urdu by T. H. Thornton, the foreign secretary of the government of India.

---

[76] R. Taylor, *The Princely Armory Being a Display for the Arms of the Ruling Chiefs of India after their Banners as Prepared for the Imperial Assemblage held at Delhi on the First Day of January, 1877*, I.O.L.R. typescript; and *Pioneer Mail*, 4 Nov. 1904 (clipping bound with Taylor, *Princely Armory* in I.O.L.R.).

[77] Burne, *Memories*, pp. 42–3.

Then a salute of 101 salvos was fired and the assembled troops fired *feux-de-joie*. The noise of the cannon and rifle fire stampeded the assembled elephants and horses; a number of bystanders were killed and injured, and a large cloud of dust was raised which hung over the rest of the proceedings.

Lytton made a speech in which, as was common in the speeches of viceroys on major occasions, he stressed the fulfilment of their empress's promise in her proclamation of 1 November 1858 of the achievement of a 'progressive prosperity' combined with the undisturbed enjoyment, on the part of the princes and peoples of India, 'of their hereditary honours', and the protection 'of their lawful interests'.

The historic basis of British authority in India was created by 'Providence' which had called upon the crown 'to replace and improve upon the rule of good and great Sovereigns', but whose successors failed

> to secure the internal peace of their dominions. Strife became chronic and anarchy constantly recurrent. The weak were the prey of the strong, and the strong the victims of their own passions.

The rule of the successors of the House of Tamerlane, Lytton continued, 'had ceased to be conductive of the progress of the East'. Now, under British rule, all 'creeds and races' were protected and guided by 'the strong hand of Imperial power' which had led to rapid advance and 'increasing prosperity'.

Lytton then referred to the proper codes of conduct for the constituent components of the empire. He first referred to 'the British Administrators and Faithful Officers of the Crown', who were thanked in the name of the empress for their 'great toil for the good of the Empire', and their 'persevering energy, public virtue, and self devotion, unsurpassed in history'. In particular, 'the district officers' were singled out for their patient intelligence and courage on which the efficient operation of the whole system of administration was dependent. All the members of the civil and military services were gratefully recognized by their queen for their capacity to 'uphold the high character of your race, and to carry out the benign precepts of your religion'. Lytton told them that they were 'conferring on all the other creeds and races in this country the inestimable benefits of good government'. The non-official European community were complimented for the benefits which India had received 'from their enterprise, industry, social energy and civic virtue'.

The princes and chiefs of the empire were thanked by the viceroy on behalf of their empress for their loyalty and their past willingness to assist her government 'if attacked or menaced', and it was to 'unite the British Crown and its feudatories and allies that Her Majesty had been graciously pleased to assume the Imperial title'.

The 'native subjects of the Empress of India' were told by their viceroy that 'the permanent interests of this Empire demand the supreme supervision and direction of their administration by English officers' who must 'continue to form the most important practical channel through which the arts, the sciences and the culture of the West...may freely flow to the East'. This assertion of English superiority notwithstanding, there was a place for the 'natives of India' to share in the administration 'of the country you inhabit'. However, appointment to the higher public service should not only go to those with 'intellectual qualifications' but must also include those who are 'natural leaders', 'by birth, rank and hereditary influence', that is, the feudal aristocracy, which was being 'created' at the assemblage.

The viceroy concluded his speech by reading a telegraphic message from 'The Queen, your Empress' who assured all assembled of her affection. 'Our rule', she cabled, was based on the great principles of liberty, equity, and justice, 'which would promote their happiness' and add to their 'prosperity and advance their welfare'.[78]

The conclusion of the viceroy's speech was greeted by loud cheering, and when this stopped, the Maharaja Scindia rose and addressed the queen in Urdu and said:

Shah in Shah, Padshah, May God bless you. The Princes of India bless you and pray that your *hukumat* [the power to give absolute orders which must be obeyed, sovereignty] may remain steadfast forever.[79]

Scindia was followed by other rulers expressing their thanks and pledging their loyalty. Scindia's statement, which appears to have been unsolicited, his failure to address the empress with the proper title 'Kaiser-i-Hind' notwithstanding, was taken by Lytton as the sign of the fulfilment of the intention of the assemblage.

The activities of the assemblage continued for another four days. These included a rifle match, the inauguration of a Royal Cup Race, won fittingly by one of the princes' horses, several more dinners and

---

[78] *Gazette of India*, Extraordinary, 1 Jan. 1877, pp. 3–7.
[79] Thornton, *op. cit.*, p. 310.

receptions, and the presentation of loyal addresses and petitions by various regional and civic bodies. There was also an extensive exhibition organized of Indian arts and crafts. The proceedings were concluded with a march by the imperial troops, followed by contingents from the armies of the princes. Long lists of new honours were announced, some princes had their gun salutes enhanced and twelve Europeans and eight Indians were awarded the title of 'Counsellor of the Empress'. Thirty-nine new members of the Star were created to mark the occasion, and large numbers of new Indian title-holders were created. Thousands of prisoners were released or had their sentence reduced, and monetary rewards were given to members of the armed forces. On the day of the proclamation ceremonies were held all over India to mark the occasion. In all, over three hundred such meetings were held in presidency capitals, in all civil and military stations down to local tahsil headquarters. In the towns, the plans for the occasion were usually drawn up by local Indian officials, and included durbars, the offering of poems and odes in Sanskrit and other languages, parades of school children and their being treated to sweets, feeding of the poor, distribution of clothes to the needy, usually winding up with a fireworks display in the evening.

CONCLUSION

Historians have paid little attention to the assemblage of 1877; at best it is treated as a kind of folly, a great *tamasha*, or show, but which had little practical consequence. It has been noted in histories of Indian nationalism as the occasion when, for the first time, early nationalist leaders and journalists from all over India were gathered in the same place at the same time, but is passed over as mere window-dressing to mask imperial realities. It is also taken as an example of the callousness on the part of imperial rulers who spent large sums of public money at a time of famine.

At the time it was planned and immediately afterwards, the assemblage received considerable criticism in the Indian-language press as well as in the English papers. It was seen by many, as were Ellenborough's attempts at imperial glorification, as being somehow or other un-English, and the expression of the wild imaginations of Disraeli and Lytton.

Yet the assemblage kept being referred to subsequently by Indians and Europeans as a kind of marker, a before and after event. It became the standard by which public ceremony was measured. It may be said the event itself recurred twice – in 1903 when Lord Curzon organized an imperial durbar in Delhi to proclaim Edward VII emperor of India on the exact location where his mother's imperial title was proclaimed, and when in 1911, also on the same spot, George V made an appearance to crown himself emperor of India. Curzon, a man of enormous energy, intelligence and almost megalomaniacal belief in his own power to rule India, spent almost six months planning 'his' durbar, and was always at pains to follow the forms which Lytton had laid down. When he did deviate from these he felt constrained to offer detailed and extensive explanations for his changes and additions. If anything, Curzon wanted the Imperial Durbar to be more 'Indian' than the assemblage, hence the design motif was 'Indo-Saracenic', rather than 'Victorian Feudal'. He also wanted more active participation in the event itself on the part of the princes, who were to offer direct acts of homage. This kind of participation became the centre piece of the 1911 Imperial Durbar, when many of the leading princes, during the durbar itself, individually kneeled before their emperor, in what was termed 'the homage pavilion', which replaced the dais of the viceroy as the centre piece of the amphitheatre.

What was the significance or consequence not only of the Imperial Assemblage and the Imperial Durbars, but also the ritual idiom created to express, make manifest and compelling the British construction of their authority over India? Did Lytton and his successors accomplish their goals? On one level they did not, as India, Pakistan and Bangladesh are independent nations today. The idea of the permanence of imperial rule is a half-forgotten curiosity, even to historians who see the events of the period of 1877 to 1947 as a fight over loaves and fishes, or the culmination of the Indian peoples' anti-imperial struggle.

I think, however, there is another way of looking at the question of success or failure, of the intentions of Lytton and his associates and the codification of the ritual idiom. I have focused almost exclusively on the British construction of authority and its representations. When Indians, particularly in the first years of their national movement, came to develop a public political idiom of their own, through their own organizations, what idiom did they use? I would suggest that in effect they used the same idiom that their British rulers employed. The early meetings of the All India Congress Committees were much like durbars, with processions and the centrality of leading figures and their speeches, which became the vehicle through which they tried to participate in the achievement of the values of 'progressive government' and the obtainment of the happiness and welfare of the Indian peoples. The British idiom was effective in that it set the terms of discourse of the nationalist movement in its beginning phases. In effect, the early nationalists were claiming that they were more loyal to the true goals of the Indian empire than were their English rulers.

The First Non-Cooperation Movement of 1920–1 is taken as marking the final establishment of Gandhi as the crucial figure in the nationalist struggle. It was the first time a new idiom was tried out in the form of non-cooperation and passive resistance. At base this was the first full-fledged and widespread rejection of British authority in India. The movement began with Gandhi's announcement that Indians should return all honours and emblems granted by the imperial government. In doing this Gandhi attacked not the institutions of government, but the capacity of that government to make meaningful and binding its authority through the creation of honours.

Most of Gandhi's contributions to the nationalist movement were concerned with the creation and representation of new codes of conduct based on a radically different theory of authority. These were represented in a series of markings. No longer were Indians to wear either western clothes or the 'native' costumes decreed by their imperial rulers, but home-spun simple peasant dress. The communal prayer meeting, not the durbar-like atmosphere of the political rallies, was where his message was expounded. The Indian pilgrimage was adapted to politics in the form of Gandhi's marches, and the idea of the *paidatra* (the walking of the politician amongst the people) is still part of the political rituals of India.

Yet, the British idiom did not die easily or quickly, and it may still be alive in various forms. The end of the empire was marked where it might be said to have begun, in 1857, with the desacralization of the Mughal's palace, with English officers drinking wine and eating pork. The moment of transfer of authority from the viceroy to the new prime minister of an independent India was marked at the Red Fort by the lowering of the Union Jack at midnight, 14 August 1947, before a huge crowd of jubilant Indians.

6. *The Invention of Tradition in Colonial Africa*

TERENCE RANGER

INTRODUCTION

The 1870s, 1880s and 1890s were the time of a great flowering of European invented tradition – ecclesiastical, educational, military, republican, monarchical. They were also the time of the European rush into Africa. There were many and complex connections between the two processes. The concept of Empire was central to the process of inventing tradition within Europe itself, but the African empires came so late in the day that they demonstrate the effects rather than the causes of European invented tradition. Deployed in Africa, however, the new traditions took on a peculiar character, distinguishing them from both their European and Asian Imperial forms.

By contrast to India many parts of Africa became colonies of white settlement. This meant that the settlers had to define themselves as natural and undisputed masters of vast numbers of Africans. They drew upon European invented traditions both to define and to justify their roles, and also to provide models of subservience into which it was sometimes possible to draw Africans. In Africa, therefore, the whole apparatus of invented school and professional and regimental traditions became much more starkly a matter of command and control than it was within Europe itself. Moreover, in Europe these invented traditions of the new ruling classes were to some extent balanced by the invented traditions of industrial workers or by the invented 'folk' cultures of peasants. In Africa, no white agriculturalist saw himself as a peasant. White workers in the mines of southern Africa certainly drew upon the invented rituals of European craft unionism but they did so partly because they were rituals of exclusiveness and could be used to prevent Africans being defined as workers.

By contrast to India, once again, Africa did not offer to its conquerors the framework of an indigenous imperial state nor existing centralized rituals of honour and degree. Ready connections

211

between African and European systems of governance could only be made at the level of the monarchy; Africa possessed, so the colonisers thought, dozens of rudimentary kings. Hence in Africa the British made an even greater use of the idea of 'Imperial Monarchy' than they did within Britain or India. The 'theology' of an omniscient, omnipotent and omnipresent monarchy became almost the sole ingredient of imperial ideology as it was presented to Africans. For the Germans, too, the Kaiser stood as the dominant symbol of German rule. The French had the more difficult task of incorporating Africans into a republican tradition.

But serviceable as the monarchical ideology was to the British, it was not enough in itself to provide the theory or justify the structures of colonial governance on the spot. Since so few connections could be made between British and African political, social and legal systems, British administrators set about inventing African traditions for Africans. Their own respect for 'tradition' disposed them to look with favour upon what they took to be traditional in Africa. They set about to codify and promulgate these traditions, thereby transforming flexible custom into hard prescription.

All this is part of the history of European ideas, but it is also very much part of the history of modern Africa. These complex processes have to be understood before a historian can arrive at any understanding of the particularity of Africa before colonialism; many African scholars as well as many European Africanists have found it difficult to free themselves from the false models of colonial codified African 'tradition'. However, the study of these processes is not only a part of historiography but of history. The invented traditions imported from Europe not only provided whites with models of command but also offered many Africans models of 'modern' behaviour. The invented traditions of African societies – whether invented by the Europeans or by Africans themselves in response – distorted the past but became in themselves realities through which a good deal of colonial encounter was expressed.

EUROPEAN INVENTED TRADITION AND THE AFRICAN EMPIRE

The traditions which were invented in Europe in the nineteenth century were very unevenly carried into Africa. In the 1880s and 1890s many whites were arriving in southern Africa from Europe,

Canada and Australia to work in the mines; very many Africans were being drawn into the labour migrant network. But European proletarian or artisanal invented traditions were not available to fit African workers into their place in the labour hierarchy, still less to help them define themselves as artisans or workers. Instead, the revived and invented rituals of craft unionism were used by white workers to *exclude* Africans from participation. Elaine Katz in her study of white trade unionism in South Africa shows how the white miners claimed craft status. Dominated by British and Australian miners, their union was 'organized on the basis of an exclusive membership restricted to white underground miners in possession of a blasting certificate'. Union leaders urged an often lethargic membership to follow the Craft Banner and the brass band in Labour Day processions – rituals of worker solidarity which in that context proclaimed élite status. As John X. Merriman, prime minister of Cape Colony, remarked in 1908, white workmen who had been regarded in Europe as the 'lower classes' were 'delighted on arrival here to find themselves in a position of an aristocracy of colour'.[1]

An extensive recent literature has shown that in the 1880s and 1890s Africans throughout East, Central and southern Africa were becoming peasants, their agricultural surplus expropriated through unequal terms of trade, tax or rent and their subordinate role in a shared cultural system defined by mission Christianity.[2] But there was little opportunity for African peasants to borrow from the invented traditions by which European peasantries had sought to defend themselves against the intrusions of capitalism. Almost everywhere in Africa white agriculturalists saw themselves not as peasants but as gentlemen farmers. Only through some of the mission churches did European peasant formulations reach Africans, and only then in transformed shape.

The closest thing to a peasant missionary church was the Basel Mission. The product of Württemberg pietism, the Basel missionaries carried with them to Africa a model of rural society derived from their defence of pre-industrial German peasant life. They proclaimed, against the threat of the industrial town, an ideal 'Christian model village', a reconstituted rural 'tradition' based on 'the pre-industrial

---

[1] Elaine N. Katz, *A Trade Union Aristocracy*, African Studies Institute Communication, no. 3 (Univ. of the Witwatersrand, Johannesburg, 1976).

[2] The two most recent accounts of 'peasantization' are: Robin Palmer and Neil Parsons (eds.), *The Roots of Rural Poverty* (London, 1978); Colin Bundy, *The Rise and Fall of the South African Peasantry* (London, 1979).

combination of crafts making use of natural products, [and] the extended family'. They stood for 'a social and economic setting "traditional" in the sense that there was direct relationship between local food production and local food supplies'. The original impulse of their entry into Africa was the desire to find free land to which German peasant communities could escape. In their approach to Africans they were 'a mission *from* the village *to* the village'. In Germany itself the pietist model only imperfectly reflected a past that had been much less organic and coherent. In Africa there had not existed 'villages' of this size or stability. The Basel Mission villages, so far from offering African cultivators a means of protecting their values, operated rather as mechanisms of authoritarian European control and of economic innovation.[3]

Few other mission churches expressed so clearly European peasant aspirations. But many carried with them features which had been produced through European ecclesiastical responses to peasant aspiration. Thus the Church of England had responded to the tensions of an increasingly class-based rural society by developing rituals of 'traditional' community, and now it introduced these harvest festivals and rogation-tide processions through the fields into Africa.[4] The Roman Catholic Church had responded to the anarchic proliferation of local peasant shrines, cults and pilgrimages by authorizing a popular Marian veneration, and centralizing it at a few shrines to which the flow of pilgrims was directed.[5] Now into Africa were introduced replicas of Fatima and Lourdes. Such centralization of ritual and cult, introduced before there was any African popular Christianity for them to respond to, acted rather to circumscribe than to stimulate African peasant imagination.

It was not the invented traditions of European workers and peasants, but those of gentlemen and professional men which were most important to whites in Africa, and which had the greatest impact upon blacks. There were two main reasons for the importance of these neo-traditions. By the 1880s and 1890s there was a surplus

[3] Paul Jenkins, 'Towards a Definition of the Pietism of Wurtemburg as a Missionary Movement', African Studies Association of the United Kingdom, Conference on Whites in Africa (Oxford, Sept. 1978).

[4] James Obelkevich, *Religion and Rural Society: South Lindsey, 1825–1875* (Oxford, 1976).

[5] Alphonse Dumont, 'La Religion – Anthropologie Religieuse', in Jacques Le Goff and Pierre Nora (eds.), *Faire de l'Histoire, Nouvelles Approches* (Paris, 1974), ii, pp. 107–36.

of neo-traditional capital in Europe waiting to be invested overseas. Production of men for service in the extended governing class of industrial democracy had been almost too successful. Younger sons, well-born orphans, the sons of the clergy had experienced the 'traditions' of the public school, the regiment, the university, but were not guaranteed secure advancement in British administrative hierarchies. Such men were deployed in Africa as soldiers, hunters, traders, store-keepers, concession-seekers, policemen, missionaries. Very often they found themselves engaged in tasks which by definition would have been menial in Britain and which only the glamour of empire building made acceptable; the emphasis which they placed on their neo-traditional title to gentility became more intense.

The second reason was that there was a desperate need in the last decades of the nineteenth century to make European activity in Africa more respectable and ordered. While life was being restructured in Britain itself, with the rise of the bureaucracy and of the service traditions in school, army, church and even commerce, most European activity in tropical Africa, whether official or unofficial, had remained tatty, squalid, rough and inefficient. With the coming of formal colonial rule it was urgently necessary to turn the whites into a convincing ruling class, entitled to hold sway over their subjects not only through force of arms or finance but also through the prescriptive status bestowed by neo-tradition.

Steps were therefore taken to ensure that the military and administrative services in Africa were related to the dominant traditions. Much use was made in the early period of colonial administration of officers of the newly efficient and honourable British army. Lugard relied upon them for 'gentlemanly' administrators in Nigeria. In 1902 Lady Lugard, writing from Lokoja on the Niger, was able to describe a veritable festival of neo-tradition. To celebrate Coronation Day – the day of the first elaborate 'traditional' coronation:

> we had the table patriotically decorated with roses... and we drank the King's health, with the band playing 'God Save the King', and a black crowd of servants and others clustering round the open windows ejaculating, 'Good King! Good King!'. I was myself struck with the thought as I looked down the table and noted the fine type of English gentleman's face which presented itself in rows on either side, that it really is a phenomenon of our Empire that we should be able in the heart of Africa to bring together for dinner

twenty well-bred English officers of as fine a type as you would hope to meet in the most civilised centres of London.[6]

Meanwhile the educational system of England began to turn out civilian colonial administrators. The headmaster of Harrow declared that

> an English headmaster, as he looks to the future of his pupils, will not forget that they are destined to be the citizens of the greatest empire under heaven; he will teach them patriotism...He will inspire them with faith in the divinely ordained mission of their country and their race.[7]

The recruiters for the colonial service testified to the success of these endeavours. 'As to the Public Schools', wrote Sir Ralph Furse, one of the chief architects of the colonial service,

> they are vital. We could not have run the show without them. In England universities train the mind; the Public Schools train character and teach leadership.[8]

But the universities too came to play their part, and soon

> the District Commissioner had to be a man of many parts. To qualify for appointment to the administrative branch of the Colonial Service he had to hold an honours degree in Arts from a recognised university...It helped the applicant's cause if, in addition to a good degree, he had some kind of athletic record.[9]

All this produced administrators who ran their districts like lordly prefects, inventing their own little traditions to keep the fags on their toes. 'D was in the habit', we are told of the district commissioner of Tunduru in southern Tanganyika,

> of going for a long walk every evening, wearing a hat. When, towards sunset, he came to the point of turning for home he would hang his hat on a convenient tree and proceed on his way hatless. The first African who passed that way after him and saw the hat was expected to bring it to D's house and hand it over to his servants, even if he was going in the opposite direction with a long journey ahead of him. If he ignored the hat he would be haunted by the fear that D's intelligence system would catch up with him.[10]

---

[6] Margery Perham, *Lugard: The Years of Authority* (London, 1960), p. 80.

[7] Cited by Cynthia Behrman, 'The Mythology of British Imperialism, 1890–1914' (Univ. of Boston doctoral dissertation, 1965), p. 47.

[8] Sir Ralph Furse, quoted by R. Heussler, *Yesterday's Rulers: The Making of the British Colonial Service* (London, 1963), p. 82; see also, D. C. Coleman, 'Gentlemen and Players', *Economic History Review*, xxvi (Feb. 1973).

[9] E. K. Lumley, *Forgotten Mandate: A British District Officer in Tanganyika* (London, 1976), p. 10.   [10] *Ibid.*, p. 55.

But it was not enough in itself to ensure the gentility of soldiers and administrators in Africa. There was also a need to believe that many of the white settlers were also actually or potentially inheritors of the neo-traditions of governance. In the end some settler communities were successful enough to set up in Africa itself replicas of the schools whose traditions validated the British governing class. Thus in 1927

a plan was discussed with Eton College to found the 'Kenya Public School', under the joint auspices of Winchester and Eton, with reciprocal staffing arrangements and scholarships for the children of poorer white parents. After a trip to Britain to test support for the project, the Director of Education decided to ask 'all the leading public schools to present us with pictures of their school buildings so that the boys may be constantly reminded of the great schools at home and old boys visiting the school may likewise remember their Alma Mater'.

As a finishing touch the school was to be named after King George V, 'as a reminder to the backward races of their participation in the Empire'.[11] But to begin with the transformation was brought about mainly by a complex system of reformulations which affected the way in which white men in Africa were regarded and the way in which they regarded themselves.

This process operated in two ways. The fact that the surplus of neo-traditional capital *was* being invested in Africa, combined with the fortune-hunting involvement of members of high society, made it possible for commentators to stress the gentlemanly element among white settlers, and to suggest that the colonial experience in itself fitted the rest to acquire gentility. Lord Bryce was struck 'by the large proportion of well-mannered and well-educated men whom one came across' in the 'tropical wilderness' of Rhodesia in the mid-1890s, and added that the colonial experience fostered 'personality developing itself under simple yet severe conditions, fitted to bring out the real force of a man'. In such circumstance Bryce was prepared to condone the rather vulgar neo-traditional enthusiasms which he himself deplored in England. He was much struck by white southern African enthusiasm for cricket, 'the national game'.

Even one who thinks that in England the passion for athletic sports has gone beyond all reasonable limits, and has become a serious injury to education and to the taste for intellectual pleasures, may

[11] M. G. Redley, 'The Politics of a Predicament: The White Community in Kenya, 1918–32' (Univ. of Cambridge doctoral dissertation, 1976), pp. 124, 125.

find in the character of the climate a justification for devotion to cricket...Our countrymen are not to be scared by the sun from the pursuit of the national game. They are as much Englishmen in Africa as in England.[12]

Alongside this process of affirming and making gentility there ran another – a redefinition of occupations, so that it became gentlemanly to be a store-keeper or a prospector. Young gentleman who migrated to Rhodesia or to Kenya may have dreamt of one day establishing a landed estate, but in the early days running a farm store and buying African agricultural produce was far more profitable than trying to grow crops oneself. It was in any case assumed that English-speaking 'farmers' would be gentleman farmers, not working the land themselves, but drawing on their neo-traditional powers of command in order to manage labour. So to begin with they relied on African – or Afrikaner – knowledge of the land and creamed off the surplus of African peasant producers through trade. By so doing they performed a vital function since the labour forces of the early colonial economies depended entirely on African produced food. Hence, for a time, it was gentlemanly to run a store or to buy grain and cattle from Africans.[13] Lord Bryce found 'cultivated and thoughtful minds' in young white store-keepers in Rhodesia in 1896, or in prospectors searching for gold. The atmosphere of these early days – and the buoyancy of the neo-traditions of gentility – emerges strikingly from Colin Harding's autobiography. Harding grew up as the son of the lord of Montacute House, a young man whose main concern was with the heroics of the hunting field. But

the death of my father revealed the unwelcome fact that neither myself nor other members of my family was as opulent as expected...Neither I nor my brothers had any profession, nor yet the means to qualify for one.

Still, 'hunting teaches a man a lot'. Harding arrived in Bulawayo in 1894 to find that 'farming was a washout' and 'men like myself were a drug on the market'. 'Experienced and reliable storekeepers', however, 'could command almost any wage they desired'. But the young gentleman did not go under. Harding set out with an old friend from the hunting field to prospect for gold. Soon he found himself

---

[12] James Bryce, *Impressions of South Africa* (London, 1897), pp. 232, 384–5.
[13] For the reliance of Rhodesian whites on African food production, see Palmer, 'The Agricultural History of Southern Rhodesia', in Palmer and Parsons (eds.), *The Roots of Rural Poverty*.

set to dig a mine shaft. 'It was useless for me to remind my friend that I knew little or nothing about sinking a shaft, for he shut me up with the observation that digging out gold was much the same as digging out a fox.' Soon Harding was in the British South Africa Police and on his way to a properly gentlemanly administrative career.[14]

Fairly soon conditions in Rhodesia and Kenya developed towards a more securely gentlemanly society. Asians and Greeks and Jews took over the task of store-keepers and 'kaffir-traders'; political action deliberately undercut African peasant production and put labour at the disposal of the gentleman farmer. M. G. Redley thus describes the nature of Kenyan white society just after the first world war.

> The main source of British immigrants with capital after the war was what has been called the 'new upper middle class'. Family wealth derived from enterprise in manufacturing, commerce and the professions had blurred the class distinctions of Victorian society. Public school education had provided the basis of a background for those who could lay no direct claim to gentility common with those who could. The background to post-war settlers owed much more to the mill and the factory owner's mansion, the rural rectory and the Indian Army officers' mess than to aristocratic lineage...However, gentility was a way of life with which they felt a close identity and in which they took an obsessive interest...The upper middle class complexion of European settlement was its greatest recommendation for those who felt their status and individuality threatened in British society.[15]

Redley describes how neo-traditions functioned to hold together the small and dispersed white rural society. Team games brought neighbours together regularly in an approved and structured way. They also allowed for symbolic expressions of protest in an idiom familiar to both settlers and administrators. Redley describes a 'fancy-dress charity football match' in Nairobi in 1907 patronized by the governor, which

> was disrupted by leading settlers dressed as colonial officials with rows of medals made of tin lids and red tape who pegged out quarantine, forest, native and game reserves until the entire pitch was 'out of bounds'.[16]

[14] Colin Harding, *Far Bugles* (London, 1933), p. 22.
[15] M. G. Redley, *op. cit.*, p. 9.   [16] M. G. Redley, *op. cit.*, p. 39.

On the other hand, every project to increase the numbers of the white settler population by bringing in thousands of small yeomen or artisans foundered on the determination of those who controlled Kenyan society to keep it in the hands of 'the public school educated with a patrimony, a military pension, investment income or an assurance of family support'.

BRINGING AFRICANS INTO THE TRADITIONS OF GOVERNANCE

The radical Kenyan journalist, J. K. Robertson, was savagely critical of Kenyan whites because he believed them to obstruct productive industry. He created a fictional settler career history to make his point.

John Smith, a London warehouse clerk, finds a clerking job in a certain office in British East Africa. John Smithers-Smith laboriously pores over books and ledgers. 'Tis the same John, only more so... He has realized the value of a double-barrelled name... John goes the pace. It is the custom of the country. He seldom pays his bills... He lives on chits and the wonderful stories of the blue blood of his ancestors. John is quite an institution in the land [and] insinuates himself into the very heart of Nairobi society.[17]

More generally, the strength of European invented traditions of governance in colonial Africa helped to produce soldiers and administrators and settlers dedicated to the 'feudal–patriarchal' ethic rather than to the 'capitalist–transformative' one.

But in many ways this is very misleading. The invented traditions of nineteenth-century Britain were a way of running an immensely complex industrial society, a way of managing and accommodating change. In Africa, too, whites drew on invented tradition in order to derive the authority and confidence that allowed them to act as agents of change. Moreover, insofar as they were consciously applied to Africans, the invented traditions of nineteenth-century Europe were seen precisely as agencies of 'modernization'.

There were two very direct ways in which Europeans sought to make use of their invented traditions to transform and modernize African thought and conduct. One was the acceptance of the idea that *some* Africans could become members of the governing class of colonial Africa, and hence the extension to such Africans of training

---

[17] Roger van Zwannenberg, 'Robertson and the *Kenya Critic*', in K. King and A. I. Salim (eds.), *Kenyan Historical Biographies* (Nairobi, 1971), pp. 145–6.

in a neo-traditional context. The second – and more common – was an attempt to make use of what European invented traditions had to offer in terms of a redefined relationship between leader and led. The regimental tradition, after all, defined the roles of both officers and men; the great-house tradition of rural gentility defined the roles of both masters and servants; the public school tradition defined the roles of both prefects and fags. All this might be made use of to create a clearly defined hierarchical society in which Europeans commanded and Africans accepted commands, but both within a shared framework of pride and loyalty. Thus if the traditions which workers and peasants had made for themselves in Europe did not exercise much influence on Africans under colonialism, invented European traditions of subordination exercised a very considerable influence indeed.

The best illustration of the first idea – that some Africans might be turned into governors by exposure to British neo-tradition – is perhaps the famous school, King's College, Budo, in Uganda. The fullest account is by G. P. McGregor, who perceptively points out that the provision of elementary education was only just being taken seriously in Britain itself in the 1870s as part of the process of bringing the majority of the population to its place in the vocational and educational hierarchy. Hence the spread of elementary schools in Buganda at the end of the nineteenth century was a remarkably little-delayed extension of the same process to the African empire. But in Buganda, while this sort of education seemed appropriate enough to the peasant cultivator majority, the Anglican missionaries did not feel that it was suitable for the Ganda aristocracy.

> So far little or nothing had been done for the children of the upper classes [wrote Bishop Tucker], who in many respects were worse off than the children of the peasants. We felt strongly that if the ruling classes of the country were to exercise in the days to come an influence for good upon their people and to have a sense of responsibility towards them, it was essential that something should be done for the education of these neglected children, on the soundest possible lines... by the discipline of work and games in a boarding school so as to build character as to enable the Baganda to take their proper place in the administrative, commercial and industrial life of their own country.[18]

In short, in Buganda the missionaries aimed to place on top of

---

[18] G. P. McGregor, *Kings College, Budo: The First Sixty Years* (London, 1967), pp. 6, 16.

British-style elementary education a structure of British-style secondary education of a neo-traditional kind. They were always clear that
their aim was 'the adaptation of our English Public School method
to the African scene'. They succeeded to an extraordinary extent
King's College was built on the Coronation Hill of the Baganda
kings, so that 'both Coronation Services of this century have been
held' in the college chapel; 'though some of the traditional ceremonies
were observed', the service 'followed many of the features of the
English coronation service'.[19] The English Public School house
spirit [was] quickly established', and the Gandan members of Turkey
House petitioned that its name be changed to Canada House so as
to go with England House, South Africa House and Australia
House – Turkey seemed 'distinctly unimperial'. The school motto,
again said to have been chosen at the request of the pupils, was a
Gandan version of Cecil Rhodes's dying words, 'So little done – so
much to do.'

McGregor quotes a letter from a Gandan pupil written in the first
year of the school's existence, which enables us to see this remarkable
process of socialization through Gandan eyes.

First in the mornings when we have got up we arrange properly
our beds. If you do not arrange it properly there is judgement or
rebuke when the Europeans make a visit...On the front of our
cups there is the likeness of a lion. That it is by which the scholars
of Budo may be known. And no-one may eat any thing in the
cubicle, nor coffee which they chew, but only in the verandah where
food is eaten. We sing one hymn and pray and then we learn
English...When we come out at four, we go and play football, on
one side eleven and on the other side eleven, and we arrange every
man in his place, goal-keeper and back men and ba-half-back and
ba-forward.[20]

Everyone agreed that Budo had managed to create that intangible
thing, 'the spirit of the school'. It was present at Budo

at its best, as we have breathed it in England after generations of
experiment – the spirit of the team, of discipline, of local
patriotism – and very remarkable has been the translation of it into
the heart of Africa.

Sir Phillip Mitchell thought that Budo was 'one of the few places here
which has a soul'. Expatriate teachers later came to criticize 'the

[19] *Ibid.*, pp. 35–6.   [20] *Ibid.*, pp. 17–18.

Budonian habit of defending worthless traditions merely on the grounds that they have always been there'.[21]

Whatever the tensions of doing so within the imperial framework which so firmly subordinated the Gandan ruling class to British administrative officers, and the Gandan monarchy to the imperial crown, there is no doubt that the missionaries created at Budo a successful complex of new traditions, which worked themselves out parallel to an increasing ceremonialism of the role of the Kabaka and the other Ugandan kings so as to achieve a synthesis not unlike that accomplished in nineteenth-century England. The Golden Jubilee ceremonies of the college – 'We had four Kings at the high table' – were also a ritual expression of the commitment of a large section of the Gandan ruling class to these by now hallowed invented traditions.[22] But the Budo experiment was not to become a general model; the British themselves came to regret their original alliance with the Ganda chiefs, and to believe that real modernizing change could not be brought about through their agency. Real modernizing change would be the product of European commanders loyally supported by African subordinates.

Various traditions of subordination were available. One was the tradition of the hierarchy of the great house. Part of the self-image of the European in Africa was his prescriptive right to have black servants – at the height of the labour crisis in the South African mines, there were more black men employed in Johannesburg as domestic servants than as mine workers.[23] In 1914 Frank Weston, bishop of Zanzibar, contrasted Islamic community in Africa with Christian differentiation. The African Christian, he wrote, has nothing to adhere to but ' a few Europeans who pass him in the street; he is beneath them; they may be kind to him; he may perhaps be a steward in their dining room, or a butler... but Brotherhood? Well, it is not yet'.[24] There was no impulse towards 'Brotherhood' in colonial Africa. For most Europeans the favoured image of their relationship with Africans was that of paternal master and loyal servant. It was an image readily transferred to industrial employment. Throughout southern Africa, African employees were not defined as

[21] *Ibid.*, pp. 54, 117, 124.
[22] *Ibid.*, p. 136.
[23] Charles van Onselen, 'The Witches of Suburbia: Domestic Service on the Witwatersrand, 1890–1914' (unpublished MS.).
[24] Frank Weston, 'Islam in Zanzibar Diocese', *Central Africa*, xxxii, no. 380 (Aug. 1914).

workers but instead controlled and disciplined under the terms of Masters and Servants Acts.

Few whites in Africa, however, maintained domestic establishments of a size which would have allowed the full 'traditional' panoply of the British servant hierarchy. A more elaborate application of European neo-traditions of subordination came with the restructuring of African armies. In Sylvanus Cookey's fascinating account of this process, the French emerge as the first and most imaginative manipulators of the military invented tradition. Faideherbe in the 1850s disbanded his demoralized pressed levies and attracted African volunteers with 'seduisant' uniforms, modern arms, Koranic oaths of allegiance and crash courses in the military glory of the French tradition.

It was even suggested from Paris, as a means of instilling at an early age a sense of the military mode in the young Africans and preparing them for a military career, that the children of the *tirailleurs* should be provided uniforms and miniature equipment similar to those of their parents.[25]

The British were slower to follow such a policy. But in the face of the French threat they also moved to regularize their African regiments. Lugard devoted his meticulous passion for detail to the transformation of his Nigerian levies from a 'rabble' to a disciplined and effective fighting force. Soon he came to esteem them highly; official praise was lavished on them for their conduct in campaigns in the Gold Coast and northern Nigeria; a regimental tradition was being built up as rapidly as the spirit of Budo. Lugard's administration was largely staffed by army officers; in East Africa, too, 'governments were largely military in character during these early years', and Professor George Shepperson has commented on

the narrowness of the line between the civilian and the military... It was through its forces as much as its missions that European culture was brought to the indigenous inhabitants of British Central Africa.[26]

This kind of admittance of Africans into the European military tradition had both the same ambiguities and the same degree of success as did the operation of the spirit of Budo. Sometimes the two

[25] S. J. Cookey, 'Origins and pre-1914 Character of the Colonial Armies in West Africa' (Univ. of California, Los Angeles, colloquium paper, 1972).
[26] George Shepperson, 'The Military History of British Central Africa: A Review Article', *Rhodes–Livingstone Journal*, no. 26 (Dec. 1959), pp. 23–33.

forms of socialization came together, as in the case of Kabaka Edward Mutesa. Mutesa became Kabaka while still a schoolboy at Budo, and remained there to complete his studies; his coronation was solemnized in the school chapel; he led the Golden Jubilee procession. But he was also admitted into the regimental tradition of the British army.

He joined the Cambridge Officers' Corps soon after arrival at the University and became an officer...He then formally applied to join the army, specifying the Grenadier Guards as his first choice...It was King George VI who, as a personal gesture of good-will, suggested that Mutesa be made a captain. Mutesa went to Buckingham Palace for the ceremony.[27]

Ali Mazrui remarks that the Kabakaship had become 'an Anglo-African institution', a fact brought out by nothing so clearly as in the ceremonies which attended Mutesa's death. He was given two funerals – one in London and one in Kampala, both marked by full military honours.

There had been a last post in the first burial of Mutesa in London in 1969. On that occasion the military component of the burial was handled by the British Grenadier Guards. Now [in Kampala] the Grenadier Guards were only part of the ceremony. The bulk of the military component was the Ugandan army. And yet the universe of discourse between that trumpet in London in 1969 and the trumpet in the Kasubi tombs in Uganda in 1971, was indeed a shared universe.[28]

But the acceptance of Mutesa into the officer ranks was a rare exception. Much more general was the production of men like Mutesa's successor as president of Uganda, Idi Amin. Mazrui argues that the rise of Amin and his 'lumpen-militariat' can be seen as a revival of pre-colonial military traditions, in abeyance since the colonial conquest. But in fact, Amin's career provides us with an excellent example of socialization through the colonial army. As Mazrui tells us, when Amin was recruited into the King's African Rifles in 1946, he showed

all the signs of colonial conditioning into dependency...Within seven years he was promoted to lance corporal and was displaying the qualities which so endeared him to his British superiors – instant

[27] Ali. A. Mazrui, *Soldiers and Kinsmen in Uganda: The Making of a Military Ethnocracy* (London, 1975), p. 173.
[28] *Ibid.*, pp. 177, 190, 191.

obedience, fierce regimental pride, reverence towards Britain and the British, a uniform which crackled with razor sharp starched creases and boots with toe-caps like black mirrors.[29]

Black mirrors of English privates and non-commissioned officers were precisely what African soldiers were intended to be. As Keegan has shown, European armies had drawn freely on the dress and romantic aura of the 'warrior' races they encountered. They do not seem to have done this in Africa, nor as a result of their military encounters with Africans. It was left to Baden-Powell, a critic of the drill-square mentality, to draw on Matabele scouting abilities so as to provide white youth with a flexible training, richly situated in Kiplingesque myths of the jungle. For a long while southern Africa presented the paradox of young Africans being trained into regimental rigidities and young whites being trained in bush-craft.[30]

Admittance of Africans into what were intended as replicas of the neo-traditions of Britain did not end with butlering or with schools like Budo or with recruitment into the army. Bishop Weston's hypothetical African Christian, in search of Brotherhood, might if he were very fortunate 'conceivably learn to be a typist',[31] and many mission-educated Africans were taken into the lower ranks of the bureaucratic hierarchy. African clerks came to value the rubber stamp and the row of pens in the breast pocket; African dance societies made use of purloined rubber stamps to authenticate their correspondence with each other, and danced in full bureaucratic as well as military array.[32] Graham Greene's madman on the river boat, with his sheaves of papers and his constant scribbling of minutes as he strove to set an uncaring world to rights, was a tribute paid to the imaginative power – if also a dramatization of the impotence – of the forms of colonial bureaucracy. And, of course, the African Christians, who were taken up as clergy into the imperfect brotherhood of the Christian churches themselves, were trained to perform the invented and re-invented rituals of nineteenth-century European ecclesiology.

There was a rough periodization in all this. European invented traditions were important for Africans in a series of overlapping

[29] *Ibid.*, pp. 206–7.
[30] For a discussion of the ambiguities of setting up Boy Scout troops in Africa and then seeking to exclude Africans from them, see Terence Ranger, 'Making Northern Rhodesia Imperial: Variations on a Royal Theme, 1924–1938', *African Affairs*, lxxix, no. 316 (July 1980).
[31] Weston, 'Islam in Zanzibar Diocese', p. 200.
[32] Terence Ranger, *Dance and Society in Eastern Africa* (London, 1975).

phases. The military neo-tradition, with its clearly visible demarcations of hierarchy and its obvious centrality to the workings of early
colonialism, was the first powerful influence. Its impact reached a
climax – particularly in eastern Africa – with the campaigns of the
first world war. Thereafter, especially in British Africa, the military
presence declined.[33] The military mode became less influential than
the modes of missionary employment or the bureaucratic build-up
of Africans in state and business employment. But the debate over
the sequence of influence or the debate over which neo-tradition was
in the end most influential – a debate that sways to and fro as African
kings, surrounded by neo-traditional trappings, dominate some new
African states; as bureaucratic élites triumph in others; and Mazrui's
'lumpen-militariat' control yet others – is less important in the end
than an assessment of the overall effect of these processes of neo-
traditional socialization.

This was surely very large indeed. European invented traditions
offered Africans a series of clearly defined points of entry into the
colonial world, though in almost all cases it was entry into the
subordinate part of a man/master relationship. They began by
socializing Africans into acceptance of one or other readily available
European neo-traditional modes of conduct – the historical literature
is full of Africans proud of having mastered the business of being
a member of a regiment or having learnt how to be an effective
practitioner of the ritual of nineteenth-century Anglicanism. The
process often ended with serious challenges to the colonial power,
often couched in terms of the socializing neo-traditions themselves.
(The boys at Budo moved from loyal celebration of the 'modernized'
coronation ceremony of Edward Mutesa to riot and protest because
the Kabaka was not treated by the authorities as though he was a
'proper' king.) This is a pattern worked out by Martin Channock
for the school-teacher traditionalists of Nyasaland, and in greater
detail by John Iliffe for Tanganyika.[34] In its varying forms it underlay
a good deal of what we call nationalism. It is distressing, but not in
the least surprising, that Kenneth Kaunda in his search for a personal
ideology to help him on the road to national leadership found solace
and inspiration in Arthur Mee's Books for Boys.[35]

[33] Tony Clayton, 'Concepts of Power and Force in Colonial Africa, 1919–1939',
Institute of Commonwealth Studies seminar (Univ. of London, Oct. 1978).
[34] Martin Channock, 'Ambiguities in the Malawian Political Tradition', *African
Affairs*, lxxiv, no. 296 (July 1975); John Iliffe, *A Modern History of Tanganyika*
(Cambridge, 1979).
[35] Kenneth Kaunda, *Zambia Shall be Free* (London, 1962), p. 31.

If we return for a moment to the question of 'modernization' through the use of European invented traditions, both their advantages and their limitations to the colonisers become plain. They *did* serve to separate out Africans into relatively specialized categories – the askari, the teacher, the servant and so on – and to provide a rudimentary professionalization of African workers. Embedded in the neo-traditions of governance and subordination, there were very clear-cut requirements for the observance of industrial time and work discipline – the neatly, even fanatically, prescribed segments of the schoolboys' day at Budo; the drill square as source and symbol of discipline and punctuality. On the other hand, the invented traditions which were introduced to Africans were those of governance rather than of production. Industrial workers may have been categorized as 'servants', but for a very long time the true domestic servant commanded a much greater prestige and could manipulate the reciprocities contained in the master/servant relationship from which the industrial worker was cut off. Industrial workers and peasants never had access to the clear-cut and prestigious ceremonials of the soldier, the teacher, the clerk – except insofar as they assumed them for themselves in the costumes of carnival or competitive dance.[36] And as we have seen, where craft union traditions did exist Africans were specifically excluded from them. African industrial workers were left to work out for themselves a consciousness and mode of behaviour appropriate to their condition.[37]

This was one of the many reasons for the relatively high prestige among Africans in colonial Africa of non-productive employment. And at the same time, if the new traditions of subordination had begun 'usefully' to define certain sorts of specializations, they gave rise later to profoundly conservative conceptualizations of these specializations, making African teachers, ministers and soldiers notoriously resistant to subsequent attempts at modernizing change.

[36] Ranger, *Dance and Society in Eastern Africa.*
[37] For a discussion of recent literature on African worker consciousness see, Peter Gutkind, Jean Copans and Robin Cohen, *African Labour History* (London, 1978), introduction; John Higginson, 'African Mine Workers at the Union Minière du Haut Katanga', American Historical Association (Dec. 1979).

NEW TRADITIONS OF MONARCHY IN COLONIAL AFRICA

Colonial governments in Africa did not wish to rule by a constant exercise of military force and they needed a wider range of collaborators than those Africans who were brought into the neo-traditions of subordination. In particular, they needed to collaborate with chiefs, headmen and elders in the rural areas. This collaboration was in essence a very practical affair of exchanged benefits.[38] But the colonial rulers felt the need for a shared ideology of Empire which could embrace whites and blacks alike, dignify the practicalities of collaboration and justify white rule. The British and the Germans found this in the concept of Imperial Monarchy.

In German East Africa the notion of the centrality of monarchy had two aspects. On the one hand, the Germans believed that Africans themselves had a rudimentary idea of kingship and especially in the first stages of interaction with African rulers they were prepared to play up to African assertions of kingliness and to decorate them with some of the stage props of nineteenth-century European ceremonial drama. Thus a German officer reported to the Kaiser in 1890 that he had presented gifts from the emperor to Chief Rindi of the Chagga: 'While the soldiers presented arms, I...encircled his shoulders with the coronation cloak...from the Berlin Opera House and placed on his head the helmet under which Niemann once sang Lohengrin'.[39] On the other hand, the Germans believed that African ideas of personal rule by a monarch could be infinitely enlarged so that the figure of an all-powerful Kaiser could come to personify German imperial authority. As John Iliffe tells us:

> The ceremony that epitomised German rule was the annual celebration of the Kaiser's birthday. At every district office the askaris paraded before a massive crowd. After inspection and drill, the Senior German official addressed the gathering, extolling his Emperor's virtues and leading a three-fold 'Hurrah' for Kaiser and Reich. And then the people danced, in circles strewn across the parade ground.[40]

But it was the British who carried the monarchical ideology to its

---

[38] For a recent account of collaborative exchanges see, Ronald Robinson, 'European Imperialism and Indigenous Reactions in British West Africa, 1890–1914', in H. L. Wesseling (ed.), *Expansion and Reaction: Essays in European Expansion and Reactions in Asia and Africa* (Leiden, 1978).

[39] Iliffe, *A Modern History of Tanganyika*, p. 100.

[40] *Ibid.*, pp. 237–8.

greatest elaborations. The British king had nothing like the very real executive power of the German Kaiser. But the British king/emperor was spoken of more in mystical than in practical terms. J. E. Hine, bishop of Northern Rhodesia, found the coronation of King George V 'a great ceremonial act of religion'. Aspects of the ritual, he found 'too theatrical and suggestive of a scene at the opera', and there was 'far too much music "especially written for the occasion"', modern music, to me noisy and unmelodious'. But

> as a whole the Coronation was a splendid sight. It was no mere piece of medieval pageantry, out of touch with modern life and the spirit of the twentieth century; no theatrical display of well staged magnificence...It was symbolism of the utmost splendour, but there was reality behind it all – the sacred unction of the Lord's anointed, an act quasi-sacramental in character, followed by the laying on the head of this one man of the Crown which is the outward sign of the awful but grand responsibility of the Government of all the English people and of the many nations beyond the seas which owe allegiance to the English King.[41]

In northern Rhodesia itself, the acting administrator summoned all the Ngoni chiefs and their people to a Coronation Day fête; the 'native police' band played; the Anglican 'representative robed and said the special prayer chosen for the occasion, standing near the saluting flag'. The enraptured missionary reported on the celebrations of that evening.

> In the valley were four huge bonfires, around which some hundreds of dusky natives capered and danced. Some had bells on their feet, and almost all carried knobkerries...The Europeans, sheltered by a grass screen, sat in a semi-circle, and between them and the fire danced the inhabitants of the soil...Then the police band came forward and in the dying flames regaled us with 'The March of the Men of Harlech', 'Onward Christian Soldiers' and other tunes.[42]

It was not only the established church, however, which spoke of the monarchy in religious terms. Secular administrators, in fact, carried the discourse still further. Their speeches presented to African audiences a king who was almost divine; omnipotent, omniscient and

[41] J. E. Hine, 'The Coronation of King George V', *Central Africa*, xxix, no. 344 (Aug. 1911), pp. 200–1.

[42] A. G. De La P., 'How the Angoni kept Coronation Day', *Central Africa*, xxx, no. 345 (Sept. 1911), pp. 242–3.

omnipresent. A series of official speeches to the Sotho, for example, stressed the royal knowledge of their situation, the royal concern for their well-being and the royal responsibility for decisions which in reality had been taken by the cabinet. In 1910 Prince Arthur of Connaught told the Sotho Paramount Chief that the new King George V 'remembers the representations you made to His late Majesty, King Edward', and that he knew 'that, if and when, He decides that the time has come for Basutoland to be included in the South African Union you will loyally obey His decision'.[43] In 1915 Lord Buxton assured the Paramount Chief that 'His Majesty never ceases to take an interest in the welfare of the Basuto', and that he appreciated their support for 'the great armies which the King has sent out against His enemies'.[44] In 1925 the Prince of Wales told the Sotho that he was

> very pleased that you still cherish the memory of my great-grandmother Queen Victoria...She is no longer with us but the King continues to watch over you with fatherly care. You must show yourselves worthy of his protection by listening to the words of the officers he has appointed to guide and educate you.[45]

And in 1927 Colonel Amery, secretary of state for the colonies, told the Sotho that 'His Majesty the King who has sent me on this journey through His dominions takes the keenest interest in every one of His people – small and great'.[46]

When the king addressed the Sotho directly – as in the Royal Message of 1910 – the officials put into his mouth words of a high patriarchal tone:

> When a child is in trouble he will go to his father, and his father after hearing all about the matter will decide what must be done. Then the child must trust and obey his father, for he is but one of a large family and his father has had great experience in settling the troubles of his older children and is able to judge what is best not only for the young child but for the peace and advantage of the whole family...The Basuto nation is as a very young child among the many peoples of the British Empire.[47]

It was little wonder in view of all this that old Chief Jonathan greeted

[43] Prince Arthur of Connaught, reply to Address, 9 Oct. 1910, file S3/28/2/2, National Archives, Lesotho, Maseru.
[44] Lord Buxton, reply to Address, Apr. 1915, S3/28/2/3, Maseru.
[45] Prince of Wales, reply to Address, 28 May 1925, S3/28/1/9, Maseru.
[46] Colonel Amery, reply to Address, Aug. 1927, S3/28/1/12, Maseru.
[47] 'The King's Message', Oct. 1910, S3/28/2/2, Maseru.

the visit of the Prince of Wales to Basutoland in 1925 in terms which
struck some of the missionaries present as almost blasphemous:

> To me this is a red-letter day. I rejoice on this day like old Simeon
> of the Holy Scriptures who rejoiced because he had seen the Lord
> Jesus before he had slept in the graves of his fathers.[48]

Everywhere else in British Africa the same rhetoric was employed.
An acute observor of the governor's indabas with chiefs in northern
Rhodesia in the 1920s remarked that they were 'designed as a parade
(in the Kintergarten sense) of His Majesty's benignity towards his
untutored African subjects'.[49] Certainly the governor was very much
concerned to derive his authority and that of the district administrators directly from the King.

> All you here are one people – subjects of the King of England. It
> is the King's wish that all his subjects shall live together in
> peace...It is to ensure this that Governors are sent out...The
> Governor who lives in Livingstone and has a large country to
> administer cannot always be in one place but the District Com-
> missioners...are representatives of the Governor and the King,
> and their work is that the King's wishes should be caried out.[50]

To give credibility to these claims colonial administrators regarded
the ceremonial side of the monarchy as crucially important. When
in 1919 the Paramount Chief of Basutoland petitioned for permission
to visit the Vatican as well as Buckingham Palace on his journey to
Europe, the high commissioner feared that he 'might be unduly
impressed by the pomp and state of reception at Vatican and might
form conclusion that Pope was more important than the King!'
Permission was refused.[51] When the Prince of Wales visited southern
and eastern Africa in 1925, his notorious dislike of ceremony was
overcome by the entreaties of colonial administrators who told him
that if he did not appear in full scarlet before the assembled African
masses it would be better for him not to appear at all. The effect was
properly gratifying. 'The Prince's arrival was a splendid affair',
reported the *Daily Telegraph* from Basutoland; 'His Royal Highness
was ablaze with medals, a sight which deeply impressed the great,
silent masses'.[52] From the Solwezi sub-district of Northern Rhodesia

[48] Chief Jonathan's speech, 28 May 1925, S3/28/1/9, Maseru.
[49] Winfrid Tapson, *Old Timer* (Capetown, 1957), p. 65.
[50] Governor Sir James Maxwell, speech at Ndola Indaba, 6 July 1928, file
ZA1/9/59/1, National Archives, Zambia, Lusaka.
[51] High commissioner, cable to secretary of state, 19 May 1919, S3/28/2/4, Maseru.
[52] *Daily Telegraph*, 30 May 1925, 'Picturesque Scenes'.

came the report that the two chiefs who had attended the indaba with
the Prince

> were highly excited when expressing the pleasure it had given them
> to meet the Prince... The two chief impressions which seem to have
> been registered on their minds... were firstly the pomp and
> ceremony connected with the visit – in Kapijimpanga's words, 'the
> *Bwana* shone so brightly in his uniform that we could not look
> upon him' – and secondly that they were able to meet in a friendly
> way with all the other chiefs of the Territory.[53]

It was the Northern Rhodesian administration's boast that the indaba
had dramatized the oneness of all the peoples of the territory, not
because they were all Africans, still less because they were all
Northern Rhodesians, but because they were all subjects of one
mighty king. Against this background it was more a sign of waning
self-confidence than of arrogance when the Northern Rhodesian
government was obliged to issue printed instructions to Africans for
the royal visit of 1947 telling them that

> King George is the biggest King in the world. He is not like an
> African chief. He does not like people crowding close all round
> Him, He expects to see His subjects on their best behaviour.[54]

But royal visits were necessarily rare occasions in colonial Africa.
In the intervals the royal cult had to be sustained by locally invented
rituals. Men could make their careers by inspired contributions to
these. A prime example is the career of Edward Twining, later
governor of Tanganyika. Twining's biographer relates that his
mother was held by her family to have married beneath her; his
clergyman father was thought no gentleman. Twining's not very
distinguished military career and his transfer to the colonial service
was a search for convincing distinction, carried out in the time-
honoured way in the imperial peripheries of gentlemanly society.
Twining found his distinction in the end – and it is quite clear that
he found it through his capacity whole-heartedly to invent tradition.

While still an administrative officer in Uganda, Twining wrote and
published a pamphlet on the English coronation ceremony, of which
The Times Literary Supplement remarked that while it was 'hardly
a book that anyone would be tempted to consult for archaeologial

---

[53] Annual Report, native commissioner, Solwezi sub-district, 1925, ZA7/1/9/2,
Lusaka.

[54] 'Northern Rhodesia. The Royal Visit. 11 April 1947. Details of the Programme
and Broadcasting Arrangements', P3/13/2/1, Lusaka.

detail', nevertheless for 'allowing the modern rite to be followed step by step nothing better could be desired'. Thus having paid tribute to other people's invented tradition, Twining proceeded in the coronation year of 1937 to invent his own. Twining was, in fact, first brought to favourable official attention by his successful organization of the 1937 celebrations in Uganda, a triumph of ceremonial creativity, vividly described by its author:

> In the evening we had the combined Tattoo and Firework Display, which was very much my own personal show, having invented it, trained 2 of the items myself, organised the whole, built a stand, sold all the tickets myself... The Governor on arrival pressed a button which did nothing actually, but pretended to set off a maroon which in turn set off an enormous bonfire across the lake which in turn set off 50 rockets. The Buglers then sounded Retreat in the dark and then on went some 40 odd spotlights, floodlights and footlights, and the drums and the band beat tattoo and the audience settled down to enjoy themselves... Then some school-boys did the Parade of the Toy Soldiers. I got the particulars of this from the Duke of York's School at Dover, and adapted it to local conditions. The boys wore white trousers, red tunics, and white pill box hats, the officer a bear-skin... The tattoo then proceeded. Fireworks. A war dance by 120 warriors in Leopard Skins. Ostrich feathers and spears and shields. Then 'From Savage to Soldier' showing the process of turning native warriors into real soldiers.

The central event, and the sensation of the evening, was a relay of the voice of the new king/emperor, broadcast to the gathering through concealed loudspeakers. And next day there was a ceremony at the high court, which involved the Kabaka, the judges, the governor, the chiefs and the bishops – 'also my invention and it turned out to be a most dignified ceremony'.[55]

The rest of Twining's adequately distinguished career displayed the same concern for invented ceremonial. He was a flamboyant governor of Tanganyika. At the end he became one of the first creation of life peers – that supreme example of invented tradition – selling off his Grand Cross Mantle of the Order of St Michael and St John in order to buy 'a second-hand robe trimmed with real ermine'.[56]

Everywhere in British colonial Africa such rituals were taken very

[55] Darrell Bates, *A Gust of Plumes: A Biography of Lord Twining of Godalming and Tanganyika* (London, 1972), pp. 102–5.   *Ibid.*, p. 286.

seriously, if only rarely with Twining's exuberance. In a recent discussion of 'State and Peasantry in Colonial Africa', John Lonsdale remarks that 'the question of the statishness of the colonial state in Africa' can perhaps best be penetrated 'by looking at its festivals'.

All over the Empire [he writes] there were celebrations on 6 May 1935, the silver jubilee of King George V, even in little Kakamega, a district headquarters in the hills of western Kenya...The *power* of the state was on view with a parade of police...The *majesty* of rule was invoked with a speech from the governor, read by the district commissioner, who observed that King George was present, even to the meanest of his subjects, in his image on their coins, on the medals of their chiefs. He was 'a very great ruler and dearly loves his people and sees that they are ruled justly. He has always shown a very deep personal concern in your welfare' – and the schoolmaster-leaders of peasant opinion were even then acting on the principles of peasant legitimism by by-passing the king's servants and petitioning his House of Commons for redress of grievances...The royal family was still further linked to the material *improvement* in peasant citizenship. In Queen Victoria's day 'very few people had any clothes except skins and blankets and hardly any knew how to read. Now you have railways and roads, schools and hospitals, towns and trading centres, which give you the opportunity for development which civilization and good government bring in their train'. Colonial improvement was linked to peasant *recreation*. The day's proceedings included a display by the local boy scout troop...The rulers sought their subjects' affection in carnival, almost indeed in *saturnalia*. There were games for Africans only, the slippery pole, a tug-of-war, blindfold football biffing; but there was inter-racial sport too, a bicycle race, a donkey derby, even a fancy dress soccer match between Europeans and Indians for the natives to gawp at. Peasant *economy* was co-opted too; there was an egg, cent and flour race...Peasant *culture* was used too; the day started off with church services. Europeans attended the high culture of an Anglican service; to Africans was left the 'low culture' of a Catholic celebration.[57]

It is plain that British administrators took all this sort of thing very seriously – Twining as governor of Tanganyika refused to negotiate

[57] John Lonsdale, 'State and Peasantry in Colonial Africa', in Raphael Samuel (ed.), *People's History and Socialist Theory* (London, 1981), pp. 113–14.

with Nyerere's Tanganyika African Union because he regarded them as disloyal to the queen. But it is very difficult to assess how seriously Africans took it. Lonsdale describes the Kakamega Silver Jubilee celebrations as part of the 'indigenization of the state', and shows how the leaders of the local African peasantry operated easily within its assumptions; in Northern Rhodesia the chiefs played up to the official 'theology' by addressing their requests for guns or uniforms to the king through his governor and sent the king presents of leopard skins or tusks; African dance associations elected their kings and Kaisers to preside over them with proper ceremony; millenarian preachers told their audiences that King George, who had hitherto been deceived by his corrupt advisers, would assume direct control and usher in the golden age.[58] Clearly the symbol of monarchy appealed to the imagination. Perhaps for a while it also contributed to some sort of ideological consensus between Europeans and their African collaborators. As we shall see, a good deal of the politics of collaboration took place within the limits set by the colonial theory of monarchy. But as Twining's fatal rigidity in Tanganyika demonstrates, the colonial manipulation of monarchy and indeed the whole process of traditional inventiveness, having served a good deal of practical purpose, eventually came to be counter-productive. Twining's apparent cheerful irreverence and readiness to manufacture tradition only thinly masked his own profound commitment to monarchy, aristocracy, to neo-tradition. It was easier to invent a tradition than to modify it and make it flexible once invented. *Invented* tradition, as distinct from unconsciously evolving custom, could only be taken seriously if it were followed to the letter. That famous 'spirit' which was so celebrated at Budo could not blow where it listed among the dry bones of colonial ceremonialism.

[58] An interesting variant, directly calling the bluff of the imperial ideology, came in a sermon preached in Bulawayo in June 1923 by a Watch Tower teacher, Kunga: 'King George V tells the truth to the English but the people of this country do not abide by what he says but make their own laws. In 1912 the King wanted to come to Rhodesia to see the natives and change the law for them, but the white people of Southern Rhodesia sent him a message and told him not to come as there was too much sickness in the country.' File N3/5/8, National Archives, Rhodesia, Salisbury.

AFRICAN ATTEMPTS TO MAKE USE OF EUROPEAN NEO-TRADITION

One of the functions of the invention of tradition in nineteenth-century Europe was to give rapid and recognizable symbolic form to developing types of authority and submission. In Africa, and under the oversimplifying influence of colonial rule, the symbolic statements themselves became simpler and more emphatic. African observers of the new colonial society could hardly miss the significance that Europeans attached to the public rituals of monarchy, the gradations of military rank, the rituals of bureaucracy. Africans who sought to manipulate these symbols for themselves, without accepting the implications of subordination within a neo-tradition of governance, were usually accused by Europeans of triviality, of confusing form with reality and of imagining that it was possible to achieve power or prosperity just by emulating ritual practice. But if this were true, the over-emphasis on the forms had already been created by colonial whites themselves, most of whom were the beneficiaries rather than the creators of wealth and power. If their monopoly of the rites and symbols of neo-tradition was so important to the whites, it was by no means foolish of Africans to seek to appropriate them.

It seems to me that there were broadly four ways in which Africans sought to draw on European invented traditions, in a relatively autonomous way and without accepting the roles which Europeans assigned to Africans within them. At one level, the aspirant African bourgeoisie sought to make its own that range of attitudes and activities which defined the European middle classes. At another level, many African rulers – and their supporters – struggled to achieve the right to express their authority through the use of the titles and symbols of European neo-traditional monarchy. Again, there were Africans who adapted European neo-traditional symbolism in a spirit of fashion, proclaiming their own sophistication not so much by 'aping' Europeans as by an impressive display of their ability to keep up to date, to discern the realities of colonial power and to comment shrewdly upon them. But in many ways the most interesting use of European neo-traditions was by Africans who found themselves uprooted and who needed to discover new ways of making a new society.

The most vivid account of African petty bourgeois aspirations and their appropriation of British middle class neo-traditions is given by

Brian Willan in his work on the mission-educated Africans of Kimberley in the 1890s. 'Kimberley in the 1890s', he writes, 'was a supremely British place: daily life in the Diamond City, indeed, perhaps expressed as clearly as anywhere in the Empire the meaning and reality of British imperial hegemony.' There existed in the city:

> a growing and increasingly coherent class of educated Africans who had been drawn to Kimberley because of the opportunities that it provided for employment and for the utilization of the skills associated with the literacy which they possessed.

These men aspired to become secure denizens of the nineteenth-century British liberal universe – a universe of freedom and equality under the common law, of secure property rights and of entrepreneurial vigour. At the same time they sought to symbolize their citizenship of this universe through their mastery of the more 'irrational' invented traditions of the late nineteenth-century British middle class.

They outdid colonial whites in their loyalty to the crown. 'One peculiarly important and pervasive symbol...which gave expression to the values and beliefs that they held, was the figure of Queen Victoria'; they celebrated the queen's Diamond Jubilee in 1897 with banquets and loyal addresses in which they dramatized their own 'progressive' achievements and their trust in the monarchy as a guarantor of them. They set up 'a network of regular activities and involvement in churches, clubs and societies'. Above all, they took to sport:

> Sport [writes Willan] was important in the life of Kimberley's African petty bourgeoisie, providing a further bond of association and the means of disseminating the hegemonic value of the society in which they lived. Tennis was played at one of three clubs: Blue Flag Tennis Club, Champion Lawn Tennis Club, and Come Again Lawn Tennis Club...Altogether more popular, however, were cricket and rugby football, the leading sports in the Cape Colony generally...Cricket was the game that Kimberley's African petty bourgeoisie really made its own. That this should have been the case is perhaps not at all surprising. Cricket, after all, was not just a game. Rather, it was a uniquely British institution that embodied so many of the values and ideals which...they aspired to. Cricket was a social training ground: the analogy between cricket and life generally was widely accepted, its value in character development unquestioned. 'Caution, care, patience and decision', so one writer

in the *Diamond Fields Advertiser* claimed in 1893, 'are inculcated by cricket's manly toil'. Cricket both embodied and disseminated the imperial idea.

In Kimberley, the two African clubs (they ran several teams each) were the Duke of Wellington Cricket Club...and Eccentrics Cricket Club: even their names are suggestive, both symbolising qualities upon which the British Empire was built.[59]

In the long run of South African history, of course, all this came to be regarded by whites as taking the imperial ideal altogether too seriously. In South Africa there was no room for a cricket-playing *black* ruling class. African cricket withered away, to be replaced later on by the proletarian association football, which is the mass sport of modern Africa. Only in such exceptional colonial societies as Sierra Leone could Creole society regularly demonstrate its real power by lavish European neo-traditional rituals.

Meanwhile, 'tribal' African rulers found themselves contesting for the visible attributes of neo-traditional monarchy because their status was everywhere threatened under middle period colonialism. In the early days colonial administrators were happy enough to recognize African rulers as kings, and to present them, like Rindi, with the properties of stage monarchy. But as the colonial régimes established themselves and became less dependent on concessions extracted from African rulers, so there began a process of deflation. Thus, much of the British South Africa Company administration's claim to north-western Rhodesia depended upon the concessions it had gained from Lewanika of Barotseland. Lewanika was described as a great king and rewarded with access to the glamour of the British crown. The symbolic climax of Lewanika's career came with his invitation to attend the coronation of Edward VII in 1902. Lewanika was received with honour by English 'society':

he had royal carriages put at his disposal, his horses were taken out of his carriage in a Dorset village so that village people could drag the carriage, he was taught to play simple games at tea parties by people like the Duchess of Abercorn.

He was encouraged to acquire for his use both in England and back home some of the symbols of British royal ceremonialism – a royal coach, the uniform of a full-dress admiral, scarlet coats for his

[59] Brian Willan, 'An African in Kimberley: Sol. T. Plaatje, 1894–8', Conference on Class Formation, Culture and Consciousness: the Making of Modern South Africa (Jan. 1980), pp. 3, 5, 14–15.

servants at Lealui. 'When Kings are seated together', proclaimed the old Lozi ruler, 'there is never a lack of things to discuss'.[60]

But soon the old man was being denied his kingliness altogether. As the Northern Rhodesian administration came to feel more secure, so it cut back Lewanika's powers, rebuffed his protestations and dramatized this withdrawal of favour through a double manipulation of royal symbolism. It was laid down that the high commissioner and the administrator must be greeted with the Lozi royal salute; it was also laid down that Lewanika himself should no longer be referred to as 'King', since this elevated him above the other chiefs and drew what was considered to be an altogether inappropriate analogy with the imperial monarch.[61] A similar pattern is apparent in the Ankole kingdom in Uganda. There, too, there was an initial period of colonial support for the Ankole monarchy, followed by a reaction in which 'officers at work in the country disliked the title of King being used for the rulers of small African states'.[62]

In this colonial middle period, African 'paramounts' strove to gain the title of king, to obtain invitations to British coronations, to dramatize their internal authority with crowns and thrones, British-style coronations and jubilees. The Omugabe of Ankole managed to acquire a throne and a coat of arms and a crown.[63] Lewanika's successor, Yeta, worked indefatigably to proclaim special royal status. He had certain advantages. Whenever a royal personage visited Northern Rhodesia, the administration looked fairly desparately around for something other than the Victoria Falls to show them. They had always to fall back on the Lozi. Reviewing the ceremonial possibilities for the Prince of Wales's visit in 1925, the governor deplored that 'generally speaking none of these Chiefs are likely to look very impressive', but consoled himself with the thought that the Lozi 'aquatic display' was likely to be 'a fairly picturesque affair as native ceremonies go'.[64] Yeta brought his fleet down the Zambesi to meet the prince, but was careful to stress in his speech that 'it would have been a great pleasure to us to receive and welcome Your Royal Highness at our home with *proper* ceremonious

[60] Henry Rangeley to 'Dear Mr Cohen', March 1938, Historical Manuscripts 20, RA1/1/1, Lusaka; G. Caplan, *The Elites of Barotseland, 1878–1969* (California, 1970).
[61] M. R. Doornbos, *Regalia Galore: The Decline and Collapse of Ankole Kingship* (Nairobi, 1975).   [62] *Ibid.*
[63] *Ibid.*
[64] Sir Herbert Stanley to Sir Geoffrey Thomas, 7 July 1925, P3/13/3/8, Lusaka.

welcome'.[65] Moreover, there were many thousands of Lozi working in the mines and towns of the south, many as clerks and supervisors. These 'new men' were fully prepared to donate money and to draft petitions in order to recover the title of 'King' for their paramount. Finally, the special status of Barotseland meant that the administration could not just impose local 'reforms' there but had to bargain with Yeta.

Drawing on all these advantages, Yeta scored a signal symbolic triumph at the end of his reign. He was determined to attend the coronation of 1937. There were formidable obstacles. The secretary of state in London had at first decided not to invite any African ruler to the ceremony, but to draw the line at the Indian princes. The administrators in Northern Rhodesia took the position that the coronation was a sacramental rite appropriate only to whites; Africans could not penetrate to this holy of holies; the coronation liturgy 'would convey nothing to the great majority of natives'.[66] But Yeta exploited all his advantages; made concessions on local government 'reform' and was invited. His progress south was triumphal as the Lozi labour migrants flocked to the line of rail to donate funds for the voyage. Yeta was received by the king; gave him the Lozi royal salute; and returned in triumph to Barotseland, where Lozi progressives expressed themselves

> very glad for the honour that the British Empire has bestowed upon Barotseland by inviting Your Highness to attend the Coronation and more than all in giving Your Highness one of the best seats in the Abbey, which is a privilege that only a few people among thousands and millions of people have enjoyed.[67]

The triumph was recorded for posterity by Yeta's secretary, Godwin Mbikusita, whose *Yeta III's Visit to England* was published in 1940.

> The Coronation [wrote Mbikusita] was the greatest event we ever saw or that we will ever see in our lives again. Nobody could think that he is really on earth when seeing the Coronation Procession, but that he is either dreaming or is in Paradise.

But he also made it very plain that Yeta made his homage to King George as one king to another, recording that Sobhuza II of Swaziland had cabled Yeta 'wishing you...to hail the King with African royal spirit and etiquette'.[68]

[65] Address of Yeta III, 18 June 1925, RC/453, Lusaka.
[66] Minute on secretary of state to governor, 6 Feb. 1937, sec. 1/1792, Lusaka.
[67] For Yeta's visit to England see file sec. 2/364, ii, Lusaka.
[68] Godwin Mbikusita, *Yeta III's Visit to England* (Lusaka, 1940).

Nor was it only great chiefs who had once enjoyed the title of 'King' who played this kind of symbolic politics. Recourse to royal neo-tradition was one of the techniques of the great invention of 'tribal' traditions which was going on everywhere in the 1920s and 1930s.[69] Leroy Vail has described what happened in the case of the Tumbuka-speakers possessed different religious and social institutions. But under colonialism a group of mission-educated Africans Tumbuka-speakers possessed different religious and social institutions. But under colonialism a group of mission-educated Africans created a Tumbuka paramountcy. Chilongozi Gondwe was appointed as chief in 1907 and commenced a campaign to impress his royal status on the minds of the Tumbuka. He celebrated each year the anniversary of his accession and began to use the title of 'King'. In this he was warmly supported by the mission élite, who were beginning to produce a myth history of the ancient Tumbuka empire. As Leroy Vail remarks:

> For the well-educated elite to accept traditional values and a hierarchical arrangement of society under chiefs is *not* to be wondered at, given the nature of the Victorian education they had received in the [mission] schools.

The district commissioner attempted to check Gondwe's acquisition of influence. 'I warned [him] that he was not to assume the title of King'. But by the time of Chilongozi Gondwe's death in 1931 things had changed. The colonial administration now favoured a policy of indirect rule and this gave an opening for the élite inventors of tradition.

An African minister, Edward Bote Manda, backed Chilongozi's son, John Gondwe, as the new chief. Manda drew up an elaborate coronation rite, including a series of 'Vows of Chieftainship' modelled on those of the British coronation – 'Do you solemnly promise to protect our Christian religion and submit to the Bible teachings which are a guide to righteous ruling of your people?' The Tumbuka paramountcy began to assume the characteristics of a progressive Christian monarchy.[70]

---

[69] Terence Ranger, 'Traditional Societies and Western Colonialism', Conference on Traditional Societies and Colonialism (Berlin, June 1979). Published as 'Kolonialismus in Ost-Und Zentral Afrika', J. H. Grevemeyer (ed.), *Traditionale Gesellschaften und europäischer Kolonialismus* (Frankfurt, 1981).

[70] Leroy Vail, 'Ethnicity, Language and National Unity' (Univ. of Zambia seminar paper, 1978). Dr Vail is editing a volume of ethnicity and political economy in southern Africa.

It will be seen that these attempts to manipulate British royal symbolism were complex. If from the point of view of the chiefs they were largely re-assertions of status, from the point of view of the mission-educated they were also an attempt to *redefine* chiefly authority. The British Coronation rite, wrote Mbikusita,

> shows great cooperation between the Crown and People, and this shows that although the people are the subjects of their King, he is also their subject...It is a great surprise to us to see that the Queen in England shares the Coronation with the King. It is a sign of irrevocable marriage and true partnership in life. European civilisation has taken centuries to appreciate this and we hope that, by the teaching and examples given to us by this civilization, this generation may come to acquire such realization.

Lozi teachers expressed the hope that Yeta's visit to the coronation would 'open a door for the Barotseland educated class' and 'uplift the country by adopting some of the civilized lines existing in England'.[71] Once again, in Africa the neo-traditions of Britain were seen as a source of modernizing change.

But just as the commitment to royal symbol proved, in the end, limiting to the colonialists, so its fruits for Africans were at best ambiguous. Educated Africans came to realize that the way towards real power to bring about modernizing change did not lie in relatively small-scale African 'kingdoms'. They began to invent nationalist rather than tribal traditions. By the time of the visit of King George VI to Northern Rhodesia in 1947, African intellectuals sought to make use of the occasion by delivering loyal addresses which made a series of nationalist points; the old pieties of such occasions were only maintained by dint of arbitrary censorship of their texts. A clear distinction had by then opened up between their concerns and those of the Lozi paramount, who put on in 1947 another reliably picturesque ceremony.[72]

Meanwhile, those African rulers who *did* succeed in acquiring some of the trappings of neo-traditional monarchy were caught up in an ironic process. What was involved, as Doornbos brings out very well for Ankole, was a transformation from flexible and adaptable customary monarchical institutions to a colonial monarchy 'fitted into the bureaucratic structure and in time adorned with a thick

---

[71] Mbikusita, *op. cit.*, pp. 56, 63–4, 145.
[72] File sec. 3/234, Lusaka contains both the original and the censored forms of Addresses.

overlay of new ceremonialism'. The essence of the change in Ankole was to turn the Omugabe 'into an instrument of bureaucratic hierarchy and to relegate the traditional values to the level of folk lore'. Aspirations to become more like the king/emperor ended in African rulers really becoming more like him, as they came more and more to occupy the ceremonial centre rather than the political or cultural centre of their societies. It was a process neatly summed up by the title of Doornbos's book, *Regalia Galore*. But unlike the ceremonial of the king/emperor, which still serves a function in shrunken, post-imperial Britain, the ceremonial of African kings turned out in the end not to mirror anything very important. The Ankole kingship was abolished without a ripple of dissent, and the local press headlined the transition to a more openly bureaucratic symbol of authority – 'The Throne Replaced by Chairman's Seat'.[73]

But it was not only African rulers and clergymen who tried to manipulate the symbols of European invented tradition. They were also seized upon by thousands of others who were experiencing the colonial economy, whether as migrant labourers or as petty clerks and functionaries. Each of these two groups sought to come to terms with the new colonial society and they did so partly by means of participation in dance associations in which one or other of the European invented traditions was drawn on to express the essence of colonialism, as a source of prestige, or as a mark of high fashion. John Iliffe has described the coastal dance associations in German East Africa just before the first world war. Dances were performed in the Kaiser's honour in 1911 by *ngoma ya kihuni* – the hooligans' dance association, a name defiantly chosen by 'low-class, up-country immigrants'. They danced the *Bom*, an imitation of German military drill, named after the sound of the machine gun. Clerks and domestic servants 'invariably celebrated the Kaiser's birthday with *chapaulinge*'. Their dance associations gathered in a house furnished in European style; they drank tea; 'and at the end of the feast they said "Hurrah!" three times'.[74] In the towns of the Kenyan coast a similar class division produced competition between the Arinoti up-country migrants and the Marini Swahili youth. The Marini rejoiced in rich aristocratic patrons and they triumphed over their plebeian opponents with processions headed by replicas of governors and their equerries; with floats of battleships, with admirals in full dress taking

[73] *Uganda Argus*, 28 Sept. 1967.
[74] Iliffe, *A Modern History of Tanganyika*, pp. 238–9.

the salute on the bridge; and on one glorious occasion still much celebrated in the photograph albums of Lamu, with a stately line of peers of the house of lords, all in full ceremonial dress.[75]

As I have argued elsewhere, these carnival occasions were very much more than a mere aping of the whites. The dance societies were descendants of older associations which had for decades, and probably centuries, reflected the changing experience of the coast and its hinterland, now marking a shift in the balance of power by taking up Omani fashions, now by adopting Indian modes. Among other things, the dance associations were very shrewd in seizing upon basic divisions within European colonial society and using these as the basis for dance competition. Before formal colonialism, French teams danced against German and British teams. Under colonialism, teams representing sea-power danced against teams representing the colonial infantry. In Kenya teams professing loyalty to the British crown – Kingi – danced against teams representing those most evident rivals of the English, the Scots. Scotchi teams paraded through the streets of Mombasa, wearing kilts and playing bag-pipes, thus celebrating the successful nineteenth-century invention of Scottish tradition. The Welsh, alas, were less present in the African empire and there were no Druids in African dance competitions![76]

These dances were performed by men who were either confident in their own coastal urban environment or who had a rural home to return to. But there were others who felt uprooted, needing not only to reflect on the colonial experience but to discover a way of organizing their whole lives. For such people, one European tradition in particular was useful – the military mode. This was the most clear-cut model available, especially in early colonialism. Its demarcations of authority were obvious, as were its methods of instilling work discipline; it formed a centrally important part of early colonial European societies, and seemed to offer a complete model of an operative community. So ready to hand was it, that the military mode and the military metaphor were extensively employed by European missionaries, who armed and drilled their early converts before formal colonial rule was established, and who continued to drill their schoolboys and organize them into drum and fife bands deep into the colonial period.[77] But an appropriate discipline was not merely

---

[75] Ranger, *Dance and Society in Eastern Africa*.   [76] *Ibid.*
[77] Terence Ranger, 'The European Military Mode and the Societies of Eastern Africa' (Univ. of California, Los Angeles, colloquium paper, 1972).

something enforced by whites; often it was something sought by Africans. After all, the adjustment to the exigencies of the new colonial system had to be made by Africans themselves. A new model of social interaction, of hierarchy and control was needed by many African groupings that wanted to become communities. The military mode could be made use of by Africans for all these purposes.

Professor Ogot cites a striking case. Bishop Willis visited scattered African converts in western Kenya in 1916.

Trained or half trained in a Mission School [wrote the Bishop], the Convert returns to his native village, and is lost to sight. Next time the missionary meets him he is in self-imposed charge of a little congregation of Readers, from which in due course a little group of candidates for the catechumenate emerges. So the work grows, but much of it in its initial stages is carried on in entire independence of the European. Again, the visitor on any Sunday to the native congregation in Kisumu will see what he will see nowhere else but in Kavirondo, a drilled and uniformed congregation. Not all, but some hundreds of them, will be found clothed in a short shirt of white with dark blue facings and a dark blue spine pad; the letters, roughly worked, C.M.K. across the breast; and on the red fez cap a blue cross on white shield. A closer inspection will reveal mysterious buttons and stripes showing that from a corporal to a colonel every rank is represented. Two little red buttons on the shoulder indicate a lieutenant, three are a captain and so on. Even the Red Cross contingent finds a place, with its own officers, outside the building before church. And throughout, in varying degrees of efficiency, the same thing. The colours vary, the shape of the cross on the cap differs with the different districts, but the same general idea is to be seen everywhere. The interesting part of the organization is that it is entirely the native Christians' own idea. They have designed and paid for their own uniforms. They drill and organize themselves without instruction or intervention from any white man; a clearer proof of natural independence it would be difficult to find.[78]

[78] F. B. Welbourn and B. A. Ogot, *A Place to Feel at Home* (London, 1966), pp. 24–5.

EUROPEANS AND 'TRADITION' IN AFRICA

The invented traditions of nineteenth-century Europe had been introduced into Africa to allow Europeans and certain Africans to combine for 'modernizing' ends. But there was an inherent ambiguity in neo-traditional thought. Europeans belonging to one or other of the neo-traditions believed themselves to have a respect for the customary. They liked the idea of age-old prescriptive rights and they liked to compare the sort of title which an African chief possessed with the title to gentlemanliness which they laid claim to themselves. A profound misunderstanding was at work here. In comparing European neo-traditions with the customary in Africa the whites were certainly comparing unlike with unlike. European invented traditions were marked by their inflexibility. They involved sets of recorded rules and procedures – like the modern coronation rites. They gave reassurance because they represented what was unchanging in a period of flux. Now, when Europeans thought of the customary in Africa, they naturally ascribed to it these same characteristics. The assertion by whites that African society was profoundly conservative – living within age-old rules which did not change; living within an ideology based on the absence of change; living within a framework of clearly defined hierarchical status – was by no means always intended as an indictment of African backwardness or reluctance to modernize. Often it was intended as a compliment to the admirable qualities of tradition, even though it was a quite misconceived compliment. This attitude towards 'traditional' Africa became more marked as whites came to realize in the 1920s and 1930s that rapid economic transformation was just not going to take place in Africa and that most Africans had to remain members of rural communities, or as some whites came to dislike the consequences of the changes which *had* taken place. The African collaborators, playing their role within one or other of the introduced European traditions, then came to seem less admirable than 'real' Africans, still presumed to be inhabiting their own, appropriate universe of tradition.

The trouble with this approach was that it totally misunderstood the realities of pre-colonial Africa. These societies had certainly valued custom and continuity but custom was loosely defined and infinitely flexible. Custom helped to maintain a sense of identity but it also allowed for an adaptation so spontaneous and natural that it was often unperceived. Moreover, there rarely existed in fact the closed corporate consensual system which came to be accepted as characteristic of 'traditional' Africa. Almost all recent studies of nineteenth-century pre-colonial Africa have emphasized that far from there being a single 'tribal' identity, most Africans moved in and out of multiple identities, defining themselves at one moment as subject to this chief, at another moment as a member of that cult, at another moment as part of this clan, and at yet another moment as an initiate in that professional guild. These overlapping networks of association and exchange extended over wide areas. Thus the boundaries of the 'tribal' polity and the hierarchies of authority within them did *not* define conceptual horizons of Africans. As Wim van Binsbergen remarks, in criticizing Africanist historians for their acceptance of something called 'Chewa identity' as a useful organizing concept for the past:

> Modern Central Africa tribes are not so much survivals from a pre-colonial past but rather largely colonial creations by colonial officers and African intellectuals...Historians fail to qualify the alleged Chewa homogeneity against the historical evidence of incessant assimilation and dissociation of peripheral groups... They do not differentiate between a seniority system of rulers imposed by the colonial freezing of political dynamics and the pre-colonial competitive, shifting, fluid imbalance of power and influence.[79]

Similarly, nineteenth-century Africa was *not* characterized by lack of internal social and economic competition, by the unchallenged authority of the elders, by an acceptance of custom which gave every person – young and old, male and female – a place in society which was defined and protected. Competition, movement, fluidity were as much features of small-scale communities as they were of larger groupings. Thus Marcia Wright has shown, in a stimulating account of the realities of late nineteenth-century society in the Lake Tanganyika corridor, that economic and political competition overrode the 'customary securities' offered to women by marriage or extended kinship relations. Women constantly found themselves being shaken out of the niches in which they had sought security, and constantly tried to find new niches for themselves. Later on, of course, and in the twentieth century, the dogmas of customary security and immutably fixed relationships grew up in these same societies, which came to

[79] Review of S. J. Ntara, *History of the Chewa*, ed. Harry Langworthy, by W. M. J. Van Binsbergen, *African Social Research* (June 1976), pp. 73–5.

have an appearance of *ujamaa* style solidarity; the nineteenth-century time of 'rapid change', in which 'formal structural factors' became relatively less important than 'personal resilience and powers of decision', gave way to stabilization. As Marcia Wright remarks:

the terms of the reconstruction were dictated by the colonial authorities in the years after 1895, when pacification came to mean immobilization of populations, re-inforcement of ethnicity and greater rigidity of social definition.[80]

Hence 'custom' in the Tanganyika corridor was much more of an invention than it was a restoration. In other places, where the competitive dynamic of the nineteenth century had given many opportunities for young men to establish independent bases of economic, social and political influence, colonialism saw an establishment of control by elders of land allocation, marriage transactions and political office. Small-scale gerontocracies were a defining feature of the twentieth rather than of the nineteenth century.

Some part of these twentieth-century processes of 'immobilization of populations, re-inforcement of ethnicity and greater rigidity of social definition' were the necessary and unplanned consequences of colonial economic and political change – of the break up of internal patterns of trade and communication, the defining of territorial boundaries, the alienation of land, the establishment of Reserves. But some part of them were the result of a conscious determination on the part of the colonial authorities to 're-establish' order and security and a sense of community by means of defining and enforcing 'tradition'. Administrators who had begun by proclaiming their support for exploited commoners against rapacious chiefs ended by backing 'traditional' chiefly authority in the interests of social control.[81] Missionaries who had begun by taking converts right out of their societies so as to transform their consciousness in 'Christian villages' ended by proclaiming the virtues of 'traditional' small-scale community. Everyone sought to tidy up and make more comprehensible the infinitely complex situation which they held to be a result of the 'untraditional' chaos of the nineteenth century. People were to be 'returned' to their tribal identities; ethnicity was to be 'restored' as the basis of association and organization.[82] The new rigidities,

[80] Marcia Wright, 'Women in Peril', *African Social Research* (Dec. 1975), p. 803.
[81] Henry Meebelo, *Reaction to Colonialism* (Manchester, 1971).
[82] Terence Ranger, 'European Attitudes and African Realities: The Rise and Fall of the Matola Chiefs of South-East Tanzania', *Journal of African History*, xx, no. 1 (1979), pp. 69–82.

immobilizations and ethnic identifications, while serving very immediate European interests, could nevertheless be seen by the whites as
fully 'traditional' and hence as legitimated. The most far-reaching
inventions of tradition in colonial Africa took place when the
Europeans believed themselves to be respecting age-old African
custom. What were called customary law, customary land-rights,
customary political structure and so on, were in fact *all* invented by
colonial codification.

There is a growing anthropological and historical literature on
these processes which it is not possible to summarize here. But a few
striking statements will give an indication of the argument. Thus
John Iliffe describes the 'creation of tribes' in colonial Tanganyika:

> The notion of the tribe lay at the heart of indirect rule in
> Tanganyika. Refining the racial thinking common in German
> times, administrators believed that every African belonged to a
> tribe, just as every European belonged to a nation. The idea
> doubtless owed much to the Old Testament, to Tacitus and Caesar,
> to academic distinctions between tribal societies based on status
> and modern societies based on contract, and to the post-war
> anthropologists who preferred 'tribal' to the more pejorative word
> 'savage'. Tribes were seen as cultural units 'possessing a common
> language, a single social system, and an established common law'.
> Their political and social systems rested on kinship. Tribal
> membership was hereditary. Different tribes were related
> genealogically...As unusually well-informed officials knew, this
> stereotype bore little relation to Tanganyika's kaleidoscopic his-
> tory, but it was the shifting sand on which Cameron and his
> disciples erected indirect rule by 'taking the *tribal* unit'. They had
> the power and they created the political geography.[83]

Elizabeth Colson describes the evolution of 'customary land law'
in much the same way:

> The newly created system was described as resting on tradition and
> presumably derived its legitimacy from immemorial custom. The
> degree to which it was a reflection of the contemporary situation
> and the joint creation of colonial officials and African
> leaders...was unlikely to be recognized.

The point is not merely that so-called custom in fact concealed new
balances of power and wealth, since this was precisely what custom
in the past had always been able to do, but that these particular

---

[83] John Iliffe, *A Modern History of Tanganyika*, pp. 323–4.

constructs of customary law became codified and rigid and unable so readily to reflect change in the future. Colson remarks that

colonial officers expected the courts to enforce long-established custom rather than current opinion. Common stereotypes about African customary law thus came to be used by colonial officials in assessing the legality of current decisions, and so came to be incorporated in 'customary' systems of tenure.[84]

Similarly, Wyatt MacGaffey has shown how the Bakongo peoples moved from a pre-colonial situation of 'processes of dispersal and assimilation'; of 'the shunting of subordinate populations of slaves and pawns'; of 'a confusion of debts, assets, scandals and grievances', into a colonial situation of much more precise and static definition of community and of land rights.

In the evolution of tradition, the touchstone of merit was very often the presiding judge's concept of customary society, derived ultimately from...a lingering European image of the African kingdom of Prester John...Court records contain evidence of the evolution for forensic purposes away from the magical in the direction of the evidential and refutable...Those whose traditions lost a case came back a year or two later with better traditions.

Once again, my point is not so much that 'traditions' changed to accommodate new circumstances but that at a certain point they had to stop changing; once the 'traditions' relating to community identity and land right were writen down in court records and exposed to the criteria of the invented customary model, a new and unchanging body of tradition had been created.

Eventually there resulted a synthesis of the new and the old, which is now called 'custom'. The main features of customary society, responding to the conditions that developed between 1908 and 1921, assumed their present form in the 1920s.[85]

Around the same time Europeans began to be more interested in and sympathetic towards the 'irrational' and ritualistic aspects of 'tradition'. In 1917 an Anglican mission theologian suggested that for the first time missionaries in the field should 'collect information with regard to the religious ideas of the black man', so that their relationship to traditional society could be understood. 'In the

---

[84] Elizabeth Colson, 'The Impact of the Colonial Period on the Definition of Land Rights', in Victor Turner (ed.), *Colonialism in Africa* (Cambridge, 1971), iii, pp. 221–51.

[85] Wyatt MacGaffey, *Custom and Government in the Lower Congo* (California, 1970), pp. 207–8.

twentieth century we are no longer contented to cut the knot, as the nineteenth century did, and say: Science has put an end to these superstitions'.[86] After the first world war, Anglicans in East Africa, faced with the need to reconstruct rural society after the ravages of the fighting and the subsequent impact of the depression, began to make anthropological analyses of those aspects of 'traditional' ritual which had contributed towards social stability. Out of such inquiry came the well-known policy of missionary 'adaptation', which produced its most developed example in the Christianized initiation ceremonies of the Masasi diocese in south-eastern Tanganyika.[87] More generally, there emerged from this kind of thought and practice – with its emphasis upon rituals of continuity and stability – a concept of immemorial 'African Traditional Religion' which did less than justice to the variety and vitality of pre-colonial African religious forms.

AFRICAN MANIPULATION OF INVENTED CUSTOM

All this could not have been achieved, of course, without a good deal of African participation. As John Iliffe writes:

The British wrongly believed that Tanganyikans belonged to tribes; Tanganyikans created tribes to function within the colonial framework...[The] new political geography...would have been transient had it not co-incided with similar trends among Africans. They too had to live amidst bewildering social complexity, which they ordered in kinship terms and buttressed with invented history. Moreover, Africans wanted effective units of action just as officials wanted effective units of government...Europeans believed Africans belonged to tribes; Africans built tribes to belong to.[88]

We have already seen in the case of the Tumbuka paramountcy how African rulers and mission-educated 'modernizers' could combine in an attempt to manipulate the symbols of monarchy. Iliffe shows how similar alliances helped to build up the ideas and structures of 'tribal' tradition.

During the twenty years after 1925 Tanganyika experienced a vast social reorganization in which Europeans and Africans combined

---

[86] 'The Study of African Religion', *Central Africa*, xxxv, no. 419 (Nov. 1917), p. 261.

[87] Terence Ranger, 'Missionary Adaptation and African Religious Institutions', in Terence Ranger and Isaria Kimambo (eds.), *The Historical Study of African Religion* (London, 1972), pp. 221–51.   [88] Iliffe, *op. cit.*, p. 324.

to create a new political order based on mythical history...Analysing the system [of indirect rule] one officer concluded that its main supporters were the progressive chiefs...It is clear that they were the key figures in indirect rule. Its chief virtue was indeed to release their energies...The native administrations employed many members of the local elite...Even educated men without native administration posts generally acknowledged hereditary authority...In return many chiefs welcomed educated guidance.

Iliffe describes progressive chiefs and mission-educated Africans combining in a programme of 'progressive traditionalism'.

Just as later nationalists sought to create a national culture, so those who built modern tribes emphasized tribal culture. In each case educated men took the lead...The problem was to synthesize, to 'pick out what is best from (European culture) and dilute it with what we hold'. In doing so, educated men naturally reformulated the past, so that their syntheses were actually new creations.[89]

One area in which African intellectuals interacted with 'adaptation' missionary theory was in the invention of 'Traditional Religion'.

It was not until missionaries studied African religions carefully during the 1920s that most Africans dared to consider their attitudes publicly. Michel Kikurwe, a Zigua teacher and cultural tribalist, envisaged a golden age of traditional African society...Samuel Sehoza pioneered the idea that indigenous religious beliefs had prefigured Christianity.

Like the missionaries these men emphasized the function of religion in stabilizing society.

In each district [wrote Kikurwe] men and women were busy to help one another, they taught their children the same laws and traditions. Every Chief tried as much as he could to help and please his people, and likewise his people did the same in turn, they all knew what was lawful and unlawful, and they knew that there was a powerful God in heaven.[90]

It is easy enough to see the personal advantages which these inventors of tradition stood to gain. The successful teacher or minister who stood at the right hand of a paramount was a man of very real power. The African clergy who constructed the model of 'Traditional Religion' as the inspiring ideology of stable pre-colonial communities were making a claim to do the same for modern African

[89] *Ibid.*, pp. 327–9, 334.
[90] *Ibid.*, pp. 335–6.

societies by means of 'adapted' Christianity.[91] Yet Iliffe concludes that

> it would be wrong to be cynical. The effort to create a Nyakyusa tribe was as honest and constructive as the essentially similar effort forty years later to create a Tanganyikan nation. Both were attempts to build societies in which men could live well in the modern world.[92]

But there was still an ambiguity in invented African tradition. However much it may have been used by the 'progressive traditionalists' to inaugurate new ideas and institutions – like compulsory education under the Tumbuka paramountcy – codified tradition inevitably hardened in a way that advantaged the vested interests in possession at the time of its codification. Codified and reified custom was manipulated by such vested interests as a means of asserting or increasing control. This happened in four particular situations; though it was not restricted to them.

Elders tended to appeal to 'tradition' in order to defend their dominance of the rural means of production against challenge by the young. Men tended to appeal to 'tradition' in order to ensure that the increasing role which women played in production in the rural areas did not result in any diminution of male control over women as economic assets. Paramount chiefs and ruling aristocracies in polities which included numbers of ethnic and social groupings appealed to 'tradition' in order to maintain or extend their control over their subjects. Indigenous populations appealed to 'tradition' in order to ensure that the migrants who settled amongst them did not achieve political or economic rights.

THE USE OF 'TRADITION' BY ELDERS AGAINST YOUTH

The colonial reification of rural custom produced a situation very much at variance with the pre-colonial situation. The pre-colonial movement of men and ideas was replaced by the colonial custom-bounded, microcosmic local society. It was important for the colonial authorities to limit regional interaction and thus to prevent a widening of focus on the part of Africans. For this reason they were prepared to back collaborators at the local level and to endorse their dominance. But at the same time the colonial powers wanted to

---

[91] Ranger, 'Missionary Adaptation and African Religious Institutions'.
[92] Iliffe, *op. cit.*, pp. 324–5.

extract labour from these rural societies, so that young men were being drawn to places of employment very much more distant than the range of journeying in the pre-colonial past. These young men were expected to be at one and the same time workers in a distant urban economy and acceptant citizens in the tightly defined microcosmic society.

This situation created many tensions. Returning migrants came back into a society tightly controlled by the elders; the elders, in turn, were alarmed at the new skills and funds possessed by the migrants. The elders stressed their customary, prescriptive rights which gave them control of land and women, and hence of patronage. MacGaffey describes the colonial Bakongo village in these terms:

> A man remains a cadet until he is about forty, perhaps longer...He is at the beck and call of his elders, whose tone towards him is often peremptory. Young men speak of their elders as jealous and fault-finding. The status of young men is that of the client...The control exercised over their dependants by the elders is a function of their managerial monopoly in routine public affairs.

This managerial monopoly is largely a function of the elders' control of 'traditional' knowledge, on which claims to land and resources are based. MacGaffey records 'the objection of elders' when 'bright young men busily took notes' at a land hearing case, and thus threatened to break the elders' monopoly.[93]

The response of young men to this manipulation of 'tradition' could take one of two forms. The key object was to outflank the elders and their sphere of local, but colonially invented, tradition. This could be done by adopting one or other of the European neo-traditions. Thus returning migrants often established themselves as catechists – whether recognized by the missions or not – and set up their own villages on new principles of organization, as it will be remembered was the case with the uniformed congregations of western Kenya. This was easier to do, however, in the earlier colonial period before both European church and European state began to insist on a proper subordination to custom. In MacGaffey's village, the young men, deprived of a real escape, took refuge in a fantasy one.

> For those who are young in years a degree of compensation is provided by the Dikembe, a social club catering to the unmarried men...Dikembe culture, an interesting caricature of the serious

---

[93] MacGaffey, *op. cit.*, pp. 208, 222–3.

magico-religious beliefs and principles of the older generation which it defies, contains the seeds of an anti-society... The doors of the bachelor huts bear such inscriptions as 'Palais d'Amour' in Gothic lettering... The culture of the Dikembe is that of *billisme*, whose heroes are the stars of romantic French and American movies [and] takes its name from Buffalo Bill, 'sheriff du quartier Santa Fe, metro d'amour'.[94]

These light-hearted absurdities conceal a serious attempt to discredit 'custom', endorsed as it is by the whites, through the subversive effects of European fantasy.

However, another path had also been open to the young in the colonial period and before the rise of the nationalist parties. This had been to outflank the reified 'custom' of the elders by appeals to more dynamic and transformative aspects of the traditional. Recent commentators have increasingly seen the very widespread witchcraft eradication movements of the colonial period, with their promise of a society freed from evil, in this sort of way. MacGaffey describes how in his Bakongo village the management of witchcraft accusation by the elders caused great discontent, and led to the arrival of a 'prophet' who undertook to eliminate witchcraft, an achievement which would deprive the elders of a potent form of social control. The result was 'the temporary paralysis of the elders'. Roy Willis has shown how in rural south-western Tanganyika in the 1950s young men tried to break the control exercised by elders over land and local 'routine public affairs', by making use of a series of witchcraft eradication movements, which outflanked invented custom by an appeal to the pre-social Golden Age.[95]

Of the many other analyses which support the argument, I will content myself with citing a particularly cogent, and as yet unpublished, account of the well-known Watch Tower sectarian movement in southern and central Africa. Sholto Cross concludes:

The three mining belts of settler Africa... provide the central focus of the movement and the migrant labourer was the main bearer... The migrant system which existed in these territories... prolonged the period in which the Africans could be regarded as bound by their tribal culture... yet at the same time policies designed to promote labour mobility were instituted which

[94] *Ibid.*, pp. 223–4.
[95] Roy Willis, 'Kamcape: An Anti-Sorcery Movement in South-West Tanzania', *Africa*, xxxi, no. 1 (1968).

undermined the economic basis of this tribal culture...The rate of change in the industrial areas far outstripped that in the rural hinterlands, yet the migrant labourers continued to move between the two worlds of town and country...The proliferation of Watch Tower villages [was caused by] the series of restraints placed upon the returning migrant. Customary authorities were jealous of the new men, whose way of life emphasized urban values...The prevalence of women and youth in the rural Watch Tower suggests that economic cleavages were reinforced by other forms of differ-entiation...The forward looking ideas of the hoped-for liberation [promised] by millenial Watch Tower were such that customary authority itself became a major object of attack.[96]

THE USE OF 'TRADITION' BY MEN AGAINST WOMEN

Denise Paulme's *Women of Tropical Africa*, though concerned to refute a stereotyped European image of oppressed African woman-hood, nevertheless brought out very clearly two things. The first was the practical breakdown under colonialism of many customary institutions regulating the relations between the sexes, a breakdown almost always disadvantageous economically to women. The second was the constant appeal by men to 'tradition'. Anne Laurentin asserted in her chapter in the collection that

remembrance of the good old days is accompanied by nostalgic regret on the part of older men...Among young and old alike there is a profoundly anti-feminist spirit which springs from a feeling of impotence upon realizing that women will refuse to return to the state of dependence they knew a century ago. The old people lay the blame for the fall in the birthrate on women.[97]

To my mind Laurentin is confusing complaints about increasing female independence with its reality. Elders reasserted their control over local affairs by their complaints of the breach of tradition by the young; men reasserted their dominance over a changing economic and social system by their complaints of the breach of tradition by women.

A more recent collection of essays on African women makes the

---

[96] Sholto Cross, 'The Watch Tower Movement in South Central Africa, 1908–1945' (Univ. of Oxford doctoral thesis, 1973), pp. 431–8.
[97] Anne Laurentin, 'Nzakara Women', in Denise Paulme (ed.), *Women of Tropical Africa* (California, 1963), pp. 431–8.

point clearly. As Caroline Ifeka-Moller reminds us, colonial records on African 'tradition', on which the new invented custom was based, were exclusively derived from male informants, so that 'indigenous female belief' remained unrecorded. Thus 'men's dominance in society, that is their control over religious beliefs and political organization' was expressed even more clearly in colonial invented custom than it had ever been before. Neither in the works of indirect rule ethnographers nor of adaptation missiologists – nor of mission-educated African intellectuals – was much attention paid to the traditions of women.[98] Moreover, African men were quite prepared to appeal to the colonial authority to enforce 'custom' upon women once it had been defined. In southern Rhodesia, and elsewhere in the zone of industrial labour migration, officials imposed punishments for adultery and enforced paternal control over marriage in response to constant complaints by male 'traditionalists'.[99] Meanwhile, in the absence of male migrants, women were playing a larger and larger part in rural production.

Once again, women had two possible means of asserting themselves against male-dominated custom. They might turn to missionary Christianity and its notions of female rights and duties, or they might seek to use the counter-propositions available within African culture. Sometimes women sought to develop rites of female initiation, which had in the past constituted a balance to male ritual influence in the microcosm. Sometimes they sought to draw on twentieth-century forms of regional cultic association and on macrocosmic prophet movements in order to challenge the constraints of the bounded society of invented custom.

One or two recent studies have sought to explore these female initiatives. Richard Stuart, in an unpublished paper, shows how Chewa women made use of a missionary import, the Mothers' Union:

An equilibrium between the equally important sphere of women and public sphere of men had developed among the Chewa of east central Africa by the end of the nineteenth century. [This] was disrupted by the impact of African and European invasions, and the effects of Christianity, Commerce and Civilization. These

[98] Caroline Ifeka-Moller, 'Female Militancy and Colonial Revolt', in S. Ardener (ed.), *Perceiving Women* (London, 1975).
[99] Eileen Byrne, 'African Marriage in Southern Rhodesia, 1890–1940' (Univ. of Manchester B.A. research thesis, 1979).

undermined the historic bases of Chewa society, and provided men with access to new forms of wealth and power denied to women. During the colonial period, neo-traditionalists attempted to maintain this disequilibrium between men and women, and to restructure society on a paternalistic and individualistic basis. One attempt to counter this process, to enable women to make the transformation from small to large scale societies on their own terms, was made by the Anglican women's organization, the Mothers' Union or *Mpingo wa Amai*. This met with an immediate response when it was introduced in the early 1930s, enabling Chewa women to redefine historic roles and institutions within the changed circumstances and to respond to novel problems raised. It achieved some success in maintaining the status of women.[100]

Sherilyn Young's 'Fertility and Famine' is a study of the alternative strategy. In summary version her account of her southern Mozambique case runs:

Colonial forced labour in the twentieth century supplemented migration in draining the labour power of the Tsonga and Chopi. Large settler plantations were carved out of their existing agricultural lands. A run of famines and ecological disasters between 1908 and 1922 ensured heavy dependence on the export of labour. The agricultural revival of the 1920s was predominantly that of a female peasantry, producing the bulk of Southern Mozambique's cashews and groundnuts...When [in] the Second World War a system of forced labour was resorted to, women had to produce cash crops, especially cotton, for four days a week, under male supervisors. Adaptation to such changes can be seen in the growth of spirit-possession cults among the people, dominated by women. Southern Mozambique society survives with a striking distinction between a local female peasantry and an emigrant male semi-proletariat.[101]

---

[100] Richard Stuart, 'Mpingo wa Amai – the Mothers' Union in Nyasaland' (unpublished MS.).

[101] Sherilyn Young, 'Fertility and Famine: Women's Agricultural History in Southern Mozambique', in Palmer and Parsons (eds.), *Roots of Rural Poverty*.

THE MANIPULATION OF 'TRADITION' AGAINST SUBJECTS AND IMMIGRANTS

The other two appeals to 'tradition' and reliance upon the relationships spelt out in the new colonial custom are more straight-forward. Ian Linden has described how the Ngoni chiefs in Nyasaland attempted to use the colonial alliance with administrators and missionaries to exert control over their Chewa subjects. To do so they adumbrated the concept of disciplined and healthy 'Ngoni culture' and of a decadent and immoral 'Chewa culture' – the very concepts which Binsbergen criticizes as so misleading for the nineteenth century; they argued that Ngoni culture had been dominant prior to the European arrival and should be supported now against the 'beastly' practices of the Chewa; they played upon the European liking for clear-cut hierarchies of status in order to firm up networks of power which had been much less clear-cut in the past. The Ngoni were also able to stiffen up their own 'tradition' of discipline and military prowess by a selective use of the European military mode.

Another Nyasaland example can be used to illustrate the use of 'tradition' by indigenes to maintain control over immigrants. Matthew Schoffeleers has shown how the Mang'anja of the Lower Shire Valley have managed to retain control of chiefship, control of land allocation, and so on, though far out-numbered by immigrants from Mozambique. They have been able to do this by a combined appeal to the 'traditions' of pre-colonial chiefship and to the 'traditions' of the local territorial cult. In fact, the nineteenth-century history of the Valley was one of enormous fluidity; well-armed adventurers came in and imposed themselves upon the Mang'anja; the shrines of the territorial cult were destroyed; there were rapid changes in the self-identification of the people, who used this or that ethnic tag according to shifting balances of prestige. It was the colonial pacification which broke up the power of the armed adventurers, restored the Mang'anja chiefs and which really stimulated the invention of Mang'anja identity. With codified colonial custom, the right of the Mang'anja chiefs to allocate land was taken as an article of faith. In the twentieth century the Mang'anja achieved a dominance in the name of tradition which they had not exercised in the past.[102]

---

[102] Ian Linden, 'Chewa Initiation Rites and Nyau Societies', in Terence Ranger and John Weller (eds.), *Themes in the Christian History of Central Africa* (London,

CONCLUSION

African politicians, cultural nationalists and, indeed, historians are left with two ambiguous legacies from the colonial invention of traditions. One is the body of invented traditions imported from Europe which in some parts of Africa still exercises an influence on ruling class culture which it has largely lost in Europe itself. In his *Prison Diary* Ngugi wa Thiong'o writes savagely of the contemporary Kenyan élite:

The members of a comprador bourgeoisie of a former settler colony count themselves lucky. They don't have to travel and reside abroad to know and copy the culture of the imperialist bourgeoisie: have they not learnt it all from the colonial settler representatives of metropolitan culture? Nurtured in the womb of the old colonial system, they have matured to their full compradorial heights, looking to the local Europeans as the alpha and omega of gentlemanly refinement and lady-like elegance. With racial barriers to class mobility thrown open, the deportment of a European gentleman – rosebuds and pins in coat lapels, spotless white kerchiefs in breast pockets, tail-coats, top-hats and gold-chained pocket watches – is no longer in the realm of dreams and wishes...The most popular columns in the old settler papers...were the social pages...Well, the columns are now back in the glossy bourgeois monthlies...The settler played golf and polo, went to horse-races or on the royal hunt in red-coats and riding-breeches...The black pupils now do the same, only with greater zeal: golf and horses have become 'national' institutions.[103]

Other new states, less open to Ngugi's charges, express their national sovereignty with the national anthems, flags and rallies which Eric Hobsbawm describes for nineteenth-century Europe in this book. Representing as they do new multi-ethnic territorial states the African nations are much less engaged in the invention of past 'national cultures' than were the Scottish or Welsh Romantics.

The second ambiguous legacy is that of 'traditional' African culture; the whole body of reified 'tradition' invented by colonial

---

1975); Matthew Schoffeleers, 'The History and Political Role of the Mbona Cult among the Mang'anja', in Ranger and Kimambo (eds.), *The Historical Study of African Religion*.

[103] Ngugi wa Thiong'o, *Detained: A Writer's Prison Diary* (London, 1981), pp. 58–9.

administrators, missionaries, 'progressive traditionalists', elders and anthropologists. Those like Ngugi who repudiate bourgeois élite culture face the ironic danger of embracing another set of colonial inventions instead. Ngugi himself solves the difficulty by embracing the tradition of Kenyan popular resistance to colonialism. As this chapter suggests, young men, women, immigrants – the exploited groups with whom Ngugi has sympathy – *have* sometimes been able to tap the continued vitality of the mingled continuity and innovation which resides within indigenous cultures as they have continued to develop underneath the rigidities of codified colonial custom.

As for historians, they have at least a double task. They have to free themselves from the illusion that the African custom recorded by officials or by many anthropologists is any sort of guide to the African past. But they also need to appreciate how much invented traditions of all kinds have to do with the history of Africa in the twentieth century and strive to produce better founded accounts of them than this preliminary sketch.

7. Mass-Producing Traditions: Europe, 1870–1914

ERIC HOBSBAWM

I

Once we are aware how commonly traditions are invented, it can easily be discovered that one period which saw them spring up with particular assiduity was in the thirty or forty years before the first world war. One hesitates to say 'with greater assiduity' than at other times, since there is no way of making realistic quantitative comparisons. Nevertheless, the creation of traditions was enthusiastically practised in numerous countries and for various purposes, and this mass-generation of traditions is the subject of this chapter. It was both practised officially and unofficially, the former – we may loosely call it 'political' – primarily in or by states or organized social and political movements, the latter – we may loosely call it 'social' – mainly by social groups not formally organized as such, or those whose objects were not specifically or consciously political, such as clubs and fraternities, whether or not these also had political functions. The distinction is one of convenience rather than principle. It is designed to draw attention to two main forms of the creation of tradition in the nineteenth century, both of which reflect the profound and rapid social transformations of the period. Quite new, or old but dramatically transformed, social groups, environments and social contexts called for new devices to ensure or express social cohesion and identity and to structure social relations. At the same time a changing society made the traditional forms of ruling by states and social or political hierarchies more difficult or even impracticable. This required new methods of ruling or establishing bonds of loyalty. In the nature of things, the consequent invention of 'political' traditions was more conscious and deliberate, since it was largely undertaken by institutions with political purposes in mind. Yet we may as well note immediately that conscious invention succeeded mainly in proportion to its success in broadcasting on a wavelength to which the public was ready to tune in. Official new public holidays, ceremonies, heroes or symbols, which commanded the growing armies of the state's employees and the growing captive public of

263

schoolchildren, might still fail to mobilize the citizen volunteers if they lacked genuine popular resonance. The German Empire did not succeed in its efforts to turn the Emperor William I into a popularly accepted founding father of a united Germany, nor in turning his birthday into a genuine national anniversary. (Who, by the way, now remembers the attempt to call him 'William the Great'?) Official encouragement did secure the building of 327 monuments to him by 1902, but within *one* year of Bismarck's death in 1898, 470 municipalities had decided to erect 'Bismarck columns'.[1]

Nevertheless, the state linked both formal and informal, official and unofficial, political and social inventions of tradition, at least in those countries where the need for it arose. Seen from below, the state increasingly defined the largest stage on which the crucial activities determining human lives as subjects and citizens were played out. Indeed, it increasingly defined as well as registered their civil existence (*état civil*). It may not have been the only such stage, but its existence, frontiers and increasingly regular and probing interventions in the citizen's life were in the last analysis decisive. In developed countries the 'national economy', its area defined by the territory of some state or its subdivisions, was the basic unit of economic development. A change in the frontiers of the state or in its policy had substantial and continuous material consequences for its citizens. The standardization of administration and law within it, and, in particular, state education, transformed people into citizens of a specific country: 'peasants into Frenchmen', to cite the title of an apposite book.[2] The state was the framework of the citizens' collective actions, insofar as these were officially recognized. To influence or change the government of the state, or its policy, was plainly the main objective of domestic politics, and the common man was increasingly entitled to take part in it. Indeed, politics in the new nineteenth-century sense was essentially nation-wide politics. In short, for practical purposes, society ('civil society') and the state within which it operated became increasingly inseparable.

It was thus natural that the classes within society, and in particular

[1] G. L. Mosse, 'Caesarism, Circuses and Movements', *Journal of Contemporary History*, vi, no. 2 (1971), pp. 167–82; G. L. Mosse, *The Nationalisation of the Masses: Political Symbolism and Mass Movements in Germany from the Napoleonic Wars through the 3rd Reich* (New York, 1975); T. Nipperdey, 'Nationalidee und Nationaldenkmal in Deutschland im 19. Jahrhundert', *Historische Zeitschrift* (June 1968), pp. 529–85, esp. 543n, 579n.

[2] Eugen Weber, *Peasants into Frenchmen: The Modernization of Rural France, 1870–1914* (Stanford, 1976).

the working class, should tend to identify themselves through nation-wide political movements or organizations ('parties'), and equally natural that de facto these should operate essentially within the confines of the nation.[3] Nor is it surprising that movements seeking to represent an entire society or 'people' should envisage its existence essentially in terms of that of an independent or at least an autonomous state. State, nation and society converged.

For the same reason, the state, seen from above in the perspective of its formal rulers or dominant groups, raised unprecedented problems of how to maintain or even establish the obedience, loyalty and cooperation of its subjects or members, or its own legitimacy in their eyes. The very fact that its direct and increasingly intrusive and regular relations with the subjects or citizens as individuals (or at most, heads of families) became increasingly central to its operations, tended to weaken the older devices by means of which social subordination had largely been maintained: relatively autonomous collectivities or corporations under the ruler, but controlling their own members, pyramids of authority linked to higher authorities at their apexes, stratified social hierarchies in which each stratum recognized its place, and so on. In any case social transformations such as those which replaced ranks by classes undermined them. The problems of states and rulers were evidently much more acute where their subjects had become citizens, that is people whose political activities were institutionally recognized as something that had to be taken note of – if only in the form of elections. They became even more acute when the political movements of citizens as masses deliberately challenged the legitimacy of the systems of political or social rule, and or threatened to prove incompatible with the state's order by setting the obligations to some other human collectivity – most usually class, church or nationality – above it.

The problem appeared to be most manageable where social structure had changed least, where men's fates appeared to be subject to no other forces than those which an inscrutable divinity had always unleashed among the human race, and where the ancient ways of hierarchical superiority and stratified, multiform and relatively autonomous subordination remained in force. If anything could

---

[3] This was conclusively demonstrated in 1914 by the socialist parties of the Second International, which not only claimed to be essentially international in scope, but actually sometimes regarded themselves officially as no more than national sections of a global movement ('Section Française de l'Internationale Ouvrière').

mobilize the peasantry of south Italy beyond their localities, it was church and king. And indeed the traditionalism of peasants (which must not be confused with passivity, though there are not many cases where they challenged the actual existence of the lords, so long as these belonged to the same faith and people) was constantly praised by nineteenth-century conservatives as the ideal model of the subject's political comportment. Unfortunately, the states in which this model worked were by definition 'backward' and therefore feeble, and any attempt to 'modernize' them was likely to make it less workable. A 'modernization' which maintained the old ordering of social subordination (possibly with some well-judged invention of tradition) was not theoretically inconceivable, but apart from Japan it is difficult to think of an example of practical success. And it may be suggested that such attempts to update the social bonds of a traditional order implied a demotion of social hierarchy, a strengthening of the subject's direct bonds to the central ruler who, whether this was intended to or not, increasingly came to represent a new kind of state. 'God save the King' was increasingly (if sometimes symbolically) a more effective political injunction than 'God bless the squire and his relations and keep us in our proper stations'. The chapter on the British monarchy throws some light on this process, though it would be desirable to see a study of the attempts by more authentically legitimist dynasties, such as those of the Habsburg and the Romanov, not merely to command the obedience of their peoples as subjects, but to rally their loyalty as potential citizens. We know that they eventually failed, but was their failure a foregone conclusion?

Conversely the problem was most intractable in states which were completely new, where the rulers were unable to make effective use of already existing bonds of political obedience and loyalty, and in states whose legitimacy (or that of the social order they represented) was effectively no longer accepted. In the period 1870–1914 there were, as it happens, unusually few 'new states'. Most European states, as well as the American republics, had by then acquired the basic official institutions, symbols and practices which Mongolia, establishing a sort of independence from China in 1912, quite rightly regarded as novel and necessary. They had capitals, flags, national anthems, military uniforms and similar paraphernalia, based largely on the model of the British, whose national anthem (datable *c.* 1740) is probably the first, and of the French, whose tricolour flag was very generally imitated. Several new states and régimes could either, like the French Third Republic, reach back into the store of earlier French republican symbolism or, like the Bismarckian German Empire, combine appeals to an earlier German Empire, with the myths and symbols of a liberal nationalism popular among the middle classes, and the dynastic continuity of the Prussian monarchy, of which by the 1860s half of the inhabitants of Bismarckian Germany were subjects. Among the major states only Italy had to start from scratch in solving the problem summarized by d'Azeglio in the phrase: 'We have made Italy: now we must make Italians'. The tradition of the kingdom of Savoy was no political asset outside the north-western corner of the country, and the church opposed the new Italian state. It is perhaps not surprising that the new kingdom of Italy, however enthusiastic about 'making Italians', was notably unenthusiastic about giving the vote to more than one or two per cent of them until this seemed quite unavoidable.

Yet if the establishment of the legitimacy of new states and régimes was relatively uncommon, its assertion against the challenge of popular politics was not. As noted above, that challenge was chiefly represented, singly or in combination, by the sometimes linked, sometimes competing, political mobilization of masses through religion (mainly Roman Catholicism), class consciousness (social democracy), and nationalism, or at least xenophobia. Politically these challenges found their most visible expression in the vote, and were at this period inextricably linked either with the existence of, or struggle for, a mass suffrage, waged against opponents who were mainly by now resigned to fighting a delaying rearguard action. By 1914 some form of extensive if not universal manhood suffrage was operating in Australia (1901), Austria (1907), Belgium (1894), Denmark (1849), Finland (1905), France (1875), Germany (1871), Italy (1913), Norway (1898), Sweden (1907), Switzerland (1848–79), the United Kingdom (1867–84) and the U.S.A., though it was still only occasionally combined with political democracy. Yet even where constitutions were not democratic, the very existence of a mass electorate dramatized the problem of maintaining its loyalty. The unbroken rise of the Social Democratic vote in imperial Germany was no less worrying to its rulers because the Reichstag in fact had very little power.

The widespread progress of electoral democracy and the consequent emergence of mass politics therefore dominated the invention of official traditions in the period 1870–1914. What made it particularly urgent was the dominance both of the model of liberal constitutional institutions and of liberal ideology. The former provided no theoretical, but only at best empirical, barriers against electoral democracy. Indeed, it was difficult for the liberal not to expect an extension of civic rights to all citizens – or at least to male ones – sooner or later. The latter had achieved its most spectacular economic triumphs and social transformations by systematically opting for the individual against the institutionalized collectivity, for market transactions (the 'cash nexus') against human ties, for class against rank hierarchy, for *Gesellschaft* against *Gemeinschaft*. It had thus systematically failed to provide for those social bonds and ties of authority taken for granted in earlier societies, and had indeed set out to and succeeded in weakening them. So long as the masses remained outside politics, or were prepared to follow the liberal bourgeoisie, this created no major political difficulties. Yet from the 1870s onwards it became increasingly obvious that the masses were becoming involved in politics and could not be relied upon to follow their masters.

After the 1870s, therefore, and almost certainly in connection with the emergence of mass politics, rulers and middle-class observers rediscovered the importance of 'irrational' elements in the maintenance of the social fabric and the social order. As Graham Wallas was to observe in *Human Nature in Politics* (1908): 'Whoever sets himself to base his political thinking on a re-examination of the working of human nature, must begin by trying to overcome his own tendency to exaggerate the intellectuality of mankind'.[4] A new generation of thinkers had no difficulty in overcoming this tendency. They rediscovered irrational elements in the individual psyche (Janet, William James, Freud), in social psychology (Le Bon, Tarde, Trotter), through anthropology in primitive peoples whose practices no longer seemed to preserve merely the childhood traits of modern humanity (did not Durkheim see the elements of all religion in the rites of the Australian aborigines?[5]), even in that quintessential fortress of ideal human reason, classical Hellenism (Frazer, Cornford).[6] The intellectual study of politics and society was transformed by the recognition

---

[4] Graham Wallas, *Human Nature in Politics* (London, 1908), p. 21.
[5] Emile Durkheim, *The Elementary Forms of the Religious Life* (London, 1976). First French publication 1912.
[6] J. G. Frazer, *The Golden Bough*, 3rd edn (London, 1907–30); F. M. Cornford, *From Religion to Philosophy: A Study of the Origins of Western Speculation* (London, 1912).

that whatever held human collectivities together it was not the rational calculation of their individual members.

This is not the place to analyse, even in the most cursory manner, this intellectual retreat from classical liberalism, in which only the economists failed to join.[7] Its relationship to the experience of mass politics is obvious, not least in the country where a bourgeoisie which had, in Burke's words, 'rudely torn off...the decent drapery of life,...the pleasing illusions which made power gentle and obedience liberal'[8] in the most irrevocable manner, now found itself nakedly confronted, at last, with the permanent necessity to rule by means of a political democracy in the shadow of social revolution (the Paris Commune). It was plainly not enough to regret the disappearance of that ancient social cement, church and monarchy, as the post-Communard Taine did, having no sympathy for either.[9] It was even less practical to restore the Catholic king as the monarchists wanted (themselves hardly the best advertisements for traditional piety and belief, as in the case of Maurras). An alternative 'civic religion' had to be constructed. The need for it was the core of Durkheim's sociology, the work of a devoted non-socialist republican. Yet it had to be instituted by less eminent thinkers, if more practical politicians.

It would be foolish to suggest that the men who ruled the Third Republic relied mainly on inventing new traditions in order to achieve social stability. Rather, they relied on the hard political fact that the right was in a permanent electoral minority, that the social-revolutionary proletariat and the inflammable Parisians could be permanently outvoted by the over-represented villages and small towns, and that the Republican rural voters' genuine passion for the French Revolution and hatred of the moneyed interest could usually be assuaged by roads suitably distributed around the arrondissements, by the defence of high farm-prices and, almost certainly, by keeping taxes low. The Radical Socialist grandee knew what he was about when he worked his electoral address, through appeals to the spirit of 1789 – nay 1793 – and a hymn to the Republic to the climax in which he pledged his loyalty to the interests of the viticulteurs of his Languedoc constituency.[10]

[7] Presumably because they were able to eliminate from their field of vision everything which could not be defined as rationally maximizing behaviour; at the cost – after the 1870s – of a considerable narrowing of their subject.

[8] Edmund Burke, *Reflections on the Revolution in France*, Everyman edn, p. 74.

[9] J. P. Mayer, *Political Thought in France from the Revolution to the 5th Republic* (London, 1961), pp. 84–8.

[10] Jean Touchard, *La Gauche en France depuis 1900* (Paris, 1977), p. 50.

Nevertheless, the invention of tradition played an essential role in maintaining the Republic, if only by safeguarding it against both socialism and the right. By deliberately annexing the revolutionary tradition, the Third Republic either domesticated social revolutionaries (like most socialists) or isolated them (like the anarchosyndicalists). In turn, it was now able to mobilize even a majority of its potential adversaries on the left in defence of a republic and a past revolution, in a common front of the classes which reduced the right to a permanent minority in the nation. Indeed, as that textbook of Third Republican politics, *Clochemerle*, makes clear, the main function of the right was to provide something for good Republicans to mobilize against. The Socialist Labour movement resisted its co-option by the bourgeois Republic to some extent; hence the establishment of the annual commemoration of the Paris Commune at the Mur des Fédérés (1880) against the institutionalization of the Republic; hence also the substitution of the new 'Internationale' for the traditional, but now official, 'Marseillaise' as its anthem during the Dreyfus affair, and especially during the controversies on socialist participation in bourgeois governments (Millerand).[11] Again, the radical Jacobin Republicans continued, within the official symbolism, to mark their separation from the moderate and dominant ones. Agulhon, who has studied the characteristic mania for putting up monuments, notably of the Republic itself, during the period 1875 to 1914, acutely notes that in the more radical municipalities Mariane bared at least one breast, while in the more moderate ones she was decently clothed.[12] Yet the basic fact was that those who controlled the imagery, the symbolism, the traditions of the Republic were the men of the centre masquerading as men of the extreme left: the Radical Socialists, proverbially 'like the radish, red outside, white inside, and always on the side the bread is buttered'. Once they ceased to control the Republic's fortunes – from the days of the Popular Front onwards – the days of the Third Republic were numbered.

There is considerable evidence that the moderate Republican bourgeoisie recognized the nature of its main political problem ('no enemies on the left') from the late 1860s onwards, and set about

[11] Maurice Dommanget, *Eugène Pottier, Membre de la Commune et Chantre de l'Internationale* (Paris, 1971), ch. 3.
[12] M. Agulhon, 'Esquisse pour une Archéologie de la République; l'Allégorie Civique Féminine'. *Annales ESC*, xxviii (1973), pp. 5–34; M. Agulhon, *Marianne au Combat: l'Imagerie et la Symbolique Républicaines de 1789 à 1880* (Paris, 1979).

solving it as soon as the Republic was firmly in power.[13] In terms of the invention of tradition, three major innovations are particularly relevant. The first was the development of a secular equivalent of the church – primary education, imbued with revolutionary and republican principles and content, and conducted by the secular equivalent of the priesthood – or perhaps, given their poverty, the friars – the *instituteurs*.[14] There is no doubt that this was a deliberate construction of the early Third Republic, and, given the proverbial centralization of French government, that the content of the manuals which were to turn not only peasants into Frenchmen but all Frenchmen into good Republicans, was not left to chance. Indeed the 'institutionalization' of the French Revolution itself in and by the Republic has been studied in some detail.[15]

The second was the invention of public ceremonies.[16] The most important of these, Bastille Day, can be exactly dated in 1880. It combined official and unofficial demonstrations and popular festivities – fireworks, dancing in the streets – in an annual assertion of France as the nation of 1789, in which every French man, woman and child could take part. Yet while it left scope for, and could hardly avoid, more militant, popular manifestations, its general tendency was to transform the heritage of the Revolution into a combined expression of state pomp and power and the citizens' pleasure. A less permanent form of public celebration were the occasional world expositions which gave the Republic the legitimacy of prosperity, technical progress – the Eiffel Tower – and the global colonial conquest they took care to emphasize.[17]

The third was the mass production of public monuments already noted. It may be observed that the Third Republic did not – unlike other countries – favour massive public buildings, of which France already had a large supply – though the great expositions left some

---

[13] Sanford H. Elwitt, *The Making of the 3rd Republic: Class and Politics in France, 1868–84* (Baton Rouge, 1975).

[14] Georges Duveau, *Les Instituteurs* (Paris, 1957); J. Ozouf (ed.), *Nous les Maîtres d'Ecole: Autobiographies d'Instituteurs de la Belle Epoque* (Paris, 1967).

[15] Alice Gérard, *La Révolution Française: Mythes et Interprétations, 1789–1970* (Paris, 1970), ch. 4.

[16] Charles Rearick, 'Festivals in Modern France: The Experience of the 3rd Republic', *Journal of Contemporary History*, xii, no. 3 (July 1977), pp. 435–60; Rosemonde Sanson, *Les 14 Juillet, Fête et Conscience Nationale, 1789–1975* (Paris, 1976), with bibliography.

[17] For the political intentions of the 1889 one, cf. Debora L. Silverman, 'The 1889 Exhibition: The Crisis of Bourgeois Individualism', *Oppositions, A Journal for Ideas and Criticism in Architecture* (Spring, 1977), pp. 71–91.

of these behind them in Paris – nor gigantic statuary. The major characteristic of French 'statuomania'[18] was its democracy, anticipating that of the war memorials after 1914–18. It spread two kinds of monuments throughout the cities and rural communes of the country: the image of the Republic itself (in the form of Marianne which now became universally familiar), and the bearded civilian figures of whoever local patriotism chose to regard as its notables, past and present. Indeed, while the construction of Republican monuments was evidently encouraged, the initiative, and the costs of, such enterprises were undertaken at a local level. The entrepreneurs catering for this market provided choices suitable for the purses of every Republican commune from the poorest upwards, ranging from modest busts of Marianne, in various sizes, through full-figure statues of varying dimensions, to the plinths and allegorical or heroic accessories with which the more ambitious citizenry could surround her feet.[19] The opulent ensembles on the Place de la République and the Place de la Nation in Paris provided the ultimate version of such statuary. Such monuments traced the grass roots of the Republic – particularly in its rural strongholds – and may be regarded as the visible links between the voters and the nation.

Some other characteristics of the official 'invented' traditions of the Third Republic may be noted in passing. Except in the form of the commemoration of notable figures from the local past, or of local political manifestos, it kept away from history. This was partly, no doubt, because history before 1789 (except perhaps for 'nos ancêtres les Gaulois') recalled church and monarchy, partly because history since 1789 was a divisive rather than unifying force: each brand – or rather degree – of Republicanism had its own corresponding heroes and villains in the revolutionary pantheon, as the historiography of the French Revolution demonstrates. Party differences were expressed in statues to Robespierre, Mirabeau or Danton. Unlike the U.S.A. and the Latin American states, the French Republic therefore shied away from the cult of Founding Fathers. It preferred general symbols, abstaining even from the use of themes referring to the national past on its postage stamps until long after 1914, though most European states (other than Britain and Scandinavia) discovered their appeal from the mid-1890s onwards. The symbols were few: the

---

[18] M. Agulhon, 'La Statuomanie et l'Histoire', *Ethnologie Française*, nos. 3–4 (1978), pp. 3–4.

[19] Agulhon, 'Esquisse pour une Archéologie'.

tricolour (democratized and universalized in the sash of the mayor, present at every civil marriage or other ceremony), the Republican monogram (RF) and motto (liberty, equality, fraternity), the 'Marseillaise', and the symbol of the Republic and of freedom itself, which appears to have taken shape in the last years of the Second Empire, Marianne. We may also note that the Third Republic showed no official hankering for the specifically invented ceremonies so characteristic of the First – 'trees of liberty', goddesses of reason and ad hoc festivals. There was to be no official national day other than 14 July, no formal mobilizations, processions and marches of the civilian citizenry (unlike the mass régimes of the twentieth century, but also unlike the U.S.A.), but rather a simple 'republicanization' of the accepted pomp of state power – uniforms, parades, bands, flags, and the like.

The Second German Empire provides an interesting contrast, especially since several of the general themes of French Republican invented tradition are recognizable in its own. Its major political problem was twofold: how to provide historical legitimacy for the Bismarckian (Prusso-Little German) version of unification which had none; and how to deal with that large part of the democratic electorate which would have preferred another solution (Great Germans, anti-Prussian particularists, Catholics and, above all, Social Democrats). Bismarck himself does not seem to have bothered much about symbolism, except for personally devising a tricolour flag which combined the Prussian black–white with the nationalist and liberal black–red–gold which he wished to annex (1866). There was no historical precedent whatever for the Empire's black–white–red national banner.[20] His recipe for political stability was simpler:

[20] Whitney Smith, *Flags through the Ages* (New York, 1975), pp. 116–18. The nationalist black–red–gold appears to have emerged from the student movement of the post-Napoleonic period, but was clearly established as the flag of the national movement in 1848. Resistance to the Weimar Republic reduced its national flag to a party banner – indeed the militia of the Social Democratic Party took it as its title ('Reichsbanner'), though the anti-republican right was divided between the imperial flag and the National Socialist flag, which abandoned the traditional tricolour design, possibly because of its associations with nineteenth-century liberalism, possibly as not sufficiently indicative of a radical break with the past. However, it maintained the basic colour scheme of the Bismarckian empire (black–white–red), while stressing the red, hitherto the symbol only of the socialist and labour movements. The Federal Republic and the Democratic Republic both returned to the colours of 1848, the former without additions, the latter with a suitable emblem adapted from the basic model of the Communist and Soviet hammer-and-sickle.

to win the support of the (predominantly liberal) bourgeoisie by carrying out as much of its programme as would not jeopardize the predominance of the Prussian monarchy, army and aristocracy, to utilize the potential divisions among the various kinds of opposition and to exclude political democracy as far as possible from affecting the decisions of government. Apparently irreconcilable groups which could not be divided – notably the Catholics and especially the post-Lassallean Social Democrats – left him somewhat at a loss. In fact, he was defeated in his head-on confrontations with both. One has the impression that this old-fashioned conservative rationalist, however brilliant in the arts of political manoeuvre, never satisfactorily solved the difficulties of political democracy, as distinct from the politics of notables.

The invention of the traditions of the German Empire is therefore primarily associated with the era of William II. Its objects were mainly twofold: to establish the continuity between the Second and First German Empires, or more generally, to establish the new Empire as the realization of the secular national aspirations of the German people; and to stress the specific historical experiences which linked Prussia and the rest of Germany in the construction of the new Empire in 1871. Both, in turn, required the merger of Prussian and German history, to which patriotic imperial historians (notably Treitschke) had for some time devoted themselves. The major difficulty in the way of achieving these objects was firstly the history of the Holy Roman Empire of the German nation was difficult to fit into any nineteenth-century nationalist mould, and secondly that its history did not suggest that the denouement of 1871 was historically inevitable, or even likely. It could be linked to a modern nationalism only by two devices: by the concept of a secular national enemy against whom the German people had defined their identity and struggled to achieve unity as a state; and by the concept of conquest or cultural, political and military supremacy, by means of which the German nation, scattered across large parts of other states, mainly in central and eastern Europe, could claim the right to be united in a single Greater German state. The second concept was not one which the Bismarckian empire, specifically 'Little German', cared to stress, though Prussia itself, as its name implied, had been historically constructed largely by expansion into Slavonic and Baltic areas outside the range of the Holy Roman Empire.

Buildings and monuments were the most visible form of establishing a new interpretation of German history, or rather a fusion between the older romantic 'invented tradition' of pre-1848 German nationalism and the new régime: the most powerful symbols being those where the fusion was achieved. Thus, the mass movement of German gymnasts, liberal and Great German until the 1860s, Bismarckian after 1866 and eventually pan-German and antisemitic, took to its heart three monuments whose inspiration was basically not official: the monument to Arminius the Cheruscan in the Teutoburg Forest (much of it constructed as early as 1838–46, and inaugurated in 1875); the Niederwald monument above the Rhine, commemorating the unification of Germany in 1871 (1877–83); and the centenary memorial of the battle of Leipzig, initiated in 1894 by a 'German patriotic League for the Erection of a Monument to the Battle of the Peoples at Leipzig', and inaugurated in 1913. On the other hand, they appear to have showed no enthusiasm for the proposal to turn the monument to William I on the Kyffhäuser mountain, on the spot where folk myth claimed the Emperor Frederick Barbarossa would appear again, into a national symbol (1890–6), and no special reaction to the construction of the monument to William I and Germany at the confluence of the Rhine and the Moselle (the 'Deutsches Eck' or German Corner), directed against French claims to the left bank of the Rhine.[21]

Leaving such variations aside, the mass of masonry and statuary which went up in Germany in this period was remarkably large, and made the fortunes of sufficiently pliable and competent architects and sculptors.[22] Among those constructed or planned in the 1890s alone, we may mention the new Reichstag building (1884–94) with elaborate historical imagery on its façade, the Kyffhäuser monument already mentioned (1890–6), the national monument to William I – clearly intended as the official father of the country (1890–7), the monument to William I at the Porta Westfalica (1892), the William I monument at the Deutsches Eck (1894–7), the extraordinary Valhalla of Hohenzollern princes in the 'Avenue of Victory' (Siegesallee) in Berlin

[21] Hans-Georg John, *Politik und Turnen: die deutsche Turnerschaft als nationale Bewegung im deutschen Kaiserreich von 1871–1914* (Ahrensberg bei Hamburg, 1976), pp. 41ff.

[22] 'Fate determined that, against his nature, he should become a monumental sculptor, who was to celebrate the imperial idea of William II in giant monuments of bronze and stone, in a language of imagery and over-emphatic pathos.' Ulrich Thieme and Felix Becker, *Allgemeines Lexikon der bildenden Künstler von der Antike bis zur Gegenwart* (Leipzig, 1907–50), iii, p. 185. See also in general entries under Begas, Schilling, Schmitz.

(1896–1901), a variety of statues to William I in German cities (Dortmund 1894, Wiesbaden 1894, Prenzlau 1898, Hamburg 1903, Halle 1901) and, a little later, a spate of Bismarck monuments, which enjoyed a more genuine support among nationalists.[23] The inauguration of one of these monuments provided the first occasion for the use of historical themes on the postage stamps of the Empire (1899).

This accumulation of masonry and statuary suggests two comments. The first concerns the choice of a national symbol. Two of these were available: a vague but adequately military 'Germania', who played no notable role in sculpture, though she figured extensively on postage stamps from the start, since no single dynastic image could as yet symbolize Germany as a whole; and the figure of the 'Deutsche Michel', who actually appears in a subordinate role on the Bismarck monument. He belongs to the curious representations of the nation, not as country or state, but as 'the people', which came to animate the demotic political language of the nineteenth-century cartoonists, and was intended (as in John Bull and the goateed Yankee – but *not* in Marianne, image of the Republic) to express national character, as seen by the members of the nation itself. Their origins and early history are obscure, though, like the national anthem, they are almost certainly first found in eighteenth-century Britain.[24] The point about the 'Deutsche Michel' is that his image stressed both the innocence and simple-mindedness so readily exploited by cunning foreigners, and the physical strength he could mobilize to frustrate their knavish tricks and conquests when finally roused. 'Michel' seems to have been essentially an anti-foreign image.

The second concerns the crucial significance of the Bismarckian unification of Germany as the *only* national historical experience which the citizens of the new Empire had in common, given that all earlier conceptions of Germany and German unification were in one way or another 'Great German'. And within this experience, the Franco-German war was central. Insofar as Germany had a (brief) 'national' tradition, it was symbolized in the three names: Bismarck, William I and Sedan.

---

[23] John, *op. cit.*, Nipperdey, 'Nationalidee', pp. 577ff.
[24] J. Surel, 'La Première Image de John Bull, Bourgeois Radical, Anglais Loyaliste (1779–1815)', *Le Mouvement Social*, cvi (Jan–Mar. 1979), pp. 65–84; Herbert M. Atherton, *Political Prints in the Age of Hogarth* (Oxford, 1974), pp. 97–100.

This is clearly exemplified by the ceremonials and rituals invented (also mainly under William II). Thus the chronicles of one Gymnasium record no less than ten ceremonies between August 1895 and March 1896 recalling the twenty-fifth anniversary of the Franco-Prussian war, including ample commemorations of battles in the war, celebrations of the emperor's birthday, the official handing-over of the portrait of an imperial prince, illuminations and public addresses on the war of 1870–1, on the development of the imperial idea (*Kaiseridee*) during the war, on the character of the Hohenzollern dynasty, and so on.[25]

A more detailed description of one such ceremony may elucidate their character. Watched by parents and friends, the boys marched into the school yard singing the 'Wacht am Rhein' (the 'national song' most directly identified with hostility to the French, though, interestingly, neither the Prussian nor the German national anthem).[26] They formed up facing representatives of each class who held flags decorated with oak leaves, which had been bought with money collected in each class. (The oak had associations with Teutonic–German folklore, nationalism and military virtues – still remembered in the oak leaves which marked the highest class of military decoration under Hitler: a suitably Germanic equivalent to the Latin laurel.) The head boy presented these banners to the headmaster, who in turn addressed the assembly on the glorious days of the late Emperor William I, and called for three ringing cheers for the reigning monarch and his empress. The boys then marched under their banners. Yet another address by the headmaster followed, before the planting of an 'imperial oak'(*Kaisereiche*) to the accompaniment of choral singing. The day concluded with an excursion into the Grunewald. All these proceedings were merely preliminaries to the actual commemoration of Sedan Day two days later, and indeed to a scholastic year amply punctuated by ritual gatherings,

---

[25] Heinz Stallmann, *Das Prinz-Heinrichs-Gymnasium zu Schöneberg, 1890–1945. Geschichte einer Schule* (Berlin, n.d. [1965]).

[26] There was in fact no official German national anthem. Of the three competing songs 'Heil Dir Im Siegerkranz' (to the tune of 'God Save the King'), being most closely associated with the Prussian emperor, roused least national fervour. The 'Watch on the Rhine' and 'Deutschland Über Alles' were seen as equal until 1914, but gradually 'Deutschland', more suited to an expansionist imperial policy, prevailed over the 'Watch', whose associations were purely anti-French. Among the German gymnasts by 1890 the former anthem had become twice as common as the latter, though their movement was particularly keen on the 'Watch', which it claimed to have been instrumental in popularizing. John, *op. cit.*, pp. 38–9.

religious and civic.[27] In the same year an imperial decree was to announce the construction of the Siegesallee, linking it with the twenty-fifth anniversary of the Franco-Prussian war, which was presented as the rising of the German people 'as one man', though 'following the call of its princes' to 'repel foreign aggression and achieve the unity of the fatherland and the *restoration* of the Reich in glorious victories' (my italics).[28] The Siegesallee, it will be recalled, represented exclusively the Hohenzollern princes back to the days of the Margraves of Brandenburg.

A comparison of the French and German innovations is instructive. Both stress the founding acts of the new régime – the French Revolution in its least precise and controversial episode (the Bastille) and the Franco-Prussian war. Except for this one point of historic reference, the French Republic abstained from historical retrospect as strikingly as the German Empire indulged in it. Since the Revolution had established the fact, the nature and the boundaries of the French nation and its patriotism, the Republic could confine itself to recalling these to its citizens by means of a few obvious symbols – Marianne, the tricolour, the 'Marseillaise', and so on – supplementing them with a little ideological exegesis elaborating on the (to its poorer citizens) obvious if sometimes theoretical benefits of Liberty, Equality and Fraternity. Since the 'German people' before 1871 had no political definition or unity, and its relation to the new Empire (which excluded large parts of it) was vague, symbolic or ideological, identification had to be more complex and – with the exception of the role of the Hohenzollern dynasty, army and state – less precise. Hence the multiplicity of reference, ranging from mythology and folklore (German oaks, the Emperor Frederick Barbarossa) through the shorthand cartoon stereotypes to definition of the nation in terms of its enemies. Like many another liberated 'people', 'Germany' was more easily defined by what it was against than in any other way.

This may explain the most obvious gap in the 'invented traditions' of the German Empire: its failure to conciliate the Social Democrats. It is true that William II initially liked to present himself as a 'social emperor', and made a clear break with Bismarck's own policy of banning the party. Yet the temptation to present the Socialist movement as anti-national ('vaterlandslose Gesellen') proved too strong to be resisted, and Socialists were more systematically excluded

---

[27] Stallmann, *op. cit.*, pp. 16–19.
[28] R. E. Hardt, *Dir Beine der Hohenzollern* (E. Berlin, 1968).

from the state service (including, by a specially passed law, from posts in higher education) than they were, for example, in the Habsburg Empire. No doubt two of the Empire's political headaches were considerably mitigated. Military glory and power as well as the rhetoric of German greatness disarmed the 'Great Germans' or pan-Germans, now increasingly divorced from their liberal or even democratic origins. If they were to achieve their ends at all, it would now be through the new Empire or not at all. The Catholics, as became clear when Bismarck's campaign against them was abandoned, caused no serious problems. Nevertheless, the Social Democrats alone, advancing with apparent inevitability towards majority status in the Empire, constituted a political force which, if other countries during this period are a guide, ought to have moved the German government towards a rather more flexible attitude.

Yet in a nation relying for its self-definition to so great an extent on its *enemies*, external and internal, this was not wholly unexpected;[29] all the more so, since the by definition anti-democratic military élite formed so powerful a device for assimilating the middle class to the status of a ruling class. Yet the choice of Social Democrats and, less formally, of Jews as internal enemies had an additional advantage, though the nationalism of the Empire was unable to exploit it fully. It provided a demagogic appeal against both capitalist liberalism and proletarian socialism which could mobilize the great masses of the lower middle class, handicraftsmen and peasants who felt threatened by both, under the banner of 'the nation'.

Paradoxically, the most democratic and, both territorially and constitutionally, one of the most clearly defined nations faced a problem of national identity in some respects similar to imperial Germany. The basic political problem of the U.S.A., once secession had been eliminated, was how to assimilate a heterogeneous mass – towards the end of our period, an almost unmanageable influx – of people who were Americans not by birth but by immigration. Americans had to be made. The invented traditions of the U.S.A. in this period were primarily designed to achieve this object. On the one hand the immigrants were encouraged to accept rituals commemorating the history of the nation – the Revolution and its founding fathers (the 4th of July) and the Protestant Anglo-Saxon tradition (Thanksgiving Day) – as indeed they did, since these now became

29 H.-U. Wehler, *Das deutsche Kaiserreich 1871–1918* (Göttingen, 1973), pp. 107–10.

holidays and occasions for public and private festivity.[30] (Conversely, the 'nation' absorbed the collective rituals of immigrants – St Patrick's Day, later Columbus Day – into the fabric of American life, mainly through the powerful assimilating mechanism of municipal and state politics.) On the other hand, the educational system was transformed into a machine for political socialization by such devices as the worship of the American flag, which, as a daily ritual in the country's schools, spread from the 1880s onwards.[31] The concept of Americanism as an act of *choice* – the decision to learn English, to apply for citizenship – and a choice of specific beliefs, acts and modes of behaviour implied the corresponding concept of 'un-Americanism'. In countries defining nationality existentially there could be unpatriotic Englishmen or Frenchmen, but their status as Englishmen and Frenchmen could not be in doubt, unless they could also be defined as strangers (*metèques*). Yet in the U.S.A., as in Germany, the 'un-American' or 'vaterlandslose' person threw doubt on his or her actual status as member of the nation.

As might be expected, the working class provided the largest and most visible body of such doubtful members of the national community; all the more doubtful because in the U.S.A. they could actually be classified as foreigners. The mass of new immigrants were workers; conversely, since at least the 1860s, the majority of workers in virtually all the large cities of the land appear to have been foreign-born. Whether the concept of 'un-Americanism', which can be traced back to at least the 1870s,[32] was more of a reaction of the native-born against the strangers or of Anglo-Saxon Protestant middle classes against foreign-born workers is unclear. At all events it provided an internal enemy against whom the good American could assert his or her Americanism, not least by the punctilious performance of all the formal and informal rituals, the assertion of all the beliefs conventionally and institutionally established as characteristic of good Americans.

[30] The history of these festivities remains to be written, but it seems clear that they became much more institutionalized on a national scale in the last third of the nineteenth century. G. W. Douglas, *American Book of Days* (New York, 1937); Elizabeth Hough Sechrist, *Red Letter Days: A Book of Holiday Customs* (Philadelphia, 1940).

[31] R. Firth, *Symbols, Public and Private* (London, 1973), pp. 358–9; W. E. Davies, *Patriotism on Parade: The Story of Veterans and Hereditary Organisations in America 1783–1900* (Cambridge, Mass., 1955), pp. 218–22; Douglas, *op. cit.*, pp. 326–7.

[32] I am obliged to Prof. Herbert Gutman for this observation.

Table 1. *First use of historical stamps before 1914*[33]

Country	First stamp	First historical stamp	Jubilee or special occasion
Austro-Hungary	1850	1908	60 years Franz Joseph
Belgium	1849	1914	War (Red Cross)
Bulgaria	1879	1901	Anniversary of revolt
Germany	1872	1899	Unveiling of monument
Greece	1861	1896	Olympic Games
Italy	1862	1910–11	Anniversaries
Netherlands	1852	1906	De Ruyter tercentenary
Portugal	1852	1894	500th anniversary of Henry the Navigator
Romania	1865	1906	40 years rule
Russia	1858	1905, 1913	War charity, tercentenary
Serbia	1866	1904	Centenary of dynasty
Spain	1850	1905	*Don Quixote* tercentenary
Switzerland	1850	1907	—

We may deal more cursorily with the invention of state traditions in other countries of the period. Monarchies, for obvious reasons, tended to link them to the crown, and this period saw the initiation of the now familiar public relations exercises centred on royal or imperial rituals, greatly facilitated by the happy discovery – or perhaps it would be better to say invention – of the jubilee or ceremonial anniversary. Its novelty is actually remarked upon in the *New English Dictionary*.[34] The publicity value of anniversaries is clearly shown by the occasion they so often provided for the first issue of historical or similar images on postage stamps, that most universal form of public imagery other than money, as Table 1 demonstrates.

Almost certainly Queen Victoria's jubilee of 1887, repeated ten

[33] Source: *Stamps of the World 1972: A Stanley Gibbons Catalogue* (London, 1972).
[34] The 'jubilee', except in its biblical sense, had previously been simply the fiftieth anniversary. There is no sign before the later nineteenth century that centenaries, single or multiple, still less anniversaries of less than fifty years, were the occasion for public celebration. The *New English Dictionary* (1901) observes under 'jubilee' 'especially frequent in the last two decades of the nineteenth century in reference to the two "jubilees" of Queen Victoria in 1887 and 1897, the Swiss jubilee of the Postal Union in 1900 and other celebrations', v, p. 615.

years later in view of its notable success, inspired subsequent royal or imperial occasions in this country and elsewhere. Even the most traditionalist dynasties – the Habsburgs in 1908, the Romanovs in 1913 – discovered the merits of this form of publicity. It was new insofar as it was directed at the public, unlike traditional royal ceremonials designed to symbolize the rulers' relation to the divinity and their position at the apex of a hierarchy of grandees. After the French Revolution every monarch had, sooner or later, to learn to change from the national equivalent of 'King of France' to 'King of the French', that is, to establish a direct relation to the collectivity of his or her subjects, however lowly. Though the stylistic option of a 'bourgeois monarchy' (pioneered by Louis Philippe) was available, it seems to have been taken only by the kings of modest countries wishing to maintain a low profile – the Netherlands, Scandinavia – though even some of the most divinely ordained rulers – notably the Emperor Francis Joseph – appear to have fancied the role of the hard-working functionary living in spartan comfort.

Technically there was no significant difference between the political use of monarchy for the purpose of strengthening effective rulers (as in the Habsburg, Romanov, but also perhaps in the Indian empires) and building the symbolic function of crowned heads in parliament- ary states. Both relied on exploiting the royal person, with or without dynastic ancestors, on elaborate ritual occasions with asso- ciated propagandist activities and a wide participation of the people, not least through the captive audiences available for official indoc- trination in the educational system. Both made the ruler the focus of his people's or peoples' unity, the symbolic representative of the country's greatness and glory, of its entire past and continuity with a changing present. Yet the innovations were perhaps more deliberate and systematic where, as in Britain, the revival of royal ritualism was seen as a necessary counterweight to the dangers of popular democracy. Bagehot had already recognized the value of political deference and the 'dignified', as distinct from the 'efficient', parts of the constitution in the days of the Second Reform Act. The old Disraeli, unlike the young, learned to use 'reverence for the throne and its occupant' as 'a mighty instrument of power and influence' and by the end of Victoria's reign the nature of the device was well under- stood. J. E. C. Bodley wrote about the coronation of Edward VII:

> The usage by an ardent yet practical people of an ancient rite to signalise the modern splendours of their empire, the recognition

by a free democracy of a hereditary crown, as a symbol of the world-wide domination of their race, constitute no mere pageant, but an event of the highest historical interest.[35]

Glory and greatness, wealth and power, could be symbolically shared by the poor through royalty and its rituals. The greater the power, the less attractive, one may suggest, was the bourgeois option for monarchy. And we may recall that in Europe monarchy remained the universal state form between 1870 and 1914, except for France and Switzerland.

II

The most universal political traditions invented in this period were the achievement of states. However, the rise of organized mass movements claiming separate or even alternative status to states, led to similar developments. Some of these movements, notably political Catholicism and various kinds of nationalism, were keenly aware of the importance of ritual, ceremonial and myth, including, normally, a mythological past. The significance of invented traditions is all the more striking when they arose among rationalist movements which were, if anything, rather hostile to them and lacked prefabricated symbolical and ritual equipment. Hence the best way to study their emergence is in one such case – that of the socialist labour movements.

The major international ritual of such movements, May Day (1890), was spontaneously evolved within a surprisingly short period. Initially it was designed as a single simultaneous one-day strike and demonstration for the eight-hour day, fixed on a date already associated for some years with this demand in the U.S.A. The choice of this date was certainly quite pragmatic in Europe. It probably had no ritual significance in the U.S.A., where 'Labour Day' had already been established at the end of summer. It has been suggested, not implausibly, that it was fixed to coincide with 'Moving Day', the traditional date for ending hiring contracts in New York and Pennsylvania.[36] Though this, like similar contractual periods in parts of traditional European agriculture, had originally formed part of the symbolically charged annual cycle of the pre-industrial labouring

[35] J. E. C. Bodley, *The Coronation of Edward VII: A Chapter of European and Imperial History* (London, 1903), pp. 153, 201.

[36] Maurice Dommanget, *Histoire du Premier Mai* (Paris, 1953), pp. 36–7.

year, its connection with the industrial proletariat was clearly
fortuitous. No particular form of demonstration was envisaged by
the new Labour and Socialist International. The concept of a
workers' festival was not only not mentioned in the original (1889)
resolution of that body, but was actively rejected on ideological
grounds by various revolutionary militants.

Yet the choice of a date so heavily charged with symbolism by
ancient tradition proved significant, even though – as Van Gennep
suggests – in France the anticlericalism of the labour movement
resisted the inclusion of traditional folklore practices in its May Day.[37]
From the start the occasion attracted and absorbed ritual and
symbolic elements, notably that of a quasi-religious or numinous
celebration ('Maifeier'), a holiday in both senses of the word.
(Engels, after referring to it as a 'demonstration', uses the term
'Feier' from 1893.[38] Adler recognized this element in Austria from
1892, Vandervelde in Belgium from 1893.) Andrea Costa expressed
it succinctly for Italy (1893): 'Catholics have Easter; henceforth the
workers will have their own Easter';[39] there are rarer references to
Whitsun also. A curiously syncretic 'May Day sermon' from
Charleroi (Belgium) survives for 1898 under the joint epigraphs
'Proletarians of all lands, unite' and 'Love one another'.[40]

Red flags, the only universal symbols of the movement, were
present from the start, but so, in several countries, were flowers: the
carnation in Austria, the red (paper) rose in Germany, sweet briar
and poppy in France, and the may, symbol of renewal, increasingly
infiltrated, and from the mid-1900s replaced by the lily-of-the-valley,
whose associations were unpolitical. Little is known about this
language of flowers which, to judge by the May Day poems in
socialist literature also, was spontaneously associated with the
occasion. It certainly struck the key-note of May Day, a time of
renewal, growth, hope and joy (we recall the girl with the
flowering branch of may associated in popular memory with the 1891
May Day shootings at Fourmies).[41] Equally, May Day played a

---

[37] A. Van Gennep, *Manuel de Folklore Français I*, iv, *Les Cérémonies Périodiques
Cycliques et Saisonnières*, 2: Cycle de Mai (Paris, 1949), p. 1719.

[38] Engels to Sorge 17 May 1893, in *Briefe und Auszüge aus Briefen an F. A. Sorge
u.A.* (Stuttgart, 1906), p. 397. See also Victor Adler, *Aufsätze, Reden und Briefe*
(Vienna, 1922), i, p. 69.

[39] Dommanget, *op. cit.*, p. 343.

[40] E. Vandervelde and J. Destrée, *Le Socialisme en Belgique* (Paris, 1903), pp. 417–18.

[41] Maxime Leroy, *La Coutûme Ouvrière* (Paris, 1913), i, p. 246.

major part in the development of the new socialist iconography of the 1890s in which, in spite of the expected emphasis on struggle, the note of hope, confidence and the approach of a brighter future – often expressed in the metaphors of plant growth – prevailed.[42]

As it happened, the First of May was initiated at a time of extraordinary growth and expansion in the labour and socialist movements of numerous countries, and might well not have established itself in a less hopeful political atmosphere. The ancient symbolism of spring, so fortuitously associated with it, suited the occasion perfectly in the early 1890s.

It thus became rapidly transformed into a highly charged annual festival and rite. The annual repetition was introduced to meet a demand from the ranks. With it the original political content of the day – the demand for an eight-hour day – inevitably dropped into the background to give way to whatever slogans attracted national labour movements in a particular year, or, more usually, to an unspecified assertion of the working-class presence and, in many Latin countries, the commemoration of the 'Chicago Martyrs'. The only original element maintained was the, preferably simultaneous, internationalism of the demonstration: in the extreme case of Russia in 1917 the revolutionaries actually abandoned their own calendar to celebrate their May Day on the same date as the rest of the world. And indeed, the public parade of the workers *as a class* formed the core of the ritual. It was, as commentators noted, the *only* holiday, even among radical and revolutionary anniversaries, to be associated with the industrial working class and no other; though – in Britain at least – specific communities of industrial workers had already shown signs of inventing general collective presentations of themselves as part of their labour movement. (The Durham miners' gala was first held in 1871.)[43] Like all such ceremonials, it was, or became, a basically good-humoured family occasion. The classical political demonstrations were not necessarily like this. (This character may still be observed in such later 'invented traditions' as the national

[42] E. J. Hobsbawm, 'Man and Woman in Socialist Iconography', *History Workshop*, vi (Autumn 1978), pp. 121–38; A. Rossel, *Premier Mai. Quatre-Vingt-Dix ans de Luttes Populaires dans le Monde* (Paris, 1977).

[43] Edward Welbourne, *The Miners' Unions of Northumberland and Durham* (Cambridge, 1923), p. 155; John Wilson, *A History of the Durham Miners' Association 1870–1904* (Durham, 1907), pp. 31, 34, 59; W. A. Moyes, *The Banner Book* (Gateshead, 1974). These annual demonstrations appear to have originated in Yorkshire in 1866.

festivals of the Italian communist newspaper *Unità*.) Like all of them it combined public and private merry-making and good cheer with the assertion of loyalty to the movement which was a basic element in working-class consciousness: oratory – in those days the longer the better, since a good speech was both inspiration and entertainment – banners, badges, slogans, and so on. Most crucially, it asserted the working-class presence by that most fundamental assertion of working-class power: the abstention from work. For, paradoxically, the success of May Day tended to be proportionate to its remoteness from the concrete every-day activities of the movement. It was greatest where socialist aspiration prevailed over the political realism and trade union calculation which, as in Britain and Germany,[44] tended to favour a demonstration on the first Sunday of the month over the annual one-day strike on the first of May. Victor Adler, sensitive to the mood of the Austrian workers, had insisted on the demonstrative strike against the advice of Kautsky,[45] and the Austrian May Day consequently acquired unusual strength and resonance. Thus, as we have seen, May Day was not so much formally invented by the leaders of the movement, as accepted and institutionalized by them on the initiative of their followers.

The strength of the new tradition was clearly appreciated by its enemies. Hitler, with his acute sense of symbolism, found it desirable not only to annex the red of the workers' flag but also May Day, by turning it into an official 'national day of labour' in 1933, and subsequently attenuating its proletarian associations.[46] We may, incidentally, observe that it has now been turned into a general holiday of labour in the E.E.C.

May Day and similar labour rituals are halfway between 'political' and 'social' traditions, belonging to the first through their association with mass organizations and parties which could – and indeed aimed to – become régimes and states, to the second because they genuinely expressed the workers' consciousness of their existence as a separate class, inasmuch as this was inseparable from the organizations of that class. While in many cases – such as Austrian Social Democracy, or

[44] Carl Schorske, *German Social Democracy, 1905–17: The Development of the Great Schism* (New York, 1965 edn), pp. 91–7.
[45] M. Ermers, *Victor Adler: Aufstieg u. Grösse einer sozialistischen Partei* (Vienna and Leipzig, 1932), p. 195.
[46] Helmut Hartwig, 'Plaketten zum 1. Mai 1934–39', *Aesthetik und Kommunikation*, vii, no. 26 (1976), pp. 56–9.

the British miners – class and organization became inseparable, it is not suggested that they were identical. 'The movement' developed its own traditions, shared by leaders and militants but not necessarily by voters and followers, and conversely the class might develop its own 'invented traditions' which were either independent of the organized movements, or even suspect in the eyes of the activists. Two of these, both clearly the product of our period, are worth a brief glance. The first is the emergence – notably in Britain, but probably also in other countries – of costume as a demonstration of class. The second is linked with mass sports.

It is no accident that the comic strip which gently satirized the traditional male working-class culture of the old industrial area of Britain (notably the North-East) should choose as its title and symbol the headgear which virtually formed the badge of class membership of the British proletarian when not at work: 'Andy Capp'. A similar equation between class and cap existed in France to some extent,[47] and possibly also in parts of Germany. In Britain, at least, icono-graphic evidence suggests that proletarian and cap were not universally identified before the 1890s, but that by the end of the Edwardian period – as photographs of crowds leaving football matches or mass meetings will confirm – that identification was almost complete. The rise of the proletarian cap awaits its chronicler. He or she, one may suspect, will find its history linked with that of the development of mass sports, since this particular type of headgear appears first as sporting wear among the upper and middle classes. Whatever its origins, it clearly became characteristic of the working class, not only because members of other classes, or those who aspired to such status, would be reluctant to be confused with proletarians, but also because manual workers did not care to choose (except no doubt for occasions of great formality) to cover their heads in any of the numerous other available fashions. Keir Hardie's demonstrative entry into parliament in a cap (1892) indicates that the element of class assertion was recognized.[48] It is not unreasonable to suppose that the masses were not unaware of it. In some obscure fashion they acquired the habit of wearing it fairly rapidly in the last decades of

[47] 'L'ouvrier même ne porte pas ici la casquette et la blouse' observed Jules Vallès contemptuously in London in 1872 – unlike the class-conscious Parisians. Paul Martinez, *The French Communard Refugees in Britain, 1871–1880* (Univ. of Sussex Ph.D. thesis, 1981), p. 341.

[48] Hardie's own deer-stalker-like cap represents a transitional stage to the eventually universal 'Andy Capp' headgear.

the nineteenth and the first decade of the twentieth century as part of the characteristic syndrome of 'working-class culture' which then took shape.

The equivalent history of proletarian costume in other countries remains to be written. Here we can only note that its political implications were clearly understood, if not before 1914 then certainly between the wars, as witness the following memory of the first National Socialist (official) May Day parade in Berlin 1933:

The workers...wore shabby, clean suits and those sailors' caps which were then a general external recognition sign of their class. These caps were decorated with an inconspicuous strap, mostly of black lacquer, but often replaced by a leather strap with buckles. Social Democrats and Communists wore this type of strap on their caps, the National Socialists another type, parted in the centre. This tiny difference suddenly leaped to the eye. The banal fact that more workers than ever before wore the parted strap on their caps carried the fatal message of a battle lost.[49]

The political association of worker and cap in France between the wars (*la salopette*) is also established, but its pre-1914 history awaits research.

The adoption of sports, and particularly football, as a mass proletarian cult is equally obscure, but without doubt equally rapid.[50] Here the timing is easier to establish. Between the middle 1870s, at the earliest, and the middle or late 1880s football acquired all the institutional and ritual characteristics with which we are still familiar: professionalism, the League, the Cup, with its annual pilgrimage of the faithful for demonstrations of proletarian triumph in the capital, the regular attendance at the Saturday match, the 'supporters' and their culture, the ritual rivalry, normally between moieties of an industrial city or conurbation (Manchester City and United, Notts County and Forest, Liverpool and Everton). Moreover, unlike other sports with regional or local proletarian bases – such as rugby union in South Wales,[51] cricket in parts of Northern England – football operated both on a local and on a national scale, so that the topic of the day's matches would provide common ground for conversation

[49] Stephan Hermlin, *Abendlicht* (Leipzig, 1979), p. 92.
[50] Tony Mason, *Association Football and English Society, 1863–1915* (Brighton, 1980).
[51] Cf. David B. Smith and Gareth W. Williams, *Field of Praise: Official History of the Welsh Rugby Union, 1881–1981* (Cardiff, 1981).

between virtually any two male workers in England or Scotland, and a few score celebrated players provided a point of common reference for all.

The nature of the football culture at this period – before it had penetrated far into the urban and industrial cultures of other countries[52] – is not yet well understood. Its socio-economic structure is less obscure. Originally developed as an amateur and character-building sport by the public-school middle classes, it was rapidly (by 1885) proletarianized and therefore professionalized; the symbolic turning-point – and recognized as a class confrontation – being the defeat of the Old Etonians by Bolton Olympic in the cup final of 1883. With professionalization, most of the philanthropic and moralizing figures from the national élite withdrew, leaving the management of the clubs in the hands of local businessmen and other notables, who maintained a curious caricature of the class relations of industrial capitalism as employers of an overwhelmingly proletarian labour force, attracted into the industry by a higher wage-rate, by the chance of windfall gains before retirement (benefit matches), but above all by the chance of fame. The structure of British football profession-alism was quite different from that of professionalism in sports with aristocratic or middle-class participation (cricket) or control (racing), or from that of the demotic entertainment business, that other means of escape from the working-class fate, which also provided the model for some sports of the poor (boxing).[53]

It is highly likely that football players tended to be drawn from skilled rather than unskilled workers,[54] probably unlike boxing, a sport which recruited in environments in which the ability to handle oneself was either useful for survival, as in big city slums, or was part of an occupational culture of masculinity, as in the mines. Though the urban and working-class character of the football crowds is patent,[55] their exact composition by age or social origin is not clear; nor is the development of the 'supporters' culture' and its practices; nor the extent to which the typical football enthusiast (unlike the

---

[52] Abroad it was often pioneered by British expatriates and the teams of local British-managed factories, but though it clearly had been to some extent naturalized by 1914 in some capital cities and industrial towns of the continent, it had hardly yet become a mass sport.

[53] W. F. Mandle, 'The Professional Cricketer in England in the Nineteenth Cen-tury', *Labour History* (Journal of the Australian Society for the Study of Labour History), xxiii (Nov. 1972), pp. 1–16; Wray Vamplew, *The Turf: A Social and Economic History of Horse Racing* (London, 1976).

[54] Mason, *op. cit.*, pp. 90–3.   [55] Mason, *op. cit.*, pp. 153–6.

typical follower of racing) was or had been an active amateur player. On the other hand, it is clear that while as the apocryphal last words of the labour militant indicate, for many of his kind belief in Jesus Christ, Keir Hardie and Huddersfield United went together, the organized movement showed a collective lack of enthusiasm for this, as for several other unpolitical aspects of working-class consciousness. Indeed, unlike central european Social Democracy, the British labour movement did not develop its own sporting organizations, with the possible exception of cycling clubs in the 1890s, whose links with progressive thought were marked.[56]

Little though we know about mass sport in Britain, we know even less about the continent. It would seem that sport, imported from Britain, remained a middle-class preserve very much longer than in its country of origin, but that otherwise the appeal of football to the working class, the replacement of middle-class (amateur) by plebeian (professional) football and the rise of mass urban identification with clubs, developed in similar ways.[57] The major exception, apart from contests closer to show-business than outdoor activity such as wrestling (suspect to the German gymnastic movement, but with a strong popular following), was cycling. On the continent this was probably the only modern mass sport – as witness the construction of 'velodromes' in big cities – four in Berlin alone before 1913 – and the institution of the Tour de France in 1903. It appears that in Germany at least the leading professional cyclists were workers.[58] Professional championships existed in France from 1881, in Switzerland and Italy from 1892, Belgium from 1894. No doubt the strong

[56] The Clarion Cycling Clubs come to mind, but also the foundation of the Oadby Cycling Club by a local radical poacher, labour activist and parish councillor. The nature of this sport – in Britain typically practised by youthful amateurs – was quite different from mass proletarian sport. David Prynn, 'The Clarion Clubs, Rambling and Holiday Associations in Britain since the 1890s', *Journal of Contemporary History*, xi, nos. 2 and 3 (July 1976), pp. 65–77; anon., 'The Clarion Fellowship', *Marx Memorial Library Quarterly Bulletin*, lxxvii (Jan.–Mar. 1976), pp. 6–9; James Hawker, *A Victorian Poacher*, ed. G. Christian (London, 1961), pp. 25–6.

[57] Of the Ruhr club Schalke 04, thirty-five out of forty-four identifiable members in 1904–13 were miners, workers or artisans, seventy-three out of eighty-eight in 1914–24, and ninety-one out of one hundred and twenty-two in 1924–34. Siegfried Gehrmann, 'Fussball in einer Industrieregion', in J. Reulecke and W. Weber (eds.), *Familie, Fabrik, Feierabend* (Wuppertal, 1978), pp. 377–98.

[58] Annemarie Lange, *Das Wilhelminische Berlin* (E. Berlin, 1967), ch. 13, esp. pp. 561–2.

commercial interest in this sport by manufacturers and other advertising interests speeded its popularity.[59]

III

To establish the class presence of a national middle-class élite and the membership of the much larger middle class was a far more difficult matter, and yet rather urgent at a time when occupations claiming middle-class status, or the numbers of those who aspired to them, were increasing with some rapidity in industrializing countries. The criterion for the membership of such classes could be nothing so simple as birth, landownership, manual labour or the receipt of wages, and while a socially recognized minimum of property and income was no doubt a necessary condition for it, it was not a sufficient one. Moreover, in the nature of things such a class included persons (or rather families) of a wide range of wealth and influence, each stratum tending to look down upon its inferiors. The fluidity of borders made clear criteria of social distinction unusually difficult. Since the middle classes were par excellence the locus of social mobility and individual self-improvement, entry to them could hardly be closed. The problem was twofold. First, how to define and separate the genuine national élite of an upper middle class (*haute bourgeoisie*, *Grossbürgertum*) once the relatively firm criteria by which subjective class membership could be determined in stable local communities had been eroded, and descent, kinship, intermarriage, the local networks of business, private sociability and politics no longer provided firm guidance. Second, how to establish an identity and a presence for the relatively large mass of those who neither belonged to this élite nor to 'the masses' – or even to that clearly inferior order of the petty-bourgeoisie of the 'lower middle classes' which at least one British observer firmly classed with the manual workers as belonging to the world of 'the Board schools'.[60] Could it be defined, could it define itself, other than as 'consisting essentially of families in the process of rising socially', as a French observer of the British scene held, or as what was left over when the more obviously recognizable masses and the 'upper ten' had been

[59] Dino Spatazza Moncada, *Storia del Ciclismo dai Primi Passi ad Oggi* (Parma, n.d.).

[60] W. R. Lawson, *John Bull and his Schools: A Book for Parents, Ratepayers and Men of Business* (Edinburgh and London, 1908), p. 39.

subtracted from the population, as an English one did?[61] A further problem arose to complicate the question: the emergence of the increasingly emancipated middle-class woman as an actress on the public scene in her own right. While the numbers of boys in French *lycées* between 1897 and 1907 rose only modestly, the number of girls increased by 170 per cent.

For the upper middle classes or 'haute bourgeoisie' the criteria and institutions which had formerly served to set apart an aristocratic ruling class provided the obvious model: they merely had to be widened and adapted. A fusion of the two classes in which the new components ceased to be recognizable as new was the ideal, though it was probably not completely attainable even in Britain, where it was quite possible for a family of Nottingham bankers to achieve, over several generations, intermarriage with royalty. What made the attempts at such assimilation possible (insofar as they were institutionally permitted) was that element of stability which, as a French observer noted of Britain, distinguished the established and arrived upper bourgeois generations from the first-generation climbers.[62] The rapid acquisition of really enormous wealth could also enable first-generation plutocrats to buy themselves into an aristocratic milieu which in bourgeois countries rested not only on title and descent but also on enough money to carry on a suitably profligate life-style.[63] In Edwardian Britain the plutocrats seized such opportunities eagerly.[64] Yet individual assimilation could serve only a tiny minority.

The basic aristocratic criterion of descent could, however, be adapted to define a relatively large new upper-middle-class élite. Thus a passion for genealogy developed in the U.S.A. in the 1890s. It was primarily a female interest: the 'Daughters of the American Revolution' (1890) survived and flourished, whereas the slightly earlier 'Sons of the American Revolution' faded away. Though the ostensible object was to distinguish native white and Protestant Americans from the mass of new immigrants, in fact their object was to establish an exclusive upper stratum among the white middle class. The D.A.R. had no more than 30,000 members in 1900, mostly in the strongholds of 'old' money – Connecticut, New York, Pennsyl-

---

[61] Paul Descamps, *L'Education dans les Ecoles Anglaises*, Bib. de la Science Sociale (Paris, Jan. 1911), p. 25; Lawson, *op. cit.*, p. 24.

[62] Descamps, *op. cit.*, pp. 11, 67.   [63] *Ibid.*, p. 11.

[64] Jamie Camplin, *The Rise of the Plutocrats: Wealth and Power in Edwardian England* (London, 1978).

vania – though also among the booming millionaires of Chicago.[65] Organizations such as these differed from the much more restrictive attempts to set up a group of families as a quasi-aristocratic élite (by inclusion in a *Social Register* or the like), inasmuch as they provided nation-wide linkages. The less exclusive D.A.R. was more likely to discover suitable members in such cities as Omaha than a very élitist *Social Register*. The history of the middle-class search for genealogy remains to be written, but the systematic American concentration on this pursuit was probably, at this period, somewhat exceptional.

Far more significant was schooling, supplemented in certain respects by amateur sports, which were closely linked to it in the Anglo-Saxon countries. For schooling provided not only a convenient means of social comparability between individuals or families lacking initial personal relations and, on a nation-wide scale, a means of establishing common patterns of behaviour and values, but also a set of interlinked networks between the products of comparable institutions and, indirectly, through the institutionalization of the 'old boy', 'alumnus' or 'Alte Herren', a strong web of intergenerational stability and continuity. Furthermore it provided, within limits, for the possibility of expanding an upper-middle-class élite socialized in some suitably acceptable manner. Indeed, education in the nineteenth century became much the most convenient and universal criterion for determining social stratification, though it is not altogether clear when it did so. Mere primary education ineluctably classified a person as belonging to the lower orders. The minimal criterion for accepted middle-class status was secondary education beyond the ages of, say, fourteen to sixteen. Higher education, except for certain forms of strictly vocational training, clearly qualified a person for the upper middle class and other élites. It incidentally follows that the traditional bourgeois–entrepreneurial practice of sending sons into business in their mid-teens, or of eschewing university education, lost ground. It certainly did so in Germany, where in 1867 thirteen out of fourteen Rhineland industrial cities had refused to contribute to the fiftieth anniversary celebration of Bonn university on the grounds that neither industrialists nor their sons used it.[66] By the 1890s the percentage of Bonn students from families

[65] Davies, *Patriotism on Parade*, pp. 47, 77.
[66] Cited in E. J. Hobsbawm, *The Age of Capital* (London, 1977), p. 59; F. Zunkel, 'Industriebürgertum in Westdeutschland', in H. U. Wehler (ed.), *Moderne deutsche Sozialgeschichte* (Cologne and Berlin, 1966), p. 323.

of the *Besitzbürgertum* had risen from *c.* twenty-three to just under forty, while those from the traditional professional bourgeoisie (*Bildungsbürgertum*) had fallen from forty-two to thirty-one.[67] It probably did so in Britain, though French observers in the 1890s still noted with surprise that the English rarely left school after 16.[68] This was certainly no longer the case in the 'upper middle class', though little systematic work has been done on the subject.

Secondary schooling provided a broad criterion of middle-class membership, but one too broad to define or select the rapidly growing, but nevertheless numerically rather small, élites which, whether we call them ruling class or 'establishment', actually ran the national affairs of countries. Even in Britain, where no national secondary system existed before the present century, a special sub-class of 'public schools' had to be formed within secondary education. They were first officially defined in the 1860s, and grew both by the enlargement of the nine schools then recognized as such (from 2,741 boys in 1860, to 4,553 in 1906) and also by the addition of further schools recognized as belonging to the élite class. Before 1868, two dozen schools at most had a serious claim to this status, but by 1902, according to Honey's calculations, they consisted of a minimum 'short list' of up to sixty-four schools and a maximum 'long list' of up to one hundred and four schools, with a fringe of perhaps sixty of more doubtful standing.[69] Universities expanded at this period by rising admissions rather than by new foundations, but this growth was sufficiently dramatic to produce serious worries about the overproduction of graduates, at least in Germany. Between the mid-1870s and the mid-1880s student numbers approximately doubled in Germany, Austria, France and Norway and more than doubled in Belgium and Denmark.[70] The expansion in the U.S.A. was even more spectacular. By 1913 there were 38.6 students per 10,000

---

[67] K. H. Jarausch, 'The Social Transformation of the University: The Case of Prussia 1865–1915', *Journal of Social History*, xii, no. 4 (1979), p. 625.

[68] Max Leclerc, *L'Education des Classes Moyennes et Dirigeantes en Angleterre* (Paris, 1894), pp. 133, 144; P. Bureau, 'Mon Séjour dans une Petite Ville d'Angleterre', *La Science Sociale* (*suivant la Méthode de F. Le Play*), 5th yr, ix (1890), p. 70. Cf. also Patrick Joyce, *Work, Society and Politics: The Culture of the Factory in Later Victorian England* (Brighton, 1980), pp. 29–34.

[69] J. R. de S. Honey, *Tom Brown's Universe: The Development of the Victorian Public School* (London, 1977), p. 273.

[70] J. Conrad, 'Die Frequenzverhältnisse der Universitäten der hauptsächlichsten Kulturländer auf dem Europäischen Kontinent', *Jahrbücher f. N. ÖK u. Statistik*, 3rd series, i (1891), pp. 376–94.

population in that country, compared with the usual continental figure of 9–11.5 (and less than 8 in Britain and Italy).[71] The problem of defining the effective élite within the growing body of those who possessed the required educational membership card was real.

In the broadest sense it was attacked by institutionalization. The *Public Schools Yearbook* (published from 1889) established the member schools of the so-called Headmasters' Conference as a recognizable national or even international community, if not of equals, then at least of comparables; and Baird's *American College Fraternities* (seven editions between 1879 and 1914) did the same for the 'Greek Letter Fraternities', membership of which indicated the élite among the mass of American university students. Yet the tendency of the aspiring to imitate the institutions of the arrived made it desirable to draw a line between the genuine 'upper middle classes' or élites and those equals who were less equal than the rest.[72] The reason for this was not purely snobbish. A growing national élite also required the construction of genuinely effective networks of interaction.

Here, it may be suggested, lies the significance of the institution of the 'old boys', 'alumni' or 'Alte Herren' which now developed, and without which 'old boy networks' cannot exist as such. In Britain 'old boy dinners' appear to have started in the 1870s, 'old boy associations' at about the same time – they multiplied particularly in the 1890s, being followed shortly after by the invention of a suitable 'old school tie'.[73] Indeed it was not before the end of the century that the practice of sending sons to the father's old school appears to have become usual: only 5 per cent of Arnold's pupils had sent their sons to Rugby.[74] In the U.S.A. the establishment of 'alumni chapters' also began in the 1870s, 'forming circles of cultivated men who would not otherwise know each other',[75] and so, a little later,

[71] Joseph Ben-David, 'Professions in the Class System of Present-Day Societies', *Current Sociology*, xii, no. 3 (1963–4), pp. 63–4.

[72] 'In consequence of the general snobbery of the English, above all of the English rising in the social scale, the education of the Middle Classes tends to model itself upon that of the Upper Middle Class, though with less expenditure of time and money.' Descamps, *L'Education dans les Ecoles Anglaises*, p. 67. The phenomenon was far from purely British.

[73] *The Book of Public School, Old Boys, University, Navy, Army, Air Force and Club Ties*, intro. by James Laver (London, 1968), p. 31; see also Honey, *op. cit.*

[74] Honey, *op. cit.*, p. 153.

[75] W. Raimond Baird, *American College Fraternities: A Descriptive Analysis of the Society System of the Colleges of the US with a Detailed Account of each Fraternity*, 4th edn (New York, 1890), pp. 20–1.

did the construction of elaborate fraternity houses in the colleges, financed by the alumni who thus demonstrated not only their wealth, and the intergenerational links but also – as in similar developments in the German student 'Korps'[76] – their influence over the younger generation. Thus Beta Theta Pi had sixteen alumni chapters in 1889 but one hundred and ten in 1913; only a single fraternity house in 1889 (though some were being built), but forty-seven in 1913. Phi Delta Theta had its first alumni association in 1876 but by 1913 the number had grown to about one hundred.

In the U.S.A. and in Germany the role of these intergenerational networks was consciously played out, possibly because in both countries their initial role as suppliers of men in public service was very clear. The 'Alte Herren' active in the 'Kösener Korps', the élite associations of this kind in the 1870s, included 18 ministers, 835 civil servants, 648 judicial officials, 127 municipal officials, 130 soldiers, 651 medical men (10 per cent of them officials), 435 secondary and university teachers and 331 lawyers. These greatly outnumbered the 257 'landowners', the 241 bankers, company directors and merchants, the 76 in technical and the 27 in scientific professions and the 37 'artists and editors'.[77] The earlier American college fraternities

Table 2. *Alumni of Delta Kappa Epsilon (Dartmouth)*[78]

	1850s	1890s
Civil service and law	21	21
Medical	3	17
Clergy	6	10
Teaching	8	12
Business	8	27
Journalism and intellectual	1	10
Other	3	5
Total	50	102

also stressed such alumni (Beta Theta Pi in 1889 prided itself on nine senators, forty congressmen, six ambassadors and fifteen governors), but, as Table 2 shows, economic and political development gave them an increasingly modest place, and in the 1900s they gave increasing

76 Bernard Oudin, *Les Corporations Allemandes d'Etudiants* (Paris, 1962), p. 19; Detlef Grieswelle, 'Die Soziologie der Kösener Korps 1870–1914', in *Student und Hochschule im 19 Jahrhundert: Studien und Materialien* (Göttingen, 1975).
77 Grieswelle, *op. cit.*, p. 357.
78 *Delta Kappa Epsilon Catalog* (1910).

prominence to their capitalists. And indeed a body like Delta Kappa Epsilon, which in 1913 included a Cabot Lodge and a Theodore Roosevelt, as well as eighteen eminent New York bankers, among them J. P. Morgan and a Whitney, nine powerful businessmen from Boston, three pillars of Standard Oil, and even in remote Minnesota a James N. Hill and a Weyerhaeuser, must have been a formidable business mafia. In Britain, it is safe to say, the informal networks, created by school and college, reinforced by family continuity, business sociability and clubs, were more effective than formal associations. How effective may be judged by the record of such institutions as the code-breaking establishment at Bletchley and the Special Operations Executive in the second world war.[79] Formal associations, unless deliberately restricted to an élite – like the German 'Kösener Korps' which between them comprised 8 per cent of German students in 1887, 5 per cent in 1914[80] – served largely, it may be suggested, to provide general criteria of social 'recognizability'. Membership of *any* Greek Letter Fraternity – even the vocational ones which multiplied from the end of the 1890s[81] – and possession of *any* tie with diagonal stripes in some combination of colours served the purpose.

However, the crucial informal device for stratifying a theoretically open and expanding system was the self-selection of acceptable social partners, and this was achieved above all through the ancient aristocratic pursuit of sport, transformed into a system of formal contests against antagonists selected as worthy on social grounds. It is significant that the best criterion for the 'public-school community' discovered is by the study of which schools were ready to play games against each other,[82] and that in the U.S.A. the élite universities (the 'Ivy League') were defined, at least in the dominant north-east, by the selection of colleges choosing to play each other at football, in that country essentially a college sport in origin. Nor is it an accident that the formal sporting contests between Oxford and Cambridge developed essentially after 1870, and especially between 1890 and 1914 (see Table 3). In Germany this social criterion was specifically recognized:

[79] R. Lewin, *Ultra Goes to War* (London, 1980 edn), pp. 55–6.
[80] Grieswelle, *op. cit.*, pp. 349–53.
[81] Baird lists forty-one fraternities in 1914 unmentioned in 1890. Twenty-eight of them formed after 1900, ten founded before 1890, twenty-eight of these were confined to lawyers, doctors, engineers, dentists and other career specializations.
[82] Honey, *op. cit.*, pp. 253ff.

Table 3. *Regular Oxford–Cambridge contests by date of institution*[83]

Date	No. of contests	Sport
Before 1860	4	Cricket, rowing, rackets, real tennis
1860s	4	Athletics, shooting, billiards, steeple-chasing
1870s	4	Golf, soccer, rugby, polo
1880s	2	Cross-country, tennis
1890s	5	Boxing, hockey, skating, swimming, water-polo
1900–13	8	Gymnastics, ice-hockey, lacrosse, motor-cycle racing, tug-of-war, fencing, car-racing, motor-cycle hill climbing (Some of these were later abandoned.)

The characteristic which singles out academic youth as a special social group (*Stand*) from the rest of society, is the concept of 'Satisfaktionsfähigkeit' [the acceptability as a challenger in duels], i.e. the claim to a specific socially defined standard of honour (*Standesehre*).[84]
Elsewhere de facto segregation was concealed in a nominally open system.

This brings us back to one of the most significant of the new social practices of our period: sport. The social history of upper- and middle-class sports remains to be written,[85] but three things may be suggested. First, the last three decades of the nineteenth century mark a decisive transformation in the spread of old, the invention of new, and the institutionalization of most sports on a national and even an international scale. Second, this institutionalization provided both a public show-case for sport, which one may (with tongue-in-cheek) compare to the fashion for public building and statuary in politics, and a mechanism for extending activities hitherto confined to the aristocracy and the rich bourgeoisie able to assimilate its life-styles to a widening range of the 'middle classes'. That, on the

---

[83] Calculated from Royal Insurance Company, *Record of Sports*, 9th edn (1914).

[84] Günter Botzert, *Sozialer Wandel der studentischen Korporationen* (Münster, 1971), p. 123.

[85] For some relevant data, see Carl Diem, *Weltgeschichte des Sports und der leibeserziehung* (Stuttgart, 1960); Kl. C. Wildt, *Daten zur Sportgeschichte. Teil 2. Europa von 1750 bis 1894* (Schorndorf bei Stuttgart, 1972).

minority to establish the sort of virtual membership of a nation-wide club which united, for example, most of those who had passed through Oxford and Cambridge, nor sufficiently united by a common destiny and potential solidarity, like the workers.[94] Negatively the middle classes found it easy to segregate themselves from their inferiors by such devices as rigid insistence on amateurism in sport, as well as by the life-style and values of 'respectability', not to mention residential segregation. Positively, it may be suggested, they found it easier to establish a sense of belonging together through external symbols, among which those of nationalism (patriotism, imperialism) were perhaps the most significant. It is, one might suggest, as the quintessential patriotic class that the new or aspiring middle class found it easiest to recognize itself collectively.

This is speculation. The present chapter does not permit us to pursue it further. Here it is only possible to point out that there is at least some prima facie evidence for it, seen in the appeal of patriotism to the white-collar strata of Britain in the South African War[95] and the role of the right-wing nationalist mass organizations – overwhelmingly of middle-class but not élite composition – in Germany from the 1880s on, the appeal of Schönerer's nationalism to the (German-speaking) university students – a middle-class stratum profoundly marked by nationalism in a number of European countries.[96] The nationalism which gained ground was overwhelmingly identified with the political right. In the 1890s the originally liberal–nationalist German gymnasts abandoned the old national colours en masse to adopt the new black–white–red banner: in 1898 only 100 out of 6501 *Turnervereine* still maintained the old black–red–gold.[97]

[94] It would be interesting, in countries whose language permits this distinction, to inquire into the changes in the mutual social use of the second person singular, symbol of social brotherhood as well as of personal intimacy. Among the higher classes its use between fellow-students (and, as with French polytechnicians, ex-students), brother-officers and the like is familiar. Workers, even when they did not know one another, used it habitually. Leo Uhen, *Gruppenbewusstsein und informelle Gruppenbildung bei deutschen Arbeitern im Jahrhundert der Industrialisierung* (Berlin, 1964), pp. 106–7. Labour movements institutionalized it among their members ('Dear Sir and Brother').

[95] Richard Price, *An Imperial War and the British Working-Class: Working-Class Attitudes and Reactions to the Boer War, 1899–1902* (London, 1972), pp. 72–3.

[96] It is to be noted that in Germany the élite student Korps resisted the principle of anti-semitism, unlike the non-élite associations, though de facto applying it (Grieswelle, *op. cit.*, p. 353). Similarly anti-semitism was imposed on the German gymnastic movement by pressure from below, against some resistance from the old National–Liberal bourgeois leadership of the movement (John, *op. cit.*, p. 65).

[97] John, *op. cit.*, p. 37.

continent, it remained confined to a fairly restricted élite before 1914 is another matter. Third, it provided a mechanism for bringing together persons of an equivalent social status otherwise lacking organic social or economic links, and perhaps above all for providing a new role for bourgeois *women*.

The sport which was to become the most characteristic of the middle classes may illustrate all three elements. Tennis was invented in Britain in 1873, and acquired its classic national tournament there (Wimbledon) in 1877, four years before the American and fourteen years before the French national championships. It acquired its organized international dimension (the Davis Cup) by 1900. Like golf, another sport which was to demonstrate an unusual attraction for the middle classes, it was not based on team-effort, and its clubs – managing sometimes rather expensive pieces of real-estate requiring rather expensive maintenance – were not linked into 'leagues' and functioned as potential or actual social centres: in the case of golf essentially for males (eventually largely for businessmen), in the case of tennis for the middle-class young of both sexes. Moreover, it is significant that competitive contests for women followed rapidly on the institution of competitive contests for men: the women's singles entered Wimbledon seven years after the men's, the American and French national championships six years after their institution.[86] Almost for the first time sport therefore provided respectable women of the upper and middle classes with a recognized public role as individual human beings, separate from their function as wives, daughters, mothers, marriage-partners or other appendages of males inside and outside the family. Its role in the analysis of the emancipation of women requires more attention than it has so far received, as does its relation to middle-class travel and holidays.[87]

It is hardly necessary to document the fact that the institutionalization of sport took place in the last decades of the century. Even in Britain it was hardly established before the 1870s – the Association football cup dates back to 1871, the county cricket championship to 1873 – and thereafter several new sports were invented (tennis, badminton, hockey, water-polo, and so on), or de facto introduced on a national scale (golf), or systematized (boxing). Elsewhere in Europe sport in the modern form was a conscious import of social

[86] *Encyclopaedia of Sports* (S. Brunswick and New York, 1969 edn): Lawn Tennis.

[87] For an early recognition of the tennis club as 'part of the revolt of sons and daughters of the middle class', see T. H. S. Escott, *Social Transformations of the Victorian Age* (London, 1897), pp. 195–6, 444. See also R. C. K. Ensor, *England 1870–1914* (Oxford, 1936), pp. 165–6.

values and life-styles from Britain, largely by those influenced by the educational system of the British upper class, such as Baron de Coubertin, an admirer of Dr Arnold.[88] What is significant is the speed with which these transfers were made, though actual institutional-ization took somewhat longer.

Middle-class sport thus combined two elements of the invention of tradition: the political and the social. On the one hand it represented a conscious, though not usually official, effort to form a ruling élite on the British model supplementing, competing with or seeking to replace the older aristocratic–military continental models, and thus, depending on the local situation, associated with conser-vative or liberal elements in the local upper and middle classes.[89] On the other it represented a more spontaneous attempt to draw class lines against the masses, mainly by the systematic emphasis on amateurism as the criterion of upper- and middle-class sport (as notably in tennis, rugby union football as against association football and rugby league and in the Olympic Games). However, it also represented an attempt to develop both a specific new bourgeois pattern of leisure activity and a life-style – both bisexual and suburban or ex-urban[90] – and a flexible and expandable criterion of group membership.

Both mass and middle-class sport combined the invention of political and social traditions in yet another way: by providing a medium for national identification and factitious community. This was not new in itself, for mass physical exercises had long been linked with liberal–nationalist movements (the German *Turner*, the Czech *Sokols*) or with national identification (rifle-shooting in Switzerland). Indeed the resistance of the German gymnastic movement, on nationalist grounds in general and anti-British ones in particular, distinctly slowed down the progress of mass sport in Germany.[91] The rise of sport provided new expressions of nationalism through the choice or invention of nationally specific sports – Welsh rugby as distinct from English soccer, and Gaelic football in Ireland (1884),

[88] Pierre de Coubertin, *L'Ecole en Angleterre* (Paris, 1888); Diem, *op. cit.*, pp. 1130f.
[89] Marcel Spivak, 'Le Développement de l'Education Physique et du Sport Français de 1852 à 1914', *Revue d'Histoire Moderne et Contemporaine*, xxiv (1977), pp. 28–48; D. Lejeune, 'Histoire Sociale et Alpinisme en France, XIX–XX s.', *ibid.*, xxv (1978), pp. 111–28.
[90] This must be distinguished from the patterns of sports and outdoor pastimes of the old aristocracy and military, even if they sometimes took to the new sports or forms of sport.
[91] John, *op. cit.*, pp. 107ff.

which acquired genuine mass support some twenty years later.[92] However, although the specific linking of physical exercises with nationalism as part of nationalist movements remained important – as in Bengal[93] – it was by now certainly less significant than two other phenomena.

The first of these was the concrete demonstration of the links which bound all inhabitants of the national state together, irrespective of local and regional differences, as in the all-English football culture or, more literally, in such sporting institutions as the cyclists' Tour de France (1903), followed by the Giro d'Italia (1909). These phenomena were all the more significant as they evolved spontane-ously or by commercial mechanisms. The second consisted of the international sporting contests which very soon supplemented nat-ional ones, and reached their typical expression in the revival of the Olympics in 1896. While we are today only too aware of the scope for vicarious national identification which such contests provide, it is important to recall that before 1914 they had barely begun to acquire their modern character. Initially, 'international' contests served to underline the unity of nations or empires much in the way inter-regional contests did. British international matches – as usual the pioneers – pitted the nations of the British Isles against each other (in football: those of Britain in the 1870s, Ireland being included in the 1880s), or various parts of the British Empire (Test Matches began in 1877). The first international football match outside the British Isles confronted Austria and Hungary (1902). International sport, with few exceptions, remained dominated by amateurism – that is by middle-class sport – even in football, where the inter-national association (F.I.F.A.) was formed by countries with little mass support for the game in 1904 (France, Belgium, Denmark, the Netherlands, Spain, Sweden, Switzerland). The Olympics remained the main international arena for this sport. To this extent national identification through sport against foreigners in this period seem to have been primarily a middle-class phenomenon.

This may itself be significant. For, as we have seen, the midd classes in the broadest sense found subjective group identificati unusually difficult, since they were not in fact a sufficiently sm

[92] W. F. Mandle, 'Sport as Politics. The Gaelic Athletic Association 1884–19 in R. Cashman and M. McKernan (eds.), *Sport in History* (Queensland U.P Lucia, 1979).
[93] John Rosselli, 'The Self-Image of Effeteness: Physical Education and Nationa in 19th Century Bengal', *Past and Present*, 86 (1980), pp. 121–48.

What is clear is that nationalism became a substitute for social cohesion through a national church, a royal family or other cohesive traditions, or collective group self-presentations, a new secular religion, and that the class which required such a mode of cohesion most was the growing new middle class, or rather that large intermediate mass which so signally lacked other forms of cohesion. At this point, once again, the invention of political traditions coincides with that of social ones.

IV

To establish the clustering of 'invented traditions' in western countries between 1870 and 1914 is relatively easy. Enough examples of such innovations have been given in this chapter, from old school ties and royal jubilees, Bastille Day and the Daughters of the American Revolution, May Day, the Internationale and the Olympic Games to the Cup Final and Tour de France as popular rites, and the institution of flag worship in the U.S.A. The political developments and the social transformations which may account for this clustering have also been discussed, though the latter more briefly and speculatively than the former. For it is unfortunately easier to document the motives and intentions of those who are in a position formally to institute such innovations, and even their consequences, than new practices which spring up spontaneously at the grass roots. British historians of the future, anxious to pursue similar inquiries for the late twentieth century, will have far less difficulty with the analysis of, say, the ceremonial consequences of the assassination of Earl Mountbatten than with such novel practices as the purchase (often at great expense) of individually distinctive number-plates for motor cars. In any case, the object of this book is to encourage the study of a relatively new subject, and any pretence to treat it other than in a tentative manner would be out of place.

However, there remain three aspects of the 'invention of tradition' in this period which call for some brief comment in conclusion.

The first is the distinction between those new practices of the period which proved lasting, and those which did not. In retrospect it would seem that the period which straddles the first world war marks a divide between languages of symbolic discourse. As in military uniforms what might be called the operatic mode gave way to the prosaic mode. The uniforms invented for the interwar mass movements, which could hardly claim the excuse of operational camouflage, eschewed bright colours, preferring duller hues such as the black and brown of Fascists and National Socialists.[98] No doubt fancy dress for ritual occasions was still invented for men in the period 1870–1914, though examples hardly come to mind – except perhaps by way of the extension of older styles to new institutions of the same type and, hopefully, status, such as academic gowns and hoods for new colleges and degrees. The old costumes were certainly still maintained. However, one has the distinct impression that in this respect the period lived on accumulated capital. In another respect, however, it clearly developed an old idiom with particular enthusiasm. The mania for statuary and allegorically decorated or symbolic public buildings has already been mentioned, and there is little doubt that it reached a peak between 1870 and 1914. Yet this idiom of symbolic discourse was destined to decline with dramatic suddenness between the wars. Its extraordinary vogue was to prove almost as short-lived as the contemporary outburst of another kind of symbolism, 'art nouveau'. Neither the massive adaptation of traditional allegory and symbolism for public purposes, nor the improvization of a new and imprecise language of vegetable or female, but in any case curvilinear, symbolism, mainly for private or semi-private purposes appears to have been suited more than temporarily to whatever social requirements gave rise to them. We can only speculate about the reasons, and this is not the place to do so.

On the other hand, it may be suggested that another idiom of public symbolic discourse, the theatrical, proved more lasting. Public ceremonies, parades and ritualized mass gatherings were far from new. Yet their extension for official purposes and for unofficial secular purposes (mass demonstrations, football matches, and the like) in this period is rather striking. Some examples have been mentioned above. Moreover, the construction of formal ritual spaces, already consciously allowed for in German nationalism, appears to have been systematically undertaken even in countries which had hitherto paid little attention to it – one thinks of Edwardian London – and neither should we overlook the invention in this period of substantially new constructions for spectacle and de facto

---

[98] The brightest such uniforms appear to have been the blue shirts and red ties of socialist youth movements. I know of no case of red, orange or yellow shirts and none of genuinely multicoloured ceremonial clothing.

mass ritual such as sports stadia, outdoor and indoor.[99] The royal attendance at the Wembley Cup Final (from 1914), and the use of such buildings as the Sportspalast in Berlin or the Vélodrome d'Hiver in Paris by the interwar mass movements of their respective countries, anticipate the development of formal spaces for public mass ritual (the Red Square from 1918) which was to be systematically fostered by Fascist régimes. We may note in passing that, in line with the exhaustion of the old language of public symbolism, the new settings for such public ritual were to stress simplicity and monumentality rather than the allegorical decoration of the nineteenth-century Ringstrasse in Vienna or the Victor Emmanuel monument in Rome;[100] a tendency already anticipated in our period.[101]

On the stage of public life the emphasis therefore shifted from the design of elaborate and varied stage-sets, capable of being 'read' in the manner of a strip cartoon or tapestry, to the movement of the actors themselves – either, as in military or royal parades, a ritual minority acting for the benefit of a watching mass public, or, as anticipated in the political mass movements of the period (such as May Day demonstrations) and the great mass sporting occasions, a merger of actors and public. These were the tendencies which were destined for further development after 1914. Without speculating further about this form of public ritualization, it does not seem unreasonable to relate it to the decline of old tradition and the democratization of politics.

The second aspect of invented tradition in this period concerns the practices identified with specific social classes or strata as distinct from members of wider inter-class collectivities such as states or 'nations'. While some such practices were formally designed as badges of class consciousness – the May Day practices among workers, the revival or invention of 'traditional' peasant costume among (de facto the richer) peasants – a larger number were not so identified in theory and many indeed were adaptations, specializations or conquests of practices originally initiated by the higher social

[99] Cf. *Wasmuth's Lexikon der Baukunst* (Berlin, 1932), iv: 'Stadthalle'; W. Scharau-Wils, *Gebäude und Gelände für Gymnastik, Spiel und Sport* (Berlin, 1925); D. R. Knight, *The Exhibitions: Great White City, Shepherds Bush* (London, 1978).

[100] Carl Schorske, *Fin de Siècle Vienna: Politics and Culture* (New York, 1980), ch. 2.

[101] Cf. Alastair Service, *Edwardian Architecture: A Handbook to Building Design in Britain 1890–1914* (London, 1977).

strata. Sport is the obvious example. From above, the class line was here drawn in three ways: by maintaining aristocratic or middle-class control of the governing institutions, by social exclusiveness or, more commonly, by the high cost or scarcity of the necessary capital equipment (real tennis courts or grouse-moors), but above all by the rigid separation between amateurism, the criterion of sport among the upper strata, and professionalism, its logical corollary among the lower urban and working classes.[102] Class-specific sport among plebeians rarely developed consciously as such. Where it did, it was usually by taking over upper-class exercises, pushing out their former practitioners, and then developing a specific set of practices on a new social basis (the football culture).

Practices thus filtering socially downwards – from aristocracy to bourgeoisie, from bourgeoisie to working class – were probably predominant in this period, not only in sport, but in costume and material culture in general, given the force of snobbery among the middle classes and of the values of bourgeois self-improvement and achievement among the working-class élites.[103] They were transformed, but their historical origins remained visible. The opposite movement was not absent, but in this period less visible. Minorities (aristocrats, intellectuals, deviants) might admire certain urban plebeian sub-cultures and activities – such as music-hall art – but the major assimilation of cultural practices developed among the lower classes or for a mass popular public was to come later. Some signs of it were visible before 1914, mainly mediated through entertainment and perhaps above all the social dance, which may be linked to the growing emancipation of women: the vogue for ragtime or the tango. However, any survey of cultural inventions in this period cannot but note the development of autochthonous lower-class sub-cultures and practices which owed nothing to models from higher social classes – almost certainly as a by-product of urbanization and mass migration.

---

[102] Professionalism implies a degree of occupational specialization and a 'market' barely if at all available among the settled rural population. Professional sportsmen there were either servants or suppliers of the upper classes (jockeys, alpine guides) or appendages to amateur upper-class competitions (cricket professionals). The distinction between the upper- and lower-class killing of game was not economic, though some poachers relied on it for a living, but legal. It was expressed in the Game Laws.

[103] A Weberian correlation of sport and Protestantism has been observed in Germany up to 1960. G. Lüschen, 'The Interdependence of Sport and Culture', in M. Hart (ed.), *Sport in the Sociocultural Process* (Dubuque, 1976).

continent, it remained confined to a fairly restricted élite before 1914 is another matter. Third, it provided a mechanism for bringing together persons of an equivalent social status otherwise lacking organic social or economic links, and perhaps above all for providing a new role for bourgeois *women*.

The sport which was to become the most characteristic of the middle classes may illustrate all three elements. Tennis was invented in Britain in 1873, and acquired its classic national tournament there (Wimbledon) in 1877, four years before the American and fourteen years before the French national championships. It acquired its organized international dimension (the Davis Cup) by 1900. Like golf, another sport which was to demonstrate an unusual attraction for the middle classes, it was not based on team-effort, and its clubs – managing sometimes rather expensive pieces of real-estate requiring rather expensive maintenance – were not linked into 'leagues' and functioned as potential or actual social centres: in the case of golf essentially for males (eventually largely for businessmen), in the case of tennis for the middle-class young of both sexes. Moreover, it is significant that competitive contests for women followed rapidly on the institution of competitive contests for men: the women's singles entered Wimbledon seven years after the men's, the American and French national championships six years after their institution.[86] Almost for the first time sport therefore provided respectable women of the upper and middle classes with a recognized public role as individual human beings, separate from their function as wives, daughters, mothers, marriage-partners or other appendages of males inside and outside the family. Its role in the analysis of the emancipation of women requires more attention than it has so far received, as does its relation to middle-class travel and holidays.[87]

It is hardly necessary to document the fact that the institutionalization of sport took place in the last decades of the century. Even in Britain it was hardly established before the 1870s – the Association football cup dates back to 1871, the county cricket championship to 1873 – and thereafter several new sports were invented (tennis, badminton, hockey, water-polo, and so on), or de facto introduced on a national scale (golf), or systematized (boxing). Elsewhere in Europe sport in the modern form was a conscious import of social

[86] *Encyclopaedia of Sports* (S. Brunswick and New York, 1969 edn): Lawn Tennis.
[87] For an early recognition of the tennis club as 'part of the revolt of sons and daughters of the middle class', see T. H. S. Escott, *Social Transformations of the Victorian Age* (London, 1897), pp. 195–6, 444. See also R. C. K. Ensor, *England 1870–1914* (Oxford, 1936), pp. 165–6.

values and life-styles from Britain, largely by those influenced by the educational system of the British upper class, such as Baron de Coubertin, an admirer of Dr Arnold.[88] What is significant is the speed with which these transfers were made, though actual institutionalization took somewhat longer.

Middle-class sport thus combined two elements of the invention of tradition: the political and the social. On the one hand it represented a conscious, though not usually official, effort to form a ruling élite on the British model supplementing, competing with or seeking to replace the older aristocratic–military continental models, and thus, depending on the local situation, associated with conservative or liberal elements in the local upper and middle classes.[89] On the other it represented a more spontaneous attempt to draw class lines against the masses, mainly by the systematic emphasis on amateurism as the criterion of upper- and middle-class sport (as notably in tennis, rugby union football as against association football and rugby league and in the Olympic Games). However, it also represented an attempt to develop both a specific new bourgeois pattern of leisure activity and a life-style – both bisexual and suburban or ex-urban[90] – and a flexible and expandable criterion of group membership.

Both mass and middle-class sport combined the invention of political and social traditions in yet another way: by providing a medium for national identification and factitious community. This was not new in itself, for mass physical exercises had long been linked with liberal–nationalist movements (the German *Turner*, the Czech *Sokols*) or with national identification (rifle-shooting in Switzerland). Indeed the resistance of the German gymnastic movement, on nationalist grounds in general and anti-British ones in particular, distinctly slowed down the progress of mass sport in Germany.[91] The rise of sport provided new expressions of nationalism through the choice or invention of nationally specific sports – Welsh rugby as distinct from English soccer, and Gaelic football in Ireland (1884),

[88] Pierre de Coubertin, *L'Ecole en Angleterre* (Paris, 1888); Diem, *op. cit.*, pp. 1130f.
[89] Marcel Spivak, 'Le Développement de l'Education Physique et du Sport Français de 1852 à 1914', *Revue d'Histoire Moderne et Contemporaine*, xxiv (1977), pp. 28–48; D. Lejeune, 'Histoire Sociale et Alpinisme en France, XIX–XX s.', *ibid.*, xxv (1978), pp. 111–28.
[90] This must be distinguished from the patterns of sports and outdoor pastimes of the old aristocracy and military, even if they sometimes took to the new sports or forms of sport.
[91] John, *op. cit.*, pp. 107ff.

which acquired genuine mass support some twenty years later.[92] However, although the specific linking of physical exercises with nationalism as part of nationalist movements remained important – as in Bengal[93] – it was by now certainly less significant than two other phenomena.

The first of these was the concrete demonstration of the links which bound all inhabitants of the national state together, irrespective of local and regional differences, as in the all-English football culture or, more literally, in such sporting institutions as the cyclists' Tour de France (1903), followed by the Giro d'Italia (1909). These phenomena were all the more significant as they evolved spontaneously or by commercial mechanisms. The second consisted of the international sporting contests which very soon supplemented national ones, and reached their typical expression in the revival of the Olympics in 1896. While we are today only too aware of the scope for vicarious national identification which such contests provide, it is important to recall that before 1914 they had barely begun to acquire their modern character. Initially, 'international' contests served to underline the unity of nations or empires much in the way inter-regional contests did. British international matches – as usual the pioneers – pitted the nations of the British Isles against each other (in football: those of Britain in the 1870s, Ireland being included in the 1880s), or various parts of the British Empire (Test Matches began in 1877). The first international football match outside the British Isles confronted Austria and Hungary (1902). International sport, with few exceptions, remained dominated by amateurism – that is by middle-class sport – even in football, where the international association (F.I.F.A.) was formed by countries with little mass support for the game in 1904 (France, Belgium, Denmark, the Netherlands, Spain, Sweden, Switzerland). The Olympics remained the main international arena for this sport. To this extent national identification through sport against foreigners in this period seems to have been primarily a middle-class phenomenon.

This may itself be significant. For, as we have seen, the middle classes in the broadest sense found subjective group identification unusually difficult, since they were not in fact a sufficiently small

---

92 W. F. Mandle, 'Sport as Politics. The Gaelic Athletic Association 1884–1916', in R. Cashman and M. McKernan (eds.), *Sport in History* (Queensland U.P., St Lucia, 1979).

93 John Rosselli, 'The Self-Image of Effeteness: Physical Education and Nationalism in 19th Century Bengal', *Past and Present*, 86 (1980), pp. 121–48.

minority to establish the sort of virtual membership of a nation-wide club which united, for example, most of those who had passed through Oxford and Cambridge, nor sufficiently united by a common destiny and potential solidarity, like the workers.[94] Negatively the middle classes found it easy to segregate themselves from their inferiors by such devices as rigid insistence on amateurism in sport, as well as by the life-style and values of 'respectability', not to mention residential segregation. Positively, it may be suggested, they found it easier to establish a sense of belonging together through external symbols, among which those of nationalism (patriotism, imperialism) were perhaps the most significant. It is, one might suggest, as the quintessential patriotic class that the new or aspiring middle class found it easiest to recognize itself collectively.

This is speculation. The present chapter does not permit us to pursue it further. Here it is only possible to point out that there is at least some prima facie evidence for it, seen in the appeal of patriotism to the white-collar strata of Britain in the South African War[95] and the role of the right-wing nationalist mass organizations – overwhelmingly of middle-class but not élite composition – in Germany from the 1880s on, the appeal of Schönerer's nationalism to the (German-speaking) university students – a middle-class stratum profoundly marked by nationalism in a number of European countries.[96] The nationalism which gained ground was overwhelmingly identified with the political right. In the 1890s the originally liberal–nationalist German gymnasts abandoned the old national colours en masse to adopt the new black–white–red banner: in 1898 only 100 out of 6501 *Turnervereine* still maintained the old black–red–gold.[97]

---

[94] It would be interesting, in countries whose language permits this distinction, to inquire into the changes in the mutual social use of the second person singular, symbol of social brotherhood as well as of personal intimacy. Among the higher classes its use between fellow-students (and, as with French polytechnicians, ex-students), brother-officers and the like is familiar. Workers, even when they did not know one another, used it habitually. Leo Uhen, *Gruppenbewusstsein und informelle Gruppenbildung bei deutschen Arbeitern im Jahrhundert der Industrialisierung* (Berlin, 1964), pp. 106–7. Labour movements institutionalized it among their members ('Dear Sir and Brother').

[95] Richard Price, *An Imperial War and the British Working-Class: Working-Class Attitudes and Reactions to the Boer War, 1899–1902* (London, 1972), pp. 72–3.

[96] It is to be noted that in Germany the élite student Korps resisted the principle of anti-semitism, unlike the non-élite associations, though de facto applying it (Grieswelle, *op. cit.*, p. 353). Similarly anti-semitism was imposed on the German gymnastic movement by pressure from below, against some resistance from the old National–Liberal bourgeois leadership of the movement (John, *op. cit.*, p. 65).

[97] John, *op. cit.*, p. 37.

What is clear is that nationalism became a substitute for social cohesion through a national church, a royal family or other cohesive traditions, or collective group self-presentations, a new secular religion, and that the class which required such a mode of cohesion most was the growing new middle class, or rather that large intermediate mass which so signally lacked other forms of cohesion. At this point, once again, the invention of political traditions coincides with that of social ones.

IV

To establish the clustering of 'invented traditions' in western countries between 1870 and 1914 is relatively easy. Enough examples of such innovations have been given in this chapter, from old school ties and royal jubilees, Bastille Day and the Daughters of the American Revolution, May Day, the Internationale and the Olympic Games to the Cup Final and Tour de France as popular rites, and the institution of flag worship in the U.S.A. The political developments and the social transformations which may account for this clustering have also been discussed, though the latter more briefly and speculatively than the former. For it is unfortunately easier to document the motives and intentions of those who are in a position formally to institute such innovations, and even their consequences, than new practices which spring up spontaneously at the grass roots. British historians of the future, anxious to pursue similar inquiries for the late twentieth century, will have far less difficulty with the analysis of, say, the ceremonial consequences of the assassination of Earl Mountbatten than with such novel practices as the purchase (often at great expense) of individually distinctive number-plates for motor cars. In any case, the object of this book is to encourage the study of a relatively new subject, and any pretence to treat it other than in a tentative manner would be out of place.

However, there remain three aspects of the 'invention of tradition' in this period which call for some brief comment in conclusion.

The first is the distinction between those new practices of the period which proved lasting, and those which did not. In retrospect it would seem that the period which straddles the first world war marks a divide between languages of symbolic discourse. As in military uniforms what might be called the operatic mode gave way to the prosaic mode. The uniforms invented for the interwar mass

movements, which could hardly claim the excuse of operational camouflage, eschewed bright colours, preferring duller hues such as the black and brown of Fascists and National Socialists.[98] No doubt fancy dress for ritual occasions was still invented for men in the period 1870–1914, though examples hardly come to mind – except perhaps by way of the extension of older styles to new institutions of the same type and, hopefully, status, such as academic gowns and hoods for new colleges and degrees. The old costumes were certainly still maintained. However, one has the distinct impression that in this respect the period lived on accumulated capital. In another respect, however, it clearly developed an old idiom with particular enthusiasm. The mania for statuary and allegorically decorated or symbolic public buildings has already been mentioned, and there is little doubt that it reached a peak between 1870 and 1914. Yet this idiom of symbolic discourse was destined to decline with dramatic suddenness between the wars. Its extraordinary vogue was to prove almost as short-lived as the contemporary outburst of another kind of symbolism, 'art nouveau'. Neither the massive adaptation of traditional allegory and symbolism for public purposes, nor the improvization of a new and imprecise language of vegetable or female, but in any case curvilinear, symbolism, mainly for private or semi-private purposes appears to have been suited more than temporarily to whatever social requirements gave rise to them. We can only speculate about the reasons, and this is not the place to do so.

On the other hand, it may be suggested that another idiom of public symbolic discourse, the theatrical, proved more lasting. Public ceremonies, parades and ritualized mass gatherings were far from new. Yet their extension for official purposes and for unofficial secular purposes (mass demonstrations, football matches, and the like) in this period is rather striking. Some examples have been mentioned above. Moreover, the construction of formal ritual spaces, already consciously allowed for in German nationalism, appears to have been systematically undertaken even in countries which had hitherto paid little attention to it – one thinks of Edwardian London – and neither should we overlook the invention in this period of substantially new constructions for spectacle and de facto

---

[98] The brightest such uniforms appear to have been the blue shirts and red ties of socialist youth movements. I know of no case of red, orange or yellow shirts and none of genuinely multicoloured ceremonial clothing.

mass ritual such as sports stadia, outdoor and indoor.[99] The royal attendance at the Wembley Cup Final (from 1914), and the use of such buildings as the Sportspalast in Berlin or the Vélodrome d'Hiver in Paris by the interwar mass movements of their respective countries, anticipate the development of formal spaces for public mass ritual (the Red Square from 1918) which was to be systematically fostered by Fascist régimes. We may note in passing that, in line with the exhaustion of the old language of public symbolism, the new settings for such public ritual were to stress simplicity and monumentality rather than the allegorical decoration of the nineteenth-century Ringstrasse in Vienna or the Victor Emmanuel monument in Rome;[100] a tendency already anticipated in our period.[101]

On the stage of public life the emphasis therefore shifted from the design of elaborate and varied stage-sets, capable of being 'read' in the manner of a strip cartoon or tapestry, to the movement of the actors themselves – either, as in military or royal parades, a ritual minority acting for the benefit of a watching mass public, or, as anticipated in the political mass movements of the period (such as May Day demonstrations) and the great mass sporting occasions, a merger of actors and public. These were the tendencies which were destined for further development after 1914. Without speculating further about this form of public ritualization, it does not seem unreasonable to relate it to the decline of old tradition and the democratization of politics.

The second aspect of invented tradition in this period concerns the practices identified with specific social classes or strata as distinct from members of wider inter-class collectivities such as states or 'nations'. While some such practices were formally designed as badges of class consciousness – the May Day practices among workers, the revival or invention of 'traditional' peasant costume among (de facto the richer) peasants – a larger number were not so identified in theory and many indeed were adaptations, specializations or conquests of practices originally initiated by the higher social

[99] Cf. *Wasmuth's Lexikon der Baukunst* (Berlin, 1932), iv: 'Stadthalle'; W. Scharau-Wils, *Gebäude und Gelände für Gymnastik, Spiel und Sport* (Berlin, 1925); D. R. Knight, *The Exhibitions: Great White City, Shepherds Bush* (London, 1978).

[100] Carl Schorske, *Fin de Siècle Vienna: Politics and Culture* (New York, 1980), ch. 2.

[101] Cf. Alastair Service, *Edwardian Architecture: A Handbook to Building Design in Britain 1890–1914* (London, 1977).

strata. Sport is the obvious example. From above, the class line was here drawn in three ways: by maintaining aristocratic or middle-class control of the governing institutions, by social exclusiveness or, more commonly, by the high cost or scarcity of the necessary capital equipment (real tennis courts or grouse-moors), but above all by the rigid separation between amateurism, the criterion of sport among the upper strata, and professionalism, its logical corollary among the lower urban and working classes.[102] Class-specific sport among plebeians rarely developed consciously as such. Where it did, it was usually by taking over upper-class exercises, pushing out their former practitioners, and then developing a specific set of practices on a new social basis (the football culture).

Practices thus filtering socially downwards – from aristocracy to bourgeoisie, from bourgeoisie to working class – were probably predominant in this period, not only in sport, but in costume and material culture in general, given the force of snobbery among the middle classes and of the values of bourgeois self-improvement and achievement among the working-class élites.[103] They were transformed, but their historical origins remained visible. The opposite movement was not absent, but in this period less visible. Minorities (aristocrats, intellectuals, deviants) might admire certain urban plebeian sub-cultures and activities – such as music-hall art – but the major assimilation of cultural practices developed among the lower classes or for a mass popular public was to come later. Some signs of it were visible before 1914, mainly mediated through entertainment and perhaps above all the social dance, which may be linked to the growing emancipation of women: the vogue for ragtime or the tango. However, any survey of cultural inventions in this period cannot but note the development of autochthonous lower-class sub-cultures and practices which owed nothing to models from higher social classes – almost certainly as a by-product of urbanization and mass migration.

[102] Professionalism implies a degree of occupational specialization and a 'market' barely if at all available among the settled rural population. Professional sportsmen there were either servants or suppliers of the upper classes (jockeys, alpine guides) or appendages to amateur upper-class competitions (cricket professionals). The distinction between the upper- and lower-class killing of game was not economic, though some poachers relied on it for a living, but legal. It was expressed in the Game Laws.

[103] A Weberian correlation of sport and Protestantism has been observed in Germany up to 1960. G. Lüschen, 'The Interdependence of Sport and Culture', in M. Hart (ed.), *Sport in the Sociocultural Process* (Dubuque, 1976).

The tango culture in Buenos Aires is an example.[104] How far they enter into a discussion of the invention of tradition must remain a matter of debate.

The final aspect is the relation betwen 'invention' and 'spontaneous generation', planning and growth. This is something which constantly puzzles observers in modern mass societies. 'Invented traditions' have significant social and political functions, and would neither come into existence nor establish themselves if they could not acquire them. Yet how far are they manipulable? The intention to use, indeed often to invent, them for manipulation is evident; both appear in politics, the first mainly (in capitalist societies) in business. To this extent conspiracy theorists opposed to such manipulation have not only plausibility but evidence on their side. Yet it also seems clear that the most successful examples of manipulation are those which exploit practices which clearly meet a felt – not necessarily a clearly understood – need among particular bodies of people. The politics of German nationalism in the Second Empire cannot be understood only from above. It has been suggested that to some extent nationalism escaped from the control of those who found it advantageous to manipulate it – at all events in this period.[105] Tastes and fashions, notably in popular entertainment, can be 'created' only within very narrow limits; they have to be discovered before being exploited and shaped. It is the historian's business to discover them retrospectively – but also to try to understand why, in terms of changing societies in changing historical situations, such needs came to be felt.

[104] Cf. Blas Matamoro, *La Ciudad del Tango* (*Tango Histórico y Sociedad*) (Buenos Aires, 1969).

[105] Geoffrey Eley, *Re-shaping the German Right* (Yale U.P., London and New Haven, 1980).

Index

abdication, 139, 141
Aberdovey, 86
Adler, Victor, 284, 286
advertising, 137, 291
Afghanistan, 175
Africa, colonial: Asians in, 219;
European neo-tradition in, 213ff,
217–19, 220–1, 226, 229ff, 237–8,
239–40; food-growing, 214, 218;
hierarchy in, 224, 227–8; indirect rule
for, 242, 258; and modernization,
223–4, 227–8, 243–4, 247–8; multiple
identities in, 248; peasants in, 211,
213–14, 218–19, 228, 235, 236; and
invented tradition, 211–12, 244ff,
247–52, 252–60; *see also*
aristocracies; clergy; unionism
Agra, 174
Agulhon, M., 270
Akbar, 174
Alaw, Owain, 77
Alexandra, Queen, 133–4
Ali, Mir Aulad, 202
allegories, national, 270, 272, 276
Allen, Admiral John Carter, 31
Allen, Thomas, 40n
All-India Congress Committees, 209
almanacks, 54; and eisteddfods, 57–8
'Alte Herren', 293, 296
Altyre, 32
'alumni chapters', 295–6
America: education in, 294–5, 296–7;
national identity for, 11, 112, 129,
279–80; Welsh emigration to, 84;
white middle class in, 292–3
Amery, Leo, 231
Amin, Idi, 225–6
Anglesey, 53, 62, 63
Anglicanism, 227, 252; in Wales, 46,
48, 65, 69, 70, 73–4, 90, 94, 95; *see
also* clergy; missionaries
Ankole, 240, 243–4
Árány, Janos, 83

Archaeologica Britannica, 68, 73
archaeology, 64, 69, 183
architects, 275–6
Arinoti, the, 244
aristocracies: in colonial Africa, 221,
223–6, 254, 260; in India, 166, 188,
189–90, 192, 194–5; and sport, 298,
300
Armistice Day, 140
army, British, 215–16; Africans in,
225–6; Highlanders in, 25
Arnold, Thomas, 295, 300
Arthur, Chester Alan, 129
Arthur, King, 46
Asiatic Society of Bengal, 182
assassinations, 129n
Austria, 288
authority, 167, 170, 180; in ritual,
178–9, 191–2, 208–9, 243; *see also*
viceregal régime

Baden-Powell, Robert, 4, 226
Bagehot, Walter, 107, 110, 119, 121,
131, 282
Bahnson, Karsten, 5
Baird's American College Fraternities,
295
Bakongo peoples, 251, 255–6
Bala, 43, 93
Baldwin, Stanley, 140
Bale, John, 62
Balfour, Lord, 128
ballads, 47, 78; or interludes, 53, 55–6
Balyney, Thomas, 77
Bangladesh, 208
banners, 63, 191, 200, 203–4, 302; craft,
213
bards, 49–50, 57, 62, 63, 65; Gorsedd
of, 60ff, 91–2; proscription of, 82, 83
Barotseland, 241
Barrington, Daines, 51, 82
Basel Mission, 213–14
Bastille Day, 271

309

Past and Present Publications

General Editor: PAUL SLACK, *Exeter College, Oxford*

* Published also as a paperback
** Published only as a paperback
† Co-published with the Maison des Sciences de l'Homme, Paris